The Child
in Latin America

*For a complete list of titles from the Helen Kellogg Institute for International Studies,
see http:www.undpress.nd.edu*

The Child
in Latin America:

*Health, Development,
and Rights*

Edited by

ERNEST J. BARTELL, C.S.C.

and

ALEJANDRO O'DONNELL

UNIVERSITY OF NOTRE DAME PRESS
Notre Dame, Indiana

University of Notre Dame Press
Notre Dame, Indiana 46556
www.undpress.nd.edu All
Rights Reserved

Set by Judy Bartlett in 10/12 Electra
Based on an original design by Wendy McMillen

Published in the United States of America

Library of Congress Cataloging-in-Publication Data
The child in Latin America : health, development, and rights / edited by
Ernest J. Bartell and Alejandro O'Donnell.
  p. cm. — (Recent titles from the Helen Kellogg Institute for International Studies)
  Based on a multidisciplinary conference at the Kellogg Institute for International
Studies at the University of Notre Dame as part of the Latin America 2000 Series.
  Includes bibliographical references.
  ISBN 0-268-02257-7 (cloth : alk. paper) — ISBN 0-268-02258-5 (pbk. : alk. paper)
  1. Children—Latin America—Social conditions. 2. Children's rights—Latin
America. 3. Children—Health and hygiene—Latin America. 4. Malnutrition in
children—Latin America. I. Bartell, Ernest J., 1932– II. O'Donnell, Alejandro.
III. Helen Kellogg Institute for International Studies. IV. Series.

HQ792.L3 C463 2001
305.23'098—dc21   00-062894

∞ *This book was printed on acid-free paper.*

Contents

Preface

In the last half of the twentieth century Latin America has undergone a transformation that ranges across the physical, social, political, economic, and cultural lives of its people. Perhaps partly because of its long historical position somewhere between the most developed and least developed regions of the world, Latin America has been a testing ground for initiatives in every aspect of human life, not only those designed for "emerging" regions but also those designed for the "advanced" nations. It has been the locus of campaigns to wipe out traditional diseases but also the home of pioneering open-heart surgery. It has been the home of socialist and capitalist models of economic development. It has been the site of anthropological fieldwork among some of the most "primitive" tribes of humankind and the home for the creation and presentation of some of the most celebrated art and literature in modern western civilization. And so, the transformations in Latin America continue to engage the attention of practitioners and scholars alike from a variety of professions and disciplines in the sciences and social sciences.

As objects of attention and study within this diversity of perspectives, the people of Latin America have been studied epidemiologically and demographically. They have been analyzed according to physical characteristics, social class, political ideology, and social participation, by economic status and roles as producers and consumers. Despite the extent of understanding that a broad range of perspectives makes possible, there is also the possibility of fragmentation, and it is easy to lose sight of people as the integral subjects of development over time. So the contributors to this volume, who together represent a wide range of disciplines and professional experience in Latin America, have sought to enhance our understanding of a special cohort of people in the development process, namely, children. It is, after all, children who, perhaps more than any other age group, embody both the results of the transformations in Latin America and the potential for its future.

This volume evolved out of a multidisciplinary conference at the Kellogg Institute for International Studies at the University of Notre Dame as part of the Latin America 2000 Series, made possible by the generous financial support of The Coca-Cola Company. The conference brought together biologists, medical specialists, social scientists, legal experts, religious and social workers, as well as administrators of public and nongovernmental sectors, all of whom demonstrated that cross-disciplinary conversation around a subject of shared human concern is possible. The chapters in this volume, which look at the physical, educational, social, legal, and economic status and progress of children in Latin America, grew out of presentations, commentaries, and discussion at the conference as well as subsequent contributions on the subject. Consequently, we are indebted not only to the authors whose names appear but to all those who helped to shape the analysis and thought included here.

We are indebted to the institutional cosponsors of this project, UNICEF and the International Life Sciences Institute (ILSI), without whose support we never would have been able to assemble so distinguished a list of conference participants and contributors to this volume. Special thanks are due to Marta Maurás and Emilio García Méndez, formerly with UNICEF, to Alex Malaspina, president of ILSI, and to Juan Méndez, now director of the Notre Dame Center for International Civil and Human Rights, for their sustained personal encouragement and commitment to the project. We also benefited from the advice and assistance of Dr. Suzanne Harris at ILSI and Paulo Sérgio Pinheiro at the University of São Paulo's Center for the Study of Violence. We are grateful to UNICEF for additional financial support and to Gabriela Mossi, Academic Coordinator of the Kellogg Institute, for her assistance with the organization of the original conference.

This volume, like so many others from the Kellogg Institute, has benefited from the professional editorial supervision of Caroline Domingo, Publications Coordinator of the Kellogg Institute, who has been ably assisted by Judy Bartlett, Kellogg's Senior Consultant, as designer and typesetter, Robert Racine as copyeditor, Linda Bigger as proofreader, and Jaime Raba, who compiled the index. We have also benefited from the cooperation and assistance of the staff of the University of Notre Dame Press. Above all, we are grateful to all the members of the administrative staff of the Kellogg Institute who have given so generously of their time, energy, and talent at every stage of this project to ensure its successful completion. With gratitude for so much support from so many sources, the coeditors are content to assume responsibility for any residual failings the reader may encounter in this volume.

— *Ernest J. Bartell, C.S.C., and Alejandro O'Donnell,*
Coeditors

Opportunities and Challenges for the Well-Being of Children in the Development of Latin America

An Overview

ERNEST J. BARTELL, C.S.C.

Introduction

The broad subject of development in Latin America is one with many dimensions, for example, geographic, industrial, agricultural, biological, economic, social, and political, which individually engage the attention of researchers and policy makers in diverse fields of expertise and responsibility. As our understanding and experience of the various elements of development expand, the connections and interdependence among the dimensions of development become increasingly apparent. This is perhaps nowhere truer than in the relationships of the development process to children, who in a special way are both targets and determinants of the process.

Economists, for example, may point out that the pace and quality of economic growth depend on labor productivity, which is largely determined by the quality of "human capital," which in turn depends on the educational attainments of workers. But biologists will demonstrate that the personal capacity to learn is dependent on determinants of health and nutrition, especially in infancy and early childhood. Social scientists and policy experts are likely to add social preconditions to the educational attainment of children that include the status and roles of mothers at home, in the larger society, and in the workforce. In addition, children's access to educational opportunities is a function of social and political structures and institutions that govern civil and human rights, as well as of economic policies and programs that determine the allocation and distribution of educational resources.

The authors who have collaborated in this volume are drawn from various fields related to medicine, biology, social science, and public policy. The individual insights from their specialties contribute to a fuller understanding of the situation of children in contemporary Latin American development. Beyond that, and perhaps more importantly, their collaboration brings into special focus the interdependence of the various dimensions of change that must be addressed if children are to be both rightful beneficiaries and effective participants in the continuing development of Latin America.

In measures of per capita income and output, almost all Latin America countries rank among the "middle-income" nations of the world.[1] Moreover, Warner points out that Latin America as a region today enjoys average rates of infant mortality and morbidity that are lower than those in Asia and Africa. Lechtig notes further that average levels of malnutrition in Latin America have declined by about two-thirds over the past three decades, even among people with incomes that fall below poverty levels. Nevertheless, his data also indicate that the Latin American average is still more than twice the U.S. average. Moreover, several of the authors identify wide disparities in all these indicators among the individual countries of Latin America. They indicate that child survival rates may vary by a factor of 8 between countries, while incomes per capita vary by a factor of more than 20 and measures of malnutrition by a factor of more than 7.

So, Latin America has traditionally been included as part of the developing world and shares many of the latter's basic attributes. Like much of the developing world, for example, Latin America lies largely in tropical and semitropical climates and so has shared the liabilities of unproductive agricultural ecology and infectious disease that characterize equatorial regions.[2]

Nutrition, Health Care, and Environmental Sanitation

Against this background, Alejandro O'Donnell in Chapter 1 reviews the history of nutritional advances in the developing world as they have affected the health and development of children in Latin America. Initial research and innovation after World War II to meet protein and amino acid requirements led to the awareness that energy, rather than protein, was the defining factor. That awareness shifted attention to food production with all of its attendant political, social, and economic complexities. The subsequent "green revolution" reached Latin America, though the manipulation of prices and exchange rates as part of inward-looking industrialization policies in major Latin

American countries sometimes acted as a market deterrent to the production of basic foods.

Meanwhile, acknowledgment and promotion of the value of breast feeding to protect infants from environmental contamination highlighted the nutritional importance of food safety and personal sanitation and raised awareness of the complementarity of health and nutrition activities. This complementarity was perhaps nowhere more evident than in the universal success of low-cost oral rehydration programs to offset the depletion of nutrients caused by infant diarrhea, the impact of which Alejandro O'Donnell describes as "similar or superior to [that of] antibiotics."

The relationships between poverty and malnutrition are complex. Poverty that is associated with the relatively high levels of income inequality in Latin America, as well as inadequate economic growth, can affect nutrition in various ways. Economic policies in the decades immediately after World War II that favored import substitute industrialization typically resulted in increased rates of urban migration that were not accompanied by increased availability of diversified foods at prices affordable by the urban poor, despite (or because of) attempts to control food prices. Structural adjustment policies introduced later in many countries to correct deficits in government budgets and in balances of payments resulted in significant increases in unemployment and poverty accompanied by rises in food prices.

Similarly, the availability of and compliance with good nutritional practice for children is related to the availability and quality of primary health care, beginning with pregnancy. This link with health care services makes effective childhood nutrition vulnerable to cutbacks in public health care budgets. Such cutbacks have not been uncommon among structural adjustments in government budgets required to deal with the effects of international debt, financial crises, and recession that have accompanied the increased globalization of Latin American economies over the past two decades.

Despite these cyclical setbacks in child nutrition and increases in infant mortality, successful long-term declines in the malnutrition and mortality of children suggest that a public commitment to child health in Latin America is not solely a function of poverty or of political and economic regimes. Alejandro O'Donnell, for example, cites the low rates of infant mortality achieved in nations as diverse as Chile, Cuba, and Costa Rica. Instead, Lechtig recommends that windows of opportunity must be identified for cost-effective strategies of child health care and nutrition, even where the problems of poverty are seemingly intractable and policy regimes are disparate. Zavaleta points out that government nutrition programs are often hampered, rather than helped, by the inconclusive and out-of-date results of lengthy programs of data collection and analysis, and she cites instead a list of sensitive, easy-to-collect indicators that are more likely to assist in identifying cost-effective strategies.

In addition, administrative obstacles can diminish the cost-effectiveness of nutrition programs. Programs of food distribution to the poor, for example, are a commonly used strategy to alleviate the impact of poverty on food security. Lechtig, however, concludes that they have "had very little to do" with the secular decline in the malnutrition of Latin American children. In his judgment this is so because of their failure to reach a high-risk target population, namely, children under 1 year of age, and because of widespread deviations in practice from the stated criteria for distribution in such programs.

And so, Zavaleta stresses the importance of integrating nutritional interventions with primary health care at the community level, utilizing a range of community-based agents and institutions, including health care institutions, schools, and NGOs. In addition, Lechtig emphasizes the importance of a broad range of strategies to enable women and improve their economic, social, and political opportunities. These points have been echoed by Freire and by Alejandro O'Donnell in his studies of child care in Tierra del Fuego and have recently been embraced by multilateral agencies like the Inter-American Development Bank.[3] Along with improving women's access to education and their labor force participation, such strategies include changing the domestic roles of women to give them greater control over the allocation of household resources, which has been shown to result in improved child care in Latin America. Such strategies will also foster increased opportunities for participation and leadership roles by women in civil society, which can increase public awareness and resolve problems related to child nutrition and health care. Beyond the negative impact of urbanization on Latin American poverty pointed out by Alejandro O'Donnell, Lechtig highlights the positive effects that urbanization has had on the expanded social, economic, and domestic management responsibilities of women in Latin America that have contributed to the quality of child care.

Relatively recently, as levels of general nutrition and child survival have risen, focus has also shifted to specific categories of nutrition and health care. Alejandro O'Donnell and Zavaleta note, for example, that in contemporary Latin America, especially in urban areas, obesity has become increasingly prevalent among both the poor and the more affluent. This is the result of increased consumption of sugar, fats, and refined flour, coupled with low levels of physical activity in a pattern that may not be unfamiliar among children in the United States. In Chile, where average incomes per capita are the second highest in Latin America, Alejandro O'Donnell estimates that over half the children who qualify for food assistance are overweight.

In many areas of Latin America, even those with relatively high levels of food consumption, the high incidence of micronutrient deficiencies in the diets of children is another current nutritional concern that is especially significant for their development. The importance of this issue, which is emphasized by several of this volume's authors, arises from the serious consequences of such deficiencies, especially of iodine, iron, Vitamin A, and zinc. It has long been known, for example, that iodine deficiency, which was once relatively widespread in the Andean regions of Bolivia, Ecuador, Argentina, and Chile, as well as in the Amazon basin, leads to severe mental retardation. Zinc deficiency leads to growth retardation, while Vitamin A deficiency weakens eyesight and can lead to blindness, as well as to reduced resistance to measles, diarrhea, and pneumonia.

Walter points out that iron deficiency inhibits cognitive skills, such as language acquisition and abstract thought, as well as the development of psychomotor functions, such as walking, body coordination, and balance. He cites recent studies which indicate that iron deficiency anemia may irreversibly retard development of the central nervous system. Freire adds that iron deficiency anemia is also associated with low birth weight and higher maternal mortality. The impact of such deficiencies on labor productivity is obvious, and Freire cites one population study that demonstrated a 30% improvement in average productivity when iron deficiency anemia was eliminated.

As the history of reduction in iodine deficiency in developed countries suggests, strategies to eliminate micronutrient deficiencies tend in principle to be relatively cost effective in comparison with other measures to improve health and nutrition. The three principal strategies for reducing micronutrient deficiencies are diversifying diets, using food supplements, and fortifying foods. However, as the examples and studies cited by several authors indicate, differences in appropriate strategies do affect rates of improvement for some relatively straightforward reasons. The diversification of diets is effective for eliminating iron and Vitamin A deficiencies. However, the strategy of diet diversification can be hampered by the lack and high cost of appropriate dietary alternatives, especially in poor urban communities, as well as by the difficulties of complying with recommended changes in eating habits. Similarly, the efficacy of food supplements is demonstrably dependent on maintaining supplementation programs over time and on the regular use of supplements by recipients.

Where food fortification is a technically feasible alternative, the results have sometimes been quite dramatic. As Alejandro O'Donnell points out, for example, the incidence of iron deficiency diseases in Bolivia declined by over

90% in little more than a decade between 1983 and 1994 as the result of iodiz-ing salt. Earlier successes like these plus recent research of the sort cited by Walter have recently helped shift professional interest to the elimination of iron deficiency. Although iron deficiency is relatively widespread in Latin America, it has been neglected in many places until recently, although Chile has had a successful program of fortifying wheat flour with iron for over a decade. The effective fortification of foods like wheat flour, unlike that of salt, entails a number of steps in the extended process of production and distribu-tion. Nevertheless, the authors agree that successful programs of fortifying food with iron are technically and economically feasible on a large scale in Latin America.[4]

Although advances in nutrition and primary health care have decreased infant mortality and improved childhood health and development, Warner points out that these successes have not been matched by a corresponding decline in morbidity rates among Latin American children. Instead, rates of illness among children from diarrhea and other diseases related to environ-mental sanitation, such as schistosomiasis, typhoid fever, dengue fever, and cholera, remain relatively high. For example, Warner points out that the first outbreak of cholera in a century that hit Peru in 1991 as a result of con-taminated seafood spread quickly, especially among the poor who lacked safe water and facilities for disposing of human waste, and cholera has now be-come endemic to the area. Similarly, dengue fever was not a significant threat in Latin America before the early 1980s, but now infects 200,000 people in 14 countries.

Average morbidity rates from contaminated water and inadequate sani-tation remain lower in Latin America than in most of Africa and Asia and are lower in Central America and the Caribbean than in South America, though with large disparities among specific countries. The index of "disability ad-justed life years" (DALYs), a somewhat controversial measure of the com-bined effects of mortality and morbidity rates on expectancy of a healthy life, also ranks Latin America and the Caribbean between sub-Saharan Africa and the developed OECD countries. The high morbidity rates in Latin America relative to rates of infant mortality reinforce the need for quality water sup-plies used for drinking, cooking, and personal hygiene and the related need of sanitarily disposing of personal and household wastes. Despite evidence that improvements in water safety and in provisions for sanitation can have a significant effect on rates of childhood illness, Warner points out that inter-ventions in these areas have still not been widely incorporated into programs for child survival.

Latin America ranks slightly better than average within the developing world in access to safe water and far above average in access to sanitation.

However, coverage in these two important dimensions of health care has not kept pace with population growth, especially in urban areas, and has been hampered by the constraints imposed by the structural adjustment economic policies adopted by many Latin American countries in recent years. In addition, despite the close interaction between water supply and waste disposal in their effects on health, there remain, according to Warner, severe institutional barriers to coordinated action in both areas of responsibility within and among government agencies, NGOs, and research institutions.

Moreover, in his opinion, the urgency of the unmet needs has also been compromised by the inconclusive nature of some inadequately designed studies of the complex and long-term impact of water and sanitation improvements. This is especially salient when the results of these studies of childhood illness are compared with studies of childhood mortality using the more directly accessible measurements of cost effectiveness of low-cost, short-term primary care health interventions, such as oral rehydration, immunizations, nutrition supplements, and breast feeding. However, as the expansion of these successful short-term interventions reaches diminishing returns, more adequate recent studies of substantial decreases in both child mortality and morbidity from programs of improved water and sanitation facilities has increased interest in such programs. Esrey cites data for Latin America, for example, that demonstrate reductions in the incidence of diarrhea of up to 47% with improved toilet and latrine facilities. Moreover, the highest rates of improvement occur where piped water is available, presumably because of the resulting reduction of pathogens in food handling, which calls attention to the relationships between sanitation and nutrition. Similarly, a Guatemalan study cited by Esrey measured a time savings of up to two hours daily for homemakers who had safe water in the home, which represents a physical energy savings sufficient to meet the lactation needs of nursing mothers and the nutritional needs of nursing children. Experiments utilizing human waste as fertilizer and compost in Mexico and sewage as nutrition for farm-raised fish in Peru vindicate for Esrey the axiom that "waste is nothing but a resource in the wrong place."

The emergence of new techniques for improving sanitation has engaged such agencies as UNICEF, the World Health Organization (WHO), and the United States Agency for International Development (USAID) in collaborative efforts in Africa, with the likelihood of expansion to Latin America. Nevertheless, the continued lack of coordination and integration of water and sanitation projects into childhood survival programs, which continue to emphasize therapeutic, rather than preventative, interventions, highlights the need for improved communication and awareness of the benefits to children's health from safe water and adequate sanitation.

Education, Work, and the Legal Status of Children

Several authors from the social science and public policy domains, especially Maurás, Minujin and Perczek, and Heisler and Anderson, agree that the gains in child survival, health, and nutrition in Latin America during the last half of the twentieth century have been impressive. They agree too that some of the challenges—for instance, reducing the incidence of persistent diseases, such as river blindness and malaria, and eliminating micronutrient deficiencies in children—that remain continue to depend strongly on technical solutions.

However, the challenge of realizing the expanded human potential that these achievements in health and nutrition have created also constitutes a challenge for legal, economic, and social policies that will shape the quality of life in Latin America. As Carol Bellamy has put it, "Having made major advances against child mortality . . . the question that has now come centre stage in this region is: survival for what? Certainly we have not succeeded in saving millions of precious lives only to see them slaughtered in wars, exploited in factories, condemned to live . . . in the streets or otherwise denied their basic human rights."[5] If the potential of a growing population of healthy and capable children and adolescents is to be realized, there must be corresponding opportunities for the exercise of citizenship, for effective participation in civil society and political life, and for an economically productive life.

In recent decades most of Latin America has experienced transitions to democracy and shared in modern advances in technology, especially in communications and information technology, along with the expansion of market economies and global trade, as Minujin and Perczek point out. These changes, along with the documented improvements in child health, nutrition, and sanitation, hold out the prospect that today's youth possess a greater potential than ever to lead dignified and productive adult lives. Unfortunately, despite these advances, Latin American countries continue to be characterized by higher levels of inequality in the distribution of income than in any other region of the world.[6] As a result, despite its "middle-income" status among the nations of the world, about one-third of the population in Latin America in 1998 had an income level equivalent in purchasing power to less than US$2 per day. If current income in Latin America could be feasibly distributed as it is in the developed countries of North America and Western Europe, the number of Latin American poor would be reduced by more than two-thirds.[7]

So, it is not surprising that, even after the renewal of economic growth following the economic crises and recessions of the 1980s, poverty levels in about half the countries of Latin America are still as high or higher than their precrisis levels. In addition, the dominance of traditional rural poverty has given way to a concentration of two-thirds of the region's poor in urban areas.

Under these circumstances of economic inequality and urbanization, it is not surprising that children, increasingly deprived of even the minimal support of traditional subsistence agriculture, make up a very large share of the Latin American poor. As Minujin and Perczek note, almost 60% of Latin American children under the age of 15 live in poverty and constitute more than one-third of the poor in Latin America. Several authors from different academic perspectives concur that the children of Latin America will not realize their human and economic potential in the open and competitive economies of modern Latin America unless the elimination of poverty becomes a policy priority for governments and a commitment within civil society itself.

Given the obvious clarity of this imperative, it is not surprising to find a focus on productive human development in the recommendations of major international development organizations, like the United Nations World Summits, UNICEF, the World Bank, the Inter-American Development Bank, and the World Health Organization. Indeed, Heisler and Anderson discern a wide-ranging consensus in policy recommendations affecting children among these organizations. Policy recommendations from a diversity of international organizations and forums, for example, are beginning to emphasize the importance of public health programs that provide basic and preventative health care services rather than costly hospital-based therapeutic services, as Warner and Esrey pointed out. And the consensus moves further into the domain of social policy with the encouragement of national policies for social development, especially in access to primary and secondary education for all children, especially girls, whose educational opportunities and attainments have traditionally lagged behind those of boys.

The Economic Commission for Latin America and the Caribbean (ECLAC) charts the progress toward meeting the social targets set by UNICEF for children in Latin America. ECLAC estimates that, at the turn of the twenty-first century, over 80% of Latin American children in urban areas will have completed four years of primary education and more than 70% will have completed a minimum of six years. Enrollment rates in rural areas, however, continue to lag significantly. Although differences in enrollment rates across socioeconomic levels have narrowed slightly, urban enrollment rates for children in the lowest income quartile are still significantly lower than the average. Moreover, according to ECLAC, countries with the greatest levels of inequality in income distribution are those that are furthest behind in meeting UNICEF targets of universal access to four years of primary education in both urban and rural areas of Latin America.[8]

Furthermore, as an indication of the educational challenge still remaining, ECLAC data indicate that during the 1990s the percentage of employed teenagers over 14 years old fell in only half the countries of Latin America and actually increased in a third of them. Moreover, the trend in child labor was even less favorable among juveniles under 14 years of age. As a result, as Salazar notes, about 20% of Latin American children between the ages of 6 and 18 are employed. Moreover, labor force participation by both children and adolescents together fell during the 1990s in only a third of the countries of Latin America.[9] On a more promising note, the percentage of urban adolescents who neither study nor participate in the labor force has declined in a majority of countries, though it still remains high, up to 50%, in the rural areas of some countries.

As Salazar demonstrates, the relationship between child labor and education is complex and varied. Traditionally, much of children's work in Latin America could be culturally understood as an educative process of personal and family identity building and as a socializing activity of transmitting survival skills suited to a subsistence rural economy, in which girls learned skills for the home and boys acquired agricultural competence. In this cultural framework, remuneration for children's work was a secondary consideration, and low or token wages could be justified by the presumed educative and socializing value of children's work. Even in today's expanding market economies, children continue to work at home. However, with the spread of macroeconomic policies to strengthen market integration, growth, and employment in a commercialized and urbanized private sector, the focus of children's work has shifted to generating income through wage labor in the marketplace.

Urban child labor tends to be concentrated in the informal sector, where most of the new jobs for unskilled workers are generated and where job security, benefits, and working conditions tend to be the least satisfactory. Where the majority of child labor is still concentrated, in rural areas of many Latin American countries, including Brazil, Colombia, and Guatemala, much child labor is still associated with traditional subsistence agriculture. However, rural child labor is also common, especially for boys, in market-oriented export agricultural production, especially of coffee, fruit, flowers, and sugar, and for girls in domestic service. Although some middle-class Latin American children do work, in both urban and rural sectors it is poor children who provide most of the child labor, and it is they who have the lowest rates of literacy and educational attainment. The lack of basic education and skills, especially for girls, is particularly acute in rural areas where, according to Salazar, the illiteracy rate is several times as high as in urban areas and where children average three years less formal education than their urban peers.

Lacking adequate formal education and confined to low-skilled jobs that are often fatiguing and hazardous, working children in Latin America face meager opportunities for the adult self-actualization needed for productive individual lives and for the success of the consensus models of market-driven development in an increasingly global economy. Moreover, without adequate private educational resources and public education programs, the need for education and the need to work for income, which ought to be complementary, in practice become mutually exclusive. School and work too often compete for children's time and energy, especially those living in poverty, with frustrating and sometimes physically and psychologically destructive effects.

Increases in the average years of primary school attendance suggest that Latin American policy makers recognize the high rates of return to investment in education, especially at the primary level, where the rate of return on educational investments is estimated to be 17% for the region. Nevertheless, studies cited by Salazar indicate that the quality of primary education in the region, especially when measured by student performance and dropout rates, remains relatively low, typically lower than in the emerging areas of Asia. Moreover, economic structural adjustment policies have shifted some educational costs, for example, books and supplies, from governments to families, creating an economic deterrent to school attendance.

Given the mixed results of global market-driven economic policy models in alleviating poverty and unemployment within Latin America, the international consensus of the 1990s on macroeconomic policy for emerging economies is increasingly subject to critical scrutiny. As several authors directly and indirectly argue, as long as the distinctive developmental and educational needs of children are ignored, no effective solutions to the deficiencies of current development models, strategies, and policies will be found.

Moreover, it is becoming increasingly apparent that there is no automatic positive relationship between the increase in democratic regimes in Latin America over the past two decades or so and improvement of children's well-being and opportunities in the region. On the contrary, the relationships among democracy, economic development, and the well-being of children have been complicated by the specific patterns of political, social, and economic changes in the individual countries of Latin America during the recent transitions to democracy and to market-driven economic development.

Every parent knows that the growth of a child is a unique, uneven, and irregular process that is vulnerable to influences within the family and society on individual and personal characteristics. It is not always so obvious that children are also distinctively vulnerable to the processes of political and social change that accompany and shape economic development. Markets, for example, do not distribute the gains from economic growth uniformly, and as suggested above, working children are especially vulnerable to the vagaries of labor markets. Public tax and transfer policies can alter the effects of market patterns of distributing income and wealth. However, lacking political voice, "invisible to society" in the words of Salazar, children remain vulnerable in the process of policy determination and administration, even under democratic institutions. Moreover, some institutional changes that have accompanied the transitions to democracy and market-driven economic growth can further complicate the integration of children as effective participants in the democratic societies of Latin America. These include, for example, a decline of the state's role in human welfare and a reduction in the capacity of labor unions and labor law to set standards of protection for wage labor.

It may be obvious that the effects of social and economic policies also depend on the quality of legal and political institutions and their administration at both national and local levels. But the distinctive force of this truism in the case of children is not always so evident. As several of the authors explain, deficiencies and irregularities in the evolution of human and civil rights and the institutions that administer and protect those rights during and after transitions to democracy in Latin America affect children differently and perhaps less obviously than they affect adults. In addition, there are severe limits on the ability of children to protect themselves and their futures from social aberrations that result from these defects, especially those often associated with poverty and socioeconomic inequality, such as violent crime, police violence, corruption, gender discrimination, and environmental degradation.

Moreover, as García Méndez points out, the earlier era of forceful intervention by the state in welfare policy dates back only to the 1950s. Although there was a tradition in many countries of state action concerning universal social needs such as health and education and state responsibility for targeted welfare, charitable assistance for children living in poverty was historically assumed largely by the Catholic Church, with some state support. Even the role of NGOs, as they are understood today, in children's concerns dates back only to the 1970s.

In addition, historically, and most notably in some countries of Europe and Latin America, children have been treated differently from adults in both criminal law and in social legislation. The concept of guardianship that evolved from this assumption came to dominate the legal treatment of children and contributed to a variety of legal alternatives for children that came to be classified under the amorphous notion of an "irregular situation." The resulting interpretation of children's legal status emphasizes the legal incapacity of minors and typically opens the way for discretionary action in the legal treatment of children under the rubric of guardianship. In effect, the "irregular situation" doctrine, especially as it evolved in Latin America, often tended in practice to exempt both criminal justice and social legislation pertaining to children from normal constitutional and legal protections and to weaken the application of democratic process to children's issues.

It is only relatively recently that, along with gains in the survival, health, and economic, political, and social potential of children, there has been a shift away from the notion of children as passive recipients of legal services and protections in their capacity as minors. In its place has emerged the principle of children as persons and active citizens with legal, civil, and human rights entitled to comprehensive legal protection. As several of the volume authors emphasize, this shift to an operating principle based on the rights of children achieved a significant milestone with the passage of the 1989 Convention on the Rights of the Child (CRC) by the UN General Assembly. The CRC identifies the rights of children to "the highest attainable standard of health . . . through the provision of adequate nutritious foods and clean drinking-water," along with "access to hygiene and environmental sanitation . . . and preventive health care."[10] However, the CRC goes beyond these material rights, indeed further than most international agreements, in formulating affirmative political, social, and economic obligations that nations have to their children, along with more easily enforceable negative obligations, such as those pertaining to the removal of barriers to civil rights.

Virtually all nations, more than 190, with the notable exception of the United States and Somalia (which has recently had no internationally recognized government), have since ratified the CRC. Juan Méndez rightly notes that this is a remarkable achievement in light of the traditional reluctance of individual nations to constrain their own discretionary action in favor of a universal agreement. García Méndez further argues that the potential of the CRC is nothing less than "revolutionary" for having generated more political-legal and, above all, social consensus than any other agreement in the history of humanity.

Moreover, the shift from a legal operating principle of children as minors in an irregular situation to an operating principle of children's rights under the law does not reflect what Mendez identifies as the evolution whereby the typical human rights treaty catches up with an existing policy consensus in practice. Instead, the CRC represents an international agreement that is intended to drive policy and practice by a set of standards or ideals to be achieved in practice.

Baratta points out the potential impact that the CRC can have on both state and civil society in a functioning democracy by focusing on the implications of the CRC principle concerning the "best interests of the child." It is this principle that becomes the "primary consideration . . . in all actions concerning children whether undertaken by public or private social welfare institutions, courts of law, administrative authorities or legislative bodies."[11] For Baratta this mandate goes far beyond the establishment of full rights and guarantees under the law for children and extends to making children's best interests a priority in the development and administration of social policy at every level in both public and private sectors, nationally and internationally.

Baratta draws upon the elaboration that García Méndez sketches of the CRC in practice to argue that the universality of this principle implies more than basic social policies and programs, for example, in health and education. The universality of the principle of children's best interests extends even further, to policies for protective support of children, correctional measures directed against crime and juvenile delinquency, and measures to ensure administrative and judicial due process. Baratta believes that a proactive interpretation such as this makes it possible to compensate for children's lack of voice in the democratic process and to make full citizenship for children compatible with the special identity that distinguishes children from adults. Acceptance of this approach, moreover, requires a change in society's perception of relationships between adults and children, implying, for example, that adults acknowledge that children have a voice from which adults themselves can learn, not only in the family, but in the larger society.

However, Guillermo O'Donnell argues that giving priority to children and their needs in law and policy is justified precisely because children do lack the autonomy and responsibilities of full citizenship. For O'Donnell it is not sufficient simply to criticize the concept of "representation without mandate" that Baratta finds in the principle of tutelage. In reality, there still remain important questions about legitimate limits to the rights and freedoms of children in democracies. These include questions about the proper balance between parental authority and children's rights, about circumstances concerning when juveniles should be treated differently from adults under the law, and about appropriate limits to children's political participation. One challenge is to define the limits to a child's rights. These can range from the minimal right of the child to be a child, as García Méndez has put it, to an upper limit of participation in the life of a democratic society appropriate to the child's age and stage of development. Given this indeterminacy, Guillermo O'Donnell finds more fruitful the application of a concept of trusteeship to the responsibilities of parents and others who represent children in some tutorial fashion in a democracy. In this framework the trustee is obliged to make informed judgments in the best interests of the child that must take into account whatever relevant understanding and views the child can express. In addition, those with trustee responsibilities for children must act in ways that are conducive to the development of the child's potential to assume the autonomy and responsibilities of full citizenship.

Several authors show how the shift in legal conceptualization of children from dependent minors in an "irregular situation" to participative persons and citizens can have significant implications for addressing the impact on children and adolescents of social aberrations, especially social violence, that have accompanied Latin America's development history. Violence against children takes many forms, from child abuse in the home to the arming of children in social conflicts. On some measures of violence, Latin America may be no more violent than other developing areas. Military and guerrilla armies in Colombia, Peru, and Paraguay have recruited thousands of children, and thousands more work as slaves in remote areas of Peru and the Brazilian Amazon, but the total numbers relative to the population may not be as great in Latin America as in Africa and Asia.[12] On the other hand, even since the transition to democracy in Latin America, violence directed by police and military authorities against children, especially street children in countries like Brazil and Guatemala, has been well documented.[13]

Still, Guerrero describes Latin America as "particularly violent," and according to Yunes and Zubarew, violence has reached "epidemic proportions" in Latin America. These judgments are supported by country homicide rates in Latin America that increased by 60% during the decade of the 1980s, while in the same period death rates from other external causes remained constant or diminished even during the economic recession that dominated the region for most of the decade. During the 1990s, homicide rates declined in the United States, but they have continued to rise in diverse countries of Latin America. Even following the end of the civil war in El Salvador, homicides continued to increase, and in Brazil by the late 1990s the increase in homicides was so marked as to spur legislative proposals for a total ban on private gun ownership.

Moreover, homicide rates among children and adolescents remain disturbingly high in Latin America, accounting for almost 30% of deaths among children between 10 and 19 years of age in the Americas. In a majority of the most populous countries (including the United States), homicide is the first or second leading cause of death from external causes among young people between the ages of 15 and 24. Because of this concentration among young people, homicides account for the loss of more active lives, as measured by DALYs, according to Yunes and Zubarew, than any health-related cause, with an economic cost estimated at $10 billion annually in direct costs and lost productivity. Not surprisingly, these authors conclude that violence has become a major public health issue facing Latin America. As a social problem, the increase of violence among children and adolescents in Latin America heightens the significance of implementing the provisions of the CRC in the region. Cillero argues persuasively that, as its principle of rights and guarantees becomes increasingly incorporated into the legal systems of Latin

America, the CRC is radically changing the legal consequences for children (defined by the UN as those under the age of 19) and older youth who violate penal law.

Many personal and social characteristics blamed by Guerrero and Yunes and Zubarew for high rates of violence among Latin American youth are also those typically identified in the United States, including access to firearms, drugs and alcohol, child-rearing practices, parental and neighborhood behavior, violence in the media, racism, and prejudice. The wide variety of these influences underscores the importance of violence prevention programs based on the systematic epidemiological research and risk analysis suggested by Yunes and Zubarew.

At the same time, differences in cultural values, especially those related to distrust of police and law enforcement procedures, as well as disrespect for legal systems, which Guerrero also identifies, also help to explain higher homicide rates in Latin America. The more merit there is in explanations based on cultural values, the more important and the more hopeful for resolving problems of violence among youth in Latin America is the acceptance and legal adoption of the CRC in the countries of Latin America.

Zaffaroni underscores this conclusion by carefully articulating the implications in the CRC of a cultural shift from the principle of guardianship to the principle of individual rights and guarantees as the basis for criminal law as it pertains to legal offenses by children and adolescents in Latin American countries. Under the principle of guardianship, a child accused of violating the law is, in effect, moved outside the protection of the law to become the ward of the court for judgment, punishment, and rehabilitation without due process of law. The court as an agent of the state is thereby assigned a relatively unlimited quasi-parental authority that lacks accountability to another public body. It is not difficult to conclude from Zaffaroni's argument that the shift of authority from family and community to the state under the principle of guardianship contributes to an institutionalized violence that evokes a culture of violence as a reaction and response in a weakened civil society.

Under the principle of individual rights and guarantees, the child offender retains the constitutional and legal rights and guarantees of any accused or convicted person, regardless of extenuating circumstances and special treatment imposed by virtue of the age of the defendant. In this perspective, the rule of law embodied in the CRC helps to define a culturally acceptable balance of authority and responsibility between state and civil society that works to mitigate the impact of other contributing forces to violence in society.

Nevertheless, Salazar reminds us that the economic setting for police violence and impunity, for violations of human rights and the denial of justice, is the life of poverty into which so many Latin American children continue to be born and in which they must survive. The sheer necessity of overcoming immediate obstacles to personal survival can simply overwhelm a child's possibility for the self-determination that Salazar rightly notes is a prerequisite for the kind of responsible citizenship envisioned in the CRC. Even the nearly unanimous consensus among governments and international multilateral agencies to support policies to raise productivity for effective competition in global markets has failed to produce coordinated action and clear results.

Moreover, Méndez points out that, even with all the possibilities for self-actualization of children envisioned by the CRC, the Convention itself remains deficient by incorporating limitations on the important right of freedom of expression that make the CRC less progressive in that respect than the American Convention on Human Rights. Latin American countries have further committed themselves to comply with the agreements reached at the World Summit for Children in 1990. They have made significant progress in implementing the provisions of the CRC through a series of accords and agreements, including the Nariño Accord in 1994 and the Santiago Accord in 1996.[14] Nevertheless, Méndez notes that the CRC's provisions for implementation remain deficient. This is especially true, he says, in the agreement's failure to provide for an international system of monitoring and enforcement of compliance.

In sum, there have been advances in children's survival, health, and nutrition, in economic restructuring and productivity, and in the support throughout Latin America for the CRC. But the analysis of all our authors suggests that the future of children in Latin America will continue to challenge governments and all sectors of society to translate those advances into the reality of human development. There are enough justified criticisms of economic inequality and poverty, of misallocated resources in public health, of denials of justice and violations of human rights to conclude that the glass is half-empty for the next generation. But as our understanding of the challenges and the interaction among them expands, we can also conclude with our authors that those interrelated challenges can be met in ways that will offer our children a half-full glass that will continue to be filled in their future.

NOTES

1. The World Bank, World Development Report: Knowledge for Development, 1998–99 (Washington: World Bank, 1999) Selected World Indicators, Table 1, 190–191.

2. See Jeffrey Sachs, "Nature, Nurture and Growth," Economist, June 14, 1997, 19–22.

3. See Inter-American Development Bank, passim. Facing Up to Inequality in Latin America: Economic and Social Progress in Latin America, 1998–1999 Report (Washington: Inter-American Development Bank, 1998).

4. Addressing micronutrient deficiencies, especially of iron, has become a priority of the International Life Sciences Institute (ILSI) in recent years. See the April and June 1997 issues of ILSI's Nutrition Review, which are dedicated to the topics of the consequences and prevention of iron deficiency.

5. Opening speech at the Third Ministerial Meeting on Children and Social Policy in the Americas, cited in UNICEF, Santiago Accord (Santiago: UNICEF, 1996), 2.

6. Vd. Inter-American Development Bank, op. cit., n. 3, 11.

7. Ibid., 22.

8. Economic Commission for Latin America, Social Panorama of Latin America, 1997 (Santiago: ECLAC, 1998), Chaps. 2 and 4.

9. Comisión Económica para América Latina y Caribe. Panorama Social de América Latina, 1998 (Santiago: CEPAL, 1999), Chap. 3.

10. United Nations. Convention on the Rights of the Child. New York: United Nations, 1989, Article 24.

11. Economic Commission for Latin America, op. cit., n. 8, 97. See also UNICEF, The State of the World's Children, 1997 (New York: Oxford University Press, 1997), Chap. 1.

12. Economist, September 21, 1996, 43; Human Rights Watch, Children in Combat (New York: Human Rights Watch, Children's Rights Project Report, 1996); and data from United Nations, Radda Barnan, and the British army cited in "Children under Arms," Economist, July 10, 1999, 19–21.

13. See Caius Brandau, "The Killings Escalate in Brazil—Street Children: More and More Killed Everyday," International Child Resource Institute Bulletin, April 1995, 1–2; Gilberto Dimenstein, Brazil: War on Children (London: Latin American Bureau, 1991); Gilberto Dimenstein, A guerra dos meninos: Assassinato de menores no Brasil (Sao Paulo: Editora Brasiliense, 1993); and W. E. Guttman, "Killing Children in Guatemala," Freedom Re-

view, 27: 26–7; as well as many reports and articles from UNICEF and Human Rights Watch.

14. Economic Commission for Latin America, Social Panorama of Latin America, 1997, Chap. 5; and UNICEF, Santiago Accord (Santiago: UNICEF, 1996).

I | Child Health in Latin America

A | The Changing Face of Malnutrition

1 | The Nutritional Status of Children in Latin America

ALEJANDRO O'DONNELL

Acknowledgments

I wish to thank Dr. Mary Penny and Dr. Nelly Zavaleta (Instituto de Investigaciones Nutricionales, Lima, Peru), Dra. Mercedez Lopez de Blanco (Fundación CAVENDES, Venezuela), and Dr. José Luis San Martín (Instituto Boliviano de Biología de Altura, La Paz, Bolivia) for providing updated information from their respective countries. I deeply appreciate the comments of Dr. Esteban Carmuega (Centro de Estudios Sabre Nutrición Infantil (CESNI), Buenos Aires) on the manuscript.

Introduction

Famine and hunger used to be considered almost natural phenomena if they occurred in Asia or Africa. Only after the Spanish Civil World and World War II, when the modern Occidental world had, for the first time, massive hunger and malnutrition in its homeland, did Westerners become conscious about the problem of malnutrition at the community level as a global health, political, and economic problem.

This prompted the scientific application of existing nutritional knowledge to mitigate hunger, malnutrition, and disease in poor countries. First was

5

the enthusiasm for alleviating the deficiency of proteins, so much so that the UN organizations created a special branch—the Protein Advisory Group (PAG)—which sponsored and coordinated many valuable investigations on protein and aminoacid requirements. There was an enormous enthusiasm among scientists because mixing different amounts of cereal and legume proteins that individually were of inferior protein quality resulted in a protein of biological value as high as milk or egg protein. The consequence was that many countries and international relief agencies developed cereal mixes for food assistance programs; these mixes never gained much acceptance by the population because of taste, culinary properties, and wrong marketing strategies. Special varieties of corn and wheat, richer in the naturally limiting aminoacids than the original plants, were bred by genetic manipulation.

The coup de grace for the protein euphoria came from dietary population studies in the Middle East and India showing that the limiting factor was energy and not protein, even among the poorest people. This produced great concern because providing energy means providing food, which has many social, political, and economical implications. The PAG soon ceased.

The "green revolution" came in help of humankind, so much so that today countries like India are wheat exporters. Unfortunately the new high-output varieties need intensive use of water and fertilizers, which is to say investments and capital to which many peasants do not have access.

Later the importance of infections in the genesis of malnutrition was realized, and sanitation and food safety programs ensued. The immense value of breast feeding for protecting small infants from contaminated environments was acknowledged, and the rediscovery and consequent promotion of breast feeding became one of the pillars of health and nutrition promotion for infants.

Meanwhile, much progress was done in nutrition and health programs at the primary care level. Countries adopted different kinds of food assistance programs, and some of them were carefully evaluated, leaving lessons to learn from. Perhaps the major lesson was that health and nutrition activities had to go hand in hand and never be separated. And the influence of economic, cultural, and sociological factors on the well-being of children was scientifically studied.

The universal implementation of oral rehydration for infectious diarrhea with the World Health Organization/United Nations Children's Fund (WHO/UNICEF) solution was another milestone in improving the health and nutrition of children. Oral rehydration has produced an impact similar or superior to that of antibiotics. Half a century of efforts to improve the nutritional and health status in less developed countries have produced results. Trends in infant mortality in the majority of Latin American countries confirm the success of such efforts (see Table 1).

These improvements in child health and nutrition have permitted us to consider less urgent matters like the quality of life of our surviving children. If we accept as a definition of "health" the condition that permits the full social and labor participation of an individual in the community where he or she lives, we must deal with many issues in the current and future situations of our children, issues such as those presented in this chapter (Myers 1993).

Recently, the importance of a child's early years for his or her adequate development has been the subject of many multidisciplinary studies, emphasizing the role of the family and caretakers. We pediatricians have always known that some families, regardless of how poor they are, generate health, while others, regardless of how privileged they are, generate disease and malnutrition (Zeittin, Ghassemi, & Mansor 1990).

Perhaps due to the relief that the increasing survival of children has produced, a lot of interest has been placed on the correction of micronutrient deficiencies, which to a greater or lesser degree affect physiological functions that can produce irreversible damage in small children (Allen 1993). This is a real challenge and a great responsibility because the tools to produce improvements exist and have been tested. The only remaining needs are an attitude of compromise and a willingness to put those improvements into work.

Table 1.   Number of Children Surviving for Every Child Dying before Its First Birthday

Country	Number
Cuba	99
Costa Rica	70
Chile	67
Mexico	47
Uruguay	46
Argentina	43
Paraguay	41
Panama	39
Venezuela	39
Colombia	25
Ecuador	25
Guatemala	19
Honduras	19
Brazil	17
Peru	17
Nicaragua	13
Bolivia	12
El Salvador	12

The Nutritional Status of Children in Latin America

In the past three decades, Latin America has suffered many transformations that have directly or indirectly influenced the health, nutrition, and well-being of children and their families. Changes can be seen in the demography of the region: the rapid rate of urbanization at the expense of rural populations, changes in the rates of child mortality and survival, widening gap between the rich and the poor, and the decreasing prevalence of infectious diseases and, in contrast, an increase in the morbidity and mortality related to chronic non-transmissible diseases, cancer, and accidents. Also, the growing percentage of women working out of the household has important implications for the care, health, and nutrition of children. And very importantly, the neoliberal economic adjustment policies implemented in almost all countries of the region have imposed a painful toll in unemployment and poverty.

Some of these changes have negatively affected children's care and, thus, their health and nutrition; others have favored access to health care and education. The balance between these explains how the nutrition and health conditions of children in Latin America have steadily improved in the past three decades, in spite of economic deterioration for large segments of the population.

Figure 1.   Changes in the Prevalence of Malnutrition (Children under 5 years) in Several Latin American Countries during the Past 25 Years (Percent)

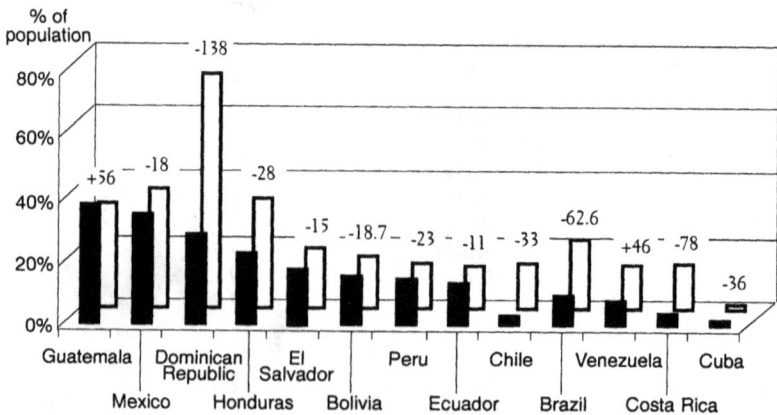

The prevalence of acute protein energy malnutrition (PEM) (defined as a low body weight for the person's length or height) is presently very low in almost all countries and negligible in some (see Figure 1 and Table 2). It is possible that the circumstances related to the accessibility of primary care, among many others, have been instrumental in this improvement.

Table 2. Prevalence of Protein Energy Malnutrition in Latin American and U.S. Preschool Children (Percent)

Country	Year	Sample	Weight/ age	Height/ age	Weight/ height
Argentina	1995	NS	2.6	5.6	0.1
Bolivia	1991	NS	11.7	38.3	2.2
Brazil	1989	NS	7.0	15.4	2.0
Chile	1989	MC	0.8	9.6	0.5
Colombia	1989	NS	10.1	16.6	2.9
Costa Rica	1990	HC	2.8	9.2	—
Ecuador	1986	NS	16.5	34.0	1.7
El Salvador	1989	NS	15.2	29.9	2.3
Guatemala	1990	NS	38.5	57.9	1.4
Honduras	1997	NS	20.6	39.4	13.1
Mexico	1988	NS	13.9	22.3	6.3
Nicaragua	1988	NS	10.9	21.9	2.3
Paraguay	1990	NS	4.2	20.3	0.4
Peru	1991	HC (rural)	10.4	35.2	1.4
Dominican Rep.	1987	NS	12.5	20.8	2.3
United States	1992	NS	2.9	4.7	1.2
Uruguay	1989	HC	6.5	14.6	1.9
Venezuela	1992	HC	8.2	17.0	5.3

NS = National Survey; HC = Health Centers; MC = Medical Centers
Source: PAHO/WHO.

Although not a sensible indicator of nutritional status, infant mortality rates give some insight into the living conditions of children in a community. In this area, there have been substantial improvements in most countries, though there still exist great disparities. Cuba, Chile, and Costa Rica are approaching the infant mortality rates of developed countries, while others, like Bolivia and Honduras still have unacceptably high figures. In others, like

Argentina and Uruguay, the downward trend observed in recent years has slowed down (see Figure 2).

Figure 2. Relation between Child Survival and Prevalence of Chronic Malnutrition

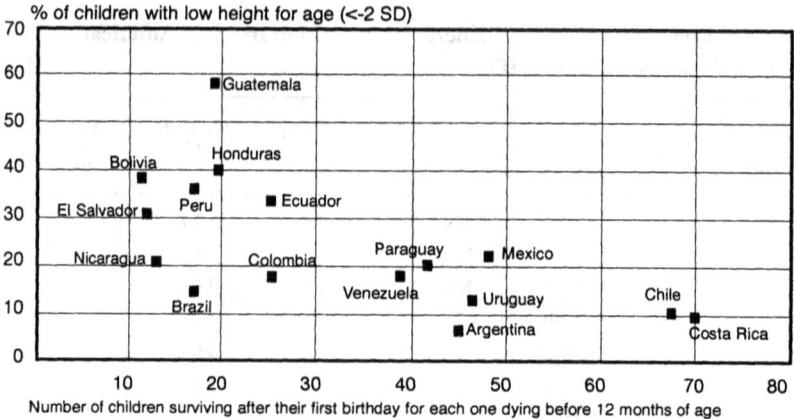

% of children with low height for age (<-2 SD)

Source: CESNI, 1996

There is a direct relationship between the prevalence of malnutrition in children expressed as deficits of height for age and the number of children surviving after the first year of life for each child dying before its first birthday. Chile has a rather moderate prevalence of chronic malnutrition but very low infant mortality rates; conversely, Argentina has lower rates of chronic malnutrition but higher infant mortality rates (see Figure 2 and Table 3). These differences reveal disparities in the quality of primary care.

Another peculiarity of the nutritional status of Latin American children is the high prevalence of chronic malnutrition—or past malnutrition—expressed as low height for age (i.e., stunting). This condition is not exclusive to countries in our region; it is a universal phenomenon that has recently been the subject of much discussion and research (Waterlow 1988) since this type of chronic malnutrition also has serious health and educational implications for children now and in the future.

Table 3 shows national prevalences of stunting in some Latin American countries. However, large differences exist among regions and communities within the same country. Stunting is always more prevalent in rural populations than in urban ones.

Table 3. Prevalence of Deficits in Height for Age in Latin American School Children (% < -2SD)

Country	Year	Prevalence
Argentina	1991	4.9
Bolivia	1988–90	35.0
Chile	1985	8.5
Costa Rica	1980	9.2
Ecuador	1990	37.5
El Salvador	1988	30.0
Guatemala	1986	37.4
Honduras	1986	39.8
Mexico	1991	18.4
Nicaragua	1989	18.7
Panama	1988	24.4
Uruguay	1987	4.0
Venezuela	1992	22.8

The high prevalence of stunting biases the interpretation of a community's nutritional status when it is based on the simplest and more popular method of nutritional assessment, which is weight for age, because children of short length or height and small body size will score low on such an indicator. On the other hand, the finding that many children in a community have adequate weight for height raises the question of whether such children are presently malnourished or simply showing the sequelae of past nutritional insults. Studies in stunted Peruvian children (Buotton et al. 1987; Trowbridge et al. 1987) found alterations in the composition of lean body mass, with larger amounts of water in the muscle tissue of stunted children of normal weight for their present height; a recent study from a very poor Brazilian community found that stunted children of normal weight for height have larger abdominal circumferences than normal children of the same height. These observations are important not only in clarifying the physiology of malnutrition, but also in defining whether stunted children qualify for food assistance programs when resources are scarce. Regardless of such considerations, the fact that children are of small size is proof that early in their lives, they have suffered nutritional insults that affected their growth potential.

The causes of growth retardation are many, and no single cause has been identified as primary. It is recognized that the future body weight of infants with low birth weight (even if proportional to body length) and/or intrauterine growth retardation (IUGR) will be compromised, especially when such infants are born to mothers who are malnourished, hypertensive, smokers, or drug addicted, or who have suffered from intrauterine infections. Such retardation occurs in developing as well as developed countries; however, the prevalence of IUGR in the former is twice that in the latter (Tennovuo et al. 1987; Villar, Belizán, Spalding & Klein 1982).

Many nutritional causes for early postnatal growth retardation have been postulated. One of the most accepted reasons is inadequate breast feeding, given the high nutritional quality of breast milk and its immunological properties, which strongly protect infants against infections in the early months of life. Many studies have confirmed its value in protecting infant health, growth, and nutrition in adverse environments, as well as in more privileged communities (Brown et al. 1989). Such observations are the foundation of efforts to promote breast feeding. All countries participating in the World Summit for Infancy and in the International Conference on Nutrition made strong commitments to achieve the exclusive breast feeding of infants during at least their first 4 months of life and ideally for their first 6 months (UNICEF 1990, 1996, 1997).

Many studies suggest that the process of stunting begins very early in life, in the first 4 or 6 months, and continues until age 3 or 4 years, when children resume normal growth velocity but remain small, regardless of the medical or nutritional interventions they might be subject to thereafter. At 3 years of age, children in a periurban community in Guatemala were already 6–8 cm shorter than the international growth norm. Another study in Guatemala traces the beginning of growth retardation in breast-fed infants as early as the first month of life; their mothers were malnourished and of very short stature. Although it is known that maternal nutritional status does not influence the amount of breast milk produced, little is known about its influence on micronutrient content, which could be one cause of growth failure in breast-fed babies. In the Institute of Nutrition of Central America and Panama (INCAP) "atole-fresco" study, the stunting of growth began in the first month of life, even though all the babies were breast fed (Brown et al. 1986; Rivera & Ruel 1997; Valdez et al. 1997).

One study in Mexico showed that although the total milk intake of slow-growing breast-fed infants was similar to that of a comparable group of infants growing normally, the energy expenditure of infants who lagged behind in growth was larger, possibly due to subclinical infections (Butte et al. 1992, 1993).

Although it can be disputed whether stunted children are concurrently malnourished, several factors should be considered in this regard. First, since individuals from all races have the same growth potential, delays in growth must be due to environmental factors, including intrauterine conditions. Individuals from different racial backgrounds raised for a few generations in favorable environments show only slight differences in body proportions and pubertal growth (Habicht et al. 1974).

Second, when stunting is prevalent in a community, it speaks of poor nutritional, health, and environmental conditions. Most children in such communities show developmental delays, whether due to malnutrition, micronutrient deficiencies, or the cluster of environmental conditions associated with extreme poverty.

Third, it has been shown that even mild degrees of malnutrition produce an increased risk of mortality (Pelletier et al. 1996). IUGR infants, even those raised in affluent communities, show long-lasting immune deficiencies, which helps explain in part the large degree to which such infants raise mortality statistics.

Fourth, today it is accepted that early growth retardation due to nutritional deficiencies produces imprints that persists throughout the life span of an individual. In humans, body size at 3 years is a good predictor of stature in adolescence; small children remain small adults. The association between stunting in children and later obesity is also well known. The "Barker hypothesis" (Barker 1994) — which is being confirmed in developed as well as in less developed countries — suggests that adults who were IUGR infants have higher risks of hypertension, obesity, and hyperinsulinism than adults who were normal newborn infants; recent studies point to similar risks for stunted, but not IUGR, slow-growing children during their first years of life.

Results from the follow-up INCAP "fresco-atole" study confirm the long-lasting impact of food supplements in the last months of pregnancy on marginally nourished mothers and their children when 15–30 months of age (with only 100 Kcal and 8.6 gr of protein per day). Adolescents who were supplemented as children were taller (especially women) and had larger muscle mass and greater work capacity. In terms of educational achievements, the supplement leveled off familial socioeconomic and educational differences, which are known to influence the educability of offsprings. All these facts emphasize the importance of nutrition in the early years of life, including during pregnancy.

The introduction of foods other than breast milk in early infancy is very critical, since babies may become exposed to foods that are of poor nutritional quality and frequently contaminated (Brown et al. 1989). It has been shown that such foods are not used to complement breast milk in fulfilling the nutritional needs of the child but rather to replace it, so that, in the short term, infants end up being totally weaned (Cohen et al. 1994).

The composition and preparation of the weaning or transitional foods typically available to poor families has been a matter of intensive study. Although household conditions can differ substantially among communities in the region, some general issues can be enunciated: iron and zinc will be limited in most instances; animal protein, particularly meats of any origin, should be given daily, not only as a protein source, but as a way to acquire and enhance the absorption of iron and zinc. It has been suggested that meats could be a source of some "nutritional fellow travelers" affecting the growth of children fed predominantly vegetables.

The fiber content of infant foods should be low because of fiber's tendency to trap water during cooking resulting in bulky foods that are low in energy and nutrient density and are difficult for the child to swallow, thus demanding a lot of time from a busy mother to feed her baby. Dietary fiber also interferes with the absorption of iron, zinc, and copper (Bell 1987).

To solve the problem of the low energy density of cereal-based weaning foods, two approaches have been used. One is to increase the energy density through the addition of sucrose (cane sugar) or oil or other fat sources. This practice only further dilutes with empty calories the concentration of micronutrients that were very likely already scarce in the original preparation, with the danger that babies may get satiated before taking in enough food to fulfill some of their micronutrient requirements.

An attempt has been made to decrease the bulk and hygroscopy of weaning foods by incubating them for several hours with amilase-rich vegetals, which predigest the starch, expelling the water retained. This has proven to be an effective alternative under controlled conditions, but the risk of contamination during incubation casts many doubts over its practicality and safety (Stephenson et al. 1994).

Calcium can in some instances be another limiting nutrient if milk or other dairy products are unavailable or if maize or wheat are not soaked in lime water, as is done for the manufacture of tortillas. Fish is a good source of calcium, but its intake must be relatively high.

It is surprising that on our continent there have been so few successful experiences with low-cost cereal-based infant foods modified and fortified during the manufacturing process. Some countries have a long tradition with so-called M-Ch programs based on the distribution of dry milk to infants and their mothers for the first 2 years of life. Infant cereals could be incorporated into those programs or subsidized to make them accessible to poorer families. The food industry and nutrition policy makers can make substantial contributions in this area of infant feeding.

Overweight and Obesity

Although lacking the ethical, health, and epidemiological relevance of malnutrition, obesity is becoming a serious health problem in all the region's countries. For small children, overweight and obesity are not existing health problems. However, obesity constitutes a cluster of risk factors for diseases of adulthood, like hypertension, insulin resistance, diabetes, coronary heart disease, stroke, osteoarticular diseases, and gout. Being obese in the early years of life does not necessarily mean that a child will be an obese adult, but the persistence of overweight during childhood makes it more and more likely. Obesity is one of the most difficult diseases to treat and results are most of the time disappointing. Prevention is of utmost importance.

In striking contrast to the obesity seen in developed countries, which is usually associated with opulence and the easy availability of food, obesity in Latin America is associated with poverty and the poor nutritional quality of the foods available in the household. In adults and older children, obesity is much more prevalent in urban than in rural communities. It is also more prevalent among women of all ages than in men.

Mothers living in shanty towns surrounding the region's big cities expend very little energy since they are confined to a few blocks around their homes most of their lives. They do not have to bring food to their family members working in the fields, as is usual in rural families. The food consumed by the family is usually of high energy density, based on pasta, sugar, fats, and oils, because these are cheaper (calorie per calorie), easier to prepare, and more energy saving than more varied diets. Moreover, these women do not have the aesthetic pressures to which more privileged classes are subject.

For older children, the same dietary considerations are valid. In Tierra del Fuego, Argentina, a community with high prevalence of infantile overweight, 20% of the total energy intake comes from sucrose (cane sugar), another 30% from pasta and bread made with highly refined wheat flour, and another 35% from fats and oils.

As already stated, inactivity adds another risk factor: the importance of TV is known by all. Poor families live in communities where sports facilities are nil, and most families do not have money to send their children to paid facilities. Mothers in the suburbs, even if open air space exists for outdoor play, do not allow their children to go because of wanting to protect them from street violence, drugs, and "bad company." To compensate, with great sacrifice, many poor families purchase video games to entertain their children. If parents work outside their home for many hours, the food they commonly prepare when they return home, tired after a day of work and suburban travel, is whatever is easiest to cook and of high energy density.

The retirement money that senior citizens get, if any, is almost charity, so a very large percentage of grandmothers are obliged to live with their daughters or sons, whose children are left under their care when parents are away from home at work. Grandmothers are generous with cookies, sweets, and TV if the children stay quiet. Middle-class parents make efforts to compensate for failures of the school system and send their children to extracurricular activities, which further aggravates parents' sedentary lifestyle.

All countries in the region report an important proportion of children who are overweight for their height. In addition to the figures in Table 1, it is interesting to comment on the results of some studies. In Chile, 56% of schoolchildren who qualify (socially and economically) for school lunch programs are overweight for their stature (J. Riumallo, personal communication). In a large sample of preschool children attending day care centers in São Paulo, Brazil, 15% were stunted, but only 0.6% were of low weight for height (Fisberg et al. 1996). In Venezuela, the prevalence of overweight school children ranges from 11 to 23% for different regions and socioeconomic status. In the suburbs of Buenos Aires, the prevalence of overweight school children (without proportional increments in height) was 17% in the first grade but increased to 48% in the seventh grade. In these suburbs, school lunch programs promoted generous gains in weight but not in height.

The first anthropometric survey of Argentina's secondary school students was done in 1938. If its information is compared with figures from the medical examination for military service (18-year-old adolescents) in 1993, average growth was 1.2 cm and 3.5 Kg/decade. The Body Mass Index (BMI) increased from 19.5 to 22.8 in the 50 years between the two series. Considering a cutoff point of BMI > 25 Kg/m2 for the definition of overweight and obesity, the prevalence was 14.7% nationwide, but as high as 18% in some provinces (Abeya & Lejarraga 1995).

In the last class examined—68,212 adolescents, 17–18 years old born in 1975—the national average BMI was 22.4, with a prevalence of overweight and obesity of 19.5 and 4.1%, respectively, representing an increase, with respect to those born in 1967, of 33 and 97% (E. B. Calvo, unpublished data). In all the series of conscripts, those with short statures had more risk of obesity (RR 1.7) relative to their normal-height counterparts.

These and many other observations confirm that obesity is a growing health and nutrition problem in Latin America and that children with short stature resulting from nutritional deprivations in the early years of life are at greater risk for becoming obese than other children.

So, malnutrition and obesity can coexist in the same countries of the region, in the same community, in the same family (obese parents with malnourished children), and even in the same individual (obesity and early growth retardation/stunting).

Micronutrient Deficiencies

Iron

Iron deficiency is the world's most prevalent nutritional deficiency (Viteri 1992). Latin America is no exception, with small infants and pregnant women being the most affected. Iron deficiency is due to a low dietary intake of iron, to dietary iron being in a poorly bioavailable form, to the presence of factors in the diet that inhibit its absorption, or to the scarcity of factors in the diet that enhance its absorption. Other causes include blood loss from uncinaria infestation and from antigenic responses of the gut induced by the early introduction of pasteurized or raw cow's milk to small infants.

Iron requirements are mainly dependent on the velocity of growth, that is, the formation of new body mass. It is therefore understandable why small infants and pregnant women have a higher than average risk of iron deficiency. Growth is most rapid in the first year of life, more than in adolescence. The growth of their reproductive organs and fetus are a challenge for the iron nutritional status of pregnant women, which is further aggravated by prolonged lactations and frequent pregnancies (Allen 1997; Viteri 1997). Female adolescents follow pregnant women in risk potential because of the rapid growth spurt of adolescence and the initiation of menses. Nonpregnant, fertile women require almost twice as much iron as men because of menstrual blood losses. Old people of both sexes are at risk because of their often inadequate diets, as well as the lower acidity of gastric juice, which render food iron less available (Beard & Piñero 1997).

Iron deficiency anemia is the final stage of iron deficiency and occurs when the body's deposits of the mineral become exhausted. Specific biochemical methods can identify the stages of iron depletion, which end in anemia. Some biological functions that depend on a good iron nutritional status can be affected before anemia becomes evident.

Iron deficiency has many biological consequences. It affects the immune system of individuals, mainly those functions related to neutrophil activity, like phagocytosis and bactericidal capacity (Walter et al. 1986, 1996). Iron deficiency is a risk factor for severe bacterial infections and for the reiteration and prolongation of common infections in children.

Iron deficiency affects physical activity, both endurance and explosive muscular activity. The first is related to the function of iron in enzymes of the mitochondrial respiratory chain and occurs with exhaustion of iron deposits even if red cell concentration is normal (Brooke 1997); the latter depends on the transport of oxygen by red cells. Anemic small children have less spontaneous activity than their nonanemic counterparts, which deprives them of the psychological stimulation provided by exploring their environment, one of the richest inputs from the point of view of infantile intellectual development. Iron deficiency has negative economic consequences for anemic laborers, since laborers' jobs require physical activity; the productivity and earnings of workers who cut sugar cane, harvest tea leaves, and mill cotton fall as a consequence of anemia and improve after treatment with iron (Hussaini, Karyadi, & Gunadi 1981; Li et al. 1994).

Severe anemia in pregnant women carries an increased risk of death during delivery. Moderate anemia and iron deficiency is associated with increased rates of preterm delivery and IUGR (Institute of Medicine 1990; NAS 1990; Scholl et al. 1992; Worthington-Roberts 1990).

There is some evidence that the correction of iron deficiency increases growth velocity in children. The mechanism for this effect is not known but is perhaps related to the increased well-being and activity of previously anemic children (Chwang, Soemantri, & Pollitt 1988; Latham et al. 1990).

But the most significant consequence of iron deficiency in children, and the most relevant for the subject of this chapter, is its effect on the intellectual development of small infants, the school performance of school children, and the mood of children of all ages. Several well-designed and controlled studies have shown that anemic infants perform less well than nonanemic infants on psychological tests. Lozoff and colleagues (1987, 1991) in Costa Rica and Walter et al. (1989, 1990) in Chile have provided strong evidence that iron deficiency anemia handicaps the development of affected infants and that the effect on mental abilities is worse when anemia is more severe and chronic (Chapter 4 in this volume).

However, as in the case of the effects of protein energy malnutrition (PEM) on intelligence, studies of the influence of iron deficiency on child development confront the fact that anemia is more prevalent among children of families with low socioeconomic status, for which many of the negative influences of poverty merge. Also, those children can be simultaneously deficient in zinc and in some vitamins, as well as be malnourished and have high lead serum concentrations, conditions common in iron-deficient children. Nevertheless, studies with experimental animals, as well as children, strongly suggest a causal relationship.

Prevalence of Iron Deficiency in Latin America

The prevalences listed in this section are national averages, which are somewhat deceiving given that large differences in prevalences can be found among regions within a country and among socioeconomic levels. In general, rural and poorer populations have the highest prevalences. For instance, the prevalence of anemia among Argentinian infants 8–24 months of age in Misiones province was 56% (Calvo et al. 1987), while in Tierra del Fuego it was 24% (CESNI 1995); in Bolivia, the prevalence in the rural altiplano was near 75%, while in the lowlands it was about 20%; the same pattern appears in Peru, where the situation is much better in Lima than in the altiplano or the Amazonian provinces (Penny, personal communication 1997; Pajuela & Ameniya 1992; see also Chapter 3 in this volume). These figures show the magnitude of iron malnutrition in the region, deserving a frontal battle for its eradication and prevention. Much has been learned about the strategies to prevent iron deficiency; developing the willingness and ingenuity to implement them is the only challenge we now face.

Strategies to Prevent Iron Deficiency

Diet

This is the most physiological of alternative strategies, but is sometimes not very effective in certain settings and for some risk groups with very high requirements, like young infants and pregnant women.

Breast feeding is a valuable method for preventing iron deficiency in infants and small children. Although the iron content of breast milk is just as low as that of cow's milk, its absorption rate is ten times greater (Garry et al. 1981; Saarinen & Siimes 1979). Exclusive breast feeding protects the immature gut of small infants from absorbing antigenic macromolecules, which can induce microscopic blood losses that further challenge the iron nutritional status of infants, who are growing rapidly; this has been shown to happen with pasteurized milk in infants in their first semester of life (Fomon et al. 1981). In one population study (Calvo & Gnazzo 1990), the early introduction of cow's milk was one of the main risk factors for the high prevalence of anemia found in Buenos Aires. Breast milk also prevents enteric infections, which produce fecal losses of blood, microscopic and macroscopic (Feachem & Koblinsky 1984).

However, the prevalence of anemia in partially breast-fed infants aged 4 to 6 months who do not receive another iron source can be as high as 30%, since iron intakes become marginal for the size and growth rates of such infants (Calvo, Galindo, & Aspres 1992). Pediatric societies worldwide recommend the incorporation of iron (medicinal iron or infant foods fortified with bioavailable iron) from that age on.

Improvements in diet consist of increasing the amount of total iron and heme-iron from animal sources, avoiding absorption inhibitors (tea, mate, coffee, perhaps milk and foods rich in phytates) during the main meals, and increasing the amount of absorption enhancers, like ascorbic acid (Lynch 1997).

In some communities the total amount of iron in the diet is not low, sometimes reaching levels as high as 30mg/day, but its bioavailability is poor because much such iron is contaminated (Lynch 1997). But in most instances the amount of iron in the diet is the limiting factor; even in Argentina, which has one of the highest levels of per capita meat consumption in the world and hence high levels of heme-iron of high bioavailability, and where meat is introduced early in the diets of normal infants, the total amount of absorbed iron is below recommended levels in 85% of infants between 8 and 24 months of age (O'Donnell, Camuega, and Durán 1997).

Ascorbic acid intake is commonly below recommended levels in urban communities, where fruits and vegetables are expensive due to the many intermediaries between producers and consumers. This is very unfortunate given that this vitamin is the most potent enhancer of iron absorption, especially when dietary iron is of poor bioavailability, that is, rich in phytates as is the case in cereals and legumes, which are staple foods in many communities. Given that its effect is on the intestinal lumen, ascorbic acid must be ingested with meals to render iron from vegetable sources more absorbable (Cook et al. 1997; Hallberg, Bruce, & Rossander 1989; Hallberg, Rossander, & Skänberg 1987).

Heme-iron, or the iron contained in meats of bovines, chicken, fish, sheep, and game animals, has high bioavailability and is little influenced by other components in meals. Compared with ascorbic acid, meats have a much less enhancing effect on the absorption of iron from vegetable sources (Hallberg et al. 1987, 1989).

Iron Supplementation

Iron was perhaps the first nutritional medicine in history. It was used to treat clorosis, the name given to the "disease" of very pale anemic adolescents and young women.

The doses and iron compounds used to treat iron deficiency anemia are well known from many controlled clinical studies. Unfortunately, the most effective and less expensive iron compounds are poorly tolerated, producing gastric discomfort, diarrhea or constipation, a disagreeable residual metallic taste, and a dark-green, blackish discoloration of the feces of small children. Better tolerated compounds are too expensive for many families and for primary programs (Cook et al. 1990).

Such unpleasant side-effects explain in part the poor compliance with the recommended daily administration of iron to children and pregnant women. Also, mothers do not feel compelled to give iron to their apparently healthy children.

In this regard, two studies of the prevalence of iron deficiency among small children in Argentina are illustrative. The two surveys, conducted 10 years apart in urban populations showed prevalences of 49% in greater Buenos Aires (Calvo & Gnazzo 1990) and 25% in Tierra del Fuego; both populations were devoid of parasites and had a similar socioeconomic level, similar dietary patterns, and the same intake of total and bioavailable iron. The only statistical difference between the many potential causes considered was the time mothers said they had given iron to their children from birth to 10 months, showing that the supplementation was instrumental in reducing the observed prevalence of iron deficiency and anemia. However, given the excellent nutrition, social programs, and medical care of children in Tierra del Fuego, it could be speculated that the low prevalence found there is the best possible when iron supplementation is the main method used to prevent iron deficiency.

To overcome the undesirable effects of daily iron doses and, so, increase compliance, it has been suggested that weekly or bi-weekly doses of iron might be as effective as daily doses in terms of preventing and even treating iron deficiency anemia (Viteri 1997). This approach is based on experimental studies in rats, which showed that daily doses equivalent to those used in humans saturated the iron transport mechanisms in the intestinal mucosa, resulting in a progressive diminution in absorption of consecutive daily iron doses (Brown et al. 1996; Wright & Sutton 1990).

The effectiveness of this approach has been shown in several studies, most of them conducted in developing countries where the prevalence of iron deficiency is high. Almost all have shown the validity of this approach; Table 4 shows the results of one study conducted with children living at high altitudes in Bolivia (Berger et al. 1996).

Table 4. Iron Supplementation in Bolivian Children Living at High Altitudes. Daily versus Weekly Doses (Hemoglobin gr/l)

	Placebo	Weekly	Daily
	(n = 57)	(n = 58)	(n = 58)
Baseline	131.7 ± 11.3[a]	135.3 ± 8.5[a]	131.7 ± 12.6[a]
5 weeks	131.0 ± 10.0[a]	142.6 ± 9.1[b]	142.8 ± 9.8[b]
10 weeks	131.6 ± 8.4[a]	146.6 ± 9.6[c]	148.4 ± 8.2[c]
16 weeks	132.2 ± 8.1[a]	150.5 ± 6.9[d]	150.1 ± 6.7[d]

Note: The supplement was 3.4 mg iron/Kg as ferrous sulphate.
a,b,c,d: $p < 0.05$ when letters change.

Some of these studies explored people's compliance using the new schedule of iron supplementation. They showed lower rates of desertion than in the groups on daily doses (Liu et al. 1995; Viteri et al. 1997). Most of the above-mentioned studies were conducted under controlled conditions in which the doses of iron were given by teachers, primary care workers, and the like. In one study, people themselves were responsible for taking the weekly dose; in this study the results were not different from those of traditional and novel iron therapies (Chew, Torún, & Viteri 1996).

There is no doubt that this new approach to iron supplementation is very attractive for its efficacy and minimal undesirable effects. However, a justified concern exists about compliance in primary care programs: forgetting to ingest the weekly dose might be detrimental to the iron nutritional status of risk groups, while forgetting several doses in the daily schedule might not. More studies are needed in field, self-dosing conditions before making recommendations for their universal implementation.

On the other hand, the weekly or bi-weekly schedules seem ideal for the prevention of iron deficiency in schools, factories, day care centers, community centers, and the like, where the administration of supplements can be closely controlled.

Food Fortification

Fortification of foods is the addition of one or more nutrients—whether already naturally present or not—to foods with the purpose of preventing or correcting a nutritional deficiency in the general population or in at-risk groups. The fortification of foodstuffs with iron compounds of good bioavailability has proved to be the most effective approach for the prevention of iron deficiency (Hurrell 1997).

The success of a food fortification program depends on several factors: (a) the selection of a food to be fortified, based on information from dietary surveys about amounts and frequency of consumption of the potential food vehicle broken into age groups, socioeconomic levels, and intrafamilial distribution, (b) the bioavailability of the fortification compound, (c) the technological feasibility of the fortification process, which includes manufacture, packaging cost, shelf life, and organoleptic changes produced by the fortification compound, (d) the economic sustainability of the intervention, (e) the legislation regulating the fortification program, (f) who has permanent control of the fortification program, (g) a continuous follow-up of the consumption of the fortified foodstuffs, and (h) evaluation of the prevalence of the deficiency before and during the implementation of the fortification program to assess its impact (FAO 1995a).

A fortification program will be more effective when targeted to special population groups at risk of deficiency (e.g., infants, school children) than to the general population. Fortification programs are also more effective when the population depends on manufactured foods, as in urban settings. For rural populations, who produce much of the foods they consume and rely less on manufactured foods, the only option is the fortification of basic foodstuffs like salt, sugar, or corn or wheat flour used in the preparation of many dishes consumed by families.

Although these general considerations apply to fortification programs with any nutrient, fortification with iron raises many problems because the iron compounds that are more bioavailable also have the greatest chemical reactivity, producing undesirable alterations in the organoleptic properties of the food vehicle they fortify, properties that can be unacceptable to consumers.

There is a tradition of fortifying food with iron in Latin America. For decades Chile has fortified wheat flour with ferrous sulphate and group B vitamins, which is the reason for Chile's low anemia rates among adolescents and adults (Olivares et al. 1996). In Guatemala, Viteri et al. (1995) demonstrated the feasibility and impact of the fortification of sugar with NaFeEDTA. Venezuela has also fortified corn and wheat flours used in the preparation of arepas with ferrous fumarate, and Layrisse et al. (1997) and Layrisse and Garcia Casal (1997) have shown the impact of this policy in lowering the rates of iron deficiency and anemia among adult women, which had increased during the economic crisis that the country has suffered since 1980.

The impact of fortifying milk powder distributed by the Chilean government through M-Ch programs has had an impact on the rates of anemia in small children; milk was fortified with ferrous sulphate and ascorbic acid (Stekel et al. 1988). In Western European countries and the United States, fortification iron provides about one-third or one-fourth of the daily intake of iron in all population groups: low rates of iron deficiency anemia (as low as 3% in children below 24 months of age) have been attributed to this "extra" iron (Block et al. 1985), while Latin America has rates ranging from 30 to 85% in the same age group.

Although evidence supporting the effectiveness of iron fortification of foods is overwhelming, its implementation is not easy and there is not a single recipe for all Latin America. The success of fortification policies in developed countries is due to several factors: the majority of the population consumes manufactured foods, and there exist strong legislative backing, and control systems, as well as a high level of consumer education. So, each country, based on dietary information from its population—or at least from the population groups at greater risk—should decide which food might be the best vehicle for iron fortification.

Three foods provide most of the energy intake for people in the region: wheat, corn, and rice. At first glance these cereals should be the candidates for fortification; however manufacturing and marketing practices differ substantially among countries and even between regions within a country. UNICEF and the World Bank are advocating an initiative leading to the fortification of wheat and corn flours in all Latin American countries; although this is a valid initiative, it is interesting to discuss the case of Argentina in this regard.

The prevalence of iron deficiency anemia is 12 to 32% in nonpregnant women of fertile age (Calvo & Sosa 1991), 37 to 45% in pregnant women, and from 23 to 56% in infants between 8 and 24 months of age (Calvo & Gnazzo 1990; CESNI 1995), varying by region and socioeconomic level of the populations studied. In infants and small children, cows' milk provides about 40% of the daily energy intake; the remaining comes from legumes, fruits, sugar, bread, pasta, and biscuits. Cows' milk is the weaning food of choice and is overwhelmingly consumed in fluid rather than in its dry (powdered) form. The consumption of infant formula is very low for cultural and economic reasons.

Fortifying pasteurized cows' milk with iron was not feasible until recently, when two new compounds were developed by an Argentinean dairy corporation—ferrous sulphate and ascorbic acid encapsulated with phospholipids (Boccio et al. 1997)—and by the National Research Council-University of Buenos Aires—ferric iron diglicinate. Both are easily absorbed and safe because they respect the physiological mechanisms regulating iron absorption (Boccio et al. 1997; Uicich et al. 1996).

These new alternatives for providing iron to small children through milk can complement a program of universal fortification of wheat flour with iron. Fortifying milk alone would benefit small children but not older population groups; conversely, the fortification of flour, bread, bakery products, and pasta would not increase significantly the iron intake of young children and infants.

The percentages of different population groups for whom the recommended intake of iron is not being fulfilled are shown in Table 5. The table also shows the percentages of individuals whose iron intake would still be below recommendations if only milk, or flour, or both were fortified (Carmuega & O'Donnell 1997).

Each country should develop its best alternatives for food fortification, aimed especially toward those groups at greatest risk. Berger et al. (1997) have shown the efficacy of fortifying a local food (api—a mixture of wheat, quinoa, and corn flours) with either NaFeEDTA or ferrous sulphate; both compounds were successful in lowering the extremely high prevalence of iron deficiency anemia among school children in the Bolivian altiplano (see Table 6).

Table 5.   Percentages of Population Groups in Argentina for Whom the Recommended Intake of Dietary Iron with the Present Diet and with the Fortification of Milk, Wheat Flour, or Both Is Not Being Fulfilled

Population group	Present diet	Fortified milk	Fortified flour	Fortified milk and flour
Infants	86	36	85	32
Preschool children	87	40	77	27
School children	78	41	55	25
Female adolescents	100	84	85	76
Male adolescents	74	58	48	34
Men	54	45	35	27
Women	100	88	88	80

Source: Carmuega and O'Donnell (1997).

Table 6.   Food (Api) Fortification with NaFeEDTA in Bolivian School Children Living at High Altitude or Ferrous Sulphate (Hemoglobin gr/l)

	Control group (n = 53)	NaFe EDTA group (n = 53)	SO4Fe group (n = 62)
Baseline	134.5 ± 6.2^a	130.4 ± 6.3^b	132.5 ± 7.2^{ab}
24 weeks	135.0 ± 7.0^a	144.9 ± 8.4^b	149.5 ± 8.3^c

a,b,c: $p < 0.05$ when letters change.

Fisberg et al. (1996) have shown impressive results with cookies and bread fortified with ferrous tri-glicinate (Albion Labs, USA) in day care centers in poor areas of São Paulo, Brazil. Dutra de Oliveira et al. (1994) fortified drinking water in Brazilian schools with ferrous sulphate, with good results. Bovine hemoglobin has been used in Chile to fortify biscuits distributed by school food assistance programs; results are excellent, but hemoglobin produces a brown discoloration of biscuits and the amount needed to provide enough iron is relatively large. Because the hygienic collection of blood at the slaughterhouse is cumbersome, this interesting approach has given way to the use of new compounds that are cheaper and easier to manipulate (Hertrampf et al. 1990).

In brief, the technology to fortify food with iron exists; many compounds have been thoroughly studied and proven effective. Consumer advocation, as well as a strong commitment from politicians, policy makers, health teams, scientific societies, and industry are needed in the war against iron deficiency. Inevitably, some population groups will not initially benefit from fortification programs. But hopefully, if Latin America progresses and access to better foods improves, they will (INACG 1992).

Prevention of Iron Fecal Losses
Due to Parasites

Some helminths, particularly A. duodenale and N. americanus, but also T. trichuria, can produce significant intestinal blood losses from the intestinal lesions produced by the parasites or by the blood sucked during their feeding and then eliminated through their feces. The threat to a person's iron nutritional status is related to his or her parasite load; a heavy load, measured by counting the amount of parasite eggs per gram of feces, produces larger intestinal blood losses (Martínez-Torres et al., 1967; Roche & Layrisse, 1966).

Uncinaria as a cause of anemia is prevalent in communities with poor sanitation and is worse when human feces is used to fertilize orchards. As a result, adults working in agriculture are more exposed than small infants; parasitic infestations are not a major cause of anemia in infants, but begin to affect children as soon as they begin to walk. For women exposed to the disease, especially if they are pregnant, uncinariasis can be deleterious for their iron nutritional status (Stephenson 1988, 1994; Stoltzfus et al. 1997). See Table 7.

Table 7. Iron Losses Produced by Intestinal Parasites and the Iron
Requirements of an Adult Woman

Requirements	Iron (mg/day)
Basal	0.72
During menstruation	0.44
During pregnancy	2.14
During lactation	0.23
Uncinaria infestation	
N. americanus	1.10
A. duodenale	2.30
Other parasites	
T. trichuria	0.16

Sources: Requirements from FAO (1988); iron losses caused by parasites from Stephenson (1988).

Improving environmental sanitation is the most obvious solution; wearing shoes is another solution, given that the parasite larvae penetrate through the skin, mainly through the naked feet. An alternative solution is periodic deparasitation with the new generation of single-dose parasiticides (Albendazole, Mebendazole), which can safely be used by pregnant women after the first trimester of pregnancy; while this alternative is theoretically very attractive, it has not yet been subject to large-scale controlled studies (WHO 1995).

Zinc

The first clinical description of zinc deficiency involved Iranian adolescents with a very delayed onset of adolescence, which responded to zinc therapy; typical Iranian foods are rich in wheat fiber, which is known to interfere with zinc absorption (Prasad et al. 1963).

Zinc is a component of many enzymes involved in different physiological processes. This explains the variety of clinical manifestations of zinc deficiency. Zinc metabolism is closely related to Vitamin A metabolism — more precisely in the synthesis of retinol-binding protein — so the deficiency of both nutrients can occur simultaneously; night blindness is a common finding in zinc deficiency (Gibson 1994).

Zinc deficiency affects several immune functions, and one of the outcomes of zinc supplementation trials in at-risk infantile populations has been the decrease in the morbidity rates from respiratory and diarrheal diseases (Castillo-Duran et al. 1987; Rosado et al. 1992; Schlesinger et al. 1992). Another common disorder accompanying zinc deficiency is anorexia, which is perhaps related to an impaired sense of taste and smell.

Zinc deficiency affects the absorption of glucose and sodium in experimental animals (Gishan 1984), and fecal losses of zinc during prolonged diarrhea negatively affect the nutritional status of children (Castillo-Durán et al. 1994; Hambridge 1992). Zinc therapy during severe diarrhea has been shown to shorten the duration of the disease, particularly in malnourished infants and small children (Behrens, Tomkins, & Roy 1990).

Animals raised, after weaning, with diets deficient in zinc but otherwise complete show delays in learning maze and other tests. Recent studies in children with zinc deficiency reveal developmental delays (Golub et al. 1995) and less motor and exploratory activity.

But the most common manifestation of zinc deficiency is growth retardation. A recent meta-analysis of the effects of zinc supplementation trials in children (Brown, Allen, & Peerson 1996) concluded that there is a small but significant effect of zinc supplementation on height gains in children; the effect is more evident in children whose height or length is less than -2 SD from normal. A small impact was also found in weight gains. This effect was inversely associated with low zinc plasma levels at the beginning of the supplementation, but not with the age of children, the level of zinc dosage, or low initial body weight. Studies conducted in Latin America confirm the conclusions of Brown and colleagues' meta-analysis (Dirren et al. 1992, in Ecuador; Castillo-Durán et al. 1994, in Chile; and Cavan et al. 1993, in Guatemala). Zinc supplements given to malnourished children have been shown to increase their weight and height gains and also to improve food efficiency, that is, the grams of weight gain per Kg per day per 100 Kcal consumed (Castillo-Duran et al. 1987; Golden & Golden 1992).

The mechanisms by which zinc deficiency affects growth are not completely understood. It is known that, in zinc deficiency, IGF-I (the peripheral mediator of growth-hormone activity) is depressed. Also, because of the important role played by zinc in the immune system, it has been suggested that improvements in zinc nutritional status allow children to deal more satisfactorily with infections, whose anorexigenic and catabolic effects are well known. Growth retardation due to zinc deficiency is usually more evident in boys than in girls, perhaps because of boys' greater growth potential and higher zinc requirements.

The study of zinc deficiency is difficult because at present there are no reliable methods to evaluate zinc nutritional status. Zinc is defined by Golden (1988) as a Type II nutrient, that is, one whose main sign of deficiency in children is the detention or slowing of growth velocity, without significant alterations in the concentration of the nutrient in body fluids—either in the excretion of its metabolites, or in the activity of zinc-dependent enzymes or their substrates. So, the method for evaluating zinc deficiency is to add zinc supplements to the diets of groups of infants and children and evaluate the response in growth and weight compared with another group receiving placebos. Supplements must be given for several months and intake needs to be supervised in order to obtain reliable conclusions (King, 1990).

The main sources of zinc are sea vegetables and meats of any source. The fiber and fitate content of foods (Allen 1993; Rosado et al. 1992), as well as excessive concentrations of copper or iron, negatively affects zinc's bioavailability and absorption; however, the common amount of iron used to fortify foods does not interfere with the absorption of zinc naturally present in that food or added during the manufacturing or fortification process.

As is the case with other minerals, the zinc content in breast milk is high during the first 3 months of lactation but decreases steadily with time, so that the concentration is very low after 6 or more months (Sievers et al. 1992). Two preliminary studies have been published in which greater gains in weight and length were observed in breast-fed male infants supplemented with zinc (Krebs, Wescott, & Butter-Simon 1996; Walravens et al. 1992).

This possibility deserves further study given the early growth failure observed in infants in developing countries. The zinc nutritional status of pregnant women should also be seriously considered, because mothers in developing countries—where intrauterine growth retardation is highly prevalent—live on diets poor in zinc; prenatal supplementation may not only benefit fetal growth, but also affect cross-generational genetic imprinting.

Based on these considerations, zinc deficiency can be suspected in a community with a high prevalence of stunting, diets based primarily on vegetal foods, and a high prevalence of diarrheal diseases. The dietary recommendations for small children are to chose foods with the lowest possible dietary fiber content and to add, whenever possible, daily small portions of meat, liver, or sea vegetables to the children's foods.

If a food fortification program targeted to infants and small children is being considered, zinc should be included. Zinc compounds to fortify foods are not expensive and are free of the technological problems of fortifying with iron compounds.

Iodine

Iodine deficiency is the major preventable cause of mental retardation. It affects a billion people worldwide. Dietary iodine is incorporated into the thyroid hormones, which in turn play a major role in the growth and development of humans.

The most severe clinical manifestation of iodine deficiency is cretinism. Deaf-mutism, spastic diplegia, neuromuscular discoordination, impaired learning secondary to brain abnormalities or to impaired hearing, and significant dwarfism are other manifestations (Stanbury 1994). Iodine deficiency in pregnant women impairs reproductive functions, leading to abortions, stillbirths, low-birth-weight babies, congenital malformations, and increased perinatal and infantile malformations. There is some evidence that iodine supplementation improves infant survival in at-risk communities (Cobra et al. 1997).

The World Health Organization (WHO) estimated in 1993 that 26 million people worldwide suffer from brain damage secondary to iodine deficiency. This figure includes 6 million cretins. It has been estimated that individuals at risk of iodine deficiency, where preventive programs have not been implemented, have on average an IQ 11 points below the median due to iodine deficiency alone (Boyages et al. 1989).

Iodine deficiency occurs in regions where the soil and water are poor in the mineral; the regions most deficient are the Bolivian, Ecuadorian, Argentinean, and Chilean altiplanes; the Amazonian River basin also has high rates of goiter and iodide deficiency. Livestock and vegetal products in the region are also iodine deficient, contributing to poor iodide intakes.

The fight against iodide-deficiency disorders (IDD) through the fortification of a staple food is one of the most successful nutritional interventions yet accomplished. Salt has been used almost universally as the vehicle for iodide, and when the fortification process is well implemented the results are superlative in terms of the reduction of IDD (Hetzal et al. 1997).

The oral or parenteral administration of iodine are alternatives to the iodination of salt in communities where iodized salt is not available or where it does not reach people. Iodine injections give better results, since the iodine is stored in the muscle and slowly released, protecting the individual for about 4 years. Oral iodine is partly stored in the thyroid gland and in the adipose tissue and partly excreted; protection is estimated to last a year. Both alternatives, although effective, are costly and labor intensive and require keeping records of the individuals because iodide overload can induce hyperthyroidism, thyroiditis, and thyroid cancer.

The iodination of drinking water is not a new idea: it was proposed about 60 years ago, though later abandoned, and is presently being reevaluated with success in Malaysia, Thailand, and Sicily. The iodination of water can be accomplished with the same equipment used to chlorinate tap water in homes or villages. China is successfully experimenting with the iodination of irrigation water, so that animals and vegetable products have an increased iodine content, which benefits humans.

The prevalence of IDD is always lower in urban settings, since people have no alternative to purchasing salt in the commercial market, where all salt is iodized. In rural populations the simultaneous utilization of all the above-mentioned strategies might be necessary.

Bolivia is a good example of what can be achieved in the prevention of IDD. In the early 1980s, Bolivia had the highest prevalence of goiter (61% nationally) and cretinism in Latin America, ranking among the highest in the world. The prevalence of cretinism was 65.3% in 1983, 20.6% in 1989, and 4.5% in 1994. This extraordinary reduction is due to a national salt iodination program (presently, 81% of households in the country consume iodized salt), and a massive intervention program of parenteral iodine supplementation that reached 1.7 million people in the areas of greater epidemiological risk. Bolivia is an example of what can be achieved with continued, coordinated, and sustainable policies.

Vitamin A

Vitamin A is an essential nutrient for all animal species because of its critical role in reproduction, immune systems, and vision, as well as in the maintenance of cellular differentiation. These are particularly critical during periods of increased growth and tissue development, as in pregnancy, infancy, and early childhood. During the early months of pregnancy the supply of Vitamin A to the fetus should be neither excessive nor insufficient, because both conditions can be teratogenic. Vitamin A deficiency during pregnancy can produce abortions and malformations, especially when severe deficiency occurs during the first trimester. Toward the end of gestation it is important for the mother to have a good Vitamin A nutritional status, since breast milk will be the only source of the vitamin for the baby. See Table 8 for prevalance of Vitamin A deficiency in children by country and region.

Table 8. Vitamin A Deficiency in Children: Prevalence of Low Serum Retinol Concentrations

Country	Year	Prevalence (percent)	Sample
Argentina	1994	10.4	Tierra del Fuego
Bolivia	1992	11.3 (19.3–9.0)	National (other)

Table 8. (*continued*)

Country	Year	Prevalence (percent)	Sample
Brazil	1983	17.5	Southwest
	1984	30.2	South
	1984	13.2	Northwest
	1986	48.8	South
Colombia	1977	24.1, 41.1	National and northern
Costa Rica	1981	1.8	National
Dominican Republic	1991	19.6	Southwest
Ecuador	1987	14.1, R 16, U 12	National; rural; urban
Guatemala	1988	21.6	National
Honduras	1987	20.0	National
Mexico	1984–90	26, 32	Yucatan and Hermosillo
Nicaragua	1994	35.8	National
Peru	1992	33, 14	Rural Piura and Rural Puno

Note: Serum retinol concentration below 20 ug/dl.
Sources: Vital (1992) and others.

The retina must have sufficient Vitamin A for a person to have night vision, and night blindness is an early sign of its deficiency. Vitamin A is also critical for the preservation of epithelia, including the conjunctiva and the cornea; corneal lesions cause opacifications and ulcerations that can progress to total blindness. Vitamin A deficiency is the main cause of blindness worldwide.

Vitamin A plays an important role in cell-mediated immunity, and early Vitamin A supplementation programs intended to prevent xeroftalmia and blindness reduced the morbidity and mortality of these diseases in small children. Later studies were designed to more precisely evaluate such findings.

The main effect of supplementing with Vitamin A was the reduction in the morbidity and mortality produced by diarrheal diseases, with a similar small effect on respiratory diseases. Another pronounced effect was the reduction of deaths due to measles and its complications, as well as a reduction in the severity of the disease, even if the vitamin was given after the disease had started. No effects were observed on the growth rates of supplemented children. The younger the children, the larger the impact; girls seemed to be benefited more than boys. A priori, a supplementation program would be more effective in a community with moderate prevalence of clinical signs of hypovitaminosis A, widespread poverty, a high prevalence of growth retardation and malnutrition in small children, and a high prevalence of diarrheal diseases and measles.

Three approaches exist for the prevention of Vitamin A deficiency (Sommer 1992). The first is to increase its intake by improving the quality of the diet. Foods rich in Vitamin A or its precursors are milk and other dairy products, eggs, fish, meat and animal viscera, leafy vegetables like spinach and cilantro, as well as ripe plantain, mangoes, papaya, zapotes, carrots, and the like. Family or community gardens are very useful in providing such foods. Educational campaigns are also important to increase their consumption.

The supply of these foods in rural settings varies seasonally; the Vitamin A status of populations at risk fluctuates with the availability of such foods and with harvests, as well as with increases in family income and an improvement in quality of diets. An example of seasonally available food is mangoes, which are plentiful for a few months and scarce the rest of the year.

Breast milk is sometimes the only source of Vitamin A for infants. It is therefore mandatory that mothers have a good nutritional status in this vitamin. This can be achieved through improvements in her diet, or by supplementation with large doses of Vitamin A given not later than 30 days after delivery to avoid the teratogenicity of the vitamin in case the mother gets pregnant again; another alternative is to give daily doses of 8,000 IU, which in many settings is impossible.

Another way of preventing Vitamin A deficiency in children is the periodic administration of high doses of the vitamin, depending on the presence of clinical signs of deficiency, obvious malnutrition, or measles. The doses are repeated every 4 to 6 months depending on the sanitary conditions of the community. Smaller and more frequent doses are more effective and have fewer undesirable effects.

Yet another alternative is the fortification of foods. The same considerations for choosing a food vehicle that were discussed in the case of iron are valid for Vitamin A, with the advantage that the latter does not produce organoleptic alterations in the supplemented food. Dr. Guillermo Arroyave of INCAP was a pioneer of interventions using fortified sugar in Guatemala. Sugar fortification programs are presently functioning in several Central American countries, with good impact; in 1996, fortified sugar was present in 85% of Guatemalan households (INCH, 1996).

But many other food vehicles can be used. The fortification of skim milk is common in most of the region's countries; infant and breakfast cereals are also being fortified; some countries have decided to massively fortify wheat flour. All these alternatives have proven to be effective, especially when implemented simultaneously.

A Final Reflection

Although differences exist in the nutritional and health status of Latin American populations, a common pattern is the coexistence of problems derived from scarcity and excess. And even in populations that have more or less successfully solved many nutritional, housing, and educational needs, some nutritional deficiencies can still be found.

For most of the region's countries, the quality of life for the growing number of surviving children is of great concern. The quality of their future life depends on the presence or absence of disease and on the sequelae of insults of any kind suffered during gestation and the early years of life. Protein energy malnutrition, inadequate breast feeding, and iron, iodine, and zinc deficiencies can individually affect the normal growth and development of our children. In conditions of poverty, all of them can act simultaneously and synergistically.

Poverty is commonplace in the region. It has been said that Latin America is the sum of the poverties of the Spanish conquerors, the aborigines living here, and the Africans brought as slaves. Ours is the region in the world with the largest social and economic differences between rich and poor, and it is known that the health of a population is affected more by differences in relative incomes within the same society than by the absolute level of average income for each society as a whole. Worldwide, the countries with the longest life expectancy and better health indicators are not the wealthiest, but those with the smallest spread of incomes and the smallest proportion of the population in relative poverty.

It is fascinating that countries so politically different as Cuba, Chile, and Costa Rica have been able to achieve very low infant and child mortality rates. Common to all of them is a long-lasting and substantial commitment to infancy and a strong tradition in primary care programs.

But these macroconsiderations are of little help for our young children who are now growing and deserve a better life than their parents had. Micronutrient deficiencies can be overcome with the strategies discussed herein, but what makes a mother choose a fortified food and not another of less nutritional quality? Is it just a matter of price? What makes a mother continue breast feeding her child in spite of difficulties posed by her work or lack of familial support? Why can many mothers raise healthy and intelligent children in very adverse situations?

As pediatricians we are used to treating malnourished infants whose parents are obese, and we are also used to seeing lovely babies whose mothers are extremely poor and even malnourished. What is the difference between them?

In a recent study in Tierra del Fuego (CESNI 1996), developmental tests were given to a large representative sample of the infantile population 6 to 60 months old, and it was found that at 24 months of age the mental development coefficient (Bayley II test) was 14 points below that of the reference population and 51% of children of this age had low developmental scores. At 5 years of age, 28% of the children had a developmental quotient (IQ) below the expected level for their age (Wechsler test). Simultaneous with these psychological outcomes, the capacity of the family to provide a stimulating environment was evaluated with the HOME inventory. Although children of better educated parents obtained higher scores in the developmental tests, at all educational and socioeconomic levels the children of families with good HOME ratings scored 8 to 10 more IQ points than children of the same socioeconomic level but lower HOME ratings.

There is no extreme poverty in Tierra del Fuego province, and it has the lowest infant mortality rate and the highest per capita expenditure in social and health services in Argentina. There is no malnutrition, and the prevalence of iron deficiency anemia is the lowest in the country. The results of developmental tests of children reveal a pattern of child care that may repeat the care received by the parents of those children, who themselves were surely raised in less favorable conditions.

Although the results of this developmental survey may cause us to worry about the school performance of these children and their future as adults, the results also leave room for hope, since it was clear that mothers did their best even if they did not know how to do better. A lot can be done to improve patterns of child care.

Child care is a concept that comprehensively includes most of the problems discussed in this chapter. Research on what makes some families better caretakers than others is needed on our continent, at all social levels and in all environments. Better child care and primary care systems are the last trenches to defend our children against the evils of poverty and ignorance (Engle & Huffman 1996).

The social sciences can make a substantial contribution in this area. My feeling is that health-generating families hold deep feelings about what is healthy and how to put those convictions into practice for protecting their children. Perhaps there are preexisting feelings about child care values in the couple that are part of the mutual attraction leading to mating and reproduction.

A review of the impact of breast-feeding promotion in Latin America done by Giuliani (1998) showed disappointing results. Perhaps the decision to breast feed a child is made unconsciously, long before the child's birth, for reasons that are worth investigating. In urban communities, those mothers who initiate breast feeding and continue it for months are those who see the primary health team as the best source of information and counseling for the good of their children. Likely, these mothers will immunize their children in due time, choose iodine-fortified salt over nonfortified salt, and monitor their children's growth and development. Why they do so is important to the improvement of the health, nutrition, and future of our children.

BIBLIOGRAPHY

Abeya, G. E., and Lejarraga, H. 1995. "Prevalencia de obesidad en 88.861 varones de 18 años, Argentina—1987." *Arch Arg Pediatr* (93): 71–9.

Acosta, A., Amar, M., Cornbluth-Szarfarc, S., Dillman, E., Fosi, M., Gongora-Bianchi, R., Grebe, G., Hertrampf, F., Kremenchuzky, S., Layrisse, M., Martínez-Torres, C., Moron, C., Pizarro, T. M., Reynafarje, C., Stekel, A., Villavicencio, D., and Zuniga, H. 1984. "Iron Absorbtion from Typical Latin American Diets." *Am J Clin Nutr* (39): 953–62.

Allen, L. H. 1993. "The Nutrition CRSP: What Is Marginal Malnutrition and Does It Affect Human Function?" *Nutr Res Rev* (51): 255–67.

_____. 1997. "Embarazo y deficiencia de hierro." In: O'Donnell, A. M., Viteri, F. E., and Carmuega, E. S. (eds.), *Deficiencia de hierro: Desnutrición oculta en América Latina.* Publicación CESNI No. 18, CESNI, Buenos Aires.

American Academy of Pediatrics-Committee on Nutrition. 1992. "The Use of Whole Cow's Milk in Infancy." *Pediatrics* (89): 1105–9

Barker, J. 1994. "Reduced Fetal Growth Increases Cardiovascular Mortality." *Health Rep* (6): 45.

Beard, I., and Piñero, D. J. 1997. "Metabolismo del hierro." In: O'Donnell, A. M., Viteri, F. E., and Carmuega, E. S. (eds.), *Deficiencia de hierro: Desnutrición oculta en América Latina.* Publicación CESNI No. 18, CESNI, Buenos Aires.

Beaton, G., Martorell, R., Aronson, K. A., Edmonston, B., McCabe, G., Ross, A. C., and Harvey, B. 1994. "La suplementación con vitamina A y la mortalidad infantil en los países en desarrollo." *Bol of Sanit Panam* (117): 506–18.

Behrens, R. H., Tomkins, A. M., and Roy, S. K. 1990. "Zinc Supplementation during Diarrhoea, a Fortification against Malnutrition?" *Lancet* (2) 442–3.

Bell, J. G., Keen, C. L., and Lönnerdal, B. 1987. "Effect of Infant Cereals on Zinc and Copper Absorption during Weaning." *Am J Dis Child* (141): 1128–32.

Bendich, A. 1993. "Folic Acid and Neural Tube Defects." Ann NY Acad Sci (678): 108–11.

Block, G., Dresser, C. M., Hartman, A. M., and Carrol, M. D. 1985. "Nutrient Sources in the American Diet: Quantitative Data from the NHANES II Survey. 1. Vitamins and Minerals" *Am J Epidemiol* (122): 13–26.

Boccio, J. R., Zubillaga, M. B., Caro, R. A., et al. 1997. "New Procedure to Fortify Fluid Milk and Dairy Products with High-Bioavailable Ferrous Sulfate." *Nutr Rev* 55(6).

Bothwell, T. I., and Charlton, R. W. (eds.). 1981. *Iron Deficiency in Women*. Washington, D.C.: Nutrition Foundation.

Boyages, S. C., Collins, J. K., Marbely, G. F., Jupp, J. J., Morris, J. G., and Eastman, C. J. 1989. "Iodine Deficiency Impairs Intellectual and Neuromotor Development in Apparently Normal Persons." *Med J Aust* (150): 676–9.

Brooks, G. A. 1997. "Hierro, metabolismo muscular y actividad física." In: O'Donnell, A. M., Viteri, F. E., and Carmuega, E. S. (eds.), *Deficiencia de hierro: Desnutrición oculta en América Latina*. Publicación CESNI No. 18, CESNI, Buenos Aires.

Brown, K. H., Alchtar, M. A., Robertson, A. D., and Ahmed, M. G. 1986. "Lactational Capacity of Marginally Nourished Mothers: Relationship between Maternal Nutritional Status and Quantity and Proximate Composition of Milk." *Pediatrics* (78): 909–19.

Brown, K. H., Allen, L. H., and Peerson, J. M. 1996. *Zinc Supplementation and Children's Growth: A Meta-Analysis of Intervention Trials*.

Brown, K. H., Black, R. E., Lopez de Romana, G., and Creed de Kanashiro, H. 1989. "Infant Feeding Practices and Their Relationship with Diarrheal and Other Diseases." *Pediatrics* (83): 31–40.

Buotton, T., et al. 1987. "Body Composition of Peruvian Children with Short Stature and High Weight-for-Height: Total Body-Water Measurements and Their Prediction from Anthropometric Values." *Am J of Clin Nutr* (45): 513–25.

Butte, N. F., Villalpando, S., Wong, W. W., Flores-Huerta, S., Hernandez-Beltran, M. de J., and O'Brian-Smith, E. 1993. "Higher Total Energy

Expenditure Contributes to Growth Faltering in Breast-Fed Infants Living in Rural Mexico." *J Nutr* (123): 1028–35.

Butte, N. F., Villalpando, S., Wong, W. W., Flores-Huerta, S., Hernandez-Beltran, M., Smith, E. O., and Garza, C. 1992. "Human Milk Intake and Growth Faltering of Rural Mesoamerindian Infants." *Am J Clin Nutr* (55): 1109–16.

Calloway, D. H., Murphy, S., Balderston, J., et al. 1992. "Functional implications of malnutrition: Village Nutrition in Egypt, Kenya, and Mexico:— Looking across the CRSP Project." Final Report of the Human Nutrition Collaborative Research Support Program. Berkeley: University of California.

Calvo, E. B., Galindo, A. C. and Aspres, N. B. 1992. "Iron Status in Exclusively Breast-Fed Infants." *Pediatrics* (90): 375–9.

Calvo, E. B., and Gnazzo, N. 1990. "Prevalence of Iron Deficiency in Children Aged 9–24 Months from a Large Urban Area of Argentina." *Am J Clin Nutr* (52): 534–8.

Calvo, E. B., Islam, J., and Gnazzo, N. 1997. "Encuesta Nutricional en Niños de Dos Años en la Provincia de Misiones: IL Indicadores Dietéticos y Hematológicos." *Arch. Arg. Pediat* (85): 260–9.

Calvo, E. B., and Sosa, E. M. 1991. "Iron Status in Non-Pregnant Women of Child-Bearing Age." *Eur J Clin Nutr* (45): 215–20.

Carmuega, E., and O'Donnell, A. M. 1997. "Fundamentos para una ley para la prevención de la deficiencia de hierro en Argentina." Documento elevado al Ministerio de Agricultura, Ganadería Pesca y Alimentación de la Nación. Documento CESNI No. 13/97.

Castillo-Durán, C., Garcia, H., Venegas, P., Torrealba, I., Panteón, E., Concha, N., and Pérez, P. 1994. "Zinc Supplementation Increase Growth of Male Children and Adolescents with Short Stature." *Acta Pediatr* (83): 833–7.

Castillo-Duran, C., Heresi, G., Fisberg, M., and Uauy, R. 1987. "Controlled Trial of Zinc Supplementation during Recovery from Malnutrition: Effect on Growth and Immune Function." *Am J Clin Nutr* (45): 602–8.

Cavan, K., Gibson, R., Grazioso, C., et al. 1996. "Growth and Body Composition of Periurban Guatemalan Children in Relation to Zinc Status: A Cross-Sectional Study." *Am J of Clin Nutr* (57): 334–43.

César, J. A., Victora, C. G., Morris, S. S. and Post, C. A. 1996. "Abdominal Circumference Contributes to Absence of Wasting in Brazilian Children." *J Nutr* (126): 2652–6.

CESNI. 1995. *Project Tierra del Fuego: Baseline Health and Nutrition Survey.* Jorge Macri Foundation Edition, Buenos Aires.

CESNI. 1996. *Project Tierra del Fuego: Baseline Child Development Survey.* Jorge Macri Foundation Edition, Buenos Aires.

Chew, F., Torún, B., and Viteri, F. E. 1996. "Comparison of Weekly and Daily Iron Supplementation to Pregnant Women in Guatemala (Supervised and Unsupervised)." *FASEB J* (10): A4221.

Chwang, L., Soemantri, A. G. and Pollitt, E. 1988. "Iron Supplementation and Physical Growth of Rural Indonesian Children." *Am J Nutr* (47): 496–501.

Cobra, C., Muhilal, R. K., et al. 1997. "Infant Survival Is Improved by Oral Iodine Supplementation." *J Nutr* (127): 574–8.

Cohen, R. J., Brown, K. H., Canahuati, J., Landa, L., and Dewey, K. G. 1994. "Effects of Age of Introduction of Complementary Foods on Infant Breast Milk Intake, Total Energy Intake, and Growth: A Randomised Intervention Study in Honduras." *Lancet* (343): 288–93.

Cook, J. D., Carriaga, M., Khan, S. G., et al. 1990. "Gastric Delivery System for Iron Supplementation." *Lancet* (335): 1136–9.

Cook, J. D., Reddy, M. B., Burry, J., Juillerat, M. A., and Hurrell, R. F. 1997. "The Influence of Different Cereal Grains on Iron Absorption from Infant Cereal Foods." *Am J Clin Nutr* (65): 964–9.

Czeizel, A. L., and Dudas, Y. 1992. "Prevention of the First Occurrence of Neural-Tube Defects by Periconceptional Vitamin Supplementation." *N Engl J Med* (327): 1832–5.

De Andraca, I., Castillo, M., and Walter, T. 1997. "Desarrollo psicomotor y conducta en lactantes anémicos por deficiencia de hierro." In: O'Donnell, A. M., Viteri, F. E., and Carmuega, E. S. (eds.), *Deficiencia de hierro: Desnutrición oculta en América Latina*. Publicación CESNI No. 18, CESNI, Buenos Aires.

Dirren, H., Barclay, D., Ramos, J. G., Lozano, R., Montalvo, M. M., Dávila, N., and Mora, J. O. 1992. *Zinc Supplementation and Child Growth in Ecuador: Zinc Supplementation and Child Growth*.

Dutra de Oliveira, J. E., Ferreira, J. F., Vasconcellos, V. P., and Marchini, J. S. 1994. "Drinking Water as an Iron Carrier to Control Anemia in Preschool Children in a Day-Care Center." *J Am Coll Nutr* (13): 198–202.

Engle, P., and Huffman, S. 1996. *Care for Life: Guidelines for Assessment, Analysis and Action to Improve Care for Nutrition*. UNICEF.

FAO (Food and Agriculture Organization). 1995a. "Food Fortification: Technology and Quality Control." Report of an FAO Technical Group. Rome, Italy.

_____. 1995b. *Sinopsis Alimentaria y Nutricional de América Latina*. Santiago de Chile, Chile.

FAO/WHO 1988. "Requirements of Vitamin A, Iron, Folate and Vitamin B12: Report of a Joint FAO-WHO Expert Consultation." Rome: Food and Agriculture Organization of the United Nations.

Feachem, R. G., and Koblinsky, M. A. 1984. *Intervention for the Control of Diarrhoeal Diseases among Young Children: Promotion of Breastfeeding.* Bull WHO (62): 271–91.

Fendrich, M., Warner, V., and Weissman, M. 1990. "Family Risk Factors, Parental Depression and Psychopathology of Offspring." *Dev Psychol* (26): 40–50.

Fisberg, M., Braga, J. A. P., Ferreira, A. M. A., Kliamca, P. E., and Berezowski, M. 1996. "The Use of Iron Enriched 'Petite Suisse' Cheese in the Prevention of Anemia in Preschool Children." (Abstract). XXXIV Meeting of the Latin American Pediatric Research Society. Iguazú, Argentina.

Fisberg, M., Braga, J. A. P., Soraggi, N. C., Vellozo, E., Cardoso, R., Graziani, E., Klianca, P. E., and Valle, J. 1996. "Fortification with Aminochelate Iron of Bread and Cookies Used in the School Meals of Preschool Children" (Abstract). XXXIV Meeting of the Latin American Pediatric Research Society. Iguazú, Argentina.

Fomon, S. J., Ziegler, E. E., Nelson, S. E., and Edwards, B. E. 1981. "Cow's Milk Feeding in Infancy: Gastrointestinal Blood Loss and Iron Nutritional Status." *J Pediatr* (98): 540–5.

Freire, W., y col. 1988. *Diagnóstico de la Situación Alimentaria, Nutricional y de Salud de la Población Ecuatoriana Menor de Cinco Años* -DANS-CONADE, MSP.

Garry, P. J., Owen, G. M., Hooper, E. M., and Gilbert, B. A. 1981. "Iron Absorption from Human Milk and Formula with and without Iron Supplementation." *Pediatr Res* (15): 822–8.

Gibson, R. S. 1994. "Zinc Nutrition in Developing Countries." *Nutr Res Rev* (7): 151–73.

Gillespie, S., and Mason, J. (eds.) 1994. *Controlling Vitamin A Deficiency.* ACC/SCN State of the Art Series. Nutrition Policy Discussion Paper No. 14. ACC/SCN, Geneva.

Gishan, F. K. 1984. "Transport of Electrolytes, Water and Glucose in Zinc Deficiency." *J Pediatr Gastr Nutr* (3): 608–12.

Giuliani, F. 1998. "Análisis de intervenciones para la promoción de la lactancia materna en América Latina." In: O'Donnell, A., Torún, B., and Caballero, B. (eds.), *Recomendaciones para la alimentación de niños menores de 5 años.* OPS-CESNI-Fundación Cavendes. Washington, DC.

Golden, B. E. and Golden, M. H. N. 1992. "Effect of Zinc on Lean Tissue Synthesis during Recovery from Malnutrition." *Europ J Clin Nutr* (46): 697–706.

Golden, M. H. N. 1988. "The Role of Individual Nutrient Deficiencies in Growth Retardation in Children, as Exemplified by Zinc and Protein."

In Waterlow, J. C. (ed.), *Linear Growth Retardation in Developing Countries*. Raven Press, New York.

Golub, M. S., Keen, C. L., Gershwin, M. E., and Hendricks, A. G. 1995 "Developmental Zinc Deficiency and Behavior." *J Nutr* (125) Suppl.: 2263–71.

Habitch, J. P., Martorell, R., Yarborough, C., Malina, R. M., and Klein, R. E. 1974. "Height and Weight Standards for Preschool Children: How Relevant Are Ethnic Differences in Growth Potential?" *Lancet* (1): 611–15.

Hallberg, L., Brune, M., and Rossander, L. 1989. "Iron Absorption in Man: Ascorbic Acid and Dose-Dependent Inhibition by Phytate." *Am J Clin Nutr* (49): 140–4.

Hallberg, L., Rossander, L., and Skänberg, A. B. 1987. "Phytates and the Inhibitory Effect of Bran on Iron Absorption in Man." *Am J Clin Nutr* (45): 988–96.

Hambidge, K. M. 1992. "Zinc and Diarrhoea." *Acta Pediatr* (381): 82–6.

Hetzel, B. S., Dunn, J. T., and Stanbury, J. B. 1997. *Prevention and Control of Iodine Deficiency Disorders*. New York: Elsevier.

Hertrampf, E., Olivares, M., Pizarro, F., Walter, T., Cayasso, M., Heresi, G., Llaguno, S., Chadud, P., and Stekel, A. 1990. "Haemoglobin Fortified Cereal: A Source of Available Iron to Breast-Fed Infants." *Europ J Clin Nutr* (44): 793–8.

Hurrell, R. 1997. "Estrategias para la prevención de la deficiencia de hierro: Fortificación de los alimentos con hierro." In: O'Donnell, A. M., Viteri, F.E., and Carmuega, E.S. (eds.), *Deficiencia de hierro: Desnutrición oculta en América Latina*. Publicación CESNI No. 18, CESNI, Buenos Aires.

Hussaini, M. A., Karyadi, H. D., and Gunadi, L. E. 1981. "Evaluation of Nutritional Anemia Intervention among Anemic Female Workers on a Tea Plantation." In: Hallberg, L., and Scrimshaw, N. S. (eds.), *Iron Deficiency and Work Performance*. Washington, DC: Nutrition Foundation.

Idjadrinata, P., and Pollitt, E. 1993. "Reversal of Developmental Delays in Iron-Deficient Anemic Infants Treated with Iron." *Lancet* (41): 1–4.

INACG (International Anemic Consultative Group). 1992. "Combating Iron-Deficiency Anemia through Food Fortification Technology." Washington, DC: Nutrition Foundation.

Institute of Medicine, Committee on Nutritional Status during Pregnancy and Lactation. 1990. *Nutrition during Pregnancy*. Washington, DC:, National Academy Press.

Keller, W. 1988. "The Epidemiology of Stunting." In: Waterlow, J. C. (ed.), *Linear Growth Retardation in Less Developed Countries*. New York:, Nestec/Raven Press (Nestlé Nutrition Workshop Series No. 14).

King, J. C. 1990. "Assessment of Zinc Status." *J Nutr* (120): 1474–9.

Krebs, N. F., Hambidge, K. M., and Walravens, P. A. 1984. "Increased Food Intake of Young Children Receiving a Zinc Supplementation." *Am J Clin Nutr* (138): 270–3.

Krebs, N. F., Westcott, J. E., and Butler-Simon, N. 1996. "Effects of a Zinc Supplement on Growth of Normal Breast-Fed Infants." *FASEB J* (10): A230 (abstr).

Latham, M. C., Stephenson, L. S., Kinoti, S. N., Zaman, M. S., and Jurz, K. M. 1990. "Improvements in Growth Following Iron Supplementation in Young Kenyan Schoolchildren." *Nutrition* (6): 159–65.

Layrisse, M., Chaves, J. F., Méndez Castellano, H., Bosch, V., Tropper, E., Bastardo, B., and González, E. 1997. "Early Response to the Impact of Iron Fortification in the Venezuela Population" (Sent to *Am J Nutr*).

Layrisse, M., and García Casal, M. N. 1997. "Estrategias para la prevención y disminución de la prevalencia de la deficiencia de hierro a través de la alimentación." In: O'Donnell, A. M., Viteri, F. E., and Carmuega, E. S. (eds.), *Deficiencia de hierro: Desnutrición oculta en América Latina. Publicación.* CESNI No. 18. CESNI, Buenos Aires.

Layrisse, M., Garcia Casal, M. N., Solarno, I., Barón, M. A., Arguello, F., Llovera, D., Ramirez, J., Leets, I., and Tropper, E. "The Role of Vitamin A on the Inhibition of Nonheme Iron Absorption." Preliminary results.

Li, R., Chen, X., Deurenberg, P., Garby, L., and Hautvast, J. G. 1994. "Functional Consequences of Iron Supplementation in Iron-Deficient Female Cotton Mill Workers in Beijing, China." *Am J Clin Nutr* (59): 908–13.

Liu, X. N., Kang, J., Zhao, L., and Viteri, F. E. 1995. "Intermittent Iron Supplementation Is Efficient and Safe Controlling Iron Deficiency and Anemia in Preschool Children." *Food Nutr Bull* (16): 139–46.

Lopez de Blanco, M., Evcus, R., de Jimenez, M., Jifontes, Y., and Machin, T. 1996. *Nutrición Base del Desarrollo: Situación Alimentaria y Nutricional de Venezuela.* Caracas: Ediciones Cavendes.

Lozoff, B., Brittenham, G. M., Wolf, A. B., et al. 1987. "Iron-Deficiency Anemia and Iron Therapy Effects on Infant Developmental Test Performance." *Pediatrics* (79): 981–95.

Lozoff, B., Jiménez, E., and Wolf, A. W. 1991. "Long-Term Developmental Outcome of Infants with Iron Deficiency." *New Engl J Med* (32)5: 687–94.

Lynch, S. 1997. "Hierro: interacción con otros nutrientes." In: O'Donnell, A. M., Viteri, F. E., and Carmuega, E. S. (eds.), *Deficiencia de hierro: desnutrición oculta en América Latina. Publicación* CESNI No. 18, CESNI, Buenos Aires.

Martínez-Torres, C., Cubeddu, L., Dillman, E., et al. 1984. "Effect of Exposure to Low Temperature on Normal and Iron Deficient Subjects." *Am J Physiol* (246): R380–3.

Martínez-Torres, C., Ojeda, A., Roche, M., and Layrisse, M. 1967. "Hookworm Infection and Intestinal Blood Loss." *Trans R Soc Trop Med Hyg* (61): 373–83.

Martorell, R. and Scrimshaw (eds.). 1995. "The Effects of Improved Nutrition in Early Childhood: The Institute of Nutrition of Central America and Panama (INCAP) Follow-Up Study." *J Nutr* (125) (Suppl.): 4s.

Mejía, L. A., and Chew, F. 1988. "Hematological Effect of Supplementing Anemic Children with Vitamin A Alone and in Combination with Iron." *Am J Clin Nutr* (48): 595–600.

Ministerio de Desarrollo Humano. Secretaría Nacional de Salud. 1996. *Situación de los desórdenes por deficiencia de yodo en Bolivia.* La Paz.

Moffatt, M. E. K., Longstaffee, S., Besant, J., and Dureski, C. 1994. "Prevention of Iron Deficiency and Psychomotor Decline in High Risk Infants through Iron Fortified Infant Formula: A Randomized Clinical Trial." *J Pediatr* (25): 527–34.

MRC Vitamin Study Research Group 1991. "Prevention of Neural Tube Defects: Results of the Medical Research Council Vitamin Study." *Lancet* (338): 131–7.

Myers, R. 1993. "Los doce que sobreviven: Fortalecimiento de los programas de desarrollo para la primera infancia en el Tercer Mundo." Publicación OPS/UNICEF. Publicación Científica No 545, Washington, DC.

National Academy of Sciences (NAS). 1990. *Nutrition during Pregnancy.* Washington, DC: National Academy Press.

O'Donnell, A. M., Carmuega, E., and Durán, P. 1997. "Deficiencia de hierro en Argentina: Qué sabemos y qué puede hacerse." In: O'Donnell, A. M., Viteri, F. E., and Carmuega, E. S. (eds.), *Deficiencia de hierro: Desnutrición oculta en América Latina.* Publicación CESNI No. 18, CESNI, Buenos Aires.

Olivares, M., Pizarro, F., Pineda, O., Name, J. J., Hertrampf, E., and Walter, T. 1996. "Bioavailability of Iron as Bis-Glycine Chelate" (Abstract). XXXIV Meeting of the Latin American Pediatric Research Society, Iguazú, Argentina.

Oski, F. A., and Honig, A. S. 1978. "The Effects of Iron Therapy on the Developmental Scores of Iron-Deficient Infants." *J Pediatr* (92): 21–5.

Pajuelo, J., and Ameniya, Y. 1992. "Anemia nutricional en la población infantil del Perú." *Revista Médica Peruana* (June–December): 50–5.

Parks, Y. A., and Warren, B. A. 1989. "Iron Deficiency and the Brain." *Acta Ped Scand* (361) Suppl.: 71–7.

Pelletier, D. L., Frongill, Jr., E. A., Schroeder, D. G., and Habicht, J. P. 1996. "Efectos de la Malnutrición en la Mortalidad de Menores de 5 Años en Países en Desarrollo." *Boletín OPS* (120): 425–32.

Pizarro, F., Uicich, R., Almeida, C., Diaz, M., Carmuega, E., and O'Donnell, A. 1996. "Biodisponibilidad de hierro de glicinato férrico en leche fluida" (Abstract). 5th Conferencia International sobre Ciencia y Tecnología de los Alimentos, Cuba.

Pollitt, E., and Oh, S. Y. 1994. "Early Supplementary Feeding, Child Development, and Health Policy." *Food Nutr Bull* (15): 3/208–13.

Pollitt, E., Saco-Pollitt, C., Leibel, R. L., and Viteri, E. 1986. "Iron Deficiency and Behavioral Development in Infants and Preschool Children." *Am J Clin Nutr* (43): 555–65.

Pollitt, E. 1997. "Deficiencia de hierro y deficiencia educacional." In: O'Donnell, A. M., Viteri, F. E., and Carmuega. E. S. (eds.), *Deficiencia de hierro: desnutrición oculta en América Latina*. Publicación CESNI No. 18, CESNI, Buenos Aires.

Ridwan, E., Schultnik, W., Dillon, D., and Gross, R. 1996. "Effects of Weekly Iron Supplementation on Pregnant Indonesian Women Are Similar to Those of Daily Supplementation." *Am J Clin Nutr* (63): 884–90.

Rivera, J., and Ruel, M. T. 1997. "Growth Retardation Starts in the First Three Months of life among Rural Guatemalan Children." *European J Clin Nutr* (51): 92–6.

Roche, M., and Layrisse, M. 1966. "The Nature and Causes of "Hookworm Anemia." *Am Trop Med Hyg* (15): 1031–100.

Rosado, J. L., López, P., Morales, M., Muñoz, E., and Allen, L. H. 1992. "Bioavailability of Energy, Nitrogen, Fat, Zinc, Iron and Calcium from Rural and Urban Mexican Diets." *Br J Nutr* (68): 45–58.

Saarinen, U. M., and Siimes, M. A. 1979. "Iron Absorbtion from Breast Milk, Cow's Milk and Iron Supplemented Formula: An Opportunistic Use of Changes in Total Body Iron Determined by Hemoglobin, Ferritin and Body Weight in 132 Infants." *Pediatr Res* (13): 143–7.

Santizo, M. C., Rivera, J., Ruel, M. T., et al. 1995. "The Impact of Zinc Supplementation on Nutrient Intake from Breast Milk among Rural Guatemalan Children." *FASEB J* (9): A116 (Abstr. 958).

Schlesinger, L., Arevalo, M., Arredondo, S., Diaz, M., Lönnerdal, B., and Stekel, A. 1992. "Effect of a Zinc-Fortified Formula on Immunocompetence and Growth of Malnourished Infants." *Am J Clin Nutr* (56) 491–8.

Scholl, T. O., Hediger, M. L., Fisher, R. L., and Schearer, J. W. 1992. "Anemia vs. Iron Deficiency: Increased Risk of Preterm Delivery in a Prospective Study." *Am J Clin Nutr* (55): 985–8.

Scholl, T. O., Hediger, M. L., Schall, J. J., Khoo, C. S., and Fisher, R. L. 1996. "Dietary and Serum Folate: Their Influence on the Outcome of Pregnancy." *Am J Clin Nutr* (63): 520–5.

Schultink, W., Gross, R., Gliwitzki, M., Karjadi, D., and Matulessi, P. 1995. "Effect of Daily vs Twice Week Iron Supplementation in Indonesian Preschool Children with Low Iron Status." *Am J Clin Nutr* (61): 111–15.

Sievers, E., Oldigs, H. D., Dörner, K., and Schaub, J. 1992. "Longitudinal Zinc Balances in Breast-Fed and Formula-Fed Infants." *Acta Pediatr* (81): 1–6.

Soewondo, S., Husaini, M., and Pollitt, E. 1989. "Effects of Iron Deficiency on Attention and Learning Processes in Preschool Children: Bandung, Indonesia." *Am J Clin Nutr* (50): 667–74.

Sommer, A. 1992. "Vitamin A Deficiency." In: *Ending hidden hunger: A Policy Conference on Micronutrient Malnutrition — The Task for Child Survival and Development*. Atlanta.

Stanbury, J. B. (ed.) 1994. *The Damaged Brain of Iodine Deficiency.* New York: Cognizant Communication Corporation.

Stekel, A., Olivares, M., Cayazzo, M., Chadud, P., Llaguno, S., and Pizzarro, F. 1988. "Prevention of Iron Deficiency by Milk Fortification. II: A Field Trial with a Full Fat Acidified Milk." *Am J Clin Nutr* (47): 265–9.

Stephenson, D. M., Gardner, J. M. M., Walker, S. P., and Ashworth, A. 1994. "Weaning-Food Viscosity and Energy Density: Their Effects on Ad-Libitium Consumption and Energy Intakes in Jamaica." *Am J Clin Nutr* (60): 465–9.

Stephenson, L. S. 1988. *Impact of Helminth Infections on Human Nutrition.* New York: Taylor and Francis.

Stoltzfus, R., Dreyfus, M. L., Jorgenson, T., Chwaya, H. M., and Albonico, M. 1997. "Control de la helmintiasis como estrategia para prevenir la deficiencia de hierro." In: O'Donnell, A. M., Viteri, F. E., and Carmuega, E. S. (eds.) *Deficiencia y hierro: Desnutrición oculta en América Latina*. Publicación CESNI No. 18, CESNI, Buenos Aires.

Temboury, M. C., Otero, A., Polanco, I., and Arribas, E. 1994. "Influence of Breast-Feeding on the Infant's Intellectual Development." *J Ped Gastr Nutr* (18): 32–6.

Tenovuo, A., Kero, P., Piekkala, P., Korvenranata, H., Silanpöö, and Erkkola, R. 1987. "Growth of 519 Small for Gestational Age Infants during the First Two Years of Life." *Acta Pediatr Scand* (76): 636–46.

Trowbridge, F. L., Marks, J. S., Romano, G. L., Madrid, S., Boutton, T. W., and Klein, P. D. 1987. "Body Composition of Peruvian Children with Short Stature and High Weight-for-Height. II Implications for the Interpretation of Weight-for-Height as an Indicator of Nutritional Status." *Am J Clin Nutr* (46): 411–18.

Uicich, R., Pizarro, F., Almaida, C., Carmuega, E., and O'Donnell, A. M. 1996. "Absorción de hierro de leche de vaca fluida fortificada con sulfato ferroso encapsulado." *Medicina Infantil* (Buenos Aires) (5):123–7.

UNICEF 1990. *First Call for the Children: World Declaration and 1990–2000 Plan of Action on the Survival, Protection and Development of Children.* New York: UNICEF.

UNICEF 1996. *El Progreso de las Naciones, 1996.* UNICEF.

UNICEF 1997. *The State of World's Children, 1997.* New York: Oxford University Press.

Valdez, C., Mazariegos, M., Romero-Abal, J. C., Grazioso, C., and Solomons, N. 1997. "Growth and Growth Faltering in a Peri-Urban Guatemalan Community." *Int Ch Health* (8): 83–91.

Victora, C. G. 1992. "The Association between Wasting and Stunting: An International Perspective." *J Nutr* (122): 1105–10.

Villar, J., Belizán, J. M., Spalding, J., and Klein, R. E. 1982. "Postnatal Growth of Intrauterine Growth Retarded Infants." *Early Human Devel* (6): 265–71.

Viteri, F. E. 1989. "Influence of Iron Nutrition on Work Capacity and Performance." In: Filer, L. J. (ed.), *Dietary Iron: Birth to Two Years.* Raven Press.

_____. 1992. "Iron: Global Perspective." In: Ending Hidden Hunger: A Policy Conference on Micronutrient Malnutrition—The Task for Child Survival and Development. Atlanta.

_____. 1995. Alvarez E., Buttes R., Torún B., Pineda O., Mejía L., and Sylvi J. 1995. "Fortification of Sugar with NaFeEDTA Improves Iron Status in Semi-Rural Population in Guatemala." *Am J Clin Nutr* (61): 1153–63.

_____. 1995. "Iron Deficiency in Children: New Possibilities for Its Control." *Int Ch. Health* (6): 49–62.

_____. 1997. "Suplementación con hierro para el control de la deficiencia de hierro en poblaciones en riesgo." In: O'Donnell, A. M., Viteri, F. E., and Carmuega, E. S. (eds.), *Deficiencia de hierro: Desnutrición oculta en América Latina.* Publicación CESNI No. 18, CESNI, Buenos Aires.

Viteri, F., Gueri, M., and Calvo, E. B. 1995. *Primer Taller Subregional sobre el control de las anemias nutricionales y la deficiencia de hierro.* GCID, ACC/SCN, IINP, ONU, OPS-OMS, CESNI- 1995. Publicación INCAP DCE/017.

Walravens, P. A., Chakar, A., Mokni, R., Denise, J., and Lemonier, D. 1992. "Zinc Supplements in Breast-Fed Infants." *Lancet* (34): 683–5.

Walter, T. 1992. "Impact of Iron Deficiency on Cognition in Infancy and Childhood." In: Fomon, S. J., and Zlotkin, S. (eds.), *Nutritional Anemias.* Nestlé Nutrition Workshop Series, Vol. 30, Nestec, Vevey, Raven Press.

Walter, T., de Andraca, I., Chadud, P., and Perales, C. G. 1989. "Iron-Deficiency Anemia: Adverse Effects on Infant Psychomotor Development." *Pediatrics* (84): 7–17.

Walter, T., Arredondo, S., Arevalo, M., and Steckel, A. 1986. "Effect of Iron Therapy on Phagocytosis and Bacterial Activity in Neutrophils of Iron Deficient Infants." *Am J Clin Nutr* (44): 897–902.

Walter, T., Hertrampf, E., Pizarro, F., Olivares, M., Llaguno, S., Letelier, A., Vega, V., and Steckel, A. 1993. "Effect of Bovine-Hemoglobin-Fortified Cookies on Iron Status of Schoolchildren: A Nationwide Program in Chile." *Am J Clin Nutr* (57): 190–4

Walter, T., Kovalskys, I., and Stekel, A. 1983. "Effects of Mild Iron Deficiency on Infant Mental Development Scores." *J Pediatr* (102): 519–22.

Walter, T., Olivares, M., Pizarro, F., and Muñoz, C. 1997. "Hierro, anemia e infección." In: O'Donnell, A. M., Viteri, F. E., Carmuega, E. S. (eds.), *Deficienia de hierro: Desnutrición oculta en América Latina*. Publicación CESNI No. 18, CESNI, Buenos Aires.

WHO. 1995. "Report of the WHO Informal Consultation on Hookworm Infection and Anemia in Girls and Women. WHO/CDS/IPI, 95, 1.

WHO/UNICEF/ICCIDD. 1992. "Technical Consultation on IDD Indicators." Report of a meeting. Geneva, Draft Document.

WHO/UNICEF/ICCIDD. 1993. "Global Prevalence of Iodine Deficiency Disorders." MDIS Working Paper No. 1.

Worthington-Roberts, B. 1990. "Maternal Iron Deficiency and Pregnancy Outcome." In: Enwonwu, C. O. (ed.), *Functional Significance of Iron Deficiency*. Nashville: Meharry Medical College.

Wright, A. J. A., and Southon, S. 1990. "The Effectiveness of Various Iron-Supplementation Regimens in Improving the Fe Status of Anemic Rats." *Bs J Nutr* (63): 579–85.

Xuan, N. N., Thissen, J. P., Collette, L., Gerard, G., Huy Khoi, H., and Ketelslegers, J. M. 1996. "Zinc Supplementation Increase Growth and Circulating Insuline-Like Growth Factor I (IGF-I) in Growth-Retarded Vietnamese Children." *Am J Clin Nutr* (63): 514–19.

Zeitlin, M., Ghassemi, H., and Mansour, M. 1990. *Positive Deviance in Child Nutrition*. New York: United Nations University.

2 | Child Undernutrition in Latin America and the Caribbean

Trends, Reasons, and Lessons

AARON LECHTIG

These comments evolve from an analysis of children's nutritional status to an analysis of their nutrition problem, in other words, by assessing trends in the prevalence of undernutrition and their main determinants, as well as by examining lessons on how to combat undernutrition.

Malnutrition should not be confounded with undernutrition. Undernutrition and overnutrition are two sides of the same coin, called malnutrition. Also, the term "protein-energy malnutrition" is misleading and it should not be used.

Problem Assessment:
What Are the Trends in Undernutrition in this Region?

Undernutrition decreased notably over the past three decades from an estimate of 21% in 1970 to 6.7% in 1997. This trend was observed in almost every country of the region. For comparison, the expected prevalence of low weight for age in the middle-class U.S. population is 3%.

Of course, this trend does not mean at all that the problem has disappeared. If there is a word that defines the current nutrition situation in Latin America and the Caribbean, that word is "disparity." The regional median rate of undernutrition (10.3%) masked countries with rates less than 5%, such as Chile, Costa Rica, Cuba, and countries such as Guatemala, Haiti, Honduras, Ecuador, and Bolivia, with rates between 15 and 33%. Gross disparity also exists within countries, such as Brazil, where the 1995 mean (5.7%) masks serious disparities between the northeast and the south and southeast. To understand why undernutrition decreased over the past three decades in the region, we will follow the UNICEF conceptual framework of assessing basic, underlying, and immediate causes.

Basic Causes

Was the Decrease Produced by Changes in Income Poverty? Probably Not.

During the past three decades, the prevalence of income poverty has not decreased: it decreased from 45 to 41% during the 1970s, increased from 41 to 46% during the 1980s, and decreased again from 46 to 44% through 1994. In Brazil, for example, prevalence of weight deficiency decreased, while the prevalence of poverty increased. This contrasting trend has been observed in almost every country for which data are available.

Although nutritionists and economists may disagree on the estimates for income poverty and undernutrition, at each point in time, most would agree that in Latin America and the Caribbean, undernutrition prevalence decreased notably during the past 30 years, while income poverty did not follow a similar trend. In fact, the prevalence of undernutrition among low-income people decreased from an estimate of 47% in 1970 to 16% in 1997. In other words, the probability of low-income people becoming undernourished decreased from 50% in 1970 to 17% in 1997. Thus, the decreasing trend in undernutrition was not caused by a decrease in income poverty.

This conclusion does not mean that income poverty is not a powerful cause of undernutrition. It should be remembered that in most countries of the region, an undernourished child is almost always growing up in a low-income family. In fact, if income poverty decreased, undernutrition would also decrease in a similar proportion. When the crunch produced by economic adjustment policies became extreme, the prevalence of low-birth-weight babies, undernutrition, and the infant mortality rate all increased. That was the case in northeast Brazil during the period 1982–84, (Becker and Lechtig 1986). It may also be the case in Venezuela and Jamaica during the 1990s.

Income poverty is not the only cause of undernutrition, and it was not the main determinant of the decrease in the prevalence of undernutrition observed in the region during the past 27 years. Being poor in terms of income does not necessarily mean becoming undernourished. This is particularly true during the 1990s. In contrast to the sixties, in the nineties the greater proportion (84%) of children from low-income families did not become undernourished. Another way of describing this situation is that the prevalence of positive deviation in weight within the low-income group has increased from 53% in 1970 to 84% in 1997.

The implication is that the strategies to combat poverty and undernutrition are not necessarily identical. A strategy to combat undernutrition will help in the long term to alleviate income poverty. A strategy to alleviate poverty will also help to combat undernutrition. Both strategies are urgently needed. The uniqueness of the strategies presents a very important window of opportunity: even in countries where there is as yet no clear way to alleviate income poverty, it is still possible to combat undernutrition effectively.

Was the Decrease in Undernutrition due to Improvements in the Area of Women's Access to Education and Employment? Yes, with High Probability.

Data on women's social condition during the past three decades is very scarce, pointing out a very important topic for research. One important change on the continent was the increase in the proportion of women who were part of the economically active population (EAP) and therefore, receiving cash income for their work. Women represented 10% of the EAP in 1970 and 37% in 1995. This regional median masks huge variations between women and men: 1:5.2 in the Dominican Republic and 1:1.2 in Jamaica. In 1995, 28% of all women regionally were in the EAP.

The education level of women in the workforce also improved notably during the same period. By 1995, there were 103 women per 100 men in professional and technical occupations. The highest values were observed in Uruguay and Jamaica and the lowest values in Bolivia and Haiti. This distribution is similar to that of undernutrition.

What Caused the Increase in the Proportion of Women in the Economically Active Population?

Families felt that one minimum-usage salary was not enough to cover their basic needs, so it was necessary for adult women to get into the cash income market. This was facilitated by women's improved educational achievements, a fact reported in almost every country of the region during the past 30 years. Although getting into the labor force was not enough to bring the family above the poverty threshold, it was probably instrumental in improving the allocation of available resources to children.

In a way, cash management by women also contributed to improve their level of empowerment. As a consequence, women were participating more in decisions that affect their lives in the 1990s than they did in the 1970s. It is more and more common to observe women leading grassroots movements in Argentina, Brazil, Chile, Ecuador, Peru, and many other countries in the region.

Studies in Latin America, Africa, and Asia have repeatedly shown that women are better than men at allocating resources to their children. The UNICEF 1996 Progress of Nations report arrived at a similar conclusion in discussing why South Asian people suffer a greater prevalence of undernutrition than populations in sub-Saharan Africa.

Education is related to this issue. Girls' education improved in almost all countries of the region during the past three decades. The regional median rates of schooling was 4.9 years in 1995, close to the boys' median of 5.3 years. As expected, the rate for girls was low for Haiti (1.3 years) and Bolivia (3.0 years) and high for Argentina (9.5 years), Uruguay (8.6 years), and Cuba (8.1 years).

The median illiteracy rate for females in 1995 reached an all-time low of 10%, 2 points above the 8% median rate for males. The rate varied from a low of 2% for Trinidad and Tobago and Uruguay, to highs of 58% for Haiti and 51% for Guatemala. The number of women per 100 men at secondary and university levels was 104 and 92, respectively, for 1995.

The key role that women's education plays in undernutrition has been reported in several countries in Africa and Latin America. This is the case in Ecuador, where most of the decrease in undernutrition observed during the 1980s could be related to the improvement in women's education (Freire 1994).

During this period, women also became effective citizens and effective leaders of their communities. As such they played a role in advancing the nutrition of children beyond their role as mothers. Women who manage their income, who are educated, and who are in positions of authority make better decisions in regard to children's nutrition than men do working with the same income level. In Latin America and the Caribbean, women have become teachers, nurses, social workers, community organizers, and political leaders, and in these roles they have played important roles in improving nutrition for children, independently of whether they were mothers or not.

This is not to say that gender discriminatory practices do not exist in the region. Discriminatory practices continue to exist, but probably to a lesser extent than before. For example, though women participation in the EAP has improved, their median labor income was still not equal to that of men in 1995: 65% for all workers, and 73% for salaried workers, with a regional range of 61 to 82%. These figures show that there is much to accomplish in gender equity.

Underlying Causes

Was this Decreasing Trend in Undernutrition Produced by an Improvement in Household Food Security? Probably not.

In fact, in this region the most important component of household food insecurity is not the lack of food availability, but insufficient money to purchase food. Income is the key determinant of food availability for 44% of the population, and this factor did not improve because income poverty did not improve.

What about the impact of the huge food distribution programs? Although they still represent an investment on the order of several billion dollars in the region, such programs probably had very little to do with the reported decrease in undernutrition. This is because the food distributed did not reach those in need, that is, high-risk children below 12 months of age, and also because of large deviations in practice from the original nutritional aim of such programs. However, the possibility remains that there was an effect produced by food supplementation for pregnant and lactating women. This remains to be demonstrated.

Was it Produced by Improved Care of Children? Probably.

In fact, child care improved as a consequence of better allocation of resources by the mothers to their children.

Was it Produced by Improved Access to and Utilization of Basic Health Services, Water, and Sanitation? Probably.

Access to and utilization of health services, including water, sanitation, and family planning, were probably key contributors to the observed decrease of undernutrition. In several analyses across countries, sanitation coverage and total fertility rate were the strongest predicting factors for undernutrition (see the chapter by Steven Esrey in this volume). A series of variables in this cluster of services did show a similar trend to that of undernutrition.

1. The decrease in total fertility rate paralleled changes in undernutrition rates. Total fertility rate is a function of access to services, education, and information.

2. There has been a steady improvement in terms of access to basic health services. Proxies to measure this include vaccinations and family planning services. In 1996, vaccination coverage against poliomyelitis was 87%, the coverage against measles in children less than 1 year of age was 83%; the coverage (ORT) was 69%, as compared with less than 20% in 1982 for polio and almost zero for measles and ORT. The regional media rate of contraception use is now estimated to be 56%, as compared with less than 10% in 1970. Yet 22% of the women of reproductive age wish to avoid a next pregnancy and do not have access to services.

3. The available data indicate that 72% of the population had access to water in 1980, 79% in 1990, but only 73% in 1995. The rate of sanitation coverage increased from 59% in 1980 to 66% in 1990 and 69% in 1995.

Two clusters of factors seem clearly responsible for the decrease in undernutrition in Latin America and the Caribbean. Basic causes include the increased management of resources by women and, therefore, their improved allocation to children. Underlying causes include improved access to, and utilization of, primary health services, including family planning and water and sanitation services, and improved child care, as a result of better allocation of available resources in the family. Two factors that were clearly not responsible for the decrease in undernutrition were income poverty and household food security, neither of which have improved.

What is a good proxy for women's management of cash, improved access to basic services, and improved child care? Probably the level of urbanization. The urban population rate in Latin American countries increased continuously from 57.4% in 1970 to 65.1% in 1980 and 74.0% in 1994, and it is projected to be 76.6% in the year 2000. Of course, the implication is not that the entire region should become urban in order to combat undernutrition.

How to Improve the Fight Against Undernutrition? The Lessons Learned

The following aspects deserve consideration for policy making.

Encourage Women's Empowerment

The empowerment of women should be encouraged as a worthy goal and a right, as well as a means to combat undernutrition in women and children. Having permeated the social fabric of the region, the movement to empower women seems irreversible. It has included legislation, political prioritization, education, and resource management at the household level, and has stopped the worst forms of exploitation of and discrimination against women. There is as yet very little quantitative information on this trend, but in almost every country in the region young women now see their role as very different and improved from that of their grandmothers.

Carefully Defined Goals and Priorities

The importance of carefully defining goals and priorities became obvious when GOBI, launched in 1982, promoted the worldwide universalization of four activities: Growth monitoring, Oral rehydration, Breast feeding, and Immunizations. Success in this approach encouraged the 1990 plan of action by the WSC to halve undernutrition and maternal mortality and to decrease the incidence of infant mortality one-third by the year 2000. In addition, the WSC established the goals of eliminating Vitamin A and iodine deficiency and decreasing by one-third the prevalence of iron deficiency anemia in women.

In terms of strategy, the emphasis on prevention paid off better and more widely than focusing on curative approaches and rehabilitation. In terms of target population, focusing on pregnant and lactating women and on children less than age 2 proved more effective than focusing on preschool or school children and was essential for success in Chile, Cuba, Costa Rica. It is also clear that such interventions as improving care of children and women and developing universal access to basic health services, including family planning, water, and sanitation, were behind almost all the success stories in the region.

Treating micronutrient deficiencies with fortified foods proved to be more sustainable than treating deficiencies with vitamin/mineral supplements. For example, iodized oil capsules improved iodine uptake for a few months, but that immediate impact did not last. On the other hand, salt iodination took longer to raise iodine levels but sustained them over the long term. Focusing on this methodology has eliminated disease associated with iodine deficiency in practically all countries in the region.

Similarly, distribution of Vitamin A supplements addressed an immediate deficiency, but had only a short-term impact. The fortification of corn flour in Venezuela with Vitamin A took three years to have an impact on deficiency, but that impact was more sustainable.

Countries such as Chile (in the case of fortifying wheat flour with iron), Guatemala (fortifying sugar with Vitamin A), and Ecuador and Bolivia fortifying salt with iodine) discovered the advantage of adding to food rather than relying on vitamin/mineral supplements. In doing so, Ecuador, Colombia, and Bolivia were also successful in avoiding negative side effects, such as inhibition of breast feeding because of liquid foods fortified with micronutrients. The success of such programs required cultivating and sustaining a political consensus for the methodology, as well as intensive effort mobilizing and building alliances throughout society.

Building on Success

There was no substitute for success in improving people's motivation and education. The history of nutrition science is plagued with failures and so the tendency is to minimize the advances achieved. Fortunately, many countries in the region avoided this tendency, and there were plenty of success histories. For example, iodine deficiency disease was eliminated through the universal iodination of salts in countries like Ecuador and Bolivia, where this achievement was considered impossible only 5 years earlier.

Contrary to common assumptions, it was learned that required resources were not out of reach. For example, even in the poorest countries there were large amounts of money allocated to food distribution, but they were used to address the wrong populations. The same resource could in fact be allocated on the basis of the credibility established by prior successful interventions. When resources were well managed, they contributed significantly to the solution of the problem. That was the case in Brazil, Chile, and Cuba, where the allocation of resources to priority cost-effective actions deserved greater attention from policy makers and donor agencies. Using available information to make better decisions was demonstrated to have a synergistic effect in improving the quality and coverage of the information as well as the management of the intervention.

The Beginning of a Movement to Favor Women and Children

The movement to benefit children and women first took form with regard to health and nutrition. Latin America has seen an increasing understanding that nutrition is a right. Begun mostly by grassroots organizations, women's groups, and opposition parties under the slogan of "Freedom from Hunger," this movement gradually permeated many countries in the region during the seventies and the eighties. During the nineties, it benefited from the groundwork established by the World Summit for Children in 1990 and the International Conference of Nutrition, which endorsed the right to nutrition.

While its original purpose was to combat child undernutrition and early childhood mortality as part of daily realities of life, the right to nutrition movement exposed the social determinants of undernutrition as a way of helping the state fulfill its obligations.

This led to better decisions for children at the family level: better public nutrition policies in Costa Rica, friendly health and nutrition services in Chile, resource mobilization in Mexico and Brazil, and committed participation by people in Bolivia, Brazil, and Peru. In fact, the decentralized grassroots efforts encouraged participation and clarified the need to approach the problem of undernutrition in several countries, including Bolivia, Colombia, El Salvador, Guatemala, Nicaragua, and Peru.

In Brazil, Chile, and Peru, women established their right to food supplements during pregnancy and lactation. Throughout the entire region, legislation to provide women with postnatal rest was the legal expression of their right to breast-feed and care for their babies.

The movement gradually extended to other issues, such as landmines and the effects of war on children, child labor, peace process, tourist use of child prostitutes, and discrimination against girl children, in Latin America. This momentum got tremendous strength from the UN General Assembly's approval of the CRC in 1989 and from the process of CRC ratification in the region's countries. Centered on children and women and sustained by people, for people as well as being the movement has evolved from projects and programs to an incipient "culture of rights." In this process, participation by all elements of society, including those who suffered need, was essential. Accomplishing this was found also to contribute to citizenship, democracy, and economic development.

BIBLIOGRAPHY

Becker, R. and A. Lechtig. 1986. *Brasil, evolução da mortalidade infantil no período 1977–1984*. Brasília: Centro de Documentação do Ministerio da Saúde.

CEPAL (Comisión Económica para América Latina y el Caribe). 1995. *Panorama social de América Latina*. Santiago de Chile: CEPAL. (Main source for estimates of poverty during the period 1970–95. Estimate to the year 2000 is from the author.)

Esrey, S. 2000. *Environmental Sanitation and Its Relation to Child Health*. In this volume.

Freire, W. 1994. *Consultant Report to UNICEF TACRO*.

UN (United Nations). 1995a. *Situation de la mujer en el mundo.* (Main source for data on women's participation in secondary education and university careers.)

_____. 1995b. *World Urbanization Prospects: The 1994 Revision,* pp. 82–5. New York: UN, Dept. of International Economic and Social Affairs. (A source for estimates on urbanization.)

UN ACC-SCN (United Nations, Administrative Committee on Coordination, Subcommittee on Nutrition). 1996. *Update on the Nutrition Situation: Summary of Results for the Third Report on the World Nutrition Situation.* Geneva: UN ACC-ASN. (Source for the data on undernutrition from 1975 up to 1995. Estimates for the period 1995–2000 and for 1970 are from the author.)

UNDP (United Nations Development Program). 1995. *Human Development Report.* New York: Oxford University Press. (Main source for data on female economic activity.)

_____. 1996. *Human Development Report: Growing Urbanization,* 176–7. New York: Oxford University Press. (A source for estimates on urbanization.)

UNESCO/UNICEF (United Nations Educational, Scientific, and Cultural Organization/United Nations Children's Fund). *Educating People.* (Main source for data on illiteracy.)

UNICEF 1990. *World Summit for Children: Plan of Action.*

UNICEF 1996. *Progress of Nations.* New York: UNICEF.

UNICEF 1997. *State of the World's Children: Nutrition.* Oxford: Oxford University Press. (Contains reference for fertility and contraception.)

UNICEF TACRO. 1996. *Victories and Upcoming Challenges.*

3 | Micronutrient Malnutrition

Overview of the Deficiencies in the Region of the Americas

WILMA B. FREIRE

Introduction

Deficiencies in iodine, iron, and Vitamin A are a widespread problem that affects more than one-third of the world's population and produces serious consequences, including learning disabilities, impaired work capacity, illness, and death. Adequate intake and availability of these micronutrients are closely related to the survival, physical and mental development, and overall well-being of individuals and populations. Many studies report on the serious adverse consequences of these deficiencies for physical and mental health, education, work capacity, and economic efficiency.

Iodine, Vitamin A, and iron deficiencies are highly prevalent in Latin American and Caribbean countries. This chapter presents the situation on micronutrient deficiencies in the region. In addition, it makes some recommendations for how to approach the problem.

Iodine Deficiency Disorders

Iodine deficiency disorders (IDDs) refer to a variety of health problems caused by insufficient iodine in the diet. Iodine is essential for thyroid function. Lack of iodine produces goiter, which is the most visible manifestation of this deficiency. Iodine deficiency in pregnant women, particularly during the first 4 months, results in increased fetal mortality, cretinism, and severe mental deficiency. Even mild or moderate deficiency produces disorders such as deafness and some degree of retarded mental development.

It is estimated that 23% of the people in the region are at risk of IDD because they live in areas where the soil is poor in iodine, so that local crops also lack iodine. This situation leads to devastating consequences because it causes thyroid function abnormalities. Where the deficiency is severe, local populations suffer endemic goiter and cretinism, mental retardation, reduced fertility, and increased prenatal and infant mortality.

Table 1.   Prevalence of Goiter

Country	Year	Prevalence (%)
COLOMBIA	1994	
Andean area		6.8
DOMINICAN REPUBLIC	1993	5.3
Azua		12.3
La Vega		7.3
EL SALVADOR	1994	
Morazan		44.0
GUATEMALA	1995	
Metropolitan		22.0
Central		22.5
Northeast		17.0
Northwest		27.0
Southwest		19.0
Southeast		18.5
Verapaces		25.0
Peten		12.0
HAITI	1992	
Central plateau		10.0
NICARAGUA	1993	
Tola		33.7
PARAGUAY	1993	
Misiones		32.4
El Chaco		42.0
VENEZUELA	1993–95	
Merida		64.7
Tachira		65.9
Trujillo		59.6

Sources: WHO/UNICEF/ICCIDD database and PAHO database.

The scanty information regarding the prevalence of goiter that is visible or palpable is rather old (Table 1). The only data less than five years old are from Tola in Nicaragua, the Andean area of Colombia, Azua and Las Vegas in the Dominican Republic, Guatemala, Misiones and El Chaco in Paraguay, and three states in Venezuela. Even though the determination of goiter is imprecise and biased, Table 1 suggests unfortunately that IDDs, expressed as a prevalence of goiter, are still a very significant problem.

Tables 2 and 3 present median urinary iodine concentrations and the proportion of the population with low levels of urinary iodine for some countries in the region. Since most iodine is excreted in the urine, urinary iodine level is a good marker of the previous day's dietary iodine intake. However, since an individual's level of urinary iodine varies daily, this indicator can be used for making a population prevalence estimate. From these tables, it can be concluded that the problem of iodine deficiency is still a major public health problem in the region in spite of successful implementation programs fortifying salt with iodine.

Thanks to such fortification programs, most countries in the region have achieved extraordinary success in the fight against IDDs. For example, Bolivia, Brazil, Colombia, Costa Rica, Cuba, Guatemala, Haiti, and Peru have acceptable values of urinary iodine (over 10 mg/dl), or are close to it (see Table 3). Nevertheless, data broken down by prevalence (Table 3) show that, in some areas, a high proportion of the population is still at risk of IDDs. Recently, Bolivia, Ecuador, and Peru, which are countries where IDDs are endemic, have achieved remarkable success. In 1995, the median urinary lev-

Table 2. Median Urinary Iodine Concentration

Country	Region	Year	mg/dl
Bolivia	National	1996	25.2
Colombia	Andean	1994	93.4
Costa Rica	National	1996	23.3
Cuba	Problem areas	1995	9.5
Guatemala	National	1995	22.2
Haiti	Central plateau	1992	10.0
Peru	Sierra and Selva	1995	13.9

Sources: WHO/UNICEF/ICCIDD data base and PAHO data base.

Table 3. Distribution of the Population by Urinary Iodine Level

Country/Region	Year	Percent <10mg/dl
BOLIVIA	1996	9.2
BRAZIL	1994	35.4**
COSTA RICA	1996	8.9
CUBA	1995	—
DOMINICAN REPUBLIC	1993	86.0
ECUADOR	1992	—
Sierra	—	19.2
Coast	—	1.5
Amazon	—	1.1
EL SALVADOR	1994	78.0
Morazan		
MEXICO (13 states)*	1993–94	1.8
Sinaloa	—	4.8
Morelos	—	0.4
NICARAGUA	1993	—
Tola		50.0
VENEZUELA	93–95	—
Andean	—	37.8
Tachira	—	37.6
Trujillo	—	37.6
Merida	—	53.8

* Expressed in mg of iodine per gram of creatinine. Cutoff point 50mg/g
** Preliminary
Sources: WHO/UNICEF/ICCIDD data base and PAHO data bank

els for the Sierra and Selva regions of Peru were 13.9 mg/dl, up from 5 mg/dl in 1986. In 1996, it was estimated that the population at risk of IDDs (urinary iodine <10 mg/dl) in Peru was 1.9 million, down from 6 million in the 1980s.

A survey conducted in Bolivia in 1996 showed a median urine excretion of iodine of 25.2 mg/dl (as compared with 20.9 in 1989). Moreover, only 9.2% of the sample had values below 10 mg/dl, down from 16.0% in 1989. Information on the situation in Ecuador from 1992 shows levels of urinary iodine over 10 mg/dl in 80.8% of highland communities. Comparable figures for the coastal and Amazon regions were 98.5% and 98.9%, respectively.

The results of a survey completed in early 1995 in Cuba confirm that IDDs are still a problem in certain areas. That study analyzed 3,027 samples of urine from children in 25 municipalities in 11 provinces. The median level was 9.5 mg/dl; however, in mountainous areas, values below 2 mg/dl were found (1).

Selected areas of Mexico surveyed in 1993 and 1994 show an average prevalence of low urinary iodine of only 1.8%, with a range from zero in the state of Mexico, to 4.8% in Sinaloa. Since then, efforts have been made in targeting interventions to isolated problem localities where iodized salt is difficult to get. In some parts of the states of Puebla, Oaxaca, Hidalgo, Veracruz, and Michoacan, it is still possible to find prevalences of low urinary iodine of 10 to 40%. However, the data is preliminary and the number of samples small and highly selected. A study carried out in Brazil in 1994 showed that 35.4% of 15,303 children presented values below 10 mg/dl, and in 21.2% of 401 municipalities the medium excretion was below 10 mg/dl (2).

Data on fortification of salt with iodine is fairly up-to-date. It shows that Argentina, Bolivia, Brazil, Chile, Costa Rica, El Salvador, Mexico, and Peru have iodized salt. However, not all the salt contains iodine in the recommended amounts.

Vitamin A Deficiency

The major cause of Vitamin A deficiency is the consumption of a diet poor in that nutrient. Vitamin A is essential for normal vision and ocular function, and deficiencies cause night blindness and other manifestations of xerophthalmia, including corneal destruction (keratomalacia) and blindness. In addition, Vitamin A deficiency has a number of other negative consequences:

- Milk produced by mothers lacking Vitamin A results in an inadequate provision of that vitamin to the infant.

- Disorders resulting from Vitamin A deficiency include growth retardation, alterations of the epithelial surfaces, increased prevalence and duration of infectious episodes, and increased mortality among children between 6 months and 6 years of age.

- Vitamin A deficiency increases the severity, complications, and risk of death from measles and the severity of infectious episodes of diarrhea and pneumonia, and infections can further accelerate the urinary loss of Vitamin A (3,4).

- Deficiency of Vitamin A interferes with iron metabolism resulting in anemia (5). The administration of Vitamin A increases hemoglobin levels, and together with iron supplements improves anemia (6,7).

Low serum or plasma retinol is widely accepted as a valid indicator of the presence and magnitude of Vitamin A deficiency (8). A prevalence greater than 10% of values of <0.35 mmol/l (<20 mg/dl) is an indication of a significant public health problem (9).

The prevalence of Vitamin A deficiency varies markedly among different segments of societies defined in terms of, for example, urban or rural residence, indigenous and nonindigenous status, and income. The lowest prevalence of the deficiency in the region was found in Panama, at 6.1%. However among indigenous children in that country the figure was 13%, compared with 5% among nonindigenous children (10; see Table 4). Panama is followed by Costa Rica, with a prevalence of 8.7% (11).

Table 4.   Serum Retinol Levels

Country	Year	Number	Group	Mean (mg/dl)	%<20mg/dl
ANTIGUA**	1996	94	1–4 years		11.7
ARGENTINA					
Great Bs. As.	1992	386	Adolescents	34.3	2.5
Tierra del Fuego	1995	1,313	All ages		—
			Infants		10.8
			Preschoolers		8.7
			Adolescents		1.7
			Pregnant women		8.7
			Adults		0.7
BOLIVIA	1991	801	12–71 months	32.3	—
Rural highlands					11.3
Eastern plains					17.0
La Paz					9.0
COLOMBIA	1996	2,187	12–69 months		13.0
Pacific region					19.1
Atlantic region					15.3
COSTA RICA	1996	961	1–6 years		8.7
DOMINICA**	1995–96	160	Preschoolers		10.7
		411	School children		1.2
		151	Pregnant women		2.0
DOMINICAN REP.	1993	1,516	—	27.6	—
		765	Preschoolers		22.7
			School children		15.0
ECUADOR	1993	1,232	12–59 months	27.6	20.0
Rural					22.0
Urban					13.0

Table 4. (*continued*)

Country	Year	Number	Group	Mean (mg/dl)	%<20 mg/dl
GUATEMALA	1995	1,517	12–59 months	15.8	15.8
Metropolitan					15.5
Highland					16.1
Southeast					14.6
Northeast					16.2
HONDURAS	1996	1,752	12–59 months		12.3
MEXICO	1993	489	Preschoolers		—
Urban					4.8
Rural					29.5
NICARAGUA	1993	1,755	12–60 months		31.0
PANAMA	1992	1,566	Preschoolers	37.4	6.1
PERU					
Lima	1993	471	<5 years		—
Urban					5.0
Slums					24.0
Libertadores/Wari	1993	193	<5 years		—
Coast					21.0
Highlands					24.0
INKA	1992–94	NR	<5 years		—
Highlands					64.0
Jungle					76.0
N.E. Maranon	1992–94	NR	<3 years		
Coast					73.0
Highland					71.0
ST. VINCENT**	1996	176	Preschoolers		2.5
		445	School children		6.2
		81	Pregnant women		1.1

* Cutoff point 20 mg/dl
** Cutoff point 25 mg/dl
Source: Mora, A., et al., "Vitamin A Deficiency in Latin America and the Caribbean: An Overview," in press.

The prevalence in Nicaragua is 31%, but the figure is higher among children of low socioeconomic status (SES) (39%). In Ecuador, serum retinol levels were associated with mother's education (children from illiterate mothers were three times more likely than literate mothers to have low serum retinol), urban/rural residence, and SES. A national Guatemalan survey found a prevalence of 15.8%, but the figure was higher among children who consume brown sugar (22.4%) than among those who consume white sugar (15.1%) because most of the latter is fortified (12). In 1994, 29.4% of 219 Mexican children living in rural areas and 4.8% of 270 urban children had low levels of retinol (13). In Peru, the figures were 5% of children in urban Lima, compared with 24% living in the shanty towns (*pueblos jovenes*) surrounding that city (14).

Using a cutoff point taken to indicate a marginal or deficient Vitamin A status of 25 mg/dl, a three-country study recently conducted in the English-speaking Caribbean (15) on b-carotene, Vitamins A and E, and iron status found prevalences of 11.7% among children aged 1 to 4 in Antigua and Barbuda; 10.7, 1.2, and 2% among preschoolers, school children, and pregnant women, respectively, in Dominica, and 6.2, 1.1, and 2.5% in corresponding groups in St. Vincent and the Grenadines.

From these data, one can conclude that the problem of Vitamin A deficiency in the Americas is still of major magnitude.

Iron Deficiency

Anemia is a significant public health problem not only in developing countries, where the prevalence is estimated to be more than 35%, but also in the industrialized world. Pregnant women and small children are the groups most affected by this disease. It is believed that more than 50% of pregnant women and more than 40% of small children in developing countries suffer from anemia, in most cases due to iron deficiency (16).

The causes of anemia are multiple and complex, including poor iron absorption or intake, folate deficiency, excessive loss of blood in women during menstruation and childbirth, low intake of other nutrients that promote iron bioavailability, parasitic infections and other chronic or repeated infections, and, more recently, acquired immunodeficiency syndrome (17). Careful studies have shown that iron deficiency is associated with factors such as neuromotor maturation, cognitive development, attention span, learning, and information processing. The severity of the effects on these factors are related to the severity and duration of the anemia and persist after the anemia has been corrected (18,19,20). The magnitude of individual intellectual deficit is small, but the deficit is greatly magnified when considering the population as a whole (21).

There is abundant evidence that anemia during pregnancy is associated with increases in maternal mortality and fetal wasting, and that it is a cause of premature delivery and consequent low birth weight (22). Iron deficiency and anemia also limit the capacity for physical work. The productivity of anemic populations increases 30% or more when iron deficiency anemia is corrected.

The cutoff point established by WHO below which anemia can be considered to exist is 11 g of hemoglobin per deciliter of blood in pregnant women and children under 5 years of age and 12 g in schoolchildren and adult, non-pregnant women. Some countries, however, have decided to adopt different cutoff points, and for populations living at high altitude the hemoglobin level below which anemia is present is not well defined as yet.

Several problems, most related to the existing sources of information, make the assessment of anemia in the region particularly challenging. In most cases, the data come from limited studies that are not representative of the national situations. Frequently the sources of data are the health services. In this case, the information may be considered to be nationally representative if health service coverage reaches most of the population, but not when coverage is low.

For selected countries, Tables 5 and 6 present the prevalence of anemia among pregnant women and preschool children, respectively. It can be seen that large variations are still present among and within countries. Thus, in the province of Buenos Aires, the prevalence of anemia among pregnant women is 8.2%, compared with 38.6% in Tierra del Fuego. In the Bolivian tableland, the prevalence is twice as high as in the valley, and while the prevalence in southeast Santiago, Chile, is 1.2%, it reaches 54.6% in Lima, Peru. No doubt these differences are in part due to the differences in the groups examined. The estimate for overall prevalence of anemia in pregnant women in the region is around 30%, although in some areas it is as high as 60% or more. The same variations can be observed among children less than 2 years of age, for whom the overall prevalence can be conservatively estimated at 40%.

Until recently, iron deficiency has received much less attention than iodine and Vitamin A deficiencies, although it is the most widespread deficiency. The only response in most countries has been the provision of iron supplements for pregnant women, with no supervision or follow up, and very little compliance. It is increasingly recognized that iron fortification of staple foods is the best long-term solution; Chile and Venezuela are two good examples of countries that have applied this approach.

Table 5. Prevalence of Anemia among Pregnant Women
(Cutoff point: Hb<11 g/dl)

Country	Region/City	Year	Sample Size	Percent	Source of Data	Ref. No.
Antigua	National	1992		24.3	HC	23
Argentina	Buenos Aires	1995	197	8.2	HC	24
	Tierra del Fuego	1995	70	38.6	LS	25
Belize	National	1995	4,661	51.7	HC	26

Table 5. (*continued*)
(Cutoff point: Hb<11 g/dl)

Country	Region/City	Year	Sample Size	Percent	Source of Data	Ref. No.
Bolivia[a]	National	1993	3,606	50.5	HC	27
	Valley	1993		33.0	HC	3
	Tableland	1993		61.8	HC	3
	Plains	1993		69.8	HC	3
Chile	S.E. Santiago	1993	342	1.2	HC	28
Cuba	Sentinel sites[b]	1993		25–35.0	LS	29
Dominica	National	1996	148	35.1	NS	30
Guatemala	National	1995		36.4[c]	NS	31
Nicaragua	National	1993		33.6[d]	NS	32
Panama	National	1994	326	8.8	HC	33
Paraguay	National	1993	385	26.2	HC	34
Peru	Lima	1992	389	54.6	LS	35

Note: HC = Data from health centers, LS = Local survey, NS = National survey
[a] Adjusted for altitude
[b] Havana and Pinar del Rio
[c] Women 18–44 years, pregnant or not
[d] Adult women, pregnant or not

Table 6. Prevalence of Anemia in Latin American Preschool Children
(Hb<11g/dl)

Country	Region/City	Year	Sample Size	Percent	Source of Data
Antigua	National	1996	81	49.4	NS
Argentina	Tierra del Fuego	1995	128[a]	28.6	LS
		1995	160[b]	10.8	LS
Brazil	São Paulo	1994–95	4,283	54.5	HS
Costa Rica	National	1996	961	26.0	NS
Dominica	National	1996	157	34.4	NS
Ecuador	Five provinces	1994	1,486	37.8	LS
Guatemala	National	1995	—	26.0	NS
Nicaragua	National	1993	1,776	28.5	NS
Peru	Libertadores	1993	186	79.6	LS
	Lima	1993	280	21.8	LS
Venezuela	Caracas	1994	307	9.3	LS

Note: HC = Data from health centers, NS = National survey, LS = Local survey
[a] Infants
[b] Preschool children

Strategies for the Control of Micronutrient Deficiencies

Countries must still take direct aim at micronutrient malnutrition through consumer education in diet diversification, the distribution of pharmaceutical supplementation, and/or the fortification of common foods. Several successful interventions have been implemented for iodine and Vitamin A deficiencies. The fortification of salt with iodine has been implemented in countries like Ecuador and Bolivia, where this deficiency is endemic, and the results have been quite dramatic. Fortification of sugar has sometimes proved to be the most appropriate and sustainable of interventions, as seen in Guatemala. Fortifying food with iron is not yet widely practiced. Nevertheless, Chile and Venezuela promote the region-wide iron fortification of popular local foods. Chile has been fortifying wheat flour for more than three decades, and now has the lowest prevalence of iron deficiency in the region. In addition, national iron supplementation for pregnant women and special complementary food enriched with iron for children have also been provided. These strategies are having a large impact on the total population, as well as on pregnant women and small children. Venezuela has been fortifying wheat and corn flour for the past 4 years and has seen impressive decreases in the prevalence of iron deficiency in its population. Corn is also fortified with Vitamin A, which enhances iron absorption.

Nevertheless, diet diversification should also be an important strategy to further improve Vitamin A levels. Large segments of the region's population need to change food consumption patterns to enhance the consumption of Vitamin A-rich products. This strategy will, in the long term, be sustainable and protect the entire population. The same recommendation is valid for iron deficiency. Foods that enhance iron absorption should also be promoted so that they are consumed on a regular basis. In addition, consumer education strategies should accompany these interventions to help the population select appropriate foods. In order to be successful in the long run, interventions also need to implement monitoring and quality assurance programs.

To formulate an integrated strategy for managing iron deficiency, an analysis of the following factors is recommended.

A. Information gathering. Collecting available information will help determine the magnitude, severity, and geographic distribution of the problem, as well as the sex, age, and diet characteristics of those affected, and the presence of other deficiencies or parasitic infestation characteristics. Most countries do not, in fact, have this information. If the information available is not sufficient to develop a baseline to support the design of interventions and subsequent impact assessment, the next step would be to design a proposal for collecting such information. For that matter, it is not necessary to resort to sophisticated or expensive research projects to construct baseline information. Instead, rapid assessment studies should be conducted to provide the minimum amount of information necessary for sustaining program implementation. Sampling techniques, indicators, or methodologies for collecting the information are separate issues. If a country needs special technical cooperation, this should be provided by international agencies.

B. Assessing technical liability. The ability to fortify food products includes the availability of food items to be fortified, the industrial capacity to process them (including equipment, laboratories, and qualified technical personnel), and the packing, distribution, and marketing of the products. With such an assessment, it will be possible to determine what modifications and improvements are needed for a successful fortification program, including when technical cooperation should be provided and what form it should take.

C. The health delivery system. To carry out a program of iron supplementation for pregnant women and small children, it is necessary to analyze the health delivery system in terms of access and coverage, as well as the level of knowledge possessed by health personnel and the work performance at each level of the system. There must also be adequate storage capacity for materials and equipment used in the supplementation programs. For this purpose, it is also essential to identify alternative means to distribute supplements and monitor consumption, such as mothers' groups, religious organizations, and schools.

D. Economic feasibility. To assess the viability of a proposed national intervention program, an economic feasibility study would determine the funding to be provided by the state, as well as the availability of private funding, donations, and loans.

E. Political commitment. The viability of a program requires that the government be willing to assign the needed funding and other resources, and that sufficient political leadership be available to ensure that governments assume responsibility for executing the project.

Once this analysis is completed, the next step is to draw up the proposal for each intervention: fortification, dietary diversification, or supplementation. It is not the purpose of this chapter to go into the specific components of each intervention, but it should be noted that the development of each intervention involves very special skills from different disciplines.

REFERENCES

1. Instituto de la Nutricón e Higiene de los Alimentos. 1996. "Informe del primer taller nacional para la discusión del cumplimiento del plan de acción para el control y la eliminación de los trastornos por deficiencia de yodo." Ministerio de Salud Pública. La Habana, 9 Julio.

2. Zonato Esteves, R. 1997. "Determinação da excreção urinária de iado em escolares brasileiros." Tese apresentada à Universidade Federal de São Paulo/Escola Paulista de Medicina pare a obtenção do título de doutor em medicine. São Paulo.

3. FAO/WHO (Food and Agriculture Organization/World Health Organization). 1988. "Requirements of Vitamin A, Iron, Folate and Vitamin B12." Report of a joint FAO/WHO expert consultation. *Food and Nutr Ser 23.* FAO, Rome.

4. Alvarez, J. O., et al. 1995. "Urinary Retinol Excretion in Children with Acute Diarrhea." *Am J Clin Nutr* 61: 1273–6.

5. Mejía, L. A., et al. 1979. "Role of Vitamin A in the Absorption, Retention and Distribution of Iron in the Rat." *J Nutr* 109: 129–37.

6. Suharno, D., et al. 1993. "Supplementation with Vitamin A and Iron for Nutritional Anemia in Pregnant Women in West Java, Indonesia." *Lancet* 342 (8883): 1325–8.

7. Mejía, L. A., and Chew, F. 1988. "Hematological Effect of Supplementing Anemic Children with Vitamin A Alone and in Combination with Iron." *Am J Clin Nutr* 48: 595–600.

8. Underwood, B., and Olson, J. (eds). 1993. "A Brief Guide to Current Methods of Assessing Vitamin A Status." International Vitamin A Consultative Group (IVACG). Nutrition Foundation, New York.

9. World Health Organization. 1994. *Indicators for Assessing Vitamin A Deficiency and Their Application in Monitoring and Evaluating Intervention Programs.* Geneva.

10. Ministerio de Salud. 1992. *Encuesta Nacional de Vitamina A, 1992.* Departamento de Nutrición y Dietética. Panama.

11. Ministerio de Salud/Instituto Costarricense de Investigación de Enseñanza en Salud y Nutrición. 1997. *Encuesta Nacional de Nutrición, 1996. Micronutrientes.* San José.

12. Ministerio de Salud Pública y Asistencia Social/INCAP (Instituto de Nutrición de Centro América y Panamá). 1995. *Informe de la Encuesta Nacional de Micronutrientes. Guatemala, 1995.* Guatemala.

13. García-Obregón, O. 1994. "Deficiencia de Vitaminos A y E en Niños en la Población Rural de México (Tésis de Grado)." Facultad de Química, Universidad Nacional Autónoma de México. México, D.F.

14. PRISMA. 1993. *Encuesta Bioquínica del Estado de Hierro y Vitamina A. Regiones Lima y Libertadores Wari, 1992–93.* Informe Final. Asociación Benéfica PRISMA. Lima.

15. Caribbean Food and Nutrition Institute. 1997. *Micronutrient study report—A three-country survey.* Kingston, Jamaica.

16. Viteri. F. E. 1993. *Report to WHO on Global Strategy for the Control of Iron Deficiency.* Nutrition Unit, World Health Organization, Geneva.

17. Viteri, F. E. 1996. "Encuesta sobre las anemias nutricionales, la deficiencia de hierro y su control." In: Viteri, F. E., Gueri, M., y Calvo, E., (eds). *Informe del I Taller Subregional sobre Control de la Anemia y la Deficiencia de Hierro.* UNU (United Nations University), PAHO/WHO (Pan-American Health Organization/World Health Organization), CESNI Centro de Estudios Sobre Nutrición Infantil), and the University of California at Berkeley, INCAP. Publication DCE/017, Guatemala.

18. Pollitt, E., Haas, J., and Levitsky, D. A., (eds). 1989. "International Conference on Iron Deficiency and Behavioral Development." *Am J Clin Nutr* 50 (Suppl): 565–705.

19. Leibel, R. L., et al. 1982. "Studies Regarding the Impact of Micronutrient Status on Behavior in Man: Iron Deficiency as a Model." *Am J Clin Nutr* 35: 1211–21.

20. Lozoff, B., et al. 1991. "Long-term Developmental Outcome of Infants with Iron Deficiency." *New Engl J Med* 325: 687–95.

21. Walter, T. 1992. "Impact of Iron Deficiency on Cognition in Infancy and Childhood." In: Fomon, S. J. and Zlotkin, S. (Eds.). *Nutritional anemias.* Nestle Nutrition Workshop Series, Vol. 30, Nestec Ltd. Vevey Raven Press, Ltd. New York.

22. Viteri, F. E. 1992. "Iron: Global Perspective." In: *Ending Hidden Hunger: A Policy Conference on Micronutrient Malnutrition.* The Task for Child Survival and Development. Atlanta.

ADDITIONAL REFERENCES

23. *Report on the Prevention and Control of Anemia in Pregnant Women in Antigua and Barbuda.* Caribbean Food and Nutrition Institute (CFNI) Document, Kingston. 1994.

24. Ortega-Soler, C. R., et al. 1995. "Relación entre la concentración elevada de hemoglobina y deficiencia de calcio en el embarazo." Abstract. XII Latin American Congress of Clinical Biochemistry, Buenos Aires.

25. CESNI. 1995. *Projecto Tierra del Fuego. Diagnóstico Basal de Salud y Nutricion.* Fundación Jorge Macri, Buenos Aires.

26. *Study of Iron Deficiency Anemia among Pregnant Women in Belize.* Ministry of Health/INCAP/PAHO-WHO/UNICEF, January 1996.

27. *Prevalencia de anemia en mujeres embarazadas y ninos pre escolares en Bolivia.* Ministerio de Desarrollo Humano, Secretaria Nacional de Salud, La Paz, 1995.

28. Hertrampf, E., et al.1994. "Situacion de la nutrición de hierro en la embarazada adolescente al principio de la gestación." *Rev Med Chi* 122: 1372–7.

29. *Plan de acción nacional pare la nutrición (Proyecto).* Follow-up of the International Conference on Nutrition (Rome 1992). Intersectorial Committee, Havana, 1994.

30. *Micronutrient Study Report—A three-country survey.* Caribbean Food and Nutrition Institute, Kingston, 1997.

31. *Informe preliminar de la encuesta nacional de micronutrientes de Guatemala, 1995.* Ministerio de Salud Pública y Asistencia Social, Guatemala, Marzo 1996.

32. *Encuesta nacional sobre deficiencia de micronutrientes.* Ministerio de Salud, Dirección General de Promoción de la Salud, Dirección de Nutrición, Managua, 1994.

33. DeAguilera, M., and DeBrandariz, F. 1994. *II Encuesta de prevalencia de desnutrición.* January 1994. Ministerio de Salud, Panamá.

34. *Taller nacional sobre estrategias de control de carencias de micronutrientes.* Ministerio de Salud y OPS, Asunción, 22–25 February 1993.

35. Zavaleta, N., et al. 1993. *Prevalencia y determinantes de la anemia por deficiencia de hierro en una muestra representativa de gestantes en Lima, Peru.* Instituto de Investigación Nutricional, Lima.

4

Effect of Iron Deficiency Anemia on Cognitive Skills and Neuromaturation in Infancy and Childhood

TÓMAS K. WALTER

Behavioral Studies

Introduction

When iron deficiency anemia ensues during the first 2 years of life, it has been associated with delayed psychomotor development and changes in behavior. These effects have been shown to persist after several months of iron therapy, despite complete correction of iron nutritional measures. Moreover, it is still uncertain whether or to what extent they are reversible after an extended period of observation, since the long-term prospective follow-up studies reported to date, to be discussed below, show the persistence of cognitive deficits at 5–6 and at 10 years of age in those who had anemia during infancy.

The inherent difficulties of identifying intervening variables in the complex field of mental development, coupled in some cases with suboptimal design of assessment programs, have prevented significant progress in the investigation of iron deficiency. However, two studies, one conducted in Costa Rica (1) and the other in Santiago, Chile (2), taking into careful consideration the potential pitfalls, confirm conclusions arising from previous work.

The study in Santiago was performed in association with a field trial of fortified infant foods. One hundred ninety-six healthy, full-term infants were assessed with the Bayley Scales of Infant Development (BSID) (3) at 12 and 15 months of age. This well-known and accepted tool is used to determine psychomotor development from age 3 to 30 months. It consists of a mental scale to evaluate cognitive skills, such as language acquisition and abstract thinking, and a motor or psychomotor scale to evaluate gross motor abilities, such as coordination, body balance, and walking. In addition it has an Infant Behavior Record (IBR) scale that is based on clinical evaluation by a psychologist.

The Costa Rican study enrolled 191 otherwise healthy infants age 12 to 23 months with heterogeneous iron status. The infants were divided into groups ranging from most to least iron deficient. The BSID was administered before treatment and after 1 week and after 3 months of iron treatment, with appropriate placebo controls.

Adverse Affects of Iron Deficiencies

At what stage of iron deficiency is infant behavior adversely affected? It was clear in both studies that a decrease in hemoglobin leading to overt anemia was necessary to significantly affect mental and psychomotor development scores. The performance of the nonanemic iron-deficient infants as a whole was indistinguishable from that of controls.

In the Chilean study, among anemic infants, *hemoglobin (Hgb) concentration* was correlated with performance. The lower the Hgb, the lower the development scores. Similarly in the Costa Rican study, infants with moderate iron deficiency anemia (Hgb < 100 g/l) had lower mental and motor test scores than appropriate controls. The Santiago study also evaluated the *effect of chronic anemia*. Infants whose anemia had a duration of 3 or more months had significantly lower mental and motor development indices than those with anemia of shorter duration.

The results of other research published to date support the conclusion of the Santiago and Costa Rican studies: iron deficiency severe and chronic enough to cause anemia is associated with impaired achievement in development tests in infancy, and as anemia becomes more severe or prolonged, deficits are more profound.

Effect of Iron Treatment

Consistent results have been obtained in studies that have included a placebo treatment group. Together, these studies indicate that short-term increases in test scores observed among iron-treated anemic infants are not significantly greater than those among placebo-treated anemic infants, and are thus likely related to a practice effect.

Although separating the effects of iron deficiency from those of anemia is important, a more pertinent question from a clinical perspective is whether iron therapy completely corrects behavioral abnormalities regardless of how soon the changes are detectable. Studies in Costa Rica (1) Chile (2), the United Kingdom (4), and Indonesia (5) included an iron treatment period of 2–4 months after which psychomotor development tests were repeated. Despite the improved iron status, most of the formerly anemic infants were unable to improve their psychomotor performance. The only study to date that shows a convincing reversal of lower BSID is the Indonesian study.

Notwithstanding this, in most of the studies of iron therapy, even complete iron repletion was ineffective in improving the psychomotor scores of anemic infants to the level of nonanemic controls. The protocol in Indonesia (5) goes to prove that studies in this field may give conflicting results and that newer and more imaginative techniques must be used to elucidate current controversies.

Specific Patterns of Failure

The Chilean study found that when examining the mental scale, items that required comprehension of language but did not involve a visual demonstration were passed by fewer anemic infants than controls. In the psychomotor scale, balance in the standing position and walking (sits from standing, stands alone, and stands up) were accomplished by significantly fewer anemic infants than controls. Similar findings were reported in the Costa Rican study.

Information about other behavioral differences has been limited. Previous work relied primarily on ratings scales during development testing, and most studies used the Bayley Infant Behavior Record. Nonetheless, observations of Guatemalan (6) infants and the results of other investigators suggested a pattern of behavior. Infants with iron deficiency anemia were rated as unusually fearful, tense, restless, hesitant, withdrawn, or unhappy during testing.

Long-Term Effects of Iron Deficiency Anemia

Cognitive Performance of Children Who Were Anemic during Infancy

The long-term persistence issue has been addressed by two follow-up studies recently described in 5-year-old Costa Rican (7) and Chilean children who had been well characterized as infants in iron status, environmental variables, and their psychomotor development. These children were the subjects of respective reports during their infancy described above (1,2). At 5 years of age an evaluation with a comprehensive set of psychometric tests showed that those who as infants had iron deficiency anemia had lower scores on many of these tests compared with children who had higher hemoglobin counts in infancy. These disadvantages persisted after statistical control of many potentially confounding variables.

Neuromaturational Studies

Iron deficiency anemia has long been thought to have central nervous system effects. However, finding direct evidence of such effects in the human infant has presented many methodological challenges. Auditory brainstem responses (ABRs), which represent the progressive activation of the auditory pathway from acoustic nerve to lateral lemniscus, provide a noninvasive means of examining an aspect of the central nervous system that is rapidly maturing during the period when iron deficiency is most common. We studied ABRs during spontaneous naps in 55 healthy 6-month-old Chilean infants (29 with iron deficiency anemia and 26 nonanemic controls). Central conduction time (CCT), the Wave I-V interpeak latency, was longer in the iron-deficient anemic group, with differences becoming more pronounced at follow-up at 12 and 18 months, despite effective iron therapy. The CCT is considered an index of central nervous system development, since myelination of nerve fibers and maturation of synaptic relays lead to an exponential reduction in CCT from birth to 24 months. The pattern of results—differences in latencies but not amplitudes, more effects on the late ABR components, and longer CTT (as an overall measure of nerve conduction velocity)—indicates that altered myelination is an appealing explanation, especially in view of recent laboratory work documenting iron's essential role in myelin formation and maintenance. This study shows that iron deficiency anemia adversely affects at least one aspect of central nervous system development in 6-month-old infants and suggests the benefits of studying other processes that are rapidly myelinating during the first 2 years of life

However, the many challenges of studying the central nervous system in human infants has meant that direct evidence of central nervous system effects has come from animal studies. That evidence is increasingly compelling. In addition to older research on iron's role in central nervous system neurotransmitter function, recent work shows that brain iron is essential for normal myelination. In the rat, there is an influx of transferrin and iron into the brain in the immediate postnatal period. As iron and its transport and storage compounds are redistributed in the brain, myelinogenesis and iron uptake are at their peak. Iron and its related proteins concentrate in oligodendrocytes and become more concentrated in white than gray matter (the majority of brain iron is found in this myelin fraction). Oligodendrocytes synthesize fatty acids and cholesterol for myelin production, a process that requires iron. Furthermore, animal studies have consistently found a lasting deficit in brain iron when iron deficiency anemia occurs early in development. Although only two studies of iron deficiency in animal models examined myelination directly, both found iron-deficient rats to be hypomyelinated.

The results of these and other animal studies indicate that iron deficiency anemia during brain growth has long-lasting central nervous system effects. Yet obtaining evidence of similar effects in the human infant has posed many methodological challenges. Over the past 20 years, research on the effects of iron deficiency anemia and iron therapy on infant development has depended heavily on standardized tests of infant development, which have serious limitations and bear unknown relations to central nervous system functions. By measuring auditory-evoked potentials, we provide more direct evidence of central nervous system alterations in iron-deficient anemic infants. Such neurophysiological measurements have not been previously conducted in the iron-deficient infant.

Perhaps the most important implication of our findings, however, is that they may further generate plausible and testable hypotheses about the effects of iron deficiency on the developing central nervous system. Many parts of the brain are becoming myelinated in the first 2 years of life, when iron deficiency is so prevalent. We are obtaining more direct and indirect noninvasive measures of myelination in the human. With the hypothesis of impaired myelination in early iron deficiency anemia, it should be possible to design studies with specific measures, using techniques such as PET-scan imaging, evoked and spontaneous potentials, and, eventually, behavioral progressions known to depend on myelination. Such hypothesis-driven research would be a substantial advance over previous studies of iron-deficient infants, which have largely depended on global tests of development. Thus, this study suggests new, promising directions for understanding some specific central nervous system mechanism by which iron deficiency anemia could alter infant behavior and development.

REFERENCES

1. Lozoff, B., Brittenham, G. M., and Wolf, A. W. 1987. "Iron Deficiency Anemia and Iron Therapy: Effect on Infant Developmental Test Performance." *Pediatrics*, 79: 981–95.

2. Walter, T., De Andraca, I., Chadud, P., et al. 1989. "Iron Deficiency Anemia: Adverse Effects on Infant Psychomotor Development." *Pediatrics*, 84: 7–17.

3. Bayley, N. 1969. *Bayley Scales of Infant Development*. New York: Psychological Corporation.

4. Aukett, M. A., Parks, Y. A., Scott, P. H., and Wharton, B. A. 1986. Treatment with Iron Increases Weight Gain and Psychomotor Development. *Arch. Dis. Child*, 61: 849–57.

5. Idjradinata, P., and Pollitt, E. 1993. "Reversal of Developmental Delays in Iron Deficient Anemic Infants Treated with Iron." *Lancet*, 341: 1–4.

6. Lozoff, B., Brittenham, G. M., Viteri, F. E., Wolf, A. W., and Urrutia, J. J. 1982. "The Effects of Short-Term Oral Iron Therapy on Developmental Deficit in Iron Deficient Anemia Infants." *J. Pediatr*; 100, 351–7.

7. Lozoff, B., Jimenez, E., and Wolf, A. 1991. "Long-Term Developmental Outcome of Infants with Iron Deficiency." *N. Engl. J. Med.* 325, 687–94.

ADDITIONAL SOURCES

De Andraca, I., Walter, T., Castillo, M., Pino, P., Rivera, P., and Cobo, C. 1991. "Iron Deficiency Anemia and Its Effects upon Psychological Development at Pre-School Age: A Longitudinal Study." *Nestlé Nutrition Annals*, 53–62.

Roncagliolo, M., Garrido, M., Walter, T., Peirano, P., and Lozoff, B. 1998. "Evidence of Altered Central Nervous System Development in Infants with Iron Deficiency Anemia at 6 Mo: Delayed Maturation of Auditory Brainstem Responses." *AJCN*; 68: 683–90.

5 | Community Intervention Programs in Latin America

NELLY ZAVALETA

The countries of Latin American are diverse in their size, economy, level of development, culture, geography, climate, and so on. At the same time the region has many similarities, like language, common history, and interest in future development.

Despite much progress in the region during recent decades, particularly in some countries, there are still nutritional problems to deal with, like household food insecurity, protein-energy deficiencies, and micronutrient deficiencies of iron, Vitamin A, and iodine. As in other transitional societies, people of the region are also facing problems of being overweight or obese.

At the last international Conference on Nutrition, held in Rome in 1992, Latin American countries signed the Declaration and Nutrition Plan in which the commitments and goals established at the World Summit for Children were ratified and the following strategies were outlined:

1. Incorporate nutritional objectives, considerations, and components in development policies and programs.

2. Improve household food security.

3. Protect consumers through improving the quality and safety of food.

4. Prevent and nutritionally manage infectious diseases.

5. Promote breastfeeding.

6. Give priority attention to socially and economically disadvantaged and nutritionally vulnerable groups.

7. Prevent and control micronutrient deficiencies.

8. Promote adequate diets and healthy lifestyles.

9. Evaluate, analyze, and monitor food and nutritional status.

In keeping with the first strategy, all Latin American countries have prepared their national plans of action in nutrition (see the various country reports under FAO/OMS/PAHO in references). Those plans include nutrition policies and programs. While the implementation of such policies can be carried out at central, regional, and community levels, virtually all of them should be implemented at the community level.

Why Invest in Nutrition?

Nowadays the role of nutrition in social and economical development is increasingly being recognized by the international community. The economic rationale for investing in nutrition stems from the social and economic implications of malnutrition, as well as the significant outcome from nutritional investment (Mora 1995).

Malnutrition in developing countries has several negative economic implications. For example, it increases risk of morbidity and mortality, which drain health budgets and decrease productivity and wages. Poor nutrition also retards cognitive and psychomotor development in children, leads to poor learning capacity and school perfomance, and, therefore, produces low rates of return from investments in education, as well as reduced adult labor productivity and income. The additional expenditures needed to address the excess morbidity associated with malnutrition is a large burden for health systems already facing financial constraints.

An important indirect effect of investing in nutrition is its ability to enhance other interventions. Better nutrition causes a reduction in morbidity, so savings within the health system can be used to meet other health and education needs.

In summary, investment in nutrition is a highly cost-effective intervention that every government should consider in promoting the social and economic development of their countries.

Demographic and Health Characteristics of the Region

Demographic indicators (Table 1) show that Argentina, Brazil, Colombia, and Mexico comprise 70% of the region's population. The rapid rate of urbanization has resulted in inadequate health and education services, housing, employment, and acceptable general living conditions for all citizens.

Fertility rates have decreased in recent decades in all Latin American countries. The mortality rates for infants and those under age 5 have also decreased substantially in the past 20 years in all Latin American countries, especially Chile, Cuba, and Costa Rica. Overall, life expectancy in the region has increased.

In Latin America, 36% of the population is under age 15. Women represent 50% of the population. According to CELADE (Latin American Center for Demographic Studies), countries can be grouped as follows:

1. initial demographic transition (Bolivia);

2. moderate demographic transition with a high birth rate and moderate mortality rate (Guatemala, Honduras, Nicaragua, and Paraguay);

3. demographic transition in progress with a moderate birth rate and moderate or low mortality rate (Brazil, Colombia, Costa Rica, Ecuador, Mexico, Panama, and Peru);

4. advanced demographic transition with an older population, because of low birth rates and moderate or low mortality rates (Argentina, Chile, Cuba, and Uruguay).

Although Latin America could be considered a middle-income region, there are remarkable differences across countries. In 1992, Argentina, Brazil, and Mexico generated 72% of the gross regional product. There are also important differences in the per capita GNP across countries, with Argentina's more than 10 times that of Bolivia or Honduras.

A large percentage of people in a majority of the region's countries are living under poverty conditions. Rural populations are the most affected.

Table 1. Current Demographic and Health Indicators of Latin American Countries

Country	Total* Population	% Population* 0–4 yrs.	% Population 5–14 yrs.	% Women 15–49 yrs.	% Urban** Population	Infant** Mortality Rate	Maternal Mortality Rate	Life** Expectancy	Total Fertility Rate
Argentina	34,586,637	10.3	20.3	46.9	86	24	5.2	73	2.7
Bolivia	7,413,832	15.5	25.7	47.4	52	73	24.7	83	4.6
Brazil	161,789,708	11.8	22.6	51.9	74	51	14.0	67	2.8
Chile	14,210,429	11.0	19.1	53.0	85	13	4.1	74	2.5
Colombia	35,100,589	11.9	23.4	53.2	69	30	14.0	70	2.6
Costa Rica*	3,423,787	13.4	23.1	51.2	47	14	4.0	77	3.0
Cuba*	11,041,263	8.2	14.6	57.0	75	9	3.2	76	1.8
Ecuador*	11,460,117	13.7	25.3	49.3	56	31	12.0	69	3.3
El Salvador*	5,767,824	15.2	28.3	46.2	47	34	14.0	67	3.8
Guatemala*	10,621,228	17.5	28.0	44.6	38	49	22.0	66	5.1
Honduras	5,653,532	17.1	28.1	45.6	41	31	22.0	69	4.6
Mexico	91,145,292	13.2	25.4	50.6	73	27	5.4	71	3.0
Nicaragua	5,169,457	18.6	29.3	45.3	55	46	15.4	68	4.8
Panama	2,631,013	12.5	22.7	51.8	53	18	6.0	73	2.8
Paraguay	4,959,713	16.0	24.7	48.5	47	28	27.0	71	4.1
Peru	23,780,034	12.9	24.9	50.1	70	41	24.0	67	3.3
Dominican Republic	7,823,318	13.3	23.7	51.6	59	37	9.0	70	2.9
Uruguay	3,185,728	8.4	17.4	46.6	89	19	3.8	73	2.3
Venezuela	21,844,496	13.8	24.3	50.6	83	20	6.0	72	3.1

* FLASCO 1995
** UNICEF 1997

Nutritional Indicators of Health in Children

Information is very important for measuring the severity and extent of nutritional problems, generating political commitment for change, planning interventions, and evaluating their impact. Information must be valid, representative, and presented in a clear and simple format (Mora 1995).

Most countries invest substantial effort and resources in nutrition programs, but the information needed to best use the invested resources is inconclusive. Frequently, much more information is generated than is needed, for which the excess costs of data collection, processing, and analysis must be borne. Often the information is obtained after long delays and is not well utilized because of its poor quality or complexity or the limited analytical capacity of decision makers. A limited number of indicators that are sensitive as well as easy to collect and interpret should be chosen. The following indicators were proposed by Mora (1995).

Socioeconomic Indicators

- Total household expenditures

- Household food expenditures

- Proportion of household expenditures for food

Health and Nutrition Indicators

- Weight for age in children (under age 3 or 5 years)

- Height for age in children (under age 3 or 5 years)

- Height for age in children entering the school system

- Newborns with birthweight less than 2,500g

- Infant mortality rate

- Preschooler mortality rate

Complementary Indicators

- Prevalence of anemia in pregnant women and children under age 5

- Prevalence of serum retinol levels of less than 20 µg/dl in children age 1 to 5

- Prevalence of goiter in school-age children

- Exclusive breastfeeding at age 4 to 6 months

- Individual and household food consumption

- Prevalence of obesity in adults or children

Interventions to Combat Malnutrition

The main objective of nutritional interventions is to prevent malnutrition, especially in the most affected population (children). A good nutritional status depends on a diet that provides the adequate nutrients for physical growth, mental development, and health. While one's health status is closely related to nutritional status, both of them have such underlying determinants as household food security, the quality of health services, environmental sanitation, quality of care (infant feeding, hygienic practices, psychosocial care, etc.). Basic determinants of nutritional status are family and community resources (economic, human, and organizational). The economic, political, cultural, and social structure strongly influences the risk of suffering malnutrition.

Nutritional Care

Nutritional care refers to the management of the available food and health resources for children's survival, growth, and development. The focus of interventions are the child from birth to age 3 years and this focus is inseparable from the well-being of women (Engle, Lhotska, and Armstrong 1997).

The equality of household practices and how well they are implemented are critical to family nutrition and health outcomes.

In concert with household food security, health services, and a healthy environment, a number of factors are necessary for the good growth and development of children under age 3: care for women, breast-feeding and feeding practices, psychosocial care, food preparation, hygienic practices, and home health practices.

Integrating Nutritional Interventions at the Community Level

The main ongoing nutritional interventions in the region are breast-feeding promotion, growth monitoring, health and nutrition education, supplementary feeding programs, food fortification, and micronutrient supplementation. Nutrition programs are usually implemented in coordination with the primary health care system.

1. Breast-feeding promotion activities have been implemented in most countries, often by nongovernmental organizations. Some countries have made progress in political commitments, legislation, and control of marketing of breast milk substitutes. While there are several successful pilot projects, the promotion of breastfeeding has yet to be implemented in large-scale national programs.

2. Supplementary feeding programs and food subsidy programs became more prevalent in most countries during the 1980s. An inventory and critique of such programs prepared by the World Bank identified 104 food distribution programs in 19 countries, with a total investment of US $1.6 billion. Of these programs, 53 were maternal and child health programs managed by or associated with health care institutions, 23 were school feeding programs, and the rest were a mixture of subsidies, community food kitchens, and other feeding programs. A total of 100 million beneficiaries were covered (24% of the total population of the region). This coverage far exceeded the estimated number of malnourished children in the countries studied, suggesting that these programs were misdirected and that greater progress could be achieved with different allocation of the same resources (Mora 1995).

3. Growth monitoring is usually carried out within the primary health care system to identify vulnerable groups that might benefit from supplementary feeding programs.

4. Health and nutrition education at the community level is often carried out by nongovernmental organizations or by the primary health care system. It is essential to consider the attitudes, habits, and practices of the target population when developing appropriate educational content.

5. Food fortification is increasingly being implemented in many countries for controlling deficiencies of such micronutrients as iodine, iron, and Vitamin A.

6. Micronutrient supplementation is used for specific vulnerable groups, such as iron supplementation for pregnant women and Vitamin A supplementation for children with malnutrition or measles.

Table 1 presents a summary of community-level nutrition interventions carried out in Latin American countries. We have selected some interventions that benefit large populations, have been ongoing for a minimum of 3 years, and have a potential to be sustained or replicated elsewhere.

It is important to note that most of these programs include supplementary food or food subsidies. Governments are usually motivated to implement such programs because of their political returns. Supplementary food could be a way to provide household food security to the substantial percentage of the population living under poverty or extreme poverty. However, these programs should be targeted to those who are most vulnerable and most in need. The participation of the organized community in these activities is extremely important.

Program Development

Targeting and Selecting of Beneficiaries

It is extremely important to define the target population, which can be accomplished in a three-tiered approach from very broad targeting to highly targeted programs. The first step should be to determine the specific areas where programs should be implemented. The second step is to identify vulnerable groups, usually children under 3 years old or pregnant and lactating women. The third step is to identify vulnerable or needy populations, for example, malnourished children or high-risk pregnancies.

Targeting is often a political issue. At the community level, targeting criteria may conflict with entitlement issues; at the national level, welfare programs may exist for reasons of political patronage and vote seeking, and thus targeting may be considered undesirable. It is important that nutrition programs consider how their targeting strategies can be accepted by those concerned.

Staff Selection, Supervision, and Training

Staff issues are complex and not easily solved. Some of the following issues common to successful nutrition interventions may not apply to all countries. Incorporating local staff in a program has several advantages, like reducing project costs and increasing community participation. However, the appropriate selection of staff is of utmost significance and their specific tasks should be well defined in order to facilitate evaluation of their perfomance.

Activities that can be successfully accomplished (with good training and supervision) by community workers include growth monitoring, identification of malnourished children, screening for supplementary feeding, and nutrition education. These activities are usually coordinated within the primary health care system. It has been observed that voluntary community workers sometimes expect to be added to the Ministry of Health payroll.

Identification of tasks, good training, and supervision of community workers are necessary for the success of the project. Workers should not be overwhelmed with too many activities. The supervisor's workload also needs to be estimated. A supervisor to worker ratio of between 1:6 and 1:12 has been suggested as appropriate, depending on local conditions. The supervisor should motivate workers in different ways: giving brief refresher training, letting workers share experiences, sending people to seminars, letting people decide/suggest about their special needs for training, organizing meetings, and recognizing good performance.

Community Participation

Community participation could be described as the involvement in decision making by the community at large and not only by its elected leaders. Community participation can be promoted by (1) creating community groups (or strengthening existing institutions), with the authority to advise, supervise, and/or manage the program, (2) selecting and training local community members as project staff, (3) linking the project with other community groups (such as small-farmers' associations, mothers' groups) and governmental services, and promoting good communication and information sharing between project staff levels.

Community participation has benefits and limitations. Among the benefits are that it

- increases a sense of ownership of the program by the community, which favors its sustainability

- decreases resistance to program innovations and helps disseminate nutrition education messages

- promotes regular attendance to program activities

- decreases dependence on external assistance and promotes self-reliance.

Among the disadvantages are that it

• increases administrative complexity

• can constrain logistics in isolated areas with weak infrastructure.

The sustainability of a project without significant external funding is the ultimate goal of any intervention, especially when resources are limited. There are differences between "functional" and "financial" sustainability; the first refers to the technical/administrative ability to run a program without external assistance, the latter to the ability to run a program without external financing.

There are no proven methodologies on how to measure community participation. Some programs quantify the amount of resources a community contributes to a nutrition program; others quantify the community's participation in project activities. This area needs more research.

NOTES

The author wishes to thank the following institutions and persons for their collaboration: Pan American Health Organization, USAID (United States Agency for International Development) Lima, USAID Ecuador, the AED (Academy for Educational Development)/USAID Washington, D.C., UNICEF Lima, Argentina: CESNI (Centro de Estudios Sobre Nutrición Infantil) (Dr. Alejandro O'Donnell and Dr. Pablo Duran). Venezuela: Dr. Ronald Evans, Instituto Nacional de Nutrición, Dr. Miguel Layrisse, Lic. María Nieves García. Chile: Inta, Professor Fernando Pizarro. Peru: AB Prisma, CARE (Cooperative for Assistance and Relief Everywhere), Caritas, ADRA OFASA (Adventist Development and Relief Agency, Obra Filantropica de Asistencia Social Adventista), Instituto de Investigación Nutricional. Dominican Republic: Secretaría de Estado de Educación, Bellas Artes y Cultos (Programa de Nutrición y Salud), Secretaría de Estado de Salud Pública y Asistencia Social (Programa de Nutrición y Alimentación), CARE, Caritas.

REFERENCES

ADRA/OFASA del Peru. 1996. *Manual de Procedimientos:* Programa Infantil. Lima, Peru.

AB Prisma. 1996. *Proyecto Kusiayllu; Vigilancia y rehabilitación nutricional a nivel del Hogar.* Lima, Peru.

Berhman, J.R. 1992. *The Economic Rationale for Investing in Nutrition in Developing Countries.* USAID. VITAL.

CARE/Peru. 1995. *Proyecto niños evaluación de impacto.* September.

CARITAS del Peru. 1996. Informe resultados del Proyecto Winay, 1996. Lima, Peru.

Center for International Health Information. 1994. *Country Health Profile: Latin American Countries—Health Situation and Statistic Report, 1994.* USAID Arlington VA.

Engle, P., Lhotska, L., and Armstrong, H. 1997. *The Care Initiative: Assessment, Analysis and Action to Improve Care for Nutrition.* UNICEF Nutrition Section. New York.

FAO/OMS (Food and Agriculture Organization of the United Nations/ Organización Mundial de la Salud). 1992. Conferencia Internacional Sobre Nutrición. *Informe final sobre la Conferencia.* Rome.

_____. 1996. *Cumbre Mundial sobre Alimentación: Declaración de Roma sobre la Seguridad Alimentaria Mundial y Plan de Acción de la Cumbre Mundial sobre la Alimentación.* Rome.

FAO/OMS/PAHO (Pan-American Health Organization). 1992. Conferencia Internacional Sobre Nutrición. *Informe de El Salvador.* San Salvador.

_____. 1992. Conferencia Internacional Sobre Nutrición. *Informe de la República Argentina.* Ministerio de Salud y Acción Social. Buenos Aires.

_____. 1992. Conferencia Internacional Sobre Nutrición. *Informe de la República Oriental de Uruguay.* Ministerio de Salud Pública. Montevido.

_____. 1992. Conferencia Internacional Sobre Nutrición. *Informe de Perú.* Ministerio de Salud/Instituto Nacional de Salud. Lima.

_____. 1992. Conferencia Internacional Sobre Nutrición. *Informe de Venezuela.* Reporte preparado por el Instituto Nacional de Nutrición. Caracas Venezuela.

_____. 1992. Conferencia Internacional Sobre Nutrición. *La Situación Nutricional de los Niños y las Madres. Plan de Acción para la Infancia en los Años 90.* Quito.

_____. 1992. Conferencia Internacional Sobre Nutrición. Ministerio de Planificación y Política Económica/Informe de Panamá. Panama.

_____. 1992. Conferencia Internacional Sobre Nutrición. *Síntesis Ejecutiva del Diagnóstico de la Situación Alimentaria y Nutricional en México.* Comisión Nacional de Alimentación. Ciudad de México.

_____. 1992. Conferencia Internacional Sobre Nutrición. *Situación Alimentaria y Nutricional de Bolivia.* Ministerio de Planeamiento y Coordinación. La Paz.

_____. 1992. Conferencia Internacional Sobre Nutrición. Situación alimentaria y Nutricional de América Latina. Santiago de Chile.

_____. 1992. Conferencia Internacional Sobre Nutrición. *Situación Alimentaria y Nutricional de Guatemala. Secretaría de Planificación* Económica. Guatemala.

_____. 1992. Conferencia Internacional Sobre Nutrición. *Situación Alimentaria y Nutricional de Paraguay.* Programa de Alimentación y Educación Nutricional. Asunción.

_____. 1992. Conferencia Internacional Sobre Nutrición. *Situación Nutricional de Nicaragua.* Nicaragua.

_____. 1992. Conferencia Internacional Sobre Nutrición. *Una Mirada a la Situación Alimentaria y Nutricional de la Población Colombiana.* Ministerio de Salud/Ministerio de Agricultura/Instituto Colombiano de Bienestar Familiar. Santa Fe de Bogotá, D.C.

FAO Proyecto Regional ALADI/FAO de Configuración de la Población de Riesgo de Inseguridad Alimentaria en América Latina. 1995. Inicio de Ejecución del Proyecto en la República de Chile. Informe de Avance - Ministerio de Planificación y Cooperación de Chile. (Mideplan) Oficina Regional de la FAO para América Latina y El Caribe, Santiago de Chile.

Jelliffe, D. B., and Jelliffe, P. 1984. "Nutritional Improvement and the Primary Health Care." *Food Nutr Bull,* 10:53–63.

Instituto Nacional de Nutrición. 1996. *Propuesta Programa Especial de Nutrición (PEN).* Caracas, Venezuela.

Instituto Nacional de Estadística/DHS (Demographic and Health Surveys)/ USAID/UNICEF/Ministerio de Salud. 1997. *Perú III Encuesta Demográfica y de Salud Familiar.* Informe Principal. Lima.

INAGG/International Anemia Consultive Group. 1997. *Iron Deficiency in Infancy and Childhood.* Nutrition Foundation, Washington, D.C.

Instituto de la Mujer, Ministerio de asuntos sociales de España. FLACSO Facultad Latinoamericana de Ciencias Sociales). 1995. *Mujeres Latinoamericanas en cifras; Tomo comparativo, Valdes y gomaris.* Instituto de la Mujer, Santiago de Chile.

McGuire, J., and Popkin, B., 1990. *Helping Women Improve Nutrition in the Developing World.* World Bank Technical Paper no. 114. Washington, D.C.

Mora, J.O. 1995. *Guidelines for Sectorial Food and Nutrition Policies in the Countries of Latin America and the Caribbean.* Prepared for USAID/ University Research Corporation/International Science & Technology Institute. Bethesda, MD.

PAHO. 1996. *Health Situation in the Americas: Basic Indicators, 1996.* Washington, D.C.

Programa Subregional Andino de Control de Desórdenes por Deficiencia de Micronutrientes. 1995. *V Reunión Aanual de Evaluación y Planificación.* Caracas, December.

República de Cuba. 1994. *Plan Nacional de Acción para la Nutrición.*

Sanchez Griñan, M. I., Fukumoto, M., Perez, F., Villasante, R., Nuñez, M., Yaeger, B., Ganoza, L. y col. 1996. *Evaluación del programa de Asistencia Alimentaria en el Perú. Título II: 1990–1995.* Instituto de Investigación Nutricional. Informe presentado a USAID. Lima, Peru.

UNU/ACC/SCN (United Nations University/Administrative Committee on Coordination/Subcommittee on Nutrition). 1996. How Nutrition Improves. ACC/SCN State of the Art Series. Nutrition policy paper no. 15.

_____. Jan/Feb 1989. *Update in the Nutrition Situation: Recent Trends in Nutrition in 33 Countries.*

B | Environmental Sanitation

6 | Environmental Sanitation and Child Health

The Missing Link in Child Survival

DENNIS B. WARNER

Introduction

For almost two decades, child survival programs have been the main vehicle for delivering selective interventions to improve the health of children. The success of this approach is shown by the fact that over the past 25 years the worldwide mortality rate of infants under 1 year of age has dropped 37% and that of children under five years has declined 40%. Morbidity rates, however, have not in general declined. In the case of diarrhea and other diseases related to poor environmental sanitation, morbidity rates have remained persistently high and often show increases. A major concern is that child survival programs do not change the environmental causes of ill health, namely unsafe drinking water and unsanitary excreta disposal. At the same time, there is a growing body of evidence that water supply and sanitation interventions, which do change the environmental determinants of disease, can have a significant effect on childhood morbidity. Nevertheless, water and sanitation interventions have not been widely adopted into child survival programs. This chapter looks at the relationship between environmental sanitation and child health and, more specifically, at why water supply and sanitation interventions are not an integral part of child survival programs.

Definition of Environmental Sanitation

In its broadest sense, *environmental sanitation* refers to measures taken to control or change the physical environment in order to prevent the transmission of diseases to human beings. Although the physical environment can be broadly interpreted to constitute many conditions for the purposes of this chapter, the environmental conditions being considered will be limited to human excreta, other household wastes, and domestic water supply, including water for drinking, cooking, personal hygiene, and general household cleanliness. These environmental conditions, and how they are managed, have a direct effect on human health through their potential for the transmission of diseases. The health outcomes of these interactions are strongly influenced by the personal behaviors and practices of people toward the management of their water and wastes.

Thus, environmental sanitation here means interventions intended to (1) improve access to safe and sufficient water supply, (2) encourage the sanitary disposal of human excreta and household wastes, and (3) change human behaviors through hygiene education. The primary purpose of these interventions is to prevent or limit the transmission of diseases arising from poor environmental sanitation.

Disease Burden due to Poor Environmental Sanitation

Diseases related to poor environmental sanitation have plagued humanity throughout recorded history. Despite major gains in public health services over the past century, rapid population growth—especially among the poorest members of society, particularly those in isolated rural communities and periurban slums—has resulted in a continual rise in the number of people suffering from poor environmental sanitation. This burden falls disproportionately on young children and infants. Of the approximately 6 billion people populating our planet today, the poorest sextile suffer seven times more mortality from infectious diseases and maternal and perinatal conditions than do the richest sextile (WHO 1997a). Among the poorest sextile, over one-half of all deaths occur among children under 5 years of age (World Bank 1993).

Morbidity and Mortality Rates

Table 1.   Infant and Child Mortality, 1996

Region	Infant mortality rate	Child mortality rate
Africa	88	130
Asia	59	74
Latin America and the Caribbean	42	51
South America	46	55
Caribbean	39	48
Central America	35	43
Europe	12	16
North America	7	9
Oceania	7	8
Global	59	78

Infant and child mortality rates clearly show the relative burden of infectious diseases that affect the regions of the world, as illustrated in Table 1. In 1996, the infant mortality rate, defined as the number of deaths before the first birthday per 1,000 live births, ranged from a high of 88 in Africa to a low of 7 in North America and Oceania. Similarly, the child mortality rate, defined as the number of deaths before the fifth birthday per 1,000 live births, ranged between 130 and 8 for the same regions. The great majority of these deaths are attributable to infectious diseases, with most caused by poor environmental sanitation. In Latin America, regional health statistics can mask the true burden of infectious diseases. While the infant mortality and child mortality rates for the region are considerably lower than global averages, great variations exist between the region's countries. In 1996, the infant mortality rate for Latin America as a whole was 42 deaths per 1,000 live births, and the child mortality rate was 51 deaths per 1,000 live births, compared with global rates of 59 and 78 deaths per 1,000 live births, respectively. The infant and child mortality rates were slightly better in the Caribbean and Central America than in South America, as shown in Table 1. However, a comparison of the countries within Latin America shows great disparities. In the worst cases, rates for infant and child mortality in the region are six to seven times those in the best cases.

Mortality statistics, however, are only one measure of overall health conditions. They provide limited information on the total disease burden and very little guidance on interventions to reduce the transmission of infectious diseases. This latter function is the role of environmental sanitation interventions, which do not directly prevent mortality. Environmental sanitation limits the occurrence of illness and hence controls morbidity, which in turn reduces the number of sick people at risk of dying from disease.

Diseases resulting from poor environmental sanitation constitute a major component of the total disease burden. WHO reports that almost half of the world's population suffers from diseases associated with insufficient or contaminated water (WHO 1996b). Currently, diarrheal diseases, including dysentery, are the leading cause of global morbidity (with over 4 billion new cases in 1996) and the sixth leading cause of mortality (with almost 2.5 million deaths in the same year). In 1996, diarrhea accounted for 2.1 million deaths in children under age 5, or 19% of the total deaths within that age group (WHO 1997a). It is estimated that approximately 90% of the diarrheal disease burden is related to poor sanitation and lack of access to clean water and safe food (WHO 1997b).

Other diseases related to poor sanitation conditions include those caused by contaminated water and food, that is, typhoid fever, cholera, and giardiasis. When contaminated water supplies are linked to inadequate general sanitation and poor personal hygiene, the health outcomes can be devastating. For example, giardiasis, which is spread by fecally contaminated water, causes 500,000 new cases a year; cholera, spread by fecally contaminated water and food, causes nearly 400,000 cases and an estimated 10,000 deaths annually; and typhoid, also carried by fecally contaminated water, causes 16 million cases and 600,000 deaths annually. Poor sanitation also contributes to vector-borne diseases. Dengue and dengue hemorrhagic fever flourish in overcrowded cities having a large accumulation of solid waste and poor drainage of surface water, where *Aedes aegypti* mosquitoes breed. These conditions account for over 3 million new cases of dengue and dengue hemorrhagic fever and almost 140,000 deaths annually. Worldwide, there are 200 million cases of and 20,000 deaths annually from schistosomiasis, which is acquired by swimming or working in freshwater bodies containing intermediate snail hosts infected by human excreta (WHO 1996b).

Improper excreta disposal also results in intestinal parasitic infections caused by worms living in fecally contaminated soil. WHO estimates that upwards of 3.5 billion people are infected by worms, with around 450 million, mostly children, becoming ill as a result. Although worm infections normally cause no more symptoms than diarrhea and abdominal pain, hookworm infections in 1995 killed 65,000 people and roundworm infections (ascariasis) killed 60,000 (WHO 1996b). Table 2 summarizes some of the morbidity and mortality rates for the main diseases related to poor environmental sanitation.

Table 2. Estimates of Morbidity and Mortality of Diseases Related to Poor Environmental Sanitation

Disease	Morbidity	Mortality (deaths/year)	Relationship of disease to environmental sanitation
Diarrheal diseases, including dysentery	4,002,000,000 episodes/yr.	2,473,000	Strongly related to unsanitary excreta disposal, poor personal hygiene, unsafe drinking water
Typhoid fever	16,000,000 episodes/yr.	600,000	Strongly related to drinking water and food contaminated by human excreta, poor personal hygiene
Dengue and dengue hemorrhagic fever	3,100,000 episodes/yr.	138,000	Strongly related to unsanitary excretal disposal
Amoebiasis	48,000,000 episodes/yr.	70,000	Related to unsanitary excreta disposal, poor personal hygiene, food contaminated by human excreta
Hookworm	151,000,000 cases	65,000	Strongly related to soil contaminated by human excreta, poor personal hygiene
Ascariasis	250,000,000 cases	60,000	Related to unsanitary disposal of human feces, food contaminated by soil containing human feces, poor personal hygiene
Schistosomiasis	200,000,000 cases	20,000	Strongly related to unsanitary excreta disposal and absence of nearby sources of safe water
Trichuriasis	45,530,000 cases	10,000	Related to soil contaminated by human feces, poor personal hygiene
Cholera	120,000 episodes/yr.	6,000	Strongly related to drinking water contaminated by human feces
Giardiasis	500,000 episodes/yr.	—	Strongly related to drinking water contaminated by human fecal matter, poor personal hygiene
Trachoma	152,420,000 cases	—	Related to poor personal hygiene, lack of soap and water
Dracunculiasis	130,000 cases	—	Strongly related to drinking water containing infected copepods

Source: WHO (1997a).

The Role of Environmental Sanitation

The unsanitary disposal of human excreta is the main cause and starting point of ill health for most of the diseases listed in Table 2. Pathogenic organisms, whether bacteria, viruses, or parasites, are frequently contained in human excreta, most often in human feces. Improper disposal of human excreta allows these pathogenic organisms to contaminate the soil and surface water, eventually spreading to drinking water, cooking utensils, food, and even people themselves. While some of the listed diseases, such as dengue fever, trachoma, and dracunculiasis, are not transmitted through human fecal matter, they tend to flourish where general cleanliness, personal hygiene, and sanitary behaviors are either poor or lacking.

The close interaction between water and wastes should be noted here. Water is a vehicle: for maintaining life, for aiding cleanliness, and for transporting pathogens. Wastes, especially human excreta, harbor the pathogens that contaminate the environment and result in sickness. Unless water is managed well, it can serve as a vehicle for spreading pathogens through fecal–oral transmission routes, contamination of the household environment, and creation of vector breeding sites.

Many pathogenic organisms, especially bacteria and some viruses, are relatively fragile and can be eliminated or at least greatly reduced through low-cost technologies and simple protective measures at the household level. The simplest measure, when available, is to use protected water sources, such as deep wells, protected springs, or rooftop rainwater collection, rather than contaminated surface sources. Low-cost water treatment measures within the household provide another line of defense. These include storing water for 24 to 48 hours before use to allow pathogen die-off and directly disinfecting water by sunlight, boiling, or treatment with low concentration chlorine solutions.

In some situations, however, the environmental causes of ill health are not organic in nature but arise from chemical contamination of drinking water sources. Two examples are groundwater containing excessive nitrates (NO_3), leading to methemoglobinemia, or "blue-baby" syndrome, which sometimes occurs in Europe and North America, and toxic levels of arsenic, which occurs in parts of India and Bangladesh. In such cases, water treatment is often complex and costly, and it may be better to seek out other water sources than remove the chemical contaminants.

From the standpoint of project design, the transport and use of water is relatively straightforward, since there exists a wealth of experience on interventions to provide water supplies. In sanitation, however, waste management and disposal is not straightforward, but to a great extent intimately associated with personal behaviors and practices. Moreover, decisions on water supply interventions tend to be made by institutions, like town councils and ministries of public works, while decisions on sanitation, especially basic measures such as latrines, washing slabs, and bathing areas, tend to be made by households. Individual and household decisions are influenced far more by culture, tradition, and personal factors than by institutional decisions, which respond more to political and financial matters. For these reasons, changes in household sanitation, excreta disposal, and personal hygiene are more difficult to achieve than improvements in the quality and quantity of community water supplies.

The Effects of Poverty

Poverty is the underlying cause of most illness and death in Latin America, where nearly 350,000 infants die annually before their first birthday for reasons that are tied to poverty but that are nonetheless preventable. In many countries of the region, diarrhea is the leading cause of death among children between ages 1 and 4. The restrictions placed on public spending in Latin America in the 1980s contributed to the deterioration of basic water and sanitation services, resulting in a resurgence of infectious diseases in overcrowded urban areas in the past two decades (WHO 1996b).

Cholera is a classic example of an infectious disease spread by poor environmental sanitation. Latin America had not seen an outbreak of cholera for at least a century, when in 1991 the disease found fertile ground in Peru, striking initially through contaminated seafood and quickly spreading throughout the region, where it has since become endemic. The areas most seriously affected were municipalities with improperly operating water treatment systems and poor areas lacking basic water supply and hygienic means of excreta disposal. In the first year almost 300,000 Peruvians came down with cholera and nearly 3,000 died (WHO 1992a). In addition to the human suffering caused by this cholera pandemic, the costs to Peru in terms of lost trade (almost a fifth of its normal yearly exports) and tourism were estimated at $770 million (WHO 1996a). By improving water disinfection and distribution, sewage treatment systems, health education campaigns, and food safety, the Peruvian government has progressively reduced the cholera caseload, which by 1996 had fallen to 4,500 cases and 21 deaths (WHO 1997c).

The spread of dengue fever is another example showing how the combination of poverty and rapid urban growth has been particularly hard on Latin America. The *Aedes aegypti* mosquito, which carries the dengue virus, often breeds in unsanitary and poorly drained urban slums. This disease had little effect on the region before 1981, but struck 14 Latin American countries in 1995, causing over 200,000 cases (WHO 1997c).

Measurements of Disease Burden

Recently, a measure combining both mortality and morbidity has been proposed for estimating the global burden of disease. This indicator, the *disability-adjusted life year* (DALY), combines into a single measure the total years of healthy life lost in a population through premature death plus the number of years of life lived with a disability. The DALY measure uses both epidemiological data and subjective judgment—including mortality and morbidity rates, life expectancy, severity of illness, age of onset of illness, and a discount rate—to estimate the loss of disability-free life in future years. It has been used to estimate losses resulting from both a specific disease and (when all ages, conditions, and illnesses are considered) the overall global burden of all diseases.

According to the World Bank, a total of 1.36 billion DALYs were lost to all diseases in 1990, which is the equivalent of 42 million deaths of newborn children. Approximately two-thirds of all DALY loss in the developing world is the result of premature death and one-third the result of disability. Regional comparisons of DALYs lost are useful. For each 1,000 of population, the World Bank found that the overall disease burden averaged 259 DALYs for the entire world, with sub-Saharan Africa highest at 574 DALYs and established market economies lowest at an average 117 DALYs. Latin America and the Caribbean came in midway with 233 DALYs (World Bank 1993).

World Bank figures also show that diarrheal diseases in 1990 accounted for 7.3% of the global burden of disease as measured by DALYs, with more than 80% of this loss occurring in children under age 5. In sub-Saharan Africa, diarrheal diseases represented 10.4% of DALY loss, while it was 6.6% in Latin America and the Caribbean and only 0.3% in established market economies. One conclusion drawn from these figures is that diseases associated with poor household environments—including poor sanitation, inadequate water supply, poor hygiene, inadequate waste disposal and drainage, and heavy indoor air pollution—account for nearly 30% of the total disease burden of developing countries. According to the World Bank (1993), modest improvements in these environmental conditions could avert nearly 25% of this burden.

It should be noted that the DALY indicator as a measure of disease burden is controversial. The focus of this indicator on death, disease, and disability underestimates the full loss of human well-being in unsanitary and poverty-stricken environments (WHO 1997b). Because the indicator obscures the socioeconomic and behavioral elements of interventions, WHO has serious reservations about its application for decision making and policy formulation (WHO 1997a). Nevertheless, the DALY indicator illustrates current efforts to develop new methods of health measurement to support health-related interventions.

Water Supply and Sanitation Service Coverage

The main factors in environmental sanitation are safe drinking water and sanitary means of excreta disposal. For over a hundred years, modern public health programs have been based on these two interventions. After a century of concerted effort to expand these services, what are the results?

Environmental sanitation was given a major boost by the UN Water Conference, held at Mar del Plata in 1977, when the concept of a global decade-long effort to meet the water supply and sanitation needs of all people of the world was initiated. At the time, only 44% of the developing world's population had access to safe drinking water and 46% had basic sanitation. This meant that around 1.8 billion people lacked potable water and nearly as many were without sanitation (UN 1990a). Concern for environmental sanitation was further expressed the following year at the International Conference on Primary Health Care, held at Alma Ata, where safe water and basic sanitation were included on the list of essential services comprising primary health care.

During the resulting International Drinking Water Supply and Sanitation Decade (1981–90), some 1.5 billion additional people were served with safe water and about 750 million with adequate excreta disposal facilities. Because of a growth in population of some 800 million people in the developing countries over the decade, however, there remained by 1990 a total of over 1 billion people without safe water and 1.75 billion without adequate sanitation (WHO 1992b).

Overall progress in reaching people who lack these services has been poor since 1990. Table 3, which contains the latest available data, shows that over 1.1 billion people, or one-quarter of the population of developing countries, still lack safe water and perhaps 2.9 billion, or two-thirds of the same population, do not have adequate excreta disposal facilities. The numbers of those unserved in Table 3 are greater than those reported in 1990. This increase is partly due to rapid population growth and to lagging rates of coverage, but also to the use of stricter national criteria for safe water and adequate sanitation.

Table 3. Water Supply and Sanitation Coverage in Developing Countries, 1994 (millions of people served and unserved)

Region	Water supply		Sanitation	
	Served	Unserved	Served	Unserved
Africa	326	381	243	464
Latin America and the Caribbean	376	97	296	177
East Asia and the Pacific	2,495	627	916	2,206
Western Asia	71	10	55	26
Global	3,268	1,115	1,510	2,873

Source: WHO/UNICEF/WSSCC (1996).

Unless the current rate of coverage is increased, the expansion of water and sanitation services will continue to be matched, or exceeded, by population growth into the foreseeable future. In other words, "business as usual" in providing water and sanitation services will result in the perpetuation of those without such services.

Table 4. Water Supply Coverage in Developing Countries: Urban and Rural Areas, 1994 (millions of people)

Region	Urban People		Rural People		Total	
	millions	%	millions	%	millions	%
Africa	153	64	173	37	326	46
Latin America and the Caribbean	306	88	70	56	376	79
East Asia and the Pacific	805	84	1,690	78	2,495	80
Western Asia	51	98	20	69	71	88
Global	1,315	82	1,953	70	3,268	75

Source: WHO/UNICEF/WSSCC (1996).

When the current coverage figures are broken down into urban and rural services levels, regional differences in urbanization and development become apparent. Table 4, showing water supply coverage, indicates that approximately

82% of the urban population in the developing world had what their governments defined as a safe drinking water supply, while only 70% of rural inhabitants had safe supplies. Urban coverage ranged from a high of 98% in the Western Pacific to a low of 64% in Africa. Rural coverage ranged from a high of 78% in East Asia and the Pacific to a low of 37% in Africa.

Table 5. Sanitation Coverage in Developing Countries: Urban and Rural Areas, 1994 (millions of people)

Region	Urban People		Rural People		Total	
	millions	%	millions	%	millions	%
Africa	131	55	112	24	243	34
Latin America and the Caribbean	254	73	42	34	296	63
East Asia and the Pacific	584	61	332	15	916	29
Western Asia	36	69	19	66	55	68
Global	1,005	63	505	18	1,510	34

Source: WHO/UNICEF/WSSCC (1996).

Table 5 shows comparable data for sanitation coverage. Overall urban coverage with what is defined by each nation as adequate means of excreta disposal extended to 63% of the population in developing countries in 1994. In rural areas, the rate was 18%. These rates varied regionally as follows: a high of 73% of urban people in Latin America and the Caribbean and a low of 55% in Africa had sanitation; a high of 60% of rural people in Western Asia and a low of 15% in East Asia and the Pacific had adequate sanitation.

It must be pointed out that in assembling these statistics, operational definitions of what constitutes safe water and adequate sanitation are determined by national governments. In general, a safe water supply is considered to be one that is potable and free of contaminants hazardous to health. The source of the water may be a household or community tap, hand pump, or other protected facility. Distances to the water may range up to a kilometer in the case of communal sources. Quantities may vary from as little as 20 liters per capita per day to several hundred.

In the case of sanitation, the main concern is to provide a sanitary means of excreta disposal, which may include a range of facilities from flush toilets with piped sewerage to various types of on-site systems including pour-flush water-seal toilets and conventional dry pit latrines. From a health standpoint, the need is to isolate human fecal matter in order to prevent contamination of water supplies, food, or people.

Table 6. Water Supply and Sanitation Coverage in Latin America and the Caribbean, 1980–94

Type	1980 (%)	1994 1990 (%)	1990 Population Coverage (%)	1990 Population not served (millions)	1994 Population not served (millions)
Urban Water	78	90	88	32	42
Rural Water	42	51	56	62	55
Total	—	79	79	94	97
Urban Sanitation	56	83	73	52	94
Rural Sanitation	20	33	34	84	83
Total	—	69	63	136	177

Source: 1980 data (WHO 1984); 1990 and 1994 data (WHO/UNICEF/WSSCC 1996).

Water and sanitation services in Latin America and the Caribbean, while generally better than global averages, have not kept pace with recent population movements. Table 6 shows that of a regional 1994 population of 473 million people, 97 million remain without safe drinking water and 177 million without adequate sanitation. The problems of providing services are becoming more acute in the rapidly expanding urban areas of the region. Since 1990, both urban and rural water and sanitation coverage have declined and the number of people lacking proper services is growing by 10 to 15% per year.

The 1990s have seen yet another round of bold pronouncements of lofty goals. The World Summit for Children in September 1990 called for universal access to safe drinking water and sanitary means of excreta disposal by the year 2000. The following year the UN General Assembly reaffirmed the decade goals of providing safe water and sanitation for all (UN 1990b). Similar sentiments were expressed at the UN Conference on Environment and Development in Rio De Janeiro in 1992, in which the Agenda 21 action plan proposed a "realistic" target of universal access to water and sanitation by the year 2025 (for urban areas it proposed that by the year 2000 all residents have access to at least 40 liters per day of safe water and that 75% of urban dwellers have proper sanitation: UNCED 1992). The Child Summit goals of universal access to safe water supply and sanitary excreta disposal by the year 2000 have been accepted by 156 nations and every UN agency.

Over the period 1990–94, global water supply coverage increased by 780 million people, but sanitation coverage registered an increase of less than 40 million people. At the same time the population of developing countries grew by 312 million. It is clear that the year 2000 Child Summit goals are not going to be achieved, and the danger is that countries may find themselves farther behind at the end of the century than they are today.

Why Such a Service Gap?

If, as seems abundantly clear, improved environmental sanitation has a direct positive effect on a variety of diseases, why haven't greater efforts been made to expand water and sanitation services, and specifically to reduce disease? Answers to this perplexing question are found in the institutional barriers that exist within and between government agencies, development organizations, and research institutions.

Water supply and sanitation services are provided to meet a variety of needs and are not always viewed as public health interventions. In most countries, water supply and sewerage systems are the responsibility of public works ministries, municipalities, and parastatal organizations. Decisions regarding system expansion and types of services are usually based on political, technological, and financial grounds. Health considerations may be included in policy and program development for the water and sanitation sector, but they rarely command priority. Most often, health concerns associated with public works are left to the ministries of health, which in any case have little control over public works agencies. Ministries of health sometimes have minor responsibilities for household and small-community sanitation systems, but are more commonly limited to regulatory roles in water quality control and to the promotion of health education programs. The general result is that capital investments in water supply and sanitation systems are not strongly influenced by health concerns, and over time, water and sanitation development becomes increasingly divorced from public health programs.

The problem is aggravated by the difficulty of interministerial cooperation within most national governments. Differing backgrounds of the professional staff in the environmental sanitation and health sectors further restrict communication. Ministries of works tend to be directed by staff with engineering and financial backgrounds, while ministries of health are dominated by those with public health and medical backgrounds. Policies and programs developed by each of these two groups generally follow the institutional and professional backgrounds of key staff.

In addition to these institutional constraints, several conceptual barriers prevent the effective application of environmental sanitation interventions to disease control programs. Over the past 20 years, a number of events have increased the perception that water supply and sanitation are not effective public health interventions. The first occurred in 1976 at a time of intense worldwide interest in health impact studies on water and sanitation improvements. Because of methodological problems and inconclusive results with some of the more prominent studies, the World Bank in 1976 convened a panel of experts to assess the overall usefulness of health impact research. Its conclusion was that the World Bank should not engage in further "attempts to isolate specific causal water supply–health relationships" because studies of such relationships were characterized by high costs, inadequate knowledge, and poor results (World Bank 1976). The general effect of this recommendation was to discourage field research by other organizations into the relationships between improved water supply and sanitation and the resulting health outcomes.

The Dominance of Selective Primary Health Care

Another and more devastating blow to the perceived link between environmental sanitation and public health programs was a paper on selected primary health care published by Dr. Julia A. Walsh and Dr. Kenneth S. Warren in 1979. This paper, published just before the launching of the International Drinking Water and Sanitation Decade, argued that community water supply and sanitation interventions were not as cost-effective in reducing mortality in the least developed countries as were a package of low-cost primary health care interventions consisting of immunizations, oral rehydration, and encouragement of breast feeding. Walsh and Warren based their arguments on the effects and costs of a variety of interventions on changes in mortality, or deaths averted, in a typical agricultural area of sub-Saharan Africa. Their calculations showed that water and sanitation services—costing an estimated $30 to $54 per capita and resulting in assumed reductions in deaths attributed to typhoid, cholera, other diarrheas, intestinal helminths and schistosomiasis—reduced mortality at a cost of $3,600 to $4,300 per infant or child death averted. In comparison, the selective primary health care package, which had an annual cost of only $0.25 per capita, was estimated to cost $200 to $250 per death averted. Other interventions, including mosquito and mollusk control and nutrition supplementation, were also assessed, and all were found to be more cost-effective than water supplies and sanitation.

The impact of the Walsh and Warren analysis had far-reaching effects that continue to influence programs in primary health care, public health, and environmental sanitation to this day. It contributed in the 1980s to the development on a global scale of vertical programs for immunizations, oral re-hydration therapy, and nutrition supplements, as WHO, UNICEF, and several bilateral agencies adopted versions of selective primary health care. Through high-level advocacy and effective promotion, national campaigns were launched for measles and diptheria immunizations, Vitamin A supplements, and other interventions. The success of these programs in reaching a large number of people became, in part, a measure of the effectiveness of the programs. This success attracted both new and existing health sector funds to selective primary health care that might otherwise have been allocated to other health programs, such as water supply and sanitation. Although the full financial impact on environmental sanitation programs is not known, investments in water and sanitation during the 1980s, a period specifically designated as the International Decade for Drinking Water Supply and Sanitation, never equaled the confident pronouncements declared at the start of the decade.

The main flaw in the Walsh and Warren analysis is that it tried to compare "apples and oranges." The selective primary health care interventions identified as being cost-effective, that is, immunizations, breast feeding, and oral rehydration, are targeted activities that generally focus on mortality reduction and on strengthening the child to resist infection but do little to improve conditions causing morbidity. Water supply and sanitation interventions, on the other hand, are broad-spectrum activities that serve many economic and social needs, including the general quality of life, as well as health concerns. More importantly, however, water and sanitation development are not undertaken to reduce mortality; their main health role is to stop or reduce the transmission of diseases and thereby reduce morbidity through changing the environment (infrastructure) and changing the behavioral practices of people (health/hygiene education). These changes are at the heart of a preventative approach to disease control, whereas most of the selective primary health interventions are based on a curative approach. By using a cost-effectiveness framework with highly restrictive assumptions, Walsh and Warren selected the more limited curative approach, which fails to address any of the fundamental environmental causes of illness. The recipients of selective primary health care, therefore, remain trapped in a cycle of sickness, followed by curative intervention, followed by sickness again.

Child Survival Programs Today

Despite the limitations of selective primary health care, it remains a dominant health care concept in developing countries to this day. In the early

1980s, international programs focused on single diseases or a small number of interventions: USAID had its "twin engines" of health development (immunizations against childhood diseases and oral rehydration therapy for diarrhea), while UNICEF promoted GOBI (Growth monitoring, Oral rehydration, Breastfeeding, and Immunizations). Later in the decade, child survival advocates began to emphasize a broader range of health interventions, including water supply and sanitation (which were never fully incorporated in child survival programs). This more inclusive approach was set out in the Convention on the Rights of the Child, adopted by the UN General Assembly in November 1989 and the plan of action from the World Summit for Children, held in September 1990 (UNICEF 1990).

Child survival programs continue to be the main framework for primary health care interventions, although the current orientation is to move beyond disease-specific programs to more integrated efforts and to develop a minimum package of cost-effective activities. The resulting programs, however, tend to exclude water and sanitation interventions. This can be clearly seen in the Sick Child Initiative of the early 1990s, in which WHO and UNICEF began to develop a new strategy based on improved case management of sick children combined with aspects of nutrition, immunizations, and community health education (WHO 1997d). The resulting strategy, the Integrated Management of Childhood Illness (IMCI), has since been adopted globally by 25 partner organizations drawn from the UN system, bilateral development agencies, nongovernmental organizations, and universities and is being implemented by some 44 countries. In Latin America, the objectives of an interagency IMCI agreement between PAHO (Pan American Health Organization) and UNICEF are to reduce mortality from the five main diseases affecting children (diarrhea, acute respiratory infections, malnutrition, measles, and malaria), to reduce the occurrence and severity of diarrhea, acute respiratory infections, and measles, and to improve the quality of care for children at health facilities (PAHO/WHO/UNICEF 1997). Although the IMCI strategy claims to promote prevention (through immunizations and infant and child nutrition), it does not formally include any water supply and sanitation activities or, indeed, any other environmental interventions.

Thus, the barriers restricting the full involvement of water and sanitation interventions in programs addressing child health are still in place. This situation is likely to continue as long as water and sanitation programs on the one hand and health programs on the other fail to clearly demonstrate the large areas of their mutual concern.

Rethinking Approaches to Environmental Sanitation

The selective primary health care approach and the more recent integrated management approach have been very successful in reducing child and infant mortality due to infectious diseases over the past two decades. They have been less successful in reducing morbidity rates, especially those linked to diseases that flourish in poor environmental conditions. Indeed, global incidence rates of diarrhea have shown no decline over the past 15 years (WHO, 1997b). A growing concern is that reductions in child mortality and morbidity rates are beginning to plateau as the limits of current approaches appear, available resources diminish, and environmental problems become more acute. Since these approaches do not attempt to change the basic environmental conditions harboring the diseases, there is some cause for concern over the long-term sustainability of current child health programs.

The obvious response to the current situation is to give greater attention and emphasis to prevention through modifications of the physical and social environment, in other words, to find ways to incorporate environmental sanitation elements in strategies and programs for child health.

Despite the fact in recent years that water and sanitation interventions have not been included in child health programs, research and development efforts to understand the link between environmental sanitation with health have continued. In the early 1980s, many studies concentrated on diarrhea, but researchers later turned their attention toward a variety of diseases related to water and sanitation. In 1991, for example, a review of 144 studies by Esrey and colleagues on the impact of improved water and sanitation services on six major diseases (ascariasis, diarrheas, dracunculiasis, hookworm, schistosomiasis, and trachoma) found reductions in mortality and morbidity ranging from 20 to almost 80% for most of these diseases, as shown in Table 7.

Table 7. Morbidity and Mortality Reductions from Improved Water and Sanitation

Disease	All studies		Better studies	
	No.	Median (%)	No.	Median (%)
Diarrhea morbidity	49	22	19	26
Diarrhea mortality	3	65	—	—

Table 7. (*continued*)

Disease	All studies		Better studies	
	No.	Median (%)	No.	Median (%)
Ascariasis	11	28	4	29
Dracunculiasis	7	76	2	78
Hookworm	9	4	—	—
Schistosomiasis	4	73	3	77
Trachoma	13	50	7	27
Overall impact on child mortality	9	60	6	55

Source: Esrey, Potash, Roberts, and Schiff (1991).

New Approaches to Environmental Sanitation Interventions

The growing evidence of measurable links between water and sanitation improvements and disease reduction is encouraging new efforts by international development institutions to make environmental sanitation programs more responsive to health needs. In particular, greater attention is being given to general sanitation and its role in preventing the generation and transmission of pathogens. Sanitation—including both excreta disposal and general cleanliness, the latter highly dependent on individual actions—needs to be defined in social, behavioral, and often cultural terms. On the other hand, water supply, which is usually provided through community or institutional action, can continue to be defined in the usual technical or engineering terms. Since 1990, research studies and field investigations on sanitation have expanded into a variety of nontraditional areas, including hygiene education and behavior change, participatory learning approaches, community management, and communications. There also has been a return to the traditional public health concern for sanitation as a means of controlling disease.

Many new techniques for implementing sanitation interventions for health purposes are now available. For example, WHO, in collaboration with other UN organizations, bilateral development agencies, nongovernmental organizations, and African ministries of health, has established the Participatory Hygiene and Sanitation Transformation (PHAST) Initiative, which is an innovative approach to promoting hygiene behaviors, sanitation improvements, and community management of water and sanitation facilities using participatory techniques (WHO 1996c). The initiative is based on the principle that no lasting change will occur in people's behavior without health awareness and understanding. It builds on the abilities of people in a community to identify and resolve their water and sanitation problems. Currently, PHAST is undergoing field trials in Africa and will soon be introduced to Asia and Latin America.

New techniques begin to influence programs in the field only when they become widely adopted as institutional guidelines. UNICEF, for example, has responded to growing demands that its water and sanitation programs provide greater support to the goals of the World Summit for Children, including those relating to infant and child health, maternal mortality, nutrition, and education. In 1995, UNICEF adopted new strategies for water and environmental sanitation with the overall objective "to contribute to child survival, protection and development by supporting efforts to achieve universal access to safe water supply and environmental sanitation services" (UNICEF 1995a). That same year, the UNICEF Executive Board urged the organization "to put greater emphasis on, and allocate resources as required, for environmental sanitation, hygiene and behavioral change" (UNICEF 1995b). In response, UNICEF, in cooperation with the USAID Environmental Health Project and a number of other UN agencies, published a handbook on sanitation programming that incorporates many of the institutional, participatory, and hygiene approaches developed in recent years (USAID/UNICEF 1997).

Increasingly, as can be seen in the case of UNICEF and WHO, environmental sanitation programs are taking on a health orientation, with emphases on disease control and child survival. In most cases, the levels of water and sanitation services being considered are relatively simple: communal water taps with household water storage, household latrines and waste disposal, and hygiene education for hand washing, food preparation, and vector control. The USAID Environmental Health Project recommends a "wellness" paradigm based on household and community-level preventative actions that should be incorporated into current child survival programs to supplement the present focus on case management and facility-based services. It recommends that the integration of preventative and curative approaches be accomplished by emphasizing risk reduction concerning the three main epidemiological pathways of disease: the generation of, transmission of, and exposure to disease agents. Representative community and household interventions can be identified to block or inhibit each of these three pathways to illness. In the case of diarrhea, for example, excreta disposal inhibits the breeding of pathogens, hand washing interrupts transmission of bacteria, and disinfection of drinking water reduces exposure to disease. According to the Environmental Health Project, incorporating such preventative environmental sanitation interventions into the curative-oriented child survival programs would lead to better and more sustainable results (Murphy, Stanton, & Galbraith 1997).

One of the more innovative efforts to compare environmental sanitation with other primary health care interventions is the recent work on cost-effectiveness by Robert C. G. Varley of the USAID Environmental Health Project (Varley, 1996). This analysis directly confronted the 1979 conclusions by Walsh and Warren that led to widespread acceptance of selective primary health care and the establishment of child survival programs lacking water and sanitation components. Using a cost-effectiveness approach, whereby the overall performance of various interventions to reduce both morbidity and mortality were compared with the costs of the interventions, the author showed that selective water supply and sanitation interventions can be more cost-effective than oral rehydration therapy (ORT).

The innovative aspects of Varley's work included breaking costs down into the "hardware" (infrastructure) costs paid by public works agencies and the "software" (hygiene education, social marketing, monitoring, and water quality regulation) costs attributable to public health agencies. Effectiveness was measured by the calculation of DALYs for both morbidity and mortality reductions in water and sanitation programs as reported in the literature by Esrey and colleagues (1991). The Varley analysis therefore went beyond the Walsh and Warren approach by including morbidity, as well as mortality, and by excluding the infrastructure costs of environmental sanitation because they are not normally a responsibility of the health sector. For the case of a hygiene education program added to existing water and sanitation systems, Varley found that the cost per death averted was $689 and the cost per DALY saved was $21. This compared favorably with ORT costs of $800 per death averted and $24 per DALY saved. Only when the costs of building the water and sanitation system were included in the analysis, the condition chosen by Walsh and Warren, was environmental sanitation clearly not cost-effective.

Closing the Gap

Although there is now a greater awareness of the close relationship between environmental sanitation and child health and there exists a growing body of data supporting the effectiveness of environmental sanitation interventions, current child survival programs have yet to adopt environmental sanitation elements to any significant degree. On the other hand, the water supply and sanitation programs of the major development organizations are increasingly responding to specific health objectives and adopting implementation techniques to achieve them. The struggle to raise health concerns to their rightful place in the environmental sanitation sector may not yet be won, but progress to date is promising.

Within the formal health sector, however, and especially within child survival programs, efforts to include long-term prevention through environmental sanitation interventions have been minimal. The expansion of child survival programs into the *integrated case management* paradigm constitutes a strengthening of the curative approach. It will improve clinical and household care for a selected group of childhood diseases, but it will have little if any effect on the recurrence of many illnesses or on the environmental and related behavioral conditions that allow these diseases to exist. Unless a better dialogue is established between the two sectors, water supply and sanitation programs will continue to be implemented without an adequate health component and child survival programs will continue on a path that is unsustainable. The costs of this failure to cooperate will be paid by the children in the cities and villages throughout the developing world and will be reflected in the unacceptable morbidity and mortality statistics published by WHO, UNICEF, and other organizations.

Conclusions

A number of major conclusions can be derived from the preceding discussion. First, children's health is very much affected by poor environmental sanitation. Diseases related to polluted drinking water, unsanitary food preparation, improper excreta disposal, and unclean household environments constitute a major burden on the health of peoples in the developing world and are the leading causes of ill-health in children. Diarrhea and dysentery alone strike young children several billion times per year and annually kill over 2 million before their fifth birthday. Environmental sanitation interventions, however, can reduce the incidence of certain illnesses by 20 to 80% by inhibiting disease generation, interrupting disease transmission, and reducing disease exposure. Sustainable child health is not possible without good environmental sanitation.

Second, existing environmental water supply, sanitation, and hygiene education interventions are not meeting the needs of the developing countries. There are currently 1.1 billion people without safe drinking water and 2.9 billion people lacking a sanitary means of excreta disposal. Countries with the highest rates of infant and child mortality and the lowest figures for income and life expectancy tend to have poor environmental sanitation services. Since water and sanitation facilities are normally provided by institutions outside the health sector, these services do not achieve optimal health benefits. Recent developmental work, however, has shown that the incorporation of hygiene education, participatory methods, communication techniques, and concepts about behavior change into environmental sanitation programs can greatly strengthen the effectiveness of such programs in improving health conditions.

Third, child survival programs have been effective vehicles for reducing childhood mortality, but have had little effect on the incidence of morbidity related to poor environmental sanitation. They are curative in nature and do not address the basic environmental conditions that foster the generation and transmission of most childhood diseases. Environmental sanitation interventions were excluded from selected primary health care and its more recent integrated management approaches because of an influential but conceptually flawed 1979 study by Walsh and Warren indicating that water and sanitation were not as cost-effective as other primary health care interventions, most notably, oral rehydration therapy and immunization. Recent investigations, however, have shown that environmental sanitation interventions can be equally cost-effective or better than the lowest-cost selective primary health care interventions. Nevertheless, the legacy of the Walsh and Warren study is that water supply and sanitation are not considered to be cost-effective health interventions and are not well integrated into the child health programs of any major development organization.

Fourth, there is great need for the integration of environmental sanitation and child health programs. Both areas would be strengthened. More importantly, the increased health benefits for the people of the developing world, especially young children, would represent a major breakthrough in global health status and, in the process, would revolutionize primary health care. Other advantages of this integration would be to make child survival programs more sustainable, to provide water and sanitation programs legitimacy within the health sector, and to encourage greater donor support. The new participatory community-based approaches being developed in the water and sanitation sector and the household-based child care approaches being adopted in the health sector offer useful entry points for this integration.

Fifth, Latin America faces a particular challenge to address the declining water and sanitation services found in many countries of the region. The impressive gains in coverage during the 1980s are now eroding, especially in the main urban centers, where, because of large population migrations from rural areas, more people are now without services than in 1990. At the same time the main child health programs do not include water and sanitation components. Linking environmental sanitation with child survival would provide child health programs with a crucial preventative basis and water and sanitation programs with a needed health focus.

REFERENCES

Esrey, S. A., Potash, J. B. Roberts, L. & Shiff, C. 1991. "Effects of Improved Water Supply and Sanitation on Ascariasis, Diarrhoea, Dracunculiasis, Hookworm Infection, Schistosomiasis, and Trachoma." *Bulletin of the World Health Organization*, 69 (5): 609–21.

Murphy, H., Stanton, B., and Galbraith, J. 1997. *Prevention: Environmental Health Interventions to Sustain Child Survival*. EHP (Johns Hopkins Employer Health Programs) Applied Study No. 3 (revised). Washington, DC: USAID.

PAHO/WHO/UNICEF (Pan-American Health Organization/World Health Organization/United Nations Children's Fund). 1997. *Interagency Agreement to Support Implementation of the Strategy for Integrated Management of Childhood Illness in the Americas*. PAHO/HCP/HCT/ARI-CDD/96.41.

UNCED. 1992. "Agenda 21: United Nations Conference on Environment and Development." Rio de Janeiro: June 3–14, 1992.

UNICEF. 1990. *First Call for Children (World Declaration and Plan of Action from the World Summit for Children; Convention on the Rights of the Child)*. New York: UNICEF.

UNICEF. 1995a. *UNICEF Strategies in Water and Environmental Sanitation*. New York: UNICEF.

UNICEF. 1995b. (As presented to the UNICEF Executive Board in May 1995). Document E/ICEF/1995/17: issued April 13, 1995 (quoted in USAID/UNICEF, 1997).

UN. 1990a. *Achievements of the International Drinking Water Supply and Sanitation Decade 1981–1990*. Report of the Secretary-General. General Assembly (A/45/327). New York: July 13, 1990.

UN. 1990b. General Assembly resolution (A/Res/45/181) New York: December 21, 1990.

UN. 1995. *Progress Made in Providing Safe Water Supply and Sanitation for all During the First Half of the 1990s*. Report of the Secretary-General (E/1995/86). Economic and Social Council, June 8, 1995.

USAID/UNICEF (US Agency for International Development/United Nations Children's Fund). 1997. *Better Sanitation Programming: A UNICEF Handbook*. EHP Applied Study No. 5. Washington, DC: USAID.

Varley, R. C. G. 1996. *Child Survival and Environmental Interventions: a Cost-Effectiveness Analysis*. EHP Applied Study No. 4. Washington, DC: USAID.

Walsh, J. A., and Warren, K. S. 1979. "Selective Primary Health Care: an Interim Strategy for Disease Control in Developing Countries." *New England Journal of Medicine*, 301: 967–74.

WHO. 1984. *The International Drinking Water Supply and Sanitation Decade: Review of National Baseline Data*. Publication No. 85. Geneva: WHO.

WHO. 1992a. *Weekly Epidemiological Record*. No. 6. 67:33–9.

WHO. 1992b. *Evaluation of the International Drinking Water Supply and Sanitation Decade, 1981–1990*. Report by the Director-General (A45/15). World Health Assembly, March 30, 1992.

WHO. 1996a. *Demographic Data for Health Situation Assessment and Projections, 1996*. WHO/HST/HSP/96.3. Division of Health Situation and Trend Assessment, Geneva: WHO.

WHO. 1996b. *The World Health Report 1996: Fighting Disease, Fostering Development*. Report of the Director-General. Geneva: WHO.

WHO. 1996c. *Participatory Hygiene and Sanitation Transformation: A New Approach to Working with Communities*. WHO/EOS/96.11. Geneva: WHO.

WHO. 1997a. *The World Health Report 1997: Conquering Suffering, Enriching Humanity*. Report of the Director-General. Geneva: WHO.

WHO. 1997b. *Health and Environment in Sustainable Development: Five Years after the Earth Summit*. WHO/EHG/97.8. Geneva: WHO.

WHO. 1997c. *Weekly Epidemiological Record*. No. 31. 72:229–34.

WHO. 1997d. *The Management of Childhood Illness in Developing Countries: Rationale for an Integrated Strategy*. IMCI Information, Division of Child Health and Development. Geneva: WHO.

WHO/UNICEF/WSSCC (World Health Organization/United Nations Children's Fund/Water Supply and Sanitation Collaborative Council). 1996. *Water Supply and Sanitation Sector Monitoring Report 1996* (sector status as of December 31, 1994). WHO/EOS/96.15. Geneva: WHO.

World Bank. 1976. *Measurements of the Health Benefits of Investments In Water Supply*. P.U. Report No. PUN 20, Public Utilities Department. Washington, DC: World Bank.

World Bank. 1993. *World Development Report, 1993: Investing in Health*. New York: Oxford University Press.

7 | Environmental Sanitation and Its Relation to Child Health

STEVEN A. ESREY

Introduction

The Convention on the Rights of the Child (CRC) (1) lays out all the rights of children, including

> the right of the child to the enjoyment of the highest attainable standard of health . . . through the provision of adequate nutritious foods and clean drinking-water . . . and . . . access to . . . hygiene and environmental sanitation and . . . preventive health care (art. 24).

While the CRC has acknowledged that children need environmental sanitation to enjoy a high standard of health, the reality is that many people are unaware of the relationship, including the scale and scope of benefits and the mechanisms to achieve them.

The five leading causes of death in Latin America are diseases of the heart, malignant neoplasms, cerebrovascular disease, accidents, and perinatal conditions (2). Seventh on the list is intestinal infections. While such an analysis implies that environmental sanitation, infectious diseases, and under-nutrition are no longer important, it masks differences across the region and recent trends. Communicable diseases remain the major cause of death in some countries in the region (2). Some of the highest rates of malnutrition in the world are found in pockets of many Latin American countries, despite a regional average far better than other parts of the world (3). The improvement in nutritional status seen in the 1980s has stalled in the 1990s (4). Environmental sanitation, while generally good in Latin America compared with other developing regions of the world, is still inadequate in nearly all countries. In rural areas half the people lack access to improved water and two out of every three people lack even basic sanitation:

> Seven years ago . . . 2.6 billion of the world's people lacked access to adequate sanitation . . . today . . . the total number of people without hygienic sanitation facilities has risen to almost 3 billion—nearly half of humanity. This is a life-and-death issue of the first order [especially for children] . . . those that survive are left underweight, stunted mentally and physically, vulnerable to even more deadly diseases—and too debilitated for the primary business of childhood: learning (5).

In addition, although urban Latin America has some of the highest rates of waterborne sewerage in the region, less than 5% of that sewage is treated in any fashion prior to discharge into the environment, causing widespread pollution and a threat to human health, and over 90% of sewage in developing countries is discharged directly into rivers, lakes, and coastal waters without treatment of any kind (6).

Warner (7) discusses many of the health benefits from environmental sanitation, identifies barriers to achieving those benefits, and recommends two courses of action to close the gap in service coverage: increased communication across sectors, specifically between the health and environmental sectors, and raising awareness of the health benefits from environmental sanitation. These two issues, which go hand in hand, will be addressed in this chapter.

Warner (7) defines environmental sanitation as "interventions [such as] . . . safe and sufficient water . . . sanitary disposal of human excreta and household wastes . . . [and] hygiene education . . . to prevent or limit the transmission of diseases." Thus, environmental sanitation encompasses a number of services, and the benefits from each vary in the nature and magnitude of the benefit. A distinction in this chapter will be made between environmental sanitation and sanitation. The former will refer to the collection of interventions, as described above, while the latter will refer to the sanitary handling/ management of human excreta.

Health and Nutrition Benefits

Environmental sanitation confers broad health and nutrition benefits through a variety of mechanisms (Figure 1). Other benefits, such as reduced environmental pollution and increased educational achievement, will not be discussed. Improvements in environmental sanitation can reduce transmission of disease agents, lead to time and energy savings by bringing water closer to homes, and improve agricultural practices and enhance food security (through reusing excreta as fertilizer). These improvements increase intake (macro- and micronutrients), reduce disease (due to bacteria, viruses, and parasites), or both. Common manifestations of undernutrition as a result of inadequate environmental sanitation include poor growth, anemia, and blindness, which exacerbate morbidity and lead to death. The vast majority of the literature and programmatic experience has been directed toward reducing the transmission of disease agents. While this may have been justified in the past, particularly during child survival interventions, it misses other key mechanisms whereby health and nutrition can be improved. More attention to the other mechanisms is now needed, particularly if the health and nutrition benefits from environmental sanitation can be maximized. Each of these three mechanisms will be discussed.

Figure 1. Environmental Sanitation and Improved Health and Nutrition: Mechanisms of Action

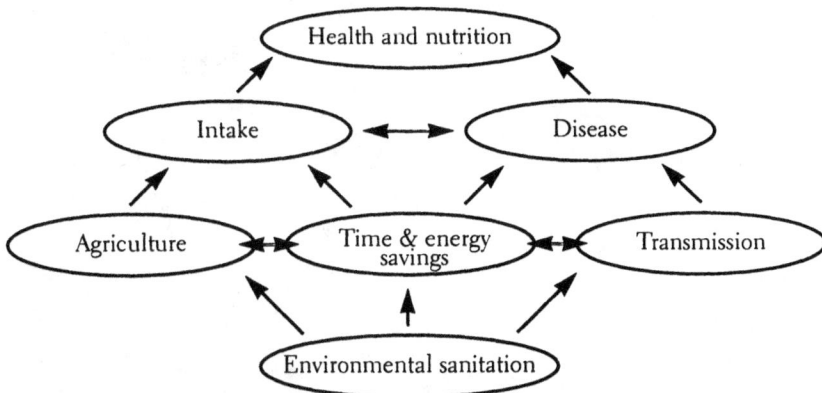

Transmission of Disease Agents

Environmental sanitation reduces the transmission of numerous disease agents, and the interventions are not specific to one disease, as are other child survival interventions. Improvements in the control of specific diseases are not only measurable, but in many cases substantial (8). This is not surprising, given historic data.

The decline in mortality rates from infectious diseases and the increase in life expectancy in Europe and the United States during the nineteenth and early twentieth centuries have been credited, in large part, to improved environmental sanitation (9, 10). While no one would claim that the reduction was due solely to improved environmental sanitation, or to any specific factor, ecological evidence does support the claim that it played a role. Long before vaccinations and the tools of curative medicine became widely used, mortality rates had already fallen substantially, largely from the reduction of infectious diseases brought about by making the environment cleaner (Figure 2).

Figure 2.   How Mortality Declined in the West

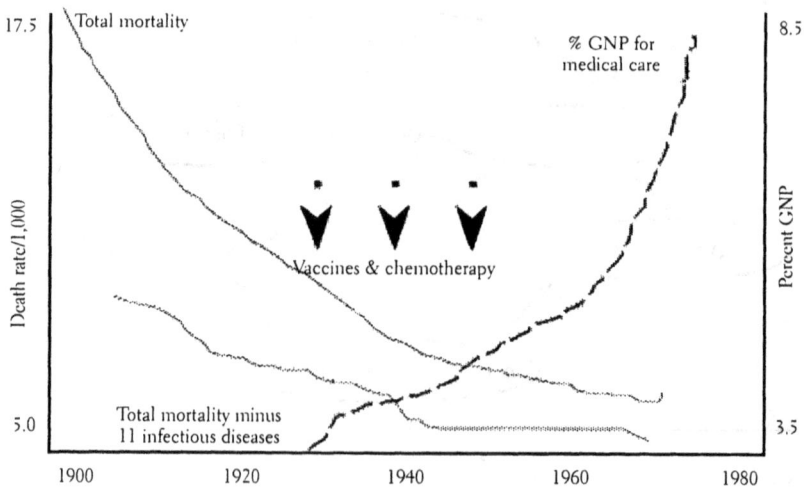

More recent evidence, based on modern epidemiological studies, substantiates the conjecture that improved environmental sanitation can reduce mortality and improve health. Reviews of studies from this century indicate that improvements in environmental sanitation confer broad health benefits—reducing the prevalence of diseases due to bacteria, viruses, and parasites (8, 11). Most of the accumulated evidence is related to diarrhea, and evidence from studies across the globe indicate that the incidence of diarrhea, a major cause of morbidity and mortality in the developing world, could be reduced by one-third from improvements in sanitation, and mortality could be halved. This is twice the reduction that can be achieved by improving the quality of drinking water and is similar to the reduction achieved by improving personal hygiene, such as hand washing.

Figure 3. Diarrhea Prevalence by Type of Environmental Sanitation among 13,642 Children, 3–36 Months of Age, from Eight Latin American Countries

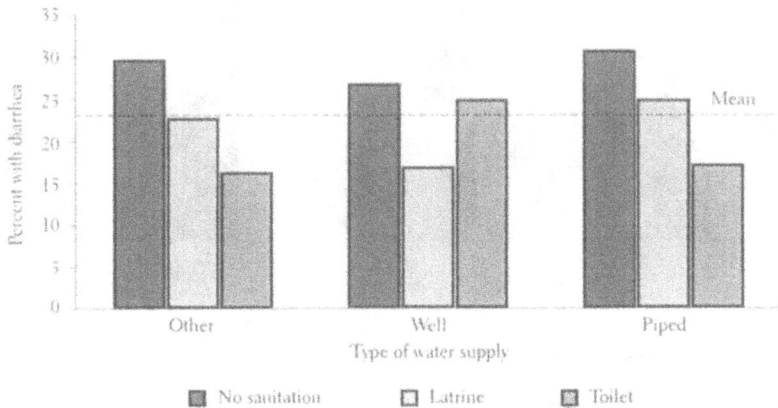

A recent analysis of data from eight Latin American countries supports this evidence (Figure 3). The selected countries provided data on water and sanitation conditions after a decade-long effort to increase coverage. "Piped water" is considered a water supply on or in the premises. Next best is some kind of community-level service (well), while "other" refers to nonimproved services. For sanitation, "toilet" refers to waterborne systems, "latrine" refers to pit latrines or chamber pots, while "no sanitation" refers to bushes, yards, or some place where excreta can spread.

Three observations can be drawn from these data. The highest rates of diarrhea (at least one episode in the preceding two weeks) were found in children without sanitation, regardless of the type of water supply. The mean prevalence of diarrhea in the sample was 23.2%, and in all cases children without sanitation experienced rates above the sample mean, ranging from 28 to 31%, even if those children came from families with water on or in the premises. Second, improvements in environmental sanitation resulted in a reduction of diarrhea by 10 to 44% depending on the level of improvement. The benefits from improved sanitation were greatest when piped water was unavailable, but were still substantial with water on or in the premises. Third, the reduction in diarrhea from improved water was virtually nil, regardless of the level of environmental sanitation.

Figure 4.   Stunting by Level of Water and Sanitation Service among 13,677 Children, 3–36 Months of Age, from Eight Latin American Countries

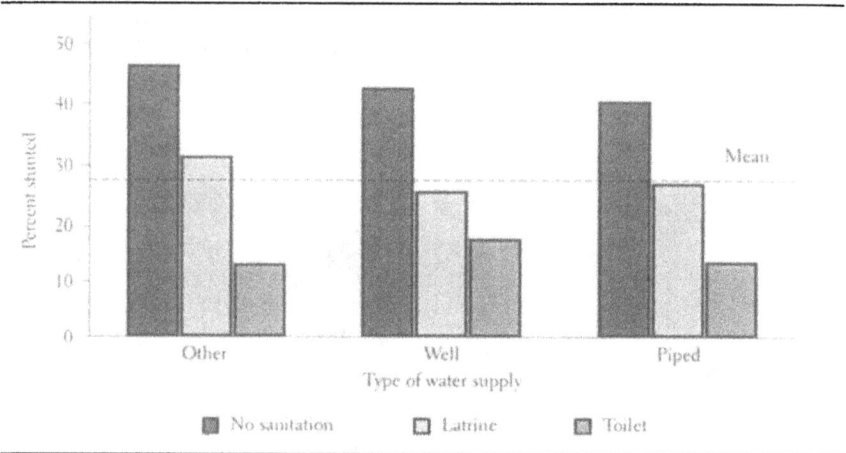

The nutrition benefits from improved sanitation using the same data, are even more striking (Figure 4). A "stunted" child was defined as one whose height-for-age Z-score was less than minus 2 standard deviations from the reference population. Overall, 27% of children were stunted, and as was found for diarrhea, the highest rates of stunting occurred among children without sanitation (41 to 46%), and the largest reductions in stunting associated with improved sanitation was found among those without improved water. Stunting may be reduced by 35 to 70% with improved sanitation and by 20 to 30% with improved water, depending on the level of service of water supplies. These results concur with a separate analysis of improved water and sanitation in 5,000 urban children from eight countries on three continents (12). The benefits in anthropometry are similar to the rates achieved by targeted nutritional supplementation programs (13).

Figure 5. Entry Points for Protecting Health

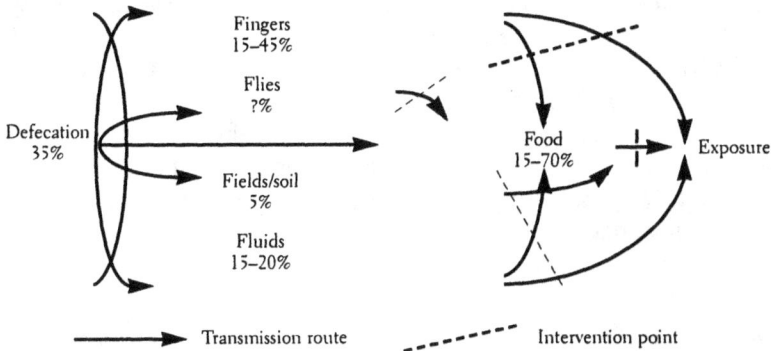

Fingers
15–45%

Flies
?%

Defecation
35%

Fields/soil
5%

Fluids
15–20%

Food
15–70%

Exposure

———→ Transmission route   - - - - - - Intervention point

Source: 18

It may seem surprising that sanitation confers larger benefits than does water supply. Examination of the routes of transmission reveals that sanitation should have the largest impact (Figure 5). If human excreta are not controlled and so gain access to the environment, pathogens may be transmitted through a variety of routes: fingers (and what they contact, including clothes and utensils), flies and domestic animals and snails, fields (e.g., vegetable gardens and household yards), and fluids (e.g., drinking water, cooking water, and beverages). People may be exposed directly through these routes or through foods. Superimposed on Figure 5 are the best estimates, based on literature reviews, for reducing diarrhea following intervention. The control of diarrhea, and by extension other fecal-borne infectious diseases, should focus on improved sanitation, personal hygiene, and food hygiene.

Why are the nutrition benefits larger and more striking than those for controlling diarrhea? Such results have been found repeatedly in a number of studies. Reports of diarrhea are subjective in nature and depend on recall, whereas anthropometry is objective, with standardized measurement techniques. Anthropometry is a summation of all nutritional insults, and diarrhea represents only one type of nutritional insult. Other diseases affected by sanitation, such as intestinal parasites, also affect anthropometry. Disease processes, even in asymptomatic children, continue to affect their nutritional status. These processes do not show up in diarrhea surveillance surveys. Thus, anthropometry more accurately measures the broader health and nutrition benefits of the disease-reducing capacity of improved environmental sanitation.

Time and Energy Savings

Providing water closer to people's homes reduces the energy and time spent collecting water and therefore fosters usage of more water for personal and domestic hygiene (Figure 6). Many studies have reported time savings from bringing safe and sufficient water closer to the home (14), and while the empirical evidence relating time savings to health benefits is scant, some studies have reported that some of the time saved was spent in other activities: commercial endeavors, preparing food and/or feeding children more frequently, and raising livestock or animals for home consumption or sale.

Figure 6. Environmental Sanitation and Improved Health and Nutrition: Mechanisms of Action

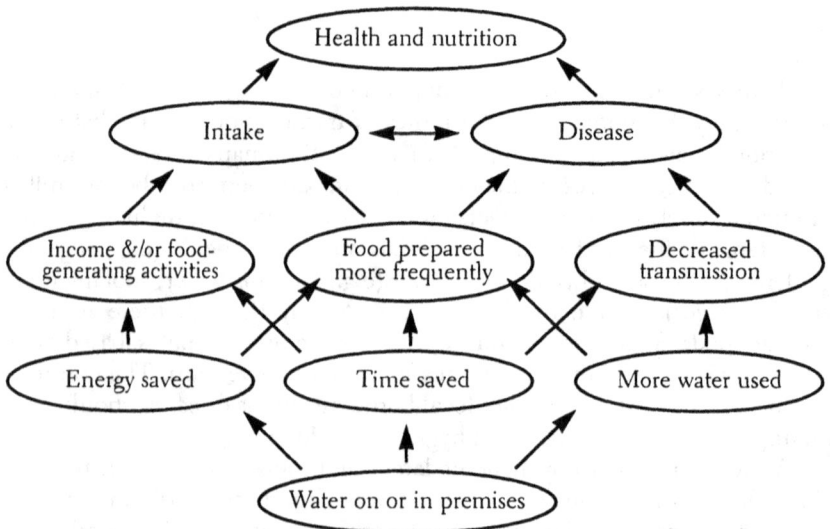

A recent study in Guatemala measured the time and energy savings of women who had water on or in their premises compared with women whose water source was 0.5 to 3 km away (15). The time saved from collecting water was 1.5 to 2 hours a day, and this "extra" time was spent in generating income

(e.g., through weaving), child care, and personal care. Women with water close to the home expended around 500 kcal less per day than the other women, and this was associated with a commensurate drop in energy consumed (16). This is equivalent to the lactation needs of nursing mothers and the complementary caloric needs of young children still breast feeding. Although these activities and time and energy savings were not associated with less diarrhea or better growth of children, the potential exists to improve health and nutrition if nutritionists helped plan and implement projects involving the provision of water supplies.

Time savings and the provision of more water can also be used to improve hygiene practices. Water could be used in personal hygiene practices, include washing hands after defecation or touching other contaminated objects (e.g., counters, ground surfaces). Food hygiene practices most likely to reduce contamination include washing of fruits and vegetables, utensils and cooking vessels, and hands prior to preparing and eating foods.

Agricultural Production

When the human–plant–animal closed loop operates, agriculture is sustainable (Figure 7a). Human excreta can be recovered and utilized as a resource for horticulture, aquaculture, livestock, and agroforestry, as has been practiced throughout history. This practice has been largely abandoned by disposing of sewage and manure, but it is reemerging in several parts of the world. The need to consider human excreta as fertilizer agents is driven by current sanitation practices, resource constraints (both physical and financial), ecosystem pollution and degradation, as well as urbanization.

Current sanitation practices 'dispose' of 'waste', which result in environmental pollution and opens up the human–plant–animal loop (Figure 7b). Latrines leak, which pollutes groundwater sources, and nearly all sewage in Latin America is discharged without any treatment (6). When the loop is opened up, chemical fertilizers are added for plant nutrition because the fertilizer value in excreta has been 'disposed.' The consequences of these practices are becoming increasingly major problems for area development: reduced availability of fresh water, coastal eutrophication, declining fish catches, coral reef destruction, red tide, reduced fertility of agricultural lands, and greater reliance on petrochemical fertilizers and pesticides (17). All of these problems affect human health in one way or another.

Figure 7.   Human Excreta, Sustainable Agriculture, and Health and Nutrition

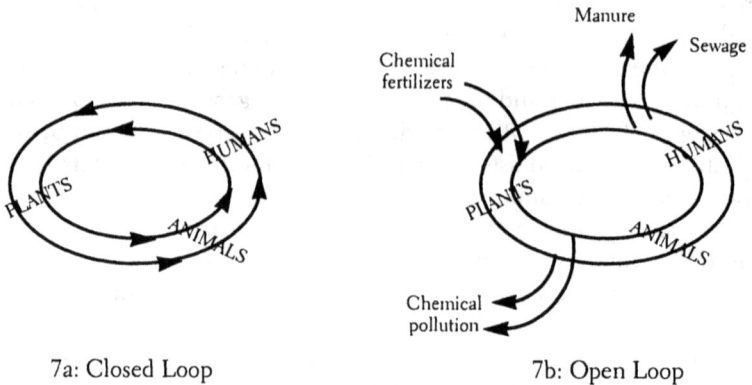

7a: Closed Loop   7b: Open Loop

Source: Adapted from 20

Most of the plant nutrients (e.g., nitrogen, phosphorous, and potassium) are found in urine, and these nutrients are in an ideal form for uptake by plants. Urine can be applied directly to plants/soil without further treatment or dilution. Only in special places would urine containing pathogens require treatment. Feces, largely undigested carbon, can enhance soil structure and waterholding capacity and promote the infusion of beneficial bacteria, enhancing plant production. In addition, the more carbon in the soil, the greater the uptake of iron for plants (18). Such practices may contribute to a sustainable solution to iron deficiency anemia. Most pathogens harmful to humans are found in feces, so feces requires treatment prior to use in agricultural production.

Sanitation pioneers in Central America and other parts of the world are developing innovative alternatives to traditional sanitation practices to capture more of the resource potential from human excreta and other organic matter (19). They are experimenting with dry systems, not mixing urine and feces, so as to recover and reuse the resource value of each. In Mexico in response to rapid inflation, high unemployment, and inadequate nutrition, Autonomía Descentralismo y Gestión (ANADEGES) (a network of nongovernment organizations [NGOs]) has perfected a method to grow vegetables in containers using domestic organic fertilizer. The project was launched in Mexico City more than 10 years ago, and it has spread to more than 1,200 urban households. In addition to household compost, urine is used to fertilize the plants. Urine is collected in 2 to 5 liter containers, mixed with soil to accelerate fermentation, covered and stored for three weeks, then diluted with water to a 10:1 ratio before being applied to plants.

Global urban agricultural practices have recently been reviewed (20), and Latin Americans are adapting practices pioneered elsewhere, while at the same time pioneering environmental sanitary practices on their own. In Peru, fish are produced using sewage, and this practice is being contemplated in Bolivia, Colombia, Cuba, and Mexico. In Brazil, a petrochemical complex is using organic waste from treated sludge to improve soils for food production. Community gardens in Lima use household compost, street waste, and livestock manure to enrich soils for food production for community kitchens (*comedores populares*).

Closing the loop by reusing resources (i.e., human excreta, household compost, animal manure, and other organic matter) means that more people can be fed, transport costs of food can be reduced, and food security can be enhanced (Figure 8). The key to capturing the resource value of these products is to keep them separate from each other by capturing each nearest to the source of their production; this is a drastic change from trying to separate them after they have been mixed together, often with huge quantities of fresh water. The modern toilet, sewers, and treatment plants are an inferior system in which to capture these resources (21). Modern sanitation methods increasingly concentrate toxic products, both human pathogens and industrial chemicals, until the end product is nearly unsafe and unusable, wasting colossal quantities of fresh water in the process.

Figure 8. Sanitation Alternatives

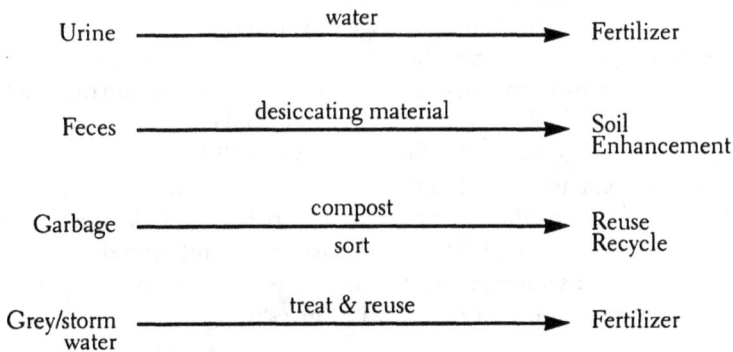

Because human excreta and the by-products of human activity are often considered waste, it is natural to think of disposing of such products. It is the concept of waste that has to be eliminated. Waste is nothing but a resource in the wrong place. The reinvention of sanitation practices would potentially result in more jobs, with resources being conserved, pollution being diminished, and people working toward sustainable communities. It is a simple matter of capturing the by-products of human activity and reusing the resources, through innovation and experimentation.

Integrating Environmental Sanitation and Health and Nutritional Programs

How can the awareness of health and nutrition benefits be raised and collaboration, not just communication, across sectors be increased? Upstream thinking (22) and systems thinking (23) need to be incorporated into project and program development. Both require a shift in how we look at problems: "All the problems afflicting either ourselves or our planet . . . [are] the result of poor thought-patterns of one kind or another. The solution . . . rearrange the insides of our heads" (24).

Upstream Thinking

Imagine you are on the side of a fast-flowing river (22). You notice someone floating by; he or she seems to be drowning. You jump in, swim over, and save the person. About the time you resume your spot on the side of the river you notice another person floating by. Again, you jump in and save the person. You're so busy saving people that you don't have the time, or perhaps the inclination, to walk upstream to see why people are falling into the river. Were they pushed in? Did their boat sink? Do they not know how to swim? Unless you go upstream to investigate the reason, you will be saving people all day, every day. Unless health and nutrition professionals move upstream to investigate why children always appear malnourished and diseased, they will forever be trying to save children who have "fallen into the river." Similarly, an environmental sanitarian, who by nature is working upstream, must walk downstream (or go beyond coverage) to investigate the effects of his or her efforts.

Figure 9.   Upstream Thinking: Entry Points for Diarrhea

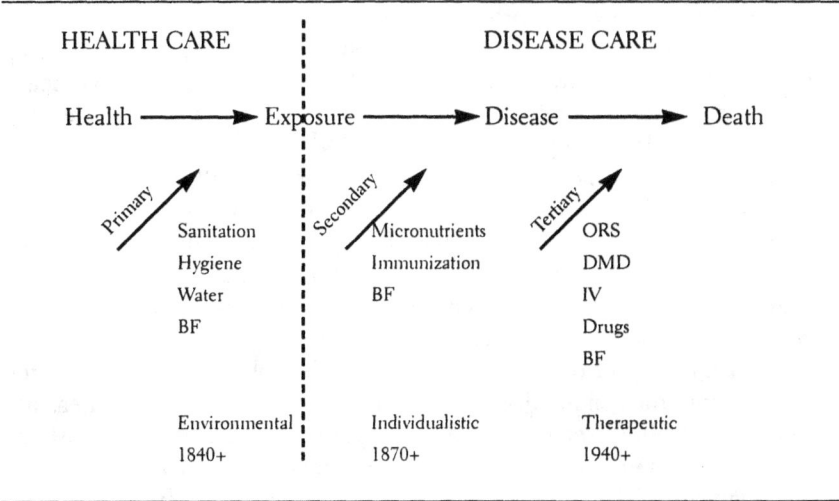

HEALTH CARE		DISEASE CARE	

Health ——▶ Exposure ——▶ Disease ——▶ Death

Primary		Secondary		Tertiary	
	Sanitation		Micronutrients		ORS
	Hygiene		Immunization		DMD
	Water		BF		IV
	BF				Drugs
					BF
	Environmental		Individualistic		Therapeutic
	1840+		1870+		1940+

Upstream thinking captures the bigger picture (Figure 9). A healthy person may be exposed to pathogens, and if the exposure is large enough, disease will occur. If the disease is severe enough, or if the pathogen is virulent, death may occur. There are three general points of intervention along this continuum. A tertiary point between disease and death prevents death by treating the disease, or at least the symptoms of disease. Secondary interventions between exposure and disease prevent disease, or at least disease severity, by treating exposure. Primary interventions prevent exposure by treating health. Primary interventions (upstream) are by definition health care, and secondary and tertiary interventions (downstream) are essentially disease care. Upstream thinking is very much in line with the CRC. Two general principles of the CRC are the indivisibility and interdependence of rights. All rights are equally important and cannot be arranged in a hierarchy. Thus, one type of intervention does not necessarily have a higher priority over another, but primary, secondary, and tertiary interventions should complement, not compensate for, each other.

Systems Thinking

Potential health and nutrition benefits can be programmed into environmental sanitation projects from the planning stages, as well as vice versa. Interdisciplinary work should not be like a relay race, whereby one discipline/

sector passes the baton off to another when its work is finished. Rather, all disciplines/sectors should run together during each leg of a race. Program and project implementation needs a conceptual framework; it needs guiding myths . . . [It] does not come as a prepared kit, all cut up and ready to process. It comes in a flood of jumbled material that needs to be picked over and sorted out by endless imaginative work (25).

Systems thinking has several characteristics (26): (1) all relevant variables are considered, (2) root causes are identified, (3) if one variable changes, assume all others change, (4) objectives are conceived, planned, and implemented in multidisciplinary rather than sectoral terms, and (5) solutions should be broad and sustainable. The first three characteristics call for the development of causal models. Characteristics 4 and 5 require that multiple disciplines plan together from the beginning with clear objectives in mind. Such efforts will minimize side effects as well as the need for palliative measures from other disciplines/sectors once the program is implemented or finished.

Mental maps, or causal models (see Figures 1, 5, 6, and 7 for examples) help explain how all the relevant variables fit into a system. In Figure 5, for example, if sanitation is not available, pathogens may be transmitted through a variety of routes. Attention to only one of these routes (e.g., safe water) will probably not alter transmission to any measurable extent, therefore failing to change morbidity rates. Thus, several transmission routes must be broken at the same time. Most environmental sanitation projects do not do this. Figure 5 is only part of the conceptual model of the health to death continuum. Causal models can (1) assist in the communication of a problem, (2) ensure that necessary linkages across disciplines/sectors have been made, (3) articulate the major objectives/focus of activities, (4) identify information gaps, (5) ensure that broader, more sustainable solutions are implemented, and (6) build alliances.

In 1996, the El Salvador UNICEF office helped the government develop a sanitation program using causal models (27). Several constraints existed in El Salvador (e.g., poverty, high rates of ill health and malnutrition, environmental problems prohibiting latrines and waterborne sewerage systems), all of which required a new approach to sanitation. Different organizations (e.g., UN agencies, NGOs, and bilateral efforts) encompassing different disciplines (e.g., engineers and health professionals) came together to develop a causal model of the factors affecting insufficient and inadequate sanitation. The conceptual framework of causes that were identified through a five-day workshop (Figure 10) produced the following results: (1) greater awareness of the current situation and the respective role of each organization, (2) emerging agreement among stakeholders to work together, (3) shared vision of the problem of sanitation and what needs to be done, (4) agreed upon definitions of terms, (5) a commonly shared and understood conceptual model, and (6) agreement on major objectives to achieve.

In Figure 10, three levels of cause are shown in bold (insufficient and inadequate sanitation, low motivation on the part of beneficiaries, and insufficient knowledge). If a program focused only on these aspects of the problem, it is unlikely that any major changes would occur. If other underlying and root causes are not addressed (e.g., distrust of institutions, insufficient maintenance), the symptoms of poor motivation may disappear, but the problem of insufficient and inadequate sanitation will not. A systematic, multi-disciplined attempt to address all causes is necessary to achieve programmatic success.

Figure 10. Causal Model: El Salvador

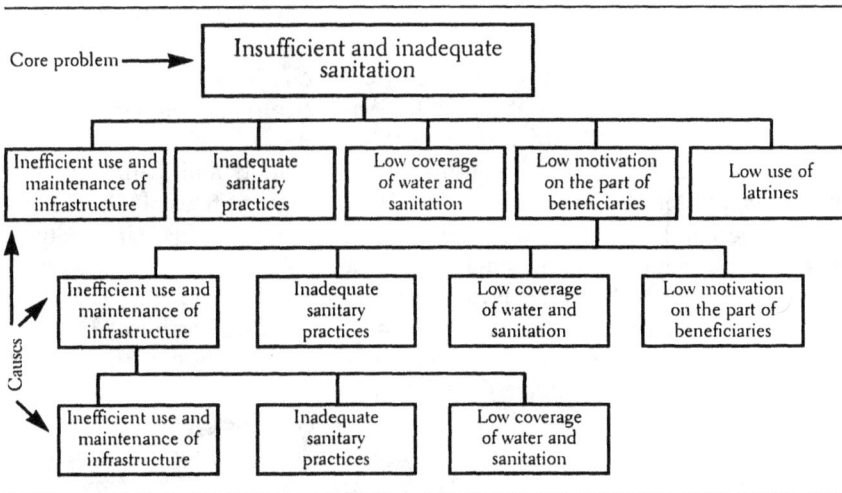

Conclusions

Environmental sanitation has, without a doubt, broad positive effects on child health and nutrition through a number of causal mechanisms. Many of the benefits can be maximized through upstream thinking, identifying root causes, and implementing complementary interventions. Achieving these benefits requires that different sectors and disciplines work together from the beginning as well as throughout projects. Finally, we need to create new and innovative solutions of how to work together in the "best interest of the child" (art. 3 of the CRC) (1).

REFERENCES

1. UN. 1989. *Convention on the Rights of the Child.* New York: UN.

2. Terris, M. 1991. "The Health Situation in the Americas." *Journal of Public Health Policy,* 12(3): 362–77.

3. de Onis, M., Monteiro, C., Akré, J., and Clugston, G. 1993. "The Worldwide Magnitude of Protein-Energy Malnutrition: An Overview from the WHO Global Database on Child Growth." *Bulletin of the World Health Organization,* 71(6): 703–12.

4. ACC/SCN (United Nations Administrative Committee on Coordination/Subcommittee on Nutrition). "Update of the Nutrition Situation, 1996: Summary of the Results for the Third Report on the World Nutrition Situation," 1997: 7–9.

5. Bellamy, C. Speech. London, July 22, 1997. "Progress of Nations."

6. World Resources Institute. 1997. *World Resources: The Urban Environment.* New York: Oxford University Press.

7. Warner, D. 1997. "Environmental Sanitation and Child Health: The Missing Link in Child Survival." In The Changing Status of Children in Latin America: Issues in Child Health and Children's Rights. University of Notre Dame, South Bend, Indiana, September 26–9.

8. Esrey, S. A., Potash, J. B., Roberts, L., and Shiff, C. 1991. "Effects of Improved Water Supply and Sanitation on Ascariasis, Diarrhoea, Dracunculiasis, Hookworm Infection, Schistosomiasis, and Trachoma." *Bulletin of the World Health Organization,* 69: 602–21.

9. McKinlay, J. B., and McKinlay, S. M. 1977. "The Questionable Contribution of Medical Measures to the Decline of Mortality in the United States in the Twentieth Century." *Milbank Memorial Fund Quarterly,* Summer: 405–28.

10. McKeown, T., and Record, R. G. 1962. "Reasons for the Decline in Mortality in England and Wales during the Nineteenth Century." *Population Studies,* 16: 94–122.

11. Esrey, S. A., Feachem, R. G., and Hughes, J. M. 1985. "Interventions for the Control of Diarrhoeal Diseases among Young Children: Improving Water Supplies and Excreta Disposal Facilities." *Bulletin of the World Health Organization,* 63: 757–72.

12. Esrey, S. A. 1996. "Water, Waste, and Well-Being: A Multicountry Study." *American Journal of Epidemiology,* 143(6): 608–23.

13. Beaton, G. H., and Ghassemi, H. 1982. "Supplementary Programs for Young Children in Developing Countries." *American Journal of Clinical Nutrition,* 35(Suppl): 863–916.

14. Burger, S. E., and Esrey, S. A. 1995. "Water and Sanitation: Health and Nutrition Benefits to Children" (Chapter 9). In: P. Pinstrup-Anderson, D. Pelletier, and H. Alderman (editors), *Child Growth and Nutrition in Developing Countries: Priorities for Action*. Ithaca: Cornell University Press, 153–75.

15. Diaz, E., Esrey, S. A., and Hurtado, E. 1995. *Social and Biological Impact Following the Introduction of Household Water in Rural Guatemala (Final Report)*. Ottawa: International Development Research Council.

16. Diaz, E., and Esrey, S. A. 1997. "Water Supply and Energy Balance in Rural Guatemalan Women" (submitted).

17. Rapaport, D. 1996. *Sewage Pollution in the Pacific and How to Prevent It*. Suva, Fija, Greenpeace Pacific Ltd.

18. Welch, R. M. 1996. "Overcoming the Limitations of Mineral Availabilities from Soils to Plants." In: G. F. J. Combs, R. M. Welch, J. M. Duxbury, N. T. Uphoff, and M. C. Nesheim (editors), *Food-Based Approaches to Preventing Micronutrient Malnutrition: An International Research Agenda*. Ithaca: Cornell International Institute for Food, Agriculture and Development, 6–7.

19. Winblad, U., Esrey, S. A., Gough, J., et al. 1997. *Ecological Sanitation*. Stockholm, Sida.

20. United Nations Development Programme. 1996. *Urban Agriculture: Food, Jobs and Sustainable Cities*. New York: United Nations Development Programme.

21. Gardner, G. 1998. "Recycling Human Waste: Fertile Ground or Toxic Legacy?" *World Watch*, January/February, 28–34.

22. Ashton, J., and Seymour, H. 1988. *The New Public Health*. Philadelphia: Open University Press.

23. Senge, P. 1990. *The Fifth Discipline: The Art and Practice of the Learning Organization*. New York: Currency Doubleday.

24. Trachtenberg, S. J. 1996. "The Triumph of Economics." *Wall Street Journal*, January 2, p. 6.

25. Midgley, M. 1991. *Wisdom, Information and Wonder: What is Knowledge for?* London: Routledge.

26. CIIFAD. 1996. "Using Systems Approaches to Prevent Micronutrient Malnutrition" (Chapter III). In: G. F. J. Combs, R. M. Welch, J. M. Duxbury, N. T. Uphoff and M. C. Nesheim (editors), *Food-Based Approaches to Preventing Micronutrient Malnutrition: An International Research Agenda*. Ithaca: Cornell International Institute for Food, Agriculture and Development, 55–6.

27. UNICEF. 1997. Better Sanitation Programming: A UNICEF Handbook. Arlington: Environmental Health Project, USAID.

II | Rights of Children and Youth in Latin America

A | Violence among Children and Youth

8 | Homicide Mortality in Adolescents and Young People

A Challenge for the Region of the Americas

JOÃO YUNES and TAMARA ZUBAREW

Introduction

During the last few decades, there has been a considerable increase in the level of violence witnessed throughout the world. Violence has reached epidemic proportions, becoming one of the most serious public health problems facing the Region of the Americas. With respect to Latin America and the Caribbean, in 1993, 456,000 deaths due to violent acts were reported (approximately 1,250 deaths per day). In fact, mortality rates from external causes (homicides, suicides, traffic accidents, and other injuries) have begun to affect the general mortality rate significantly. The situation is particularly alarming among adolescents and young people age 10 to 24 (1). Violence affects the entire population of the Americas. However, in conditions of poverty and social deprivation, certain social sectors are especially at risk.

According to the Pan American Health Organization, adolescents are defined as being age 10 to 19, and young people as being age 15 to 24. Adolescents constitute 20.3% and young people 11.3% of the population in the Americas. (2).

Of all the homicides reported in the region, 28.7% happened to those age 15 to 24. Young men are the principle victims and perpetrators of homicidal violence. In 10 of the region's 21 countries with populations greater than a million, homicide is the second leading cause of death in the 15- to 24-year-old age group, and one of the five leading causes of death in 17 of those 21 countries (3).

The premature death of young people due to violence results in high economic and social costs. The concentration of homicides and other external causes of death among adolescents and young people indicates that violence is the primary cause of life-years lost in the majority of the region's countries, an average loss of 30 to 40 years per death (2). The direct economic cost of deaths and disability as a result of violent acts is estimated to be $10 billion dollars annually. This represents approximately 20% of the region's total health expenditure (1).

Deaths due to violence, however, constitute only a small portion of the problem. The World Health Organization (WHO) estimates that for every child and adolescent that dies due to injury, 15 are left severely affected by the violent incident, and another 30 to 40 report injuries requiring medical or psychological treatment or rehabilitation.

Adolescents are not only victims of violence, but also perpetrators or intermediaries of violence. Violent acts affect the victim directly, as well as members of their families, classmates, colleagues, and the community at large. All forms of violence have short- and long-term damaging effects on the physical and mental health of those involved, thus limiting the functioning of individuals and society. Furthermore, violent acts are responsible for enormous costs to society in terms of health care and diminished productivity. Violence among adolescents and young people is avoidable and preventable (4). Individual characteristics, family experiences, relationships, access to weapons, alcohol and drug use, exposure to violence in the media, and other political, cultural, and social factors interact and play a fundamental role in the incidence of violence among young people.

The region's adolescents and young people are exposed to a great deal of violence portrayed in the media. There is now a consensus that this exposure is one of the causes of aggressive conduct, crimes, and violence among young people. Although it does not constitute the sole cause of violence, the influence of the media is one of the contributing factors that can most feasibly be controlled (5).

Given its multifaceted nature, violence should be prevented through the coordinated and active participation of all societal sectors using a multidisciplinary and intersectoral focus. Despite the fact that violent deaths provoke the loss of a great many lives of young people, limit individual and societal functioning, and negatively impact the economy, the implementation of epidemiological surveillance systems and violence prevention programs for adolescents and young people is scarce in the region. The programs that currently exist are fragmented and incomplete, lacking an integrated and intersectoral focus, as well as evaluation mechanisms.

Materials and Method

Our analysis is based on population data and mortality rates compiled by the Pan American Health Organization (PAHO) data bank from annual mortality reports submitted by all of the countries of the region. The causes of death have been classified according to the International Classification of Diseases, Ninth Revision (ICD-9). In each age and sex group the following causes of death are analyzed:

- Mortality Rates from All External Causes (Code E800–E999)

- Mortality Rates from Homicides and Intentional Injuries and Injuries Resulting from War or Legal Interventions (Code E960–E969; E970–E978; E990–E999)

For comparison, mortality rates from the entire population were also analyzed utilizing the same categories to establish the relative weight for each cause of mortality in the population of adolescents and young people.

Study Parameters

The factors that determined the inclusion of the 16 countries analyzed in the study were the existence of information available in the PAHO data bank: population size, quality of vital statistics (measured by the proportion of external deaths attributed to injuries that would not be counted were they to be accidental or intentionally inflicted), the availability of information over the total period analyzed, and availability of information for subcategories of external causes. The countries that fulfilled those criteria were Costa Rica, El Salvador, and Panama (in Central America), Canada, Mexico, and the United States (in North America), Argentina, Brazil, Chile, Colombia, Ecuador, Uruguay, and Venezuela (in South America), and Cuba, Puerto Rico, and Trinidad and Tobago (in the Caribbean). Mortality rates specific to age and sex were analyzed in the following age groups: all ages, 10 to 14, 15 to 19, 20 to 24, 10 to 19, and 15 to 24 years.

Results

Countries of Central America

Costa Rica

In Costa Rica there was a 4.2% decrease in mortality rates from external causes among the total population between 1981 and 1991. The largest decrease was observed in male adolescents and young people, with a 36% decrease among males aged 10 to 14, a 16% decrease among males aged 15 to 19, and a 33% decrease among males aged 20 to 24. Similar decreases were observed among the female adolescent population, with the mortality rates from external causes being two to three times less among women aged 10 to 19, and up to six times less among those aged 20 to 24 than rates for the respective male age groups.

The homicide rate for the total population has remained stable throughout the period studied at 4.1 per 100,000 in 1991 (6.6 among males and 1.6 among females). The homicide rate among adolescents and young people in Costa Rica is low and actually decreased between 1981 and 1991 for all of the age and sex groups. Among those aged 15 to 19, the rate decreased from 4.2 to 1.3 per 100,000 males, and from 2.9 to 0.7 per 100,000 females.

In conclusion, the slow decline in mortality rates from external causes in adolescents and young people in Costa Rica is a result of the decline in mortality rates from traffic accidents and homicides. Costa Rica is one of the countries with the lowest mortality rate due to homicide among adolescents and is the only country in this study with a decreasing mortality rate for this age group.

El Salvador

Although the data available from El Salvador is inadequate, the country has been included in this study because of the magnitude of the mortality rates from external causes and homicides due to the armed conflict that occurred from 1981 to 1991. However, information is available only from 1981 to 1984 and from 1990 to 1991.

Information regarding trends in homicide rates among adolescents and young people during the period studied is not available. Homicide rates in 1991 among 10- to 14-year-olds were 4.7 per 100,000 males and 2.8 per 100,000 females; among 15- to 19-year-olds, 109.7 per 100,000 males and 3.1 per 100,000 females; and among 20- to 24-year-olds, 244.5 per 100,000 males and 4.2 per 100,000 females.

In conclusion, although a decrease occurred between 1981 and 1991, El Salvador continues to be one of the region's countries with the highest mortality rates from external causes and homicides among adolescents and young people, surpassed only by Colombia. This is primarily a result of the warlike conflict that the country experienced during the period of observation.

Panama

Trends in the mortality rates from external causes among males, aged 10 to 14 and 15 to 19, showed a decline between 1980 and 1989. On the other hand, among males, aged 20 to 24, there was a decrease until 1987, followed by a 44% increase between 1988 and 1989. Mortality rates from external causes for all females did not undergo significant changes in the period studied.

Mortality rates due to homicides among the entire population nearly quadrupled between 1980 and 1988, rapidly increasing by 103% between 1988 and 1989, a year of warlike conflict. There was a progressive and dramatic increase in homicides among male adolescents and young people during the period studied.

Mortality rates among males aged 15 to 19 quadrupled between 1980 and 1988, and rose 39% between 1988 and 1989 alone. In males aged 20 to 24 years, there was a 413% increase between 1980 and 1988, and a 103% increase between 1988 and 1989. There was also an increase in homicide rates among females aged 15 to 24, although significantly less than that for males.

In conclusion, the mortality rates from external causes for adolescents and young people from Panama have remained relatively stable as a result of a simultaneous decrease in mortality rates from traffic deaths and an increase in homicide and suicide rates between 1980 and 1988. The rapid increase in deaths among young people (aged 20 to 24) from external causes between 1988 and 1989 is attributable to the increase in homicides and other intentional injuries as a result of the warlike conflict suffered by the country.

North America

Canada

Mortality rates from external causes among Canadian adolescents and young people are progressively declining in all age and sex groups. There was a 50% decrease among males and a 29% decrease among females aged 10 to 14, a 40% decrease among both males and females aged 15 to 19, and 39% and 43% decreases among males and females, respectively, aged 20 to 24. Males aged 20 to 24 had the highest mortality rate (81.5 per 100,000) from external causes in 1994.

Homicide rates are low in Canada for all of the age groups studied. The rate among the entire population decreased by 15% (from 2 to 1.7 per 100,000) between 1980 and 1994. The rates have remained stable for adolescents and young people during the same period (0.3 and 0.7 per 100,000 males and females aged 10 to 14, respectively; 2.9 and 1.3 per 100,000 males and females aged 15 to 19, and 4.0 and 2.3 per 100,000 males and females aged 20 to 24).

In conclusion, Canada has one of the region's lowest mortality rates from external causes and homicides for adolescents. The decrease in mortality rates from external causes for both adolescents and young people between 1980 and 1994 is largely the result of a decrease in traffic deaths. Nevertheless, Canada has the highest suicide rate among adolescents and young people of all the countries analyzed in this study.

Mexico

In general, adolescents and young people in Mexico have experienced a decrease in mortality rates from external causes, though certain subgroups experienced an increase in homicide rates during the period under study. Homicide rates increased by 21% among males and females aged 15 to 19 years, while the rates remained stable among those aged 20 to 24.

The decrease in mortality from external causes among adolescents and young people is primarily due to a decrease in traffic deaths. Death from homicide is the principle category of mortality from external causes among males aged 15 to 24 years of age, and this trend is increasing, especially among adolescents aged 15 to 19.

United States

All age and sex groups of adolescents and young people from the United States experienced a slight and progressive decline in mortality from external causes: 19 and 11% decreases among males and females aged 10 to 14, respectively; 10 and 16% decreases among those aged 15 to 19; and 20 to 23% decreases among those aged 20 to 24.

Among U.S. adolescents and young people, homicide is the second leading cause of death from external causes, and there was a progressive increase among all subgroups by age and sex between 1980 and 1994: 88 and 15% increases among males and females aged 10 to 14, respectively; 114 and 8% increases for those aged 15 to 19; and a 29% increase among males aged 20 to 24. Mortality rates from homicides between 1980 and 1994 increased dramatically, up 163% (from 13.2 to 34.7 per 100,000) among males aged 15 to 19 and up 77% (from 23.6 to 41.7 per 100,000) among males aged 20 to 24.

In conclusion, the decrease in mortality rates from external causes among adolescents and young people in the United States is a result of a decrease in traffic deaths. However, it must be noted that there has been a considerable increase in deaths from homicide among adolescents, particularly among males aged 15 to 19.

South America

Argentina

Homicide rates increased in all groups of adolescents and young males, doubling in males aged 15 to 19 between 1981 and 1993. In women aged 15 to 24, rates decreased by 47% during the same period.

Mortality from external causes for the entire Argentine population is primarily due to traffic accidents. Nevertheless, among adolescents and young males aged 15 to 24, the increase in mortality from external causes is primarily the result of increasing homicides and suicides.

Brazil

The mortality rate from external causes for the entire population of Brazil progressively increased 20% from 1980 to 1994 as a result of an increase in the male population and increasing mortalities among male adolescents and young people. The group most affected is males aged 15 to 19, who experienced a 51% increase in mortality rate from external causes, reaching 122.9 per 100,000 in 1994. Young people aged 20 to 24 have the highest rate of mortality from external causes (197.7 per 100,000 in 1994), increasing by 47% during the time of the study. Females aged 15 to 24 have maintained a stable mortality rate of approximately 24 per 100,000.

Homicides and traffic deaths are the two leading categories of mortality from external causes for the entire population. The mortality rate from homicides increased for the entire population by 84% between 1980 and 1994. After 1991, the homicide rate surpassed the mortality rate from traffic accidents for the entire population. Homicide is the leading external cause of death for adolescents and young people. There has been a significant increase in homicides in all age and sex groups examined. Between 1980 and 1984, homicide rates for adolescents aged 10 to 14 doubled. Homicide rates for adolescent males aged 15 to 19 increased 174% to 52.9 per 100,000 in 1994. Females aged 15 to 19 suffered a 52% increase to 5.4 per 100,000. The highest homicide rate is found among males aged 20 to 24 at 93.3 per 100,000 in 1994 (a 114% increase since 1980). The disparity between the sexes is quite significant in this age group, with a male to female ratio of 16:1 in 1994.

In conclusion, the increase in mortality from external causes among Brazilian adolescents and young people is primarily due to traffic deaths and homicides and secondarily from an increase in suicides. The increase in the homicide rate is especially noteworthy in those aged 15 to 19.

Chile

In Chile, homicide rates were low and stable at close to 3 per 100,000 for the entire population. The same trend was observed for Chile's adolescents and young people. Low homicide rates among adolescents and young people were revealed in the analysis, with a slight increase for males aged 15 to 24 between 1980 and 1992. However, it should be noted that Chile may have skewed data, given that it has a high percentage of deaths classified as "injuries that are ignored were they to be accidental or intentionally inflicted," which would call into question the certification of the causes of death.

In conclusion, the decrease in mortality from external causes for adolescents and young people in Chile is due to the decrease in traffic deaths. Reported homicide and suicide rates are low, although a slight increase in homicides among males aged 15 to 24 was observed.

Colombia

Mortality rates from external causes among adolescents and young people aged 10 to 14 remained stable at approximately 34 per 100,000 boys and 12.5 per 100,000 girls, between 1984 and 1994. However, there has been a dramatic increase in mortality rates among both males and females aged 15 to 24. There was a 176% increase in the rates among males aged 15 to 19 (92.2 to 254.2 per 100,000) and a 61.6% increase among females aged 15 to 19 (21.9 to 35.4 per 100,000). There was a 92% increase among males (226.2 to 439.9 per 100,000) and a 31% increase among females (29.3 to 38.4 per 100,000) aged 20 to 24. While males aged 20 to 24 have the highest mortality rates from external causes among adolescents and young people, the greatest increase in mortality rates was seen among males aged 15 to 19. In 1994, the ratio of male to female mortalities from external causes was 2.8:1 for those aged 10 to 14; 7:1 for those aged 15 to 19; and 11:1 for those aged 20 to 24.

Homicide is the largest category of external causes of death in Colombia for the entire population: the homicide rate increased by 177% between 1984 and 1992 and decreased by 11% through 1994 to 80.1 per 100,000.

A dramatic increase in homicide rates among adolescents and young people was also observed, similar to increases from other external causes of death during the period studied. Homicide rates tripled among boys aged 10 to 14, reaching 12.9 per 100,000 in 1994. The rate among girls in the same age group tripled, reaching 3.2 per 100,000 in 1994. In 1994, males aged 15 to 19 suffered the greatest increase in mortality rates from homicide of all the groups analyzed, with a rate of 199 per 100,000, almost five times the 1984 rate. The rate for females of the same age tripled, reaching 18.6 per 100,000 in 1994. Males aged 20 to 24 had the highest of all homicide rates (342 per 100,000 in 1994), a tripling of the 1984 rates. The rates for females of the same ages doubled, similar to rates of females ages 15 to 19. The ratio of male to female mortalities was 3:1 for those aged 10 to14; 10:1 for those aged 15 to 19; and 18:1 for those aged 20 to 24. The observed decrease in homicide rates among the total population between 1992 and 1994 is not reflected in the adolescent mortality rates.

In conclusion, of the countries analyzed, Colombia had the highest mortality rates from external causes and homicides for the entire population, adolescents, and young people. The dramatic increase in mortality from external causes is a result of the increase in homicides. The group with the highest homicide rate among adolescents and young people is males aged 20 to 24. Between 1984 and 1994, males aged 15 to 19 suffered the greatest increase in mortality rates.

Ecuador
Mortality rates from external causes among adolescents and young people decreased by 17% for males aged 15 to 24, down to 100.8 per 100,000. However, Ecuador has suffered a 63% increase in mortality from homicides among the total population, and a 47% increase among males aged 15 to 24. In 1980, the mortality rate from traffic deaths among males aged 20 to 24 was twice that of homicides. In 1990, the rate from homicides surpassed that from traffic accidents (37.7 versus 36.7 per 100,000). The ratio of male to female homicides for those aged 15 to 24 was 14:1.

In conclusion, the decrease in the mortality rates from external causes for adolescents and young people is due to a decrease in traffic accidents. The mortality rate due to homicides is increasing for these groups and has surpassed the mortality rate from traffic accidents in young people aged 20 to 24.

Uruguay
Homicides were low among adolescents and young people in Uruguay, but increased by 68% in males aged 15 to 24, and by 21% in females of the same age (5.7 per 100,00 males, 3.3 per 100,000 females). The greatest increase was observed in males aged 20 to 24, reaching a rate of 7.9 per 100,000 in 1990. Rates decreased for males aged 15 to 24 and increased for females of the same age. Homicides in Uruguay are rare, although there is some evidence of a slight increase in their occurrence.

Venezuela
There was no significant change in the mortality rates from external causes among all groups of adolescents and young people between 1980 and 1991.

For those aged 15 to 24, a decrease in mortality rates between 1980 and 1988 and a 75% increase between 1988 and 1994 averaged out to a 15% increase during the entire period studied.

Between 1987 and 1994, there was a 216% increase in the mortality rate from homicide among adolescent males aged 15 to 19, up to 4.9 per 100,000 at the end of the study. Among males aged 20 to 24, there was a 150% increase, reaching a rate of 85.4 per 100,000 in 1994. Between 1980 and 1994, there was a 65% increase for young people aged 15 to 24. The ratio of male to female mortalities for those aged 15 to 24 was 20:1.

In conclusion, mortality from external causes for Venezuelan adolescents and young people is due to traffic accidents and homicides. Both causes have similar trends, with a decrease from 1980 to 1989, followed by an increase after 1989. The increase is particularly notable in the homicide rate among males aged 15 to 24.

Caribbean

Cuba

The mortality rates from external causes for adolescents and young people decreased during the period studied for females of all ages: 81% for those aged 10 to 14, 109% for those aged 15 to 19, and 65% for those aged 20 to 24. The rate increased by 12% during the same period among males aged 15 to 19, and remained stable, with only slight oscillations, among males aged 20 to 24.

Among males 15 to 24 years, homicides, suicides, and traffic deaths all produced similar mortality rates in 1994 (traffic deaths: 18 per 100,000; homicides: 18.4 per 100,000; and suicides: 14.3 per 100,000). However, among females aged 15 to 24, the suicide rate of 16 per 100,000 in 1994 dominated, in comparison with the 9.9 per 100,000 rate from traffic accidents and 6.5 per 100,000 rate from homicides. Homicide does not appear to be the most significant cause of death among adolescents and young people in Cuba.

Puerto Rico

The principle reasons for the high mortality rate from external causes for the entire Puerto Rican population are traffic deaths and homicides. Homicide rates for the entire population increased by 57% during the period examined, with an initial decrease until 1984 followed by an increase until 1992.

Among adolescents and young people, homicide is the primary category of mortality from external causes. The same trends are witnessed in males and females aged 15 to 24 years, with an initial decrease in homicides until 1984, followed by an increase. Homicide rates increased by 238% between 1983 and 1992 for males aged 15 to 19 (65.3 per 100,000). The rate for females aged 20 to 24 increased by 178% by 1992 (125.7 per 100,000). After 1984, the rates for males were at least 10 times greater than those for females. Homicide rates for adolescents aged 10 to 14 were low, with periodic oscillations.

In conclusion, the increase in the mortality rate from external causes among adolescents and young people in Puerto Rico is primarily due to homicides. The greatest increase was observed between 1983 and 1992 among males aged 15 to 19. The highest homicide rates were found in males aged 20 to 24.

Trinidad and Tobago
Between 1980 and 1994, homicide rates in Trinidad and Tobago increased fivefold for the total population. Among adolescents and young people, the mortality rate from external causes is primarily due to homicides, followed very closely by suicides and traffic deaths. However, it should be noted that homicide rates in Trinidad and Tobago are low, although they did increase from 1980 to 1993 among young males aged 15 to 24 from 2.4 to 21.4 per 100,000. Homicides in the female population are rare.

In conclusion, the decrease in the mortality rate from external causes in adolescents and young people from Trinidad and Tobago is due to the decline in traffic deaths. Definite increases are noted in the mortality rates from homicides and suicides among young people aged 15 to 24.

Discussion and Conclusion

Precaution must be taken when extrapolating conclusions from this chapter's data concerning mortality trends in the region of the Americas. The 16 countries that had the population and information necessary to fulfill the minimum requirements for statistical analysis represent 90% of the population for the region.

Variations exist in mortality rates from external causes among subgroups in the countries examined. For the entire population, the leading cause of mortality is traffic accidents in all of the countries except: El Salvador and Colombia (where homicide dominates), Cuba (in which suicides dominate), Panama in 1989 (in which homicides, as a result of the country's warlike conflict, dominated), Mexico (where homicide has dominated since 1984); and Brazil (in which homicides dominate since 1991).

Homicide is a critical cause of mortality among adolescents and young people. It is the greatest contributing factor to mortality rates among adolescents and young people in Argentina, Mexico, and Puerto Rico, in contrast with traffic deaths, which constitute the primary category of mortality from external causes for the entire populations of these countries. Since 1991, homicide is the primary cause of mortality from external causes for both the adolescents and the entire population in Brazil, Colombia, and El Salvador.

Homicide rates in general are greater for adolescents and young people than for whole populations. They are also greater for males than females and increase with age for 10- to 24 year-olds. The ratio of mortality between the sexes is quite varied and increases parallel with increases in homicides. The greatest ratios between the sexes exist in Colombia, El Salvador, and Puerto Rico.

The countries with the highest homicide rates among whole populations, in decreasing order, are Colombia, El Salvador, Puerto Rico, Brazil, and Venezuela. Colombia's rate is three times that of El Salvador.

Using males ages 15 to 24 as a reference group, the countries analyzed can be categorized by homicide rates: high, intermediate, and low. Countries with a high homicide rate (greater than 50 per 100,000), in decreasing order, are Colombia, El Salvador, Puerto Rico, Venezuela, and Brazil. Countries with intermediate homicide rates (from 10 to 50 per 100,000) are Mexico, the United States, Panama, Ecuador, Trinidad and Tobago, Cuba, and Argentina. Countries with low homicide rates (less than 10 per 100,000) are Chile, Uruguay, Costa Rica, and Canada.

It should be noted that in most countries analyzed, homicide rates increased during the period under study. In 10 of the countries analyzed, homicide rates increased in both the adolescent and total populations: Argentina, Brazil, Colombia, Ecuador, Panama, Puerto Rico, Trinidad and Tobago, the United States, Uruguay, and Venezuela (Cuba and El Salvador were excluded from this analysis due to a lack of data).

In Mexico, homicide rates for the entire population decreased slightly. Nevertheless, an increase in adolescent homicide rates was observed in 15- to 19-year-olds. In Chile, homicide rates remained stable for the entire population, but increased among adolescents aged 15 to 24. In Canada, the rate decreased for the entire population and remained stable among adolescents.

The only country with a decreasing homicide rate among adolescents was Costa Rica. However, this decline is small, and an analysis of trends is difficult, due to the small population and few deaths.

Homicide is a growing problem in the region. In 10 of 16 countries analyzed, homicide rates are increasing for whole populations, as well as for adolescents.

Homicide is the primary cause of mortality from external causes in the general populations of Colombia, El Salvador, and Mexico. It is also the primary cause of mortality from external causes among adolescents and young people in those three countries, as well as, in Argentina, Brazil, and Puerto Rico. Although males aged 20 to 24 have the highest homicide rate, an alarming increase was observed in males aged 15 to 19, particularly in Brazil and the United States.

Results from this analysis reveal that violence and its manifestations are a growing problem for the region. The increasing homicide rate, particularly alarming among adolescents and young people, reflects the need for violence prevention programs targeting this population. The health sector can contribute to the development of the regional plan of action for violence prevention by implementing epidemiological surveillance systems with the purpose of providing information to better understand trends in violence in the region, as well as risk factors. This is of critical importance because in order to effectively intervene and provide solutions to this problem, the health sector must thoroughly understand what risk factors are contributing to this increase in homicides among the region's youth, particularly in those countries and areas experiencing alarming increases.

REFERENCES

1. Pan American Health Organization. 1994. "International Conference on Society, Violence and Health." November. Washington, D.C.

2. Pan American Health Organization. 1994. *Health Conditions of the Americas*, Vol. 1. Washington, D.C.; PAHO, Scientific Publication No. 549.

3. Maddaleno, M., Munist, M., Serrano, C. V., Silber, T. J., and Yunes, J. (1994). *La salud del adolescente y del joven*. Washington, D.C.: Pan American Health Organization, Scientific Publication No. 549.

4. Eron, L. D., Gentry, J. H., and Schlege, P. *Reason to Hope: A Psychological Perspective on Violence and Youth*. 1994. Washington, D.C.: American Psychological Association.

5. American Academy of Pediatrics, Committee on Communications. "Media Violence." 1995. *Pediatrics*. 95: 949–51.

6. Yunes, J. 1993. "Mortalidad por causas violentas en la región de las Américas." *Bol. Of. Sanit. Panam.* 114(4): 302–16.

7. Yunes, J., and Rajs, D. "Tendencia de la Mortalidad por Causas Externas en la Población General y entre Adolescentes y Jóvenes de la Región de las Américas." *Ad. Aude Publi.*, Rio de Janeiro, 10 (Supl 1):88–125.

9 | The Epidemic of Youth Violence in the Americas

A Public Health Approach

RODRIGO GUERRERO

Introduction

Violence has been present in human societies since the beginnings of recorded history. Wars and massive genocide are part of human history, but the question of whether they are inevitable or preventable has been raised only recently.

"Identifying violence as a public health issue is a relatively new idea," wrote Surgeon General C. Everett Koop in 1985.[1] In 1992, Koop also declared that violence was a public health emergency.[2] The ministers of health of the Americas declared the prevention of violence to be a public health priority in 1993,[3] and the World Health Assembly passed a similar resolution in 1996.[4] Preventing violence is not only front-page news now, but also very high on the political agenda of city mayors and other decision makers.

Violence is no longer considered the exclusive concern of the police and the criminal justice system. Social, political, and behavioral scientists, as well as mental and public health specialists, are actively interested in this issue. The Interamerican Development Bank and the World Bank currently consider violence and insecurity to be major obstacles for development.[5]

The public health sector has recently come into the forum of violence prevention.[6] Public health concepts such as multicausality, causal complexity, and risk factor strategy, together with a practical approach to studying diseases of an unknown nature, may contribute to the study and control of violence.

The public health strategy of reducing disease by controlling its risk factors has been successfully applied in the case of cardiovascular and other diseases. In contrast to the genetic risk factor (for which little can be done at the present time), other risk factors like dietary habits, cigarette smoking, and physical exercise are susceptible to alteration by education and other means. Violence similarly has many risk factors, some of which can be manipulated to varying degrees. A successful strategy for controlling violence seems to be that of reducing its most important risk factors.

For public health purposes, violence can be broadly defined as *the use (or the threat of use) of physical force with the intent to cause harm to oneself or others.* This working definition is convenient because it facilitates the gathering of information from injury or death registries; however such registries do not track other forms of violence that may be more frequent, like psychological, sexual, or negligent violence. For example, approximately 25,000 homicides occur in the United States every year, between 1.8 and 4.0 million U.S. women are abused in their homes, and nearly 3 million U.S. children are reported abused or neglected.[7]

Violence in the Americas

Using homicides as an indicator of violence, it can be observed that the Americas is a particularly violent region. The overall rate of homicides increased from 10 to 16 per 100,000 from 1980 to 1991. Detailed analysis indicates that overall rates began to increase around 1980 for most countries, while rates for other external causes of death, like suicides and traffic accidents, either decreased or remained constant (see Table 1).

In Colombia, of the 5.5 million disability-adjusted life years (DALYs) lost during 1994, 25% were exclusively due to homicides, more than double the amount lost due to cardiovascular diseases, the second largest cause of death.[8] Other forms of nonhomicidal violence also occur frequently. In the United States, an estimated 2.9 million serious violent crimes (rapes, personal robberies, and aggravated assaults) occurred in 1990, according to the National Crime Victimization Survey.[9]

It should be noted that most of the homicidal violence in the Americas predominantly affects young males of low socioeconomic status. In some U.S. cities and some Central American countries, this is exacerbated by gang violence.

Table 1. Homicide and Traffic Accident Death Rates in the Americas Region[a] (per 100,000)

| Region | Homicide and Traffic Accident Deaths | | | |
	1980	1991	1980	1991
North America[b]	—	9.7	22.7	16.4
Latin America and the Caribbean	**12.5**	**21.3**	**17.0**	**15.5**
Latin America	12.8	21.4	17.1	15.6
Mexico	18.1	19.6	22.8	16.5
Central America	35.6	27.6	15.1	13.5
Latin Caribbean	5.1	8.8	13.2	14.7
Brazil	11.5	19.0	16.4	19.1
Andean Countries	12.1	39.5	18.3	13.2
Southern Cone	3.5	4.2	9.5	9.2
Caribbean	3.1	3.5	10.2	7.6
Whole Region	**11.4**	**16.6**	**19.4**	**15.8**

[a] Haiti and Bolivia are not included.

[b] Within North America, rates differ between Canada (2.6:100,000) and the United States (10.1:100,000).

Sources: See *Health in the Americas: Basic Indicators, 1995,* PAHO (Washington, D.C.), for aspects related to registered mortality.

See UN, *World Population Prospects, 1994* (revision), for aspects related to population.

Youth Violence

Rapid urban population change, community and family disintegration, increasing poverty (relative and absolute), and social isolation contribute to institutional failures and the consequent development of youth gangs. The interplay of social disorganization and lack of access, through legitimate means, to social resources, figure in the development of seriously deviant groups.

Gangs are loosely defined organizations that may play a role in the normal process of adolescents gaining independence and autonomy from parental authorities, and range from rather innocent street corner groups to highly criminal organizations. The gang is an extension of the family in which members frequently find values such as loyalty, honor, and comradeship. Reasons for joining gangs include a need for recognition, status, and safety in violent neighborhoods, as well as a desire for power and excitement. The pressing need for income may be an important factor moving gang members into illegal activities such as robbery, assault, and drug distribution.

Of all homicides reported in the region of the Americas, 28.7% are attributed to young people aged 10 to 19; in 10 of the 21 countries with a population greater than 1 million, homicide is the second leading cause of death for those aged 15 to 24 and one of the five leading causes of death in 17 of the same 21 countries.[10] In Colombia, homicide is the leading cause of death in adolescents and young adults.[11]

The homicide rates for U.S. males of all races increase dramatically in late adolescence and early adulthood. The combined homicide rate for males of all races aged 15 to 19 (32.8 per 100,000) is 10.3 times greater than the rate for those aged 10 to 14 (2.9 per 100,000).[12] In Cali, Colombia (a city with reliable data concerning crime and homicides), young males are the predominant victims of homicide, but at a higher order of magnitude than in the United States. The rates for females in Cali, although very high in comparison with U.S. rates, are considerably lower than those for males.[13]

Because there is little consensus on the definition of gangs or gang-related incidents, the magnitude of the gang problem may not be known reliably. In 1980, there were 286 U.S. cities with gang problems, and it was estimated that there were 2,000 gangs with approximately 100,000 members. For 1995, the corresponding estimates were 2,000 cities with problems, 25,000 gangs, and 650,000 members.[14] African-Americans (54.6%) and Hispanics (32.6%) are the most frequent ethnic groups reported to be involved in gangs.[15] Salvadoran youth deported from the United States frequently keep their original gang affiliation, for example, the "Salvatrucha" and "18th Street" gangs from Los Angeles that are operating in the capital city of San Salvador.[16] Gang activities have also been reported in many capital cities of Latin America.[17]

Los Angeles, using a broad definition of gangs, reports that between 25 and 30% of the city's homicides are gang related, while Chicago and Cali, using a more restrictive definition of gang incidents, report about 10%[18] and 5%,[19] respectively. Gang-related homicide on U.S. streets is more likely to grow out of turf violence than wars over drug markets, but drug markets indirectly influence violence by bringing rival gang members into proximity.[20]

Risk Factors for Violence

Firearms

There seems to be no doubt that the proliferation of firearms in the civilian population is associated with increased homicide rates. In the United States,

80% of youth homicides are caused by firearms, and the observed increase in youth homicides is due to firearms, since other types of homicides have remained constant.[21] Those who keep firearms in their households increase by a factor of 2.7 their risk of dying from firearm injuries.[22] Abundant firearms remaining from the armed conflict are thought to explain the very high and rising homicide rates that have occurred after peace agreements were signed in El Salvador.[23] Restricting the carrying of firearms has reduced the number of homicides in Cali[24] and Bogotá.[25]

Consumption of Alcohol and Other Drugs

The consumption of alcohol, particularly in the form of "binge drinking," has been associated with elevated homicide rates. One review of five U.S. homicide studies showed that 47 to 68% of homicide victims had been consuming alcohol,[26] and other studies have shown similar results for aggressors.[27] Blood alcohol levels above 25mg have been found in homicide victims in Colombia.[28] On the other hand, policies restricting the late-night sale of alcoholic beverages have reduced homicides in Cali and, more recently, in Bogotá.[29] The relationship between violence and the consumption of drugs other than alcohol is not well explored, but there are several studies indicating that the use of cocaine[30] and opioids[31] are also associated with violent behavior and crime.

Education and Cultural Factors

Most of the current literature points to the fact that violent behavior is a learned process that begins at the earliest stages of psychosocial development. Parental behavior and, at a later stage, teacher behavior are important milestones in determining later violent behavior. Inadequate child-rearing practices may convey to children the acceptability and desirability of violence as a normal and expected form of behavior. The role of the family, the role of the mother offering loving care from the first moments after delivery, and the role of the father have been mentioned as crucial for the prevention of youth violence.[32]

Patterson and colleagues[33] have identified children who, from very young ages, are more likely to engage in tantrums, fights, and rejection by peers. They found this group of "early starters" to be more likely to exhibit violent behavior at later stages in life.

Children may experience violence directly in the form of physical abuse or may witness neighborhood violence involving family acquaintances, which greatly heightens the emotional impact. For example, 17% of a sample of murders in Detroit in 1985 were witnessed by children, and in one-quarter of these cases, the victim was a family member.[34]

Society tends to model the response to conflict through cultural attitudes and normative beliefs. When some kind of reaction is deemed necessary in disputes, the selection of responses is influenced by attitudes toward alternative approaches to conflict resolution. When there is no credibility in the police or the legal system, the response may be to take justice into one's own hand. Different cultural values are thought to explain the differences in homicides rates between the southern and the northern parts of the United States.

Violence in the Media

By the time a typical U.S. adolescent graduates from high school, he or she will have been exposed to 18,000 murders and 800 suicides on the television screen. For the American Psychological Association, there is no doubt that violence in the media stimulates violent behavior, particularly in the young.[35] Media violence is a risk factor for violent behavior at least in young children. The media can also teach that violence is a normal way of solving conflicts and also contribute to desensitizing children to violent acts. The recent killing of a rap entertainer brought attention to the violence-stimulating role of some of the lyrics and music to which youngsters are exposed.

There are ways in which emotions such as anxiety and anger can be adequately portrayed in the media without stimulating violence, and violence in the news, if properly framed, need not stimulate violent behavior.[36]

Violence Prevention: Successful Strategies

Of the many attempts to cope with the problem of juvenile crime and delinquency, unfortunately very few have been adequately evaluated. In addition to the difficulty of evaluating social interventions, most interventions were not designed to be evaluated, but rather were the result of pressing needs. Fortunately there are enough programs that have been evaluated and have a sound scientific basis to allow for interventions.

In general, successful programs involve a combination of prevention, intervention, and repression strategies. Successful programs must take into account that juvenile violence occurs in a broader social context, and that there are no isolated solutions to this problem. As a rule, interventions must be multisectoral and require considerable coordinating skills between agencies. The success of intervention efforts may be limited if society continues to accept violence and aggression in certain contexts or continues to view violence as a reasonable response to conflict. The role of violence in the media, availability of firearms, acceptance of any forms of prejudice and racism, and lack of faith in the judiciary and police systems have been identified as societal risk factors for violence.[37]

A partnership between police and community is important in reducing youth violence. In the city of Bogotá, Colombia, police officers have been trained in community policing and human rights as part of a larger effort to reduce crime.[38] The continuum from youngsters "hanging out" on a street corner to hard core criminal gangs must be borne in mind. This is of particular importance to the police authorities, who are frequently misled by the similar external appearance (color, signs, dress codes, etc.) of these groups.

Effective preventive interventions must begin early in childhood. Some of the most promising programs are interventions designed to assist and educate families who are at risk, even before a child is born.[39] Evidence indicates that early childhood interventions can reduce aggressive and antisocial behavior, and also contribute to prevent other risk factors associated with antisocial behaviors, such as low educational achievement and inconsistent and inappropriate parenting practices.

Usually, aggression is just one of a set of problem behaviors, and preventive programs must address the needs of the child in everyday social contexts: family, school, peer group, media viewing, and community. Since aggressive children have been found to be less creative in finding nonviolent solutions to conflictive situations and more prone to attribute hostile intentions to others in ambiguous situations, a cognitive mediation training intervention has been found to positively affect the behavior of such youngsters.[40]

Intervention strategies require intensive personal interaction with the young, equivalent to a "reparenting" experience, like the one carried out by Father Gregory Doyle at Mission Dolores in Los Angeles.[41] Income-generating activities and special schooling opportunities for gang members have also been shown to be of extraordinary value.[42] Peer involvement in the rehabilitation of gangs also seems useful, as shown by the experience of Hommies Unidos in El Salvador or the group Los Especiales in Bogotá, Colombia.[43] Another example of this approach is the Gang Violence Reduction Project in East Los Angeles, which employs gang members to mediate between gangs whose rivalries may result in violence.[44]

An integral component of the problems of juvenile violence, in addition to prevention and intervention, is the punishment of those who have transgressed the law. Correctional interventions or repression is also needed, but in the case of juvenile violence, special efforts have to be made to incorporate rehabilitation. Different methods of social control like probation and surveillance should be attempted in conjunction with incarceration. Handling juvenile criminals in traditional adult jails has shown to be of little or no value. Because ethnic minorities make up a large proportion of juvenile delinquents, the importance of cultural sensitivity must be emphasized.

NOTES

1. Koop, C. E. 1989. *Injury Prevention: Meeting the Challenge.* A report of the National Committee for Injury Prevention and Control. Oxford University Press, Oxford.

2. Koop, C. E., and Lundeberg, G. D. "Violence in America: A Public Health Emergency—Time to Bite the Bullet Back." *JAMA* 267: 3075–6.

3. PAHO (Pan American Health Organization). Resolution 19, approved by the 37th Meeting of the Directing Council. Washington, D.C.

4. WHO (World Health Organization), Resolution WHA49.25, approved by the 49th World Health Assembly, May 25, 1996. Geneva.

5. See, e.g., Ratinoff, L. (ed.) 1996. "Toward an Integrated Approach to Development: Ethics, Violence and Citizen Safety." Report of colloquium held at the Interamerican Development Bank, February 16–17, Washington, D.C.; Londono, J.L. 1996, "Violence, Psychics and Social Capital," and Guerrero, R. 1996, "Epidemiology of Violence: The Colombian Case," papers presented at the Second Annual Conference of the World Bank for the Development of Latin America and the Caribbean, Bogotá, Colombia, June 30–July 2; and World Bank 1997, "Crime and Violence as Development Issues in Latin America and the Caribbean," presented at the seminar The Challenge of Urban Criminal Violence, Interamerican Development Bank, Rio de Janeiro, March 2–4.

6. Foege, W. H., Rosenberg, M. L., and Mercy, J. A. 1995. "Public Health and Violence Prevention." *Current Issues in Public Health*, 1: 2–9.

7. Hofford, M., and Harrell, A.V. 1993. *Family Violence: Interventions for the Justice System*—Program Brief. Office of Justice Programs, U.S. Department of Justice, Washington, D.C.

8. Ministerio de Salud. 1994. "La carga de la enfermedad en Colombia." Ministerio de Salud, República de Colombia, Bogotá, Colombia.

9. Roth, J.A. 1994. "Understanding and Preventing Violence. National Institute of Justice." Research brief, U.S. Department of Justice, National Institute of Justice, Washington, D.C. (February).

10. Yunes, J., and Zubarew, T. 1997. "Mortality from Violent Causes in Adolescents and Young People: A Challenge for the Region of the Americas." Paper sent for publication.

11. PAHO. 1990. "Health Conditions in the Americas," 1: 210–11. Washington, D.C.

12. National Adolescent Health Information Center. 1995. "Fact Sheet on Adolescent Homicide." Division of Adolescent Medicine and Institute for Health Policy Studies, University of California, San Francisco, Calif.

13. Espitia, V. E., Concha A., and Guerrero, R. 1995. "Patterns of Homicide in Cali, Colombia," *MMWR* 44: 734–7.

14. Office of Juvenile Justice and Delinquency. 1997. "Youth Gangs in America." OJJDP National Satellite Teleconference, March 21.

15. Spergel, I., Curry, D., Chance, R., et al. 1994. *Gang Suppression and Intervention: Problem and Response.* Office of Justice Programs, U.S. Department of Justice, Washington, D.C.

16. Report from El Salvadoran authorities at a meeting on gang related violence, organized by the Pan American Health Organization, San Salvador, May 7–9, 1997.

17. Concha-Eastman, A., Carrión, F., and Cobo, G. (eds.) 1994. *Ciudad y violencias en América Latina.* Programa de Gestión Urbana PGU. (Series Gestión Urbana, Vol. 2). Quito, Ecuador.

18. Spergel, I., et al., op. cit., n.15.

19. Espitia, V. E. 1997. *Muertes violentas en Cali., 1993–1996.* Secretaría de Gobierno Convivencia y Seguridad de Cali. Alcaldía de Santiago de Cali.

20. Illinois Criminal Justice Information Authority. 1996. *Street Gangs and Crime: Patterns and Trends in Chicago.* Chicago, Ill. (February).

21. Carter Center. 1994. *Not Even One.* Report of the Carter Center Consultation on the Crisis of Children and Firearms., Atlanta, Ga.

22. Kellerman, A. L., Rivara, F. P., Rushford, N. B. Banton, J. G. et al. 1993. "Gun Ownership as a Risk Factor for Homicide in the Home." *NEJM* 329: 1084–91.

23. Cruz, J. M. 1997. Presentation made at the meeting on gang related violence, organized by the Pan-American Health Organization, El Salvador, May 7–9.

24. Villaveces, A., Espitia, V. E., and Kellermann, A. 1994. "Effect of a Disarmament Strategy on Homicides in Cali, Colombia." Paper sent for publication.

25. Centro de Referencia Nacional sobre Violencia. 1996. "Evaluación de la efectividad de las medidas de control adoptadas en Santafé de Bogotá en 1995." *Boletín CRNV* 6 (January). Instituto Nacional de Medicina Legal y Ciencias Forenses, Bogotá.

26. Pernanen, K. 1991. *Alcohol in Human Violence.* Guilford, New York.

27. Wiesczorek, W. F., Welte, J. W., and Abel, E. L. 1990. "Alcohol, Drugs and Murder: A Study of Convicted Homicide Offenders." *Journal of Criminal Justice* 18(3): 217–27.

28. Mora, R., Sánchez, M. D., Suarez, G. I., and Hernández, W. H. 1994. "Reporte del comportamiento de las lesiones fatales en Colombia, 1994." Centro de Referencia Nacional sobre Violencia, Instituto Nacional de Medicina Legal y Ciencias Forenses, Bogotá.

29. Centro de Referencia Nacional sobre Violencia, op. cit., n. 25.

30. Hanzlick, R., and Gowitt, G. T. 1991. "Cocaine Metabolite Detection in Homicide Victims." *JAMA* 265(6): 760–1.

31. Hammersley, R., Forsyth, A., Morrison, V., and Davies, J. B. "Relationship between Crime and Opioid Use." *British Journal of Addiction* 84(9): 1029–43.

32. Prothrow-Stith, D., and Weissman, M. 1991. *Deadly Consequences: How Violence Is Destroying Our Teenage Population and a Plan to Begin Solving the Problem.* HarperCollins, New York.

33. Patterson, G. R., Capaldi, D., and Bank, L. 1991. "An Early Starter Model for Predicting Delinquency," in Peppler, D., and Rubin, K. H., *The Development and Treatment of Childhood Aggression.* Earlbaum, Hillsdale, N.J.

34. Batchelow and Wicks. 1985. quoted in Slaby, R. G., Roedell, W. C., Arezzo, D., and Hendrix, K. 1995. *Early Violence Prevention.* National Association for the Education of Young Children, Washington, D.C.

35. Donnerstein, E., Slaby, R. G., and Eron, L. D. 1994. "The Mass Media and Youth Aggression," in *Reason to Hope: A Psychological Perspective on Violence and Youth.* American Psychological Association, Washington, D.C.

36. PAHO, paper presented at the conference Prevention of Violence: Creative Media Opportunities. Cartagena, Colombia.

37. PAHO. 1996. *Study on Attitudes and Cultural Norms Related to Violence.* ACTIVA study. Washington, D.C.

38. Acero, H. 1997. "Alcaldía de Santafé de Bogotá." Paper prepared for the Interamerican Development Bank, Washington, D.C.

39. American Psychological Association. 1993. *Report of the Commission on Violence and Youth.* Vol. 1. American Psychological Association, Washington, D.C.

40. Guerra, N. G., and Slaby, R. G. 1990. "Cognitive Mediators of Aggression in Adolescent Offenders." *Developmental Psychology* 26(2): 269–77.

41. Boyle, G. 1997. "An Alternative Approach to Juvenile Gang Violence." Paper presented at the conference on Juvenile violence, organized by the Pan-American Health Organization, San Salvador, El Salvador (May).

42. Concha-Eastman, A., Carrión, F., and Cobo, G. (eds.), op. cit., n.17.

43. The experience of Hommies Unidos and Los Especiales was presented at the Juvenile Gang Violence Conference held in El Salvador.

44. Goldstein, A. P., and Huff, C. R. (eds.). 1993. *The Gang Intervention Handbook*. Research Press, Champaign, Ill.

B | Child Labor

10 Child Work and Education in Latin America

MARÍA CRISTINA SALAZAR

Overview

This chapter addresses the relationship between child work and education in Brazil, Colombia, Ecuador, Guatemala, and Peru, countries that aspire — with others in the region — to balanced, equitable, and sustainable development, with benefits that should be widely shared.[1] Unfortunately, economic growth in the region has too often resulted in maldistribution of the means and fruits of development between and among classes and between cities and countrysides, and natural resources have been pilfered. Only too late is it recognized that the stability arising from a more balanced and equitable development is important for general social progress. For example, a strategy for alleviating rural poverty and fostering rural economic growth must confront a history of neglect that has led to extreme poverty and the marginalization as well as exploitation of children, as shown in many studies since 1990.[2]

The lack of attention to education by most Latin American governments has limited the region's capacity to compete in international markets, where comparative advantages are increasingly defined by productivity based on scientific and technological advances. As is known, the high concentration of income in this region of the world is a result of traditional discriminatory patterns of property ownership combined with the decline of the labor market and levels of remuneration, the regressive nature of the tax structure, and the rapid impairment—even elimination—of social services. Social polarization has increased in recent years, with the middle classes suffering heavy losses.

The informal labor sector has expanded. Four out of every five new jobs generated from 1990 to 1992 were located in this sector, where many working children are concentrated. Women suffer with particular intensity this degradation of employment. The adoption of "labor flexibility" policies, the decomposition of complex processes into simple operations, and the more frequent use of individual versus collective contracts have contributed to maintain wages at very low levels (Vidich 1994).

During the 1980s, those living in poverty in Latin America and the Caribbean increased by 60 million, reaching about 200 million people. The region produced poor people at twice the rate of total population growth. Urbanization of poverty accelerated essentially in response to faulty government policies. Moreover, concerning child work, which is concentrated mainly in the region's rural areas, some striking facts related to rural poverty have to be recalled:

- In 6 countries the rural population still makes up over half the national total.

- The majority of the poor, including many Blacks and Indians, live rurally in at least 12 countries.

- In all countries the majority of the people in the poorest deciles, that is, the poorest 10%, live rurally (Valdes & Wiens 1996).

These unfavorable statistics have severe consequences for politics and the consolidation of democratic regimes. States devote very few resources to creating conditions that would allow the poor to participate in national and/or world development, that is, for democracy to flourish. The idea that a country should belong to all its citizens is not defensible when there is ample evidence that it is owned or controlled by only a few.

The world of poverty in which so many children live and work is the setting of police violence and impunity, the denial of justice, the greatest violations of human rights, ethnic and gender discrimination, and everyday insecurity. The sheer necessity of solving the problems of daily survival reduces the scope of rationality to immediate demands. The possibility of achieving self-determination, which is a central ingredient in the concept of responsible citizenship, cannot be seriously pursued.

However, throughout the region there is now a new awareness of the consequences that hazardous work and working while still young bring to millions of children.[3] Governments and civil society have started to respond to this problem with better-focused social policies and programs, many of them inspired by the 1989 UN Convention on the Rights of the Child (CRC).

Distribution, Extension, and Characteristics of Child Work

International Labor Office (ILO) figures indicate that there are around 17 million child workers in the region between ages 6 and 18 (Tokman 1997). That is, around 20% of the children in this age group are workers; around half of them work full time and the work of younger children (under age 12) is widespread.

In Guatemala, for example, 27% of child workers are age 7 to 12. In Ecuador, 12% of the economically active children are age 10 or 11. In Peru, 16% are age 6 to 11. In rural Colombia, 1 out of 3 children age 10 to 11, and 1 of every 4 children age 6 to 9, work in secondary activities.[4] In large Colombian cities, 1 out of 6 children age 10 to 11, and 1 of every 10 children age 6 to 9, participate in the labor market (Flórez, Knaul, & Méndez 1995: 108). However, in the region the work of those under age 12 is less than that of the child workers age 15 to 17.

The most visible of these are the street children who work as ragpickers and vendors, children in small industrial workshops and service establishments, and a few (almost always over age 14) in formally constituted businesses, while a majority perform heavy agricultural work and are exposed to the hazards associated with modern machinery and chemicals. Hundreds of thousands of very young girls are concentrated in services, particularly in domestic service. Many working boys and girls are invisible to society, the government, and the labor unions. They do not even know their rights.

Rural Child Work

The traditional work of some children in agriculture supports a precarious family subsistence; other children are involved in commercial export-oriented plantations (raising coffee, fruits, flowers, sugarcane). In Guatemala, for example, 65% of child workers engage in agriculture; more Indian than non-Indian children are involved in this type of work. In Ecuador and Peru, 48 and 40% of the child workers, respectively, also engage in agriculture. These proportions are even higher for Brazil (78%) and Colombia (82% of male children and 36% of female children). All these children belong to poor rural families.

The rural poor tend to be less educated and have larger families and higher dependency ratios, as well as less access to services and worse health indicators than those who are not poor. For example, illiteracy rates among rural children over age 15 are still extraordinarily high in several countries, such as Guatemala and Brazil. Overall, the illiteracy rate in rural areas is two to six times that in urban areas. On average, rural children attend school three years less than urban children. As well, poor rural and urban children attend school three years less than those who are not poor. The differences are not as evident for primary schooling, but the already low average rates of completing secondary school are even lower for the rural poor. In addition to supply factors (availability and quality of schools), these patterns may also reflect demand factors: where children work on the farm or, indeed, as wage laborers, the opportunity cost of sending a teenager to school—not to mention school fees and living expenses—since secondary students must often board in town—is considerably higher than that in urban areas (Valdes & Wien 1996: 5).

The poor tend to be found in areas that are agriculturally marginal in the absence of such improvements as fertilizing, leveling of land, or irrigation. In the case of indigenous peoples, the historical loss of their most fertile lands and water rights to conquerors and usurpers is well known. The rural poor often lack access to adequate roads, potable water, electricity, communications, secondary schools, public health services, and other developments. In this respect, their standard of living compares quite unfavorably with the urban poor.

Most of the rural poor, to a greater or lesser extent, supplement farm income with earnings off the farm. Usually one or more household members migrate during part or all of the year to earn income as wage laborers, either for commercial farmers or as casual laborers or domestic servants in the cities. Households may have sidelines in petty commerce, handicrafts, or services, where many of the children work. Nonagricultural or off-farm earnings may account for an important proportion of cash earnings.

In rural areas children as young as age 5 help their parents in tending flocks of small animals; they also participate in off-farm activities and, as they advance in age, assume other tasks during planting and harvesting. As they reach adolescence, the work they do becomes more differentiated according to gender. Boys take charge of the tasks that require greater physical effort, while girls concentrate their attention in the domestic sphere and give less attention to tasks directly related to production.[5]

The working population of children includes substantially more boys than girls. However, the picture changes when taking into account domestic work performed by adolescent girls, both in and outside their own home. Many more girls than boys are dedicated exclusively to household jobs. This is an important fact to consider, for those who work do not attend school. It can be assumed that household jobs are carried out on a full time basis.

The figures mentioned earlier and several case studies analyzed for this book point to a change in purpose as the most significant transformation in child work during the past 20 or 30 years. Formerly an essentially socializing activity intended to impart skills, child work has become a way to earn income for the family.

This change has altered the meaning of child work, which has always been associated with poverty. A distinction should be made between market-oriented productive labor and nonmarket domestic labor. Furthermore, access to schooling has been limited. As a result, work was seen as a "natural" and highly valued part of children's socialization. On the other hand, the demands of a developing urban market economy and greater access to and need for schooling have put work at odds with education. The need for schooling, the impossibility of eliminating child work as a direct or indirect source of income, and consumerism exert an enormous influence on poor children by making them parties to economic input. The increase in self-employed workers to the detriment of unpaid family workers and the decline in agricultural workers in favor of those in other areas of activity reflect this influence. Thus, unpaid family work and farm production for self-subsistence continue to be part of the socialization process for many children.

The presence or absence of an Indian population is one of the basic regional differences, and the use of native languages is one of its identifying features. According to data for Ecuador, labor participation rates among children who speak a native language (Quichua or Shuar) are higher than for the rest of the population. The labor participation rate is 34.6% among the Spanish-speaking population 89.1% for those who speak a native language or are bilingual. This is even higher than the labor rate in the rural sector (58.7%).

In all the region's countries, the percentage of urban and rural boys who work exclusively at household jobs has remained low and stable, while the participation of rural girls in such activities has declined significantly. Figures on urban girls who work exclusively at household jobs reflect a downward trend similar to that observed among all working girls.

Children have more job stability in rural areas than in cities. For example, in Ecuador, 77% of the boys and 86% of the girls living and working in the countryside say their work is permanent. This is explained of course by the predominance of agricultural employment.

In the urban area, job stability varies with age. The youngest children have fewer stable jobs than older children, although the difference is not that great. There is almost no such difference in rural areas, and a larger percentage of permanent employees is found among the youngest children. Clearly, the burden of economic adjustment continues to fall on the poorest members of society. In most countries, the few social programs created by governments to make amends for this situation have done little or nothing to alter circumstances for the most vulnerable groups.

Cultural Factors

Child work is also influenced by cultural factors. In rural areas there is no discrimination between market-oriented and domestic labor, according to Western standards. Neither time nor space separates the two. Both are part of the child's rights and responsibilities. Peasant children begin their working life at a very early age. Education does not take place separate from work; both converge in a single process. Work is an important vehicle for conveying knowledge about the environment and society. The standards and pace of this instruction are established culturally to ensure development suited to the traditional environment. Consequently, at a very young age, children begin to "help" their parents with both household chores and market-oriented activities. This is considered part of the process of learning to work and becoming familiar with rules for harmonious social relations. The conflict between education and work begins when the school is seen as a specialized institution of learning. Moreover, criteria on when childhood ends vary according to social class and culture. Rural people are likely to consider a 15-year-old boy or girl an adult and, therefore, a person who is made to work. Premodern notions of infancy are accentuated, particularly in rural areas, where boys and girls are simply considered "mini-adults." In these cases, children are burdened with chores since these are thought to form part of their role.

Parents also defend child work as instructive. They say it teaches children to be responsible, to appreciate the value of things and the effort required to obtain them. On the other hand, many believe it enables the young to learn an occupation or trade with which to support themselves as adults. The instructive nature of work is particularly evident in the case of indolent boys who disobey rules at home, do not attend school, and may be in danger of becoming gang members. Parents see work as a way to reverse this trend. In these cases, the value of productive activity on character formation is more important than any income to be earned.

The underlying conception seems to be that all family members are economic providers and that undertaking this responsibility prepares children for their future roles as adults. All Latin American countries have forms of production in which the family acts as an economic unit and children's labor participation is accepted. Parents justify child work by saying that it contributes to children's responsibility, autonomy, and strength to endure difficulties and sacrifices. Work is seen as a protection against vice and indolence, which lead to delinquency. Very little value is attached to children's play and leisure, which are seen by most parents as a waste of time.

Perceptions about schooling are ambiguous. Parents appreciate the possibility for children to learn how to read and write, but some peasant parents regard education as irrelevant. When school and labor schedules conflict, parents tend to give more importance to work, which has immediate benefits for the subsistence of the family. Many parents are afraid of schools because children may there learn how to rebel against the family's traditions and norms. Others fear that children will learn bad habits. On the other hand, some parents see children's work as a solution to their problems with poor school performance: if children are not successful in school, it is better to put them to work than to have them at home doing nothing. School performance is related to a variety of factors, all of which become more prevalent as family poverty increases. However, even in families that are not poor, performance is a powerful reason for parents to take children out of school and to put them to work, or for children themselves to reach this decision. Considering the large number of children who repeat a grade, particularly in urban areas, this can be considered one of the causes explaining a significant proportion of child work.

Parents also attribute child work to the need for income or labor, to socialization, and to the building of identity (García & Hernández 1992). It is often defined as a strategy for survival, that is, as a way for families to compensate for insufficient income. In this respect, it is important to recall that child work resolves two related but not necessarily equal family problems: the need for monetary income and the need for labor. In the first case, children work as wage earners and, in the second as paid or unpaid family workers.

Parents believe that full-time, paid employment is acceptable for boys, but only occasionally so for girls. Reasons for this view include first of all the perception of girls' roles, which are associated more with household activities than with remunerative labor. Of course, many girls over age 12 are responsible for most household chores, and in some families their role as collaborators in household maintenance is irreplaceable. Second, it is felt that girls are more vulnerable than boys and, therefore, should be protected from exposure to job-related risks. And third, the labor market offers more opportunities for boys. Education is viewed as girls' only possibility for entering the labor market under decent conditions.[6] In other cases, parents encourage children to enter the working world as a way to continue their studies; children's income is used to pay their school expenses (uniforms, supplies, transportation, and food). If these expenses cannot be paid, children are forced to leave school.

Child work also creates problems for parents. The poor place their hopes for social mobility in the possibility of new generations gaining a better position in society. Most people still believe this depends on education or instruction. Parents are clear about the fact that work hampers and eventually prevents children from studying. They may also know of its negative repercussions on health, safety, and morals.

Just as trends toward concentration and dispersion exist in domestic units, relations between parents and their children revolve around issues of dependence and independence. Dependency refers not only to the psychological processes of personality building, but to a pattern of social relations that places family interests above personal ones. One of the objectives of children's socialization is the building of a family identity rather than an individual identity. Independence is expressed when children begin to work outside the family environment, since their employment is a potential source of conflict between individual and collective interests. Parents want children to respond to family perspectives and needs, but the work environment and use of income from employment may prompt children to adopt an attitude contrary to the interests of the family unit, as expressed in what their parents want. The split between generations is a difference in the perspectives that lend meaning to personal values and practices (García & Hernández 1992:80).

There is little information on working children's perceptions regarding their work, which would relate to family, school, personal independence, and identity. For many, work is part of their function within the family. The child has to work in order to belong to the family; work is not an option but an obligation. Work may also be seen as a way to escape from a family milieu that is too restrictive or repressive. Personal independence may be the result gained by some children who work, and it may even lead to their leaving home. Finally, work may be a way to build up an identity and strengthen children's self-esteem, particularly concerning skills that are passed on within the family from one generation to another.

For some children, working is an alternative to schooling. If school is seen as useless, work is regarded positively by many children. Perceived school performance is perhaps the most important factor in children's positive perceptions of education. Aptitude for academic work is a factor that parents take into account when deciding whether or not a child should go to school and, if so, to what extent. Sooner or later, children who fail in school are compelled to work. In reality, they have no other option.

Employers also think that they are helping children by giving them work at an early age, a fact that leads them to think that there is no reason for them to pay a just price for such work. The attitude that work "saves" children tends to legitimize the work of poor children. It makes eradicating child work difficult by shifting the discussion from the sphere of the rights of citizens and placing it in the sphere of ideology or philanthropy, thus concealing the buying–selling relationship within the labor market, as well as the employer–employee relation (Rodríguez 1996).

Demographic variables associated with the early incorporation of children into the labor market vary across countries. There is a relatively greater impoverishment of Brazilian households headed by women alone and a larger probability that their children will drop out of school and go to work. In Guatemalan households headed by women, children who do not study drop out of school and may be concentrated in domestic activities in their homes. Also, rural schools are sometimes located far away from homes, making it more difficult for children to attend school.

Child Work and Poverty

While poverty is always a necessary factor in the work of children, additional cultural and demographic traits are also relevant. They clearly explain why only a limited sector of poor families send their very young children to work. We cannot say that child work is a determining factor in the intergenerational transmission of poverty, but it does maintain poverty levels for some social groups. We know that early entry into the labor market contributes to the future poverty of child workers. There is a negative correlation between family income and child labor participation: the lower the family per capita income, the larger the proportion of children who say that they work to add income to the family budget.

The working world of children and adolescents is heterogeneous, as are the reasons why they work. However, the notion that these children work due to paternal irresponsibility still exists in nonprofessional circles. From such a perspective, the cause of child work would be lazy fathers who use their children's labor. However, this would incorrectly mean that the exploitation or irresponsibility would lie exclusively on the side of the poor and that middle-class and wealthy fathers would not be irresponsible and, therefore, their children would not work. Of course, this is not true. For example, statistics have shown that some children who work come from families above the poverty line. In this sense, the data for Peru are interesting: 30% of working children and adolescents belong to families that are not poor. This does not mean that children of the upper classes usually work. They do not. These data point out the reality of middle-class working families.

Child Work and Gender

As stated earlier, gender is an important variable in child work: more males than females are in the child labor force. The information from Guatemala shows that 84% of workers age 7 to 17 are males. In Ecuador 64% of workers age 10 to 14 are male. In Brazil 63% of workers age 10 to 14 are male. The same pattern is seen in Colombia and Peru.

Nevertheless, the participation of girls, especially those under age 12, is underestimated, since they usually work in their own homes and are not registered as workers, although it is presumed that in doing such work girls have dropped out of school and work excessive hours. In some countries, a significant percentage of girls under age 18 "do not work and do not study." This group is largely composed of girls who stay at home while their parents go out to work. The basic problem is that exhausting participation in domestic chores in their own homes violates the basic rights of children. Despite this fact, official statistics in general still do not consider such domestic roles as work.

Consequently, a large percentage of girls have a double workload. They work outside the home, but they also do domestic chores upon returning to their own homes. If the 21 hours that Guatemalan girls dedicate to household chores are added to their average 40-hour work week, a total workload of 61 hours per week is obtained.

Data from a Brazilian study are important. In comparing groups of girls "who do not work" with those "who do work," school attendance is more important among the former. In summary, we find that domestic work by girls in their own homes seems to be more widespread than was thought.

Economic Contribution of Children

The work of children is hardly ever an individual strategy; it is rather framed within the family economy and takes place in a variety of modalities. The most common employment is nonpaid domestic work in their own homes (which frees adults, essentially mothers, to find paid jobs.) This type of work is most detrimental to girls, who then do not have the time to attend school and/or to do their homework.

In some cases children work for wages to supplement family income or use their wages to buy goods that their parents would otherwise have to purchase, such as school books, clothing, and food. In many cases there is a combination of both modalities.

This diversity of visible and invisible links with the family budget makes it extremely difficult to estimate children's and adolescents' contribution to the family economy. In contrast to children (under age 12), older children usually hand over more money to their family. When younger children work close to or with their parents, they usually receive only a tip for their work, and sometimes no type of recompense at all. As they grow up they acquire more autonomy and direct pay begins to be more important. Therefore, it is with older working children that direct contribution to the family economy becomes visible.

In Colombia, the contribution of child work to families does not seem to be significant. A Peruvian study shows that the monetary contribution of early childhood work accounts for 10% of total income among the poor families of Lima. Data from Guatemala indicate that children's contribution reaches 15% of the budget in poor and indigent families. In Brazil, children's economic contribution becomes significant to the degree that families descend into deeper levels of poverty.

Some analysts have tried to justify the presence of child work by claiming that, without it, families simply would not be able to subsist. It seems that this effect is being overestimated. This point requires reliable surveys on family income and disaggregated data according to age groups. Since this information is not available, the only statement that can be made with some certainty is that the magnitude of monetary contribution is linked to age. But we do not know whether this contribution is vital to the immediate subsistence of poor families. Because the income from children's work is so low, in most of Latin American countries it represents only half the income of wage earners age 35 to 54 who have little formal education, that is, about 7 years of school (CEPAL 1995).

In some cases, as in southern Brazil and Chile, a large proportion of children keep their earnings for themselves (Salazar & Gárate 1996). But we must recall that the work of children is basically categorized as "nonpaid family work"; in Ecuador and Peru, respectively, 57 and 44% of children who work are nonpaid family workers. In Colombia, 44.2% of workers age 12 to 13 and 26.8% of those age 14 to 17 are nonpaid family workers (Flórez et al. 1995 Table 8.1).

Hazardous Work

Many of the activities that children carry out are dangerous to their health and development. Children have to face long working hours, filth, and non-functional rest facilities, as well as malnutrition and harsh climates. Examples of such hazardous work have been documented throughout the region: in agriculture, weeding, cutting, loading, and spraying chemicals; in construction, digging earth, mixing mud in brickmaking, shoveling sand and cement, and carrying loads; in Brazil, making charcoal; in Colombia and Peru, mining gold and coal; and in many countries of the region in street trades such as hawking goods and rag picking. In Guatemala and Colombia, fireworks manufacturing is another dangerous activity involving many children. However, other potentially hazardous activities such as domestic work have not been studied. All these occupations impede attendance and performance at school and they should be eradicated for all children under age 18, as stated in national laws. But legislation refers mainly to formal employment, whereas child workers operate mainly in the informal sector and do family work for which there are no specific laws (Nieuwenhuys 1996). Moreover, in all countries of the region it is recognized that enforcement measures are lacking.

From a physical and psychological standpoint, extremely hazardous employment deserves special treatment. Domestic service can entail serious psychological risks for girls and boys who work as servants, including discrimination, isolation, and disdain. Frequently, they are locked in and not paid appropriately, which resemble conditions of slavery. Little reliable information is available on this occupation, owing to the difficulty of reaching girls at home or on the job. In many Latin American countries, this type of work is believed to be on the increase. Girls employed as maids live among adults who show little or no affection and regard them as inferior. They work long days under various kinds of pressure and are virtually isolated from their families and friends. In Colombia, Knaul (1995) found that girls under age 15 who are employed as domestics work an average of 50 hours a week. Evidence points to the physical, mental, and sexual abuse of girls who work in homes other than their own. All this is damaging to their self-esteem and may lead to depression.

Child Work and Education

In recent years many studies have pointed out that education and child work tend to be mutually exclusive. This relationship especially affects the poorest population. Dropping out of school, repeating grades, having low academic achievement, being overage students, and failing in school characterize working children. There continue to be many children who never go to school.

There is a clear relationship between the labor activities of children and their school attendance. Nonworking children attend school in higher proportions than working children. In Ecuador, for example, these proportions are 89 and 58%, respectively, and half of the urban working children work 30 or more hours per week, which means that they do not attend school, frequently miss school, or have low performance rates as indicated in home surveys. Of those who attend school, even though working 30 or more hours per week, their teachers comment on the difficulties that impede their academic performance.

Some studies indicate that school performance varies according to the number of hours worked, age, quality of teaching, and the value that both parents and children attribute to education. For Ecuador, it is known that girls working as domestics and boys working in construction hardly ever attend school.

Throughout the region, the majority of working children attend public schools, although about one-third of them are in private schools, often sponsored by religious groups. The quality of the latter is considered by many parents to be better than that of public education. The money earned by the children is often used to pay school registration and other education costs.

Preschool: Off to a Good Start?

Preschool education exists in all the countries of the region, although its availability is low: only 14% of the preschool-age population attends such schooling and there is great inequality of opportunities. Coverage ranges between a meager 7% in Central America and 32% in the English-speaking Caribbean countries. Greater opportunities for preschool attendance exist in urban areas, favoring the middle and upper classes; children of working-class families are typically excluded. Facilities do not exist in rural areas where the greatest number of working children are concentrated, nor do they extend to indigenous groups. In some countries, including Colombia and Guatemala, privately sponsored preschool education exceeds the public offering, once again privileging higher-income groups. Failure to get off to a good educational start in preschool increases disadvantaged children's chances of later failure, grade repetition, and dropping out of school. Greater attention to more equitable, accessible, and adequate preschool education constitutes an indispensable basis for improving primary education (UNICEF 1992b).

Primary School: Still a Long Way to Go

The high correlation between national investment in primary education and economic growth is well known. A recent evaluation undertaken in 14 countries in Latin America and the Caribbean demonstrated that the average rate of social return on primary education surpassed 17% (BID 1993). Although governments have recognized the importance of investing in education, the allocation of economic and human resources is still inadequate, as are education policies. Studies have shown that the academic quality of primary schools is poor (inferior to that found in many Asian nations), the school day is short (4–5 hours, often less than $3^{1}/_{2}$ hours in many urban schools), the actual number of days of school (often as few as 120) does not correspond to the official calendar (180 days),[7] and textbook provision remains grossly inadequate.

Relatively high coverage has been achieved at the primary school level in Latin America as a result of policies instituted since the 1950s to promote the expansion of the school system. According to the latest available data, most countries of the region have succeeded in making primary school accessible to nearly all school-age boys and girls: on average, 92% of children enroll in primary school at some point during the school period (UNICEF 1992b). An estimated 20%, however, begin school late in relation to the entrance age set for each country. Sharp differences in both enrollment and attendance also persist according to family income level and urban versus rural location. In only four countries of the region (El Salvador, Guatemala, Haiti, and Nicaragua) enrollment rates continue to fall below 80%. In countries with large indigenous populations, like Ecuador, Guatemala, and Peru, enrollment is lower for the children of these groups. On a more positive note, differences by gender have diminished.

Limitations rooted in the failure to achieve more efficient uses of available capacity explain to some extent the shortcomings of providing universal primary school education. UNICEF (1992b) calculations estimate that enrollment rates for the six years of primary school education reach 108%, thus indicating that almost all countries of Latin America already have sufficient capacity to respond to the demand for primary school education among the school-age population.

Failing: Children or the System?

If the school systems of Latin America are examined on the basis of outcomes, it is hard to avoid the conclusion that they are failing. Analysts refer to the "failed" school, and educational indexes explain why: grade repetition rates continue to be high, starting in the first years of primary school, academic levels continue to be low, and an alarmingly large number of children continue to give up on school, deserting the classrooms even though they have not—or perhaps because they have not—acquired the necessary skills to assure them a reasonable job and livelihood.

A review of the literature on factors affecting primary school achievement in Latin America and the Caribbean shows that urban, non-coeducational and full-time schools tend to obtain the best results. In schools that have a double schedule, "The students attending the morning program tend to be better, perhaps due to the fact that students from lower-income families work in the morning and attend school in the afternoon."

Studies and evaluations undertaken by the World Bank and other institutions emphasize the poor quality of the school system as children's main barrier to acquiring a useful education in Latin America. Inadequate management capability, lack of efficiency, unequal access, and insufficient resource allocations are some of the factors that combine to make school irrelevant to many children. The outcome is that Latin American workers have an average of 5.2 years of formal education, falling short of the compulsory level of schooling by 2 or more years. There is thus a pressing need to examine the problem of child work from the perspective of how work impedes school attendance, but also from the perspective of how Latin American schools fail to satisfy the needs, demands, and expectations of students and their families.

Research findings for the seven principal cities of Colombia, based on the opinions of working children themselves, established that the severe limitations of school constitute the main cause for dropping out; only 2% of the children who were questioned mentioned work as the reason. The need to work, however, does become a more decisive factor for older children: it was found that dropping out of secondary school was due to the need to work for 21% of male and 11% of female students, although it is worth pointing out that 40% of the boys and 18% of the girls did not want to stay in school—statistics that once again point all too clearly to the poor quality of secondary schools.[8]

In Guatemala, a 1994 survey of 600 children who had left school showed that their decision to drop out was based on deficiencies of the school (irresponsible teachers, insufficient resources, uselessness of curricula; 40%), economic motives (28%), and the need to work (24%). Thus, the results of this survey indicate that the need to work is often not the main cause for dropping out of school. Nevertheless, the determining nature of economic factors in decisions to drop out of school has been underestimated in child work studies, not so much in terms of children's necessary contribution to household income, but because of the high costs of schooling and the higher value awarded to alternative uses of their time, even when it is not remunerated. Much more needs to be known about the attitudes of parents concerning education, which appear to be crucial in child work in all countries of the region.

Secondary Education

The availability of a secondary education is far less than that of primary school, and differences between urban and rural areas continue to exist. In Colombia, for example, women account for a larger share of enrollment (53.7% in 1991) than men (46.3%). There are serious problems with dropping out and grade repetition at the secondary level. Studies in each country indicate that dropping out of secondary school in rural areas is a generalized phenomenon caused by the family's need for manpower and the inability of schools to adapt to the realities of rural life.

Investing in Education

Structural adjustment policies have led to the privatization of many government services and to reductions in social spending, which in turn have resulted in rising education costs for families. More expensive tuition, fees, uniforms, school-bus transport, books, and other supplies have created additional pressures on a large number of already overburdened families, particularly those headed by women. The children of poor families are often forced to work to cover these costs.

The education budget in Ecuador, for instance, has decreased constantly over the past 15 years, dropping from 33% of public expenditure in 1980 to 22% in 1985, 17% in 1990, and 16% in 1995. Ninety percent of this allocation covers teachers' salaries, with only 10% remaining for developing and maintaining infrastructure, training, educational research, and so on.

In Guatemala, education spending has never exceeded 2% of GNP during the past 20 years. Operating expenditures absorb between 90 and 97% of the resource allocation. Government spending per student (in constant quetzals) was decreased in 1991 at the preschool, primary, and secondary levels; costs per student at the secondary level are almost three times higher than those at the primary level.

In Colombia, government spending represented 2.8% of GNP in 1992, and the present government has promised to boost it to 3.8% of GNP by 1998. While government spending has increased at both the primary and secondary levels over the past 20 years, there are nonetheless symptoms of stagnation and decreased per capita spending. Government subsidies do make some attempt, however, to help children of the poorest households by covering more than 15% of their enrollment and tuition.

Between 1980 and 1989, public spending on primary education per student per year for the countries of Latin America and the Caribbean as a whole dropped from US$164 to US$118. It is, however, important to note that marked variations exist across countries: while the proportion of GNP allocated to education in Brazil fell from 3.5 to 2.7% between 1980 and 1988, it rose from 3.1 to 3.4% for the 1980–87 period in Peru.

Studies argue that a viable and effective financial effort on the part of Latin American governments could provide nine years of education for the labor force as a whole in less than two decades. The adoption of dynamic policies to promote the development of human capital, which would represent considerable savings for families if accompanied by global policies to stimulate growth and innovation in the economy as a whole, could substantially accelerate economic growth and improve the standard of living of 70% of the poor in Latin America.

Policies

Immediate action and positive interventions are needed to change the situation of child work in the region. International action is needed for the effective safeguard of human rights and for other issues such as the protection of the biosphere. The only effective way to prevent illegal migration from the south to the north is through the joint pressure of workers and others on both sides to improve working and living conditions in the countries of the south. This must lead to the elimination of hazardous child work in all countries, that is, work that impedes the education and the full development of children, as stated in article 32 of the Convention on the Rights of the Child.

The definition and rapid implementation of socioeconomic policies to decrease poverty levels are urgently needed, as are social and wage policies to promote democratic access to income and an increase in the minimum legal salary.

Significantly higher investments in human capital for the poor are also needed. Poor children need to have more access to preschool education and to receive nutritional and other in-kind subsidies or direct financial aid to improve their nutritional intake.

Strengthening the traditions of participatory action research in the universities may lead to better information and analysis of child work and the educational system needed to formulate policies and promote advocacy work. Analysis of current programs to eliminate child work is also needed.

Parents of working children also have to become more involved in educational decisions, such as the kind of education they want for their children and which subsidies will reduce family expenditures for schooling. Income replacement and substitution mechanisms that have been carried out in some countries of the region, particularly in Brazil, have to be further analyzed, since they may be important in reducing the extent of child work.

Long-Term Policy Proposals

1. Reduce adult underemployment and unemployment. The well-being of families is possible within a socioeconomic framework that makes the use of child work unnecessary. Poverty is the social setting of child work. This situation demands a change in development paradigms and a more equitable distribution of society's wealth.

2. Foster a children's culture based on the principles of the Convention. Children must no longer occupy last place on the list of family and social priorities. Daily life is full of customs that reflect disregard for children.

3.   Stop poor families' exploitation or abuse of their children. Being poor does not mean that parents are entitled to mortgage their children's future. Parents' first responsibility is to safeguard their children's present life and future as adults.

Medium-Term Policy Proposals

1.   Recognize the essential need for radical and qualitative change in schooling. More efforts are needed to establish schools (even in the most remote areas), programs, and curriculums suited to local and regional needs and cultural diversity. Teachers must be properly trained and their salaries should be raised according to their performance as teachers.

2.   Develop a system of schooling that acts as a magnet for children. Education is the core of the struggle against child work. The eradication of child work must be linked to universal, efficient, and useful primary education.

3.   Design the basic social policies needed to gradually discourage adults from using child and adolescent labor.

4.   Combine policies intended to gradually eradicate work among boys and girls under age 12 (or 14, depending on national legislation) with structural changes in the educational system. These require the following:

     a.   More government investment in education is essential, particularly at the primary school level. This includes supplying textbooks to children, giving schools adequate libraries, space, and equipment, training teachers in innovative classroom methods, and creating suitable environments for schools within the community.

     b.   The curriculum should be more flexible to ensure grade promotion and avoid grade repetition and dropping out, in addition to encouraging family participation in school processes and establishing subsidies, scholarships, and other ways to replace children's income and their contribution to the family budget.

     c.   Governments must establish quantitative indicators of good education, such as minimum standards for public spending on education, investment per student, or investment in physical infrastructure, textbooks, and teaching guides.

d. Ministries of education will have to propose goals for different groups of boys and girls, namely, those who work and attend school, those who work and are not in school, those who "do nothing" (neither work nor study),[9] those who have never been in school, those who are overaged, and those who have dropped out.

e. Formal education should be attractive rather than a burden. A serious effort is required to universalize primary education and to reduce high rates of repeating grades and dropping out, which especially affect children in the early grades.

f. Child workers must be encouraged to participate in all that regards their work.

Short-Term Policy Proposals

1. Learn more about child work by promoting participatory research designed to transform unsuitable conditions.

2. Eradicate hazardous child and adolescent labor. Domestic work performed by girls should be included in the category of hazardous occupations.

3. Eliminate hazardous work that prevents children from attending or performing adequately in school through efficient social control (exercised by teachers, authorities, families, and the community), coupled with state implementation of labor laws specific to child work. Ministries of labor must fulfill their obligation to supervise the work of children at least in the public sector.

4. Disseminate national and international legislation on the rights of children, particularly Convention 138 and Recommendation 146 of the International Labor Organization (ILO). Governments should participate in the new ILO Convention on Child Work, which was launched in 1998.

5. Find ways and means to improve family income in order to guarantee that children have access to school, stay in or reenter school, and achieve academic performance.

6. Develop children's access to good public services (education, health, culture, sports, recreation). Such activities are crucial to their development and

training for adult life and must consider ethnic, gender, regional, and cultural differences.

7. Establish better labor legislation and control measures to ensure that every working child has the right to be protected against all forms of exploitation on the job. Access to professional job training as a child's right (from 12 to 17 years of age) should be part of that protection, but with more emphasis on education than production (Himes, Colbert de Arbolleda, & García Méndez 1994).

8. Inform and mobilize the general public about child work in the interest of formulating policy and controlling public spending. This applies specifically to sectors involved in the struggle against child work (governments, employer and worker organizations, NGOs, and other influential groups).

9. Instruct children, parents, and teachers about children's rights as workers, the high cost of their early entry into labor, and possible alternatives.

10. Urge children to participate in the fulfillment of their rights. Efforts to organize child workers are crucial for increased appreciation of their work, for defense of their rights, and for an end to exploitation.

Conclusions: Can Work and Study Meet?

The evidence in Latin America demonstrates that a significant proportion of children do not attend school with any regularity. It would certainly be misleading to conclude that work is the only factor preventing children from attending school. Yet the evidence does alert us to the fact that child work by and large competes with, rather than facilitates, schooling.

The gap between available educational opportunities and the real need of families is most evident in rural areas. Many rural parents perceive education as irrelevant to their children's future, and thus prefer them to work. There is also a deep rift between the possibilities of future social mobility offered by an education and the urgent demands of the present. The children of impoverished peasants are the most vulnerable to the harsh demands of family survival.

The nature of the work that children carry out, especially in rural areas, is hardly conducive to successful study. Children have to fight exhaustion to concentrate in class, and they have very little time to study or do their homework. In short, the burden of work makes a burden of school, compromising children's motivation and performance.

Working children are condemned to compete from a disadvantaged position in the labor market. Child work becomes a factor in the intergenerational transmission of poverty. Millions of unpaid children, even those under age 12, accompany their parents on the job, without making any significant monetary contribution to family subsistence. It is essential to encourage parents to withdraw these children from work, while reinforcing their school attendance and academic performance. The necessary coordination and pressure will have to be developed to ensure that education for these youngsters is not a burden to anyone concerned. It is essential that families regain their faith in public school as an institution of instruction, socialization, and the building of citizenship.

The work of children in Latin American and Caribbean countries is one of the main sources of child exploitation and violation of their human rights today. Several national and international meetings of high government officials have unanimously condemned the exploitation of children and have called for immediate action to eradicate it. UNICEF and the ILO, especially, as well as other international agencies, have urged programs of action to eliminate child exploitation and immediately end the most intolerable forms of child labor, such as slave-like practices, forced or compulsory labor, the use of children in prostitution, pornography, and the drug trade, and their employment in any type of work that is harmful or hazardous or that interferes with their education. These and other institutions and NGOs have called for total prohibition of work by those under age 12 and special protection for girls.

As stated in the *Report of the Amsterdam Child Labor Conference* in 1997 (ILO, 1997), the struggle against child labor requires a firm expression of political will at the highest level and concerted action at all levels by governments, employers' organizations and trade unions, NGOs, representatives of working children and their families, and other members of society united in a coherent multidisciplinary program. This program should focus on key areas such as education, the enactment and enforcement of child labor legislation, and the alleviation of poverty. Policies should be targeted at:

- the immediate removal of all children under age 12 or 14 (according to the legislation of each country) from any kind of work that impedes their formal basic education

- the immediate removal of all children, whatever their age, from the most intolerable forms of child labor

- the prevention of child labor through the universal provision of access to quality education and to an adequate social infrastructure providing health care, social protection for families, and enhanced opportunities for adult employment

- the creation of full awareness and understanding of the rights of children and the need to end child labor.

NOTES

1. The chapter is based on case studies carried out in Brazil, Colombia, Ecuador, Guatemala, and Peru. See UNICEF (1996a) for complete reports in Spanish and Salazar & Alarcón (1996) for an abridged English version. On the concept of development and its shortcomings, see papers presented at the World Congress for Participatory Convergence (Cartagena, June 1997) in Escobar (forthcoming).

2. "Exploitation" in an economic context is defined as a situation in which a worker is paid less than his or her marginal product (Hammer et al., 1997: 22).

3. "Hazardous work" has been defined in many ways and in English is associated with child labor; UNICEF and others define it, according to article 32 of the CRC, to include any economic activity that impedes or hinders the child's full development and/or schooling.

4. "Secondary activities," consisting of taking care of animals, working in family vegetable gardens, making improvements, and helping out in a grocery store or business are only measured in rural areas and without taking account of the number of hours worked.

5. One weakness in specialized studies on this topic is precisely the vacuum of information on child work in rural areas. What is known on this subject is insufficient. For this reason, assessments should leave room for the formulation of hypotheses to be tested in the future.

6. In the cities, there are a number of private institutes offering one- or two-year courses in a particular trade, such as sewing, cosmetology, or manual arts. Usually, the only requirement is a primary education. Many parents see these courses as a genuine alternative to secondary education.

7. In European countries, the average school year is 220 six-hour days. In Japan and some of the recently industrialized countries of Asia, the school year averages 220 nine-hour days.

8. Indirect means of measuring these factors are the indexes of grade repetition, dropouts, and grade promotion. In Peru, 18% of children repeat at least one grade in primary school and just over 30% repeat the first grade; in Guatemala and Brazil the latter rises to almost 55%.

9. In some countries, the percentage of children who "neither work nor study" is substantial. Children (especially girls) who perform household jobs within their own homes are considered part of this category.

BIBLIOGRAPHY

BID (Banco Interaméricano del Desarrollo). 1993. *Mejoramiento de la Calidad de Educación Primaria en América Latina y El Caribe: Hacia el Siglo XXI*. Consultants: L. Wolff, E. Schiefelbein, and J. Valenzuela. Informe No. 28. Programa de Estudios Regionales. Latin America and the Caribbean, Technical Department.

CEPAL (Comisión Económica Para América Latina y el Caribe). 1995. *Panorama social de América Latina*. United Nations, Santiago de Chile.

Defensa de los Niños Internacional—Chile. 1995. "Diagnóstico sobre los Niños Trabajadores en Chile." Manuscript.

Flórez, C. E., Knaul, F., and Méndez, R. 1995. *¿Niños y jóvenes: Cuántos y dónde trabajan?* Ministerio de Trabajo y Seguridad Social. CEDE, Universidad de los Andes. Bogotá.

García, M., and Hernández, C. 1992. *¿Tiempo de jugar? Niños y jóvenes trabajadores de las familias populares urbanas*. CEPLAES. Quito.

García Méndez, E., and Araldsen, H. 1994. *El Debate Actual sobre el Trabajo Infanto-Juvenil en América Latina y El Caribe: Tendencias y Perspectivas*. UNICEF, Santa Fe de Bogotá, Colombia.

Himes, J. R., Colbert de Arboleda, V., and García Méndez, E. 1994. "Child Labor and Basic Education in Latin America and the Caribbean: A Proposed UNICEF Initiative." Innocenti Essay, no. 6. UNICEF International Development Centre. Florence.

ILO [Ministry of Foreign Affairs, Ministry of Social Affairs and Employment]. 1997. *Report of the Amsterdam Child Labor Conference*. Amsterdam.

Knaul, F. M. 1995. "Young Workers, Street Life and Gender: The Effect of Education and Work Experience on Earnings in Colombia." Ph.D. Dissertation (Cambridge, MA, Harvard University).

Londoño, J. L. 1995. *Pobreza, Desigualdad, Política Social y Democracia.* World Bank, Technical Department for Latin America.

Nieuwenhuys, O. 1996. "The Paradox of Child Labor and Anthropology." *Annual Review of Anthropology,* 25: 237–51.

Petras, J. 1995. La Recuperación Económica de América Latina, El Mito y la Realidad, Nueva Sociedad (Caracas), 137: pp. 164–79.

Rodríguez, B. dos Santos. 1996. *Trabalho infantil no Brasil: Um estudo das estrategias e políticas para sua eliminação.* DNI/ISPCAN/IWGCL. São Paulo.

Salazar, M. C., and Alarcón, W. 1996. *Better Schools: Less Child Work. Child Work and Education in Brazil, Colombia, Ecuador, Guatemala and Peru.* Innocenti Essay, no. 7. UNICEF. Regional Office for Latin America and the Caribbean, Bogotá and International Child Development Centre. Florence.

Salazar, M. C., and Gárate, M. 1996. *Trabajo infantil en América Latina. Defensa de los Niños Internacional.* DCI/ISPCAN/IWGCL. International Working Group on Child Labor. Amsterdam.

Tokman, V. 1997. *Erradicación del trabajo infantil. La experiencia del IPEC en América Latina.* Primera Reunión Iberoamericana tripartita de nivel ministerial sobre erradición del trabajo infantil. OIT/IPEC. Cartagena, 8–9 de Mayo 1997.

UNICEF. 1992a. *Latin America Special Report 5,* 10: pp. 2–3.

UNICEF. 1992b. *Los Niños de las Américas.* UNICEF, Santa Fe de Bogotá.

UNICEF. 1996a. *Mejores escuelas: Menos trabajo infantil. Trabajo infantil y educación en Brasil, Colombia, Guatemala, Ecuador y Perú.* UNICEF. Oficina Regional para América Latina y el Caribe, Bogotá and International Child Development Centre. Florencia.

UNICEF. 1996b. *State of the World's Children.* New York.

UN. 1995. *Estudio Económico y Social Mundial.* New York.

Valdes, A., and Wiens, T. 1996. "Rural Poverty in Latin America and the Caribbean." Second Annual World Bank Conference on Development in Latin America and the Caribbean. June 30–July 2, 1996. Bogotá.

Vidich, A. 1994. "The Growing Marginality of Latin America in the World Economy," in *Politics, Culture and Society,* edited by A. Vidich, vol. 8, no. 2.

White, B. 1995. "Globalization and the Child Work Problem." Manuscript, Institute of Social Studies, The Hague.

C | Rights of Children and Penal Law

11 | Adolescents and the Penal System

Proposals Based on the Convention on the Rights of the Child

MIGUEL CILLERO BRUÑOL

Introduction

In most modern justice systems, the legal penalties for criminal offenses are differentiated according to whether the offenders are juveniles or adults. As far back as ancient times, there were provisions that exempted children from certain penalties or reduced their severity, and this practice was continued during the Middle Ages.[1]

A historical overview reveals the existence of three major systems that have arisen in succession but are nonetheless interwoven. The first is a *mitigated penal doctrine*. This system, whose origins go far back in history, was consolidated in the legal codes of the nineteenth century that incorporated the criterion of *discernment*.[2] This was followed by a system based on the concept of *guardianship*, whose founding principles included the age-old humanitarian aspiration to treat juveniles differently than adults. Some aspects of this system were found in judicial institutions of the eighteenth century, but it reached its apex in the *guardianship-based* systems for minors developed in the late nineteenth and early twentieth centuries throughout the Americas and in some parts of Europe.

The twentieth century has also seen the development of a *juvenile justice system* — perhaps best exemplified by the Juvenile Penal Act of the former

West Germany—that seeks to combine the tradition of penal doctrine with the humanitarian and correctional approaches predominating in guardianship-based systems.

This general picture remained virtually unchanged until existing juvenile justice systems gradually began to incorporate a *human-rights-based* approach and, more specifically, the provisions contained in legal instruments expressly concerned with the rights of children, particularly the Convention on the Rights of the Child (CRC), which was adopted by the UN General Assembly in 1989 and classifies all persons under 18 years of age as children. In line with a system of classification whose use is becoming increasingly widespread in Latin America, here we will be speaking about children and adolescents, with the latter being defined as persons over age 12 and under 18.

An analysis of the historical and legal aspects of this subject provides sufficient grounds for the statement that the system that attributes legal consequences for the violation of penal law by children and adolescents has been radically changed by a progressive recognition of their rights.[3] Consequently, the argument that will be developed here is based on the observation that the social system for controlling the commission of criminally punishable acts by children and adolescents is heavily influenced by—among a wide variety of other factors—the predominant legal concept of childhood and the corresponding normative position in which the legal order places children and adolescents.

Hence, despite their differences, mitigated and guardianship-based penal systems both regard minors as lacking legal capacity, as persons who are defined by what they are not, that is, by their lack of certain characteristics required of a legally defined adult. Within the penal system, the theory of *legal incapacity* is manifested in a view of children as nonliable, or inculpable, and in the development of a complex system of supervision and protection in which the child is a passive subject of state intervention who has virtually no guarantees on which to rely in dealing with a justice system that investigates and passes judgment untrammeled by any checks or balances.

The consolidation of the guardianship-based system for dealing with juveniles ushered in a situation in which two types of systems—guardianship itself, and a punitive approach—overlapped; although they might seem to run counter to one another, these two systems actually turned out to be complementary. Laws applying to juveniles, especially in the Americas, laid the foundations, under the aegis of naturalist positivism,[4] for the application of punitive methods for correctional purposes, to be administered within a jurisdictional framework based on the authority of the magistrate and the discretionary application of the criterion of whether juveniles were a threat to social welfare. This entailed a great deal of confusion between the state's function in guarding welfare or providing assistance, and its adjudicatory functions.

With the emergence of a human-rights-based approach to the treatment of children and adolescents, earlier concepts based on the assumption that childhood and adolescence are a period of legal incapacity have given way to a concept of children and adolescents as subjects at law. In penal terms, this change is manifested in the recognition of a special form of responsibility starting at a specified age (the commencement of adolescence), in a reinforcement of the legal position occupied by children and adolescents in the courts, and, in general, in the incorporation of a series of guarantees or safeguards that limits the punitive power of the state and that opens the way for a different kind of response to juvenile offenders—one that promotes social integration and upholds the rights of children and adolescents.

A pivotal role in this evolutionary change has been played by the CRC, which has marked a fundamental change in juvenile rights and represents a qualitative leap in terms of how society views childhood.[5] Following ratification of the CRC, an interesting and as yet unfinished legislative reform process has been taking place throughout Latin America, and one of the central components of this process has been the establishment of a new system for responding to violations of penal law committed by adolescents.[6]

The key element of this new system is its incorporation of the idea of responsibility, whose counterpart is the legitimacy of the courts' right to censure acts constituting criminal offenses, while at the same time acknowledging that minors cannot be held criminally responsible in the same way as adults would be.

This rights-based approach, as applied to the subject of penal offenses committed by juveniles, has given rise to an alternative legal model to the correctional or guardianship model for juveniles; this new model, which may be described as a model of legal responsibility, is founded on the doctrine of the integral protection of the rights of children and adolescents that has grown out of the CRC and related legal instruments.

Laws Applying to Juveniles in the Twentieth Century: Emergence and Breakdown of Guardianship-Based Systems

Virtually all the specialized literature on the subject identifies the starting point for legislation based on the guardianship or protection of minors as the establishment of the Juvenile Court of Chicago in 1899, although of course there were many examples of differentiated treatment of juveniles and adults by the penal system prior to its founding.[7]

The model developed in Chicago rapidly came into widespread use, in both the United States and Europe, and systems for the protection of minors involving legislative, judicial, and administrative mechanisms were rapidly created. The hallmark of this new system was the creation of juvenile courts.[8]

These juvenile courts were not, however, based on the same principles as those underlying modern-day courts of justice, especially in terms of criminal matters; rather than functioning as courts designed to ascribe legal consequences for violations of the law, they were designed to control/protect a specific, residual category of minors who were classified as neglected or problem children.

Following this line of reasoning, a system was developed that justified the administration of the same legal treatment to penal offenses to situations in which children were socially at-risk or in which their rights were being threatened or violated. This type of legislation put penal offenders on the same footing as children who were neglected by their families or by society and, with no more than negligible variations, was to be found in all the legal codes of that period. The following statutes are cited by way of example.

The relevant statute of the state of Illinois (1907) stated:

A delinquent is [defined as] any minor who infringes any law or regulation of the State; or who is incorrigible; or who knowingly associates with thieves; or who, without just cause or permission from his parents or guardians, leaves his home; or who lapses into sloth or crime; or who manifestly frequents a house of ill repute or an establishment that sells inebriating drink; or who wanders the night.

The Guardianship Act of Argentina (1919) read:

For the purposes of the preceding articles, material or moral abandonment or moral danger shall be defined as the incitement of a minor by his or her parents or guardians to engage in acts detrimental to his or her physical or moral health, mendicancy or vagrancy on the part of the minor, the frequenting of immoral or gaming establishments or association with thieves or persons of corrupt habits or of ill repute, or, in the case of minors under eighteen years of age, the selling of periodicals, publications or objects of any nature whatsoever in streets or public places or the practice in such places of trades far from the supervision of their parents or guardians or the practice of trades or jobs detrimental to their moral welfare or health.

Chile's Act 4.447 for the Protection of Minors (1928) was applied to persons under the age of 20 in special situations:

1. Unimputable juveniles charged with having committed a crime, minor offense or misdemeanor (art. 18);

2. Abandoned juveniles (art. 22);

3. Juveniles whose parents are physically or morally incapacitated (art. 22);

4. Juveniles in material or moral danger (in which case both parents shall be deemed to be incapacitated (art. 22).

The Chilean courts could apply a uniform list of measures to all these children, with such measures ranging from the child's return to his or her parents to incarceration in a reformatory (art. 21).

Spain's Juvenile Welfare Act (1948) reads:

Art. 9. The jurisdiction of the courts shall include:

B. Infractions committed by juveniles of the same age (16 years);

C. The cases of juveniles of sixteen years of age who have been prostituted, are licentious, or are vagrant, provided that the relevant Court finds that they are in need of its reformatory powers.

Art. 11. Unruly juveniles under sixteen years of age who are declared to be such by their parents or guardians . . .

All such persons in Spain were subject to the application of measures that would deprive them of their liberty.

A reflection of the mainstream trend in guardianship-based legal theory applying to juveniles is the assertion by Cuello Calón that "when dealing with children who are not going to be sentenced or harmed, but rather to whom protective measures and methods of guardianship are to be applied, for whom favorable measures are to be taken, there is no such thing as excess or abuse. In doing good, there is no excess."[9] In the same vein, Jiménez de Asúa stated that

"all formality and publicity in the proceedings should be abolished . . . since it is not a matter of litigation, there is no role to be played by lawyers, no need for a defense counsel, nor for a judge to listen to both sides. In such cases there is simply a man who examines the cases of juveniles and attempts to help them . . . [and to whom] the widest possible discretion should be accorded . . . in

> determining the manner in which the investigation should be con-
> ducted. [The judge] . . . is not going to investigate facts; (s)he is not
> going to solve the questions as to whether the crime was committed
> in one way or another, whether there was some justification, whether
> there were aggravating or mitigating circumstances. What (s)he is
> going to do is to examine the character of the minor."[10]

This type of argument dominated the legal debate on the issue, and even managed to outweigh the doubts that were expressed as to the constitution-ality of the degree of procedural flexibility permitted by such provisions,[11] until, in 1967, the U.S. Supreme Court handed down a decision in the *Gault* case wherein it objected, among other key aspects, to the lack of guarantees of due procedure and, in particular, to the absence of legal defense.[12] This finding was a milestone decision that marked the beginning of a new era in the protection of young persons' rights.

In 1979, the Human Rights Commission reaffirmed this new doctrine when it stated that what determines the applicability of the rights and guar-antees of the individual in relation to the penal system is not whether or not the law of the land recognizes such applicability as penal law or classifies the conduct in question as criminal, but rather the implications of the appli-cation of such rights and guarantees for the party in question.[13] Accordingly, the penal system's substantive and procedural guarantees are to be respected in any proceeding that could affect the interested party's personal liberty or cause some other sort of punitive measure to be applied to that party.

This rules out the possibility of denying juveniles procedural safeguards on the grounds that they are subject to the application of protective measures rather than punishments, thereby putting an end to the accusation that the juvenile justice system had been practicing fraud or sleight of hand, and curtailing one systemic source of denial of juvenile rights.

The Constitutional Court of Spain also upheld such guarantees when, in Judicial Finding No. 36/1991, it declared article 15 of the Juvenile Welfare Act to be unconstitutional because it dispensed with constitutionally man-dated procedural guarantees in proceedings involving offenses committed by minors.[14]

In Latin America, criticisms based on legal doctrine and on constitu-tional grounds have been reinforced by a series of studies on the penal system that take a multidisciplinary approach to the justice systems in the region. These research projects have identified the juvenile justice system as one of the most seriously flawed components of the entire judicial system.

In 1985 the Inter-American Institute of Human Rights issued a report on criminal justice systems which asserted that one of the basic characteristics of guardianship-based legislation was its dispersed nature and lack of coherence, with striking differences existing between the stated purposes of the juvenile justice system and the means employed to achieve those ends.[15] One typical example of this situation is that, despite the fact that juvenile courts have been in existence for a long time now, they are still not widespread.

The most compelling argument against the line of reasoning that bases the concept of procedural flexibility on the purportedly special nature of the magistrates in juvenile courts and the measures they apply is the absence of resources for establishing special courts and measures. Specific studies on the guardianship-based system have also shown that it is a system that, as of the 1980s, had still not achieved its goal of judicial specialization and that had suffered from an extreme shortage of resources for the "specialized treatment of juveniles."[16]

The 1985 report criticizes such legislation on the grounds that it is based on a concept of "social irregularity"—a vague and inexact term that permits an array of divergent situations to be equated with one another and backs up the idea of having a body of law intended for all minors as a group. This criticism should be viewed in conjunction with the wealth of evidence indicating that guardianship-based systems for minors are used solely for the social control of certain segments of children and young people belonging to the most underprivileged sectors of society.

In terms of its normative aspects, the system's most glaring flaws appear to be the lack of procedural guarantees and the indeterminate nature of both the presumptions made and the duration of protective measures. Most of the studies done on the subject have found that the guardianship-based system employs concepts that have been discarded by criminal law theorists because they have been found to infringe on certain human rights (such concepts include, e.g., the nonimputability of the author of an act, measures adopted prior to criminal proceedings, criteria referring to a situation of danger or imperilment, and procedures used in questioning).[17]

In sum, during the 1980s the criticism leveled at the guardianship-based juvenile justice system revealed the existence of a crisis in terms of the system's legal legitimacy, due to the unconstitutionality of its underlying precepts, and of its social legitimacy, due to its unsatisfactory results and an increasing awareness of the fact that it was an extremely discriminatory and authoritarian system used for controlling of a given segment of the young population.

Within this legislative and social context, the passage into law of the CRC in Latin American countries and the processes by which these countries regained or made the transition to democratic systems of government joined forces during the late 1980s and early 1990s, sparking a powerful legislative reform movement. In terms of the scope of human rights, this movement can be seen as an active process of expansion that has worked to the benefit of persons under age 18, who constitute a significant percentage of the region's inhabitants.

The Current Debate: Public Safety, Public Policy, and Legislative Reform

At the present time, the system for dealing with juvenile delinquency or criminality in Latin America is an issue that commands a great deal of interest on the part of the media, scientific and legal circles, political and judicial authorities, and the general public.

The above-mentioned crisis in guardianship-based juvenile justice systems has had two adverse affects: a feeling of insecurity and impunity in the face of juvenile delinquency, and a discrediting of state response mechanisms owing to the irrationality of existing sanctions and the absence of safeguards. Thus, an urgent need exists for debate, for the design of new types of policies to address these issues, and for a reform of the legal system's institutional structure.

Unfortunately, the discussion of these issues has often been distorted and reduced to nothing more than a marginal debate about public safety and a call for police action or correctional mechanisms; social alarm—sparked by serious crimes, prison uprisings, or the practices of specialized centers for juveniles—would appear to be what triggers the adoption of new measures and, worse yet, the main motivating force behind new bills of law.[18]

To gain a clear understanding of this subject, it is best to put aside the idea of this matter as a "public issue" open to so many interpretations, distortions, and mystifications, so that we can delve more deeply into the fundamental principles underlying this phenomenon, which merit the attention of legal and political authorities at the highest levels.[19]

The cornerstones for a focused policy on juvenile criminality must foster social coexistence and provide a justifiable basis for the control of criminality in a democratic society; this means that they relate directly to the foundational elements of the legal system as such, the organization of state power, mechanisms to settle disputes, and the boundaries of state intervention.

Public policies designed to prevent and control juvenile criminality are complex mechanisms involving value judgments, political variables, and legal factors, each of which influences all the others.

In regard to *value judgments*, as so aptly stated by Antonio Carlos Gomes Da Costa,[20] only a society that learns to respect the "worst" of its members will be capable of respecting all individuals. Thus, a society's level of ethical development may be measured by how it treats the worst of its members, those who commit acts that run counter to the norm.

Thus, the way in which the justice system, as a mechanism of societal control, reacts to criminal behavior (particularly in the case of juveniles) reflects the degree to which society respects the personal dignity of its members and serves to indicate its justice system's stage of development.

Another point that should be addressed concerns how adolescent offenders are regarded. For a long time, and especially in the twentieth century, specialists have been divided on this issue. At one end of the spectrum, adolescent offenders have been viewed as culpable and dangerous, making it both legitimate and necessary to punish and repress them; at the other, adolescent offenders are regarded as victims of societal neglect who therefore deserve to be protected and, if possible, rehabilitated. The exact content of these positions is what determines the character and areas of emphasis of existing systems for dealing with juvenile criminality.

The *political* aspect of the issue refers to the specific kind of relationship established by law between the adolescent and the state. This relationship has been redefined as a consequence of the CRC, since that instrument expressly regulates the rights of children and adolescents in their dealings with the criminal justice system, and it is therefore directly related to the concept of law and order and respect for socially accepted and judicially sanctioned rules for living together in society.

With the democratization of society, however, the structuring of that order has ceased to be confined to the sphere of politics and the state and has become a social matter as well, one whose very foundations come under the control of society. This order also finds expression in laws and institutions, that is, in juridical structures.[21] Thus, an indivisible assemblage of social, political, and legal aspects underlie the concept of such an order.

Following this line of reasoning, the problem of how to structure such a system, particularly as regards society's reaction to transgressions against the social order and to violence, can be addressed on the basis of a juridical-normative concept that rests on two basic pillars: power and the rights of individuals. The systems through which society responds to and controls delinquency can be classified according to which of these two elements predominates.

A system that puts its emphasis on the concept of sovereignty, understood as the use of force by the authorities, will tend toward the use of authoritarian forms of reactive control based on the idea of the authorities' power to inhibit or censure people's behavior; in contrast, a system based on the ideas of citizenship and the rights of the individual will tend toward active forms of societal control that seek to induce certain types of behavior rather than prohibiting others.[22]

Under guardianship-based juvenile justice systems, the citizenship of children and adolescents has been denied or undermined, and they have consequently been subjected to the unbridled control of an authoritarian system that focuses on repressing illicit acts on their part and promoting, through coercive measures, modifications of their behavior.[23]

Political history shows us that tension invariably exists between sovereign power and the rights of the individual, between violence legitimized by the law and the right to limit violence.[24] By reinforcing the position of juveniles as subjects at law, the Convention on the Rights of the Child (CRC) offers children the hope of witnessing a move away from authoritarian systems that wield untrammeled power over their person and their rights, and toward systems that provide a series of safeguards that set limits on state action.

Within the Latin American context, the foundation for dealing with juvenile offenders is, then, the construction of a peaceful social order—in opposition to the violent order generated by criminality—and the consolidation of a democratic order, in opposition to the authoritarian order engendered by legislation based on the idea of the legal incapacity of the child. Such an order recognizes the right of all persons to be protected by the justice system and the state against acts of violence and acknowledges children's right to limit and to contest, by legal means, the state's attempt to punish or correct them. In short, the idea is to create a system of safeguards for both perpetrators and victims.

The potential effectiveness of the CRC in bringing about political and legal change is not limited to acknowledging a list of rights, however. It also offers an approach for dealing with infringements of penal law from the standpoint of children's and adolescents' participation in social life, as well as their progressive development as citizens with both rights and responsibilities. It is also felt, in this regard, that in order for adolescents to develop and become integrated into society, they must gradually acquire a feeling of ownership with regard to their own actions and a sense of responsibility, and this process needs to be fostered by means of a formalized system for dealing with violations of the law.

These factors make the CRC a key consideration in any conceptualization of the issue of effective political and legal change, not only because of its legal value as a guarantee of limitations on the punitive power of the state, but also because of the valuable contribution it makes to the development of a social response that will encourage the social integration of adolescent offenders and promote social coexistence.

Thus, in contradistinction to the model of "law and order" that is sometimes pursued at any cost (by lowering the age of legal imputability, placing adolescents in prisons for adults, ignoring social factors), the CRC points to the existence of a different solution. This solution bases public safety on rebuilding a pattern of harmonious coexistence as part of a system that, even though it may be severe in its requirements, is founded on recognizing human dignity and on legitimate judicial methods of settling the conflicts that may arise in society: a social order or system in which children and adolescents are recognized, in all spheres, as subjects at law with both rights and duties.

Another important element is that the phenomenon of juvenile delinquency should be classified within the domain of civil and political rights rather than that of social rights and social justice. This is a crucial difference between the responsibility-based model associated with the CRC and other human rights instruments, and the legal grounds that have generally been used to conceptualize the problem of so-called juvenile offenders in the laws directed at Latin American minors.

Under present conditions in the region, the objectives of social welfare or assistance are pursued by means of a disparate array of "protective" mechanisms that range all the way from social support to the deprivation of liberty.[25]

This tangle, or confusion, of levels leads to two forms of dissimulation; on the one hand, the discourse of social welfare theory rejects judicial and penal controls, while, on the other, the discourse of protection-oriented legal theory denies the existence of actual juridical conflicts, lumping together such vastly different acts as abandonment and infringement of penal law under the heading of "irregular situations."

A thorough analysis of the content of laws designed for application to juveniles, together with the economic and social role such laws play, has made it possible to separate legal issues from political-social matters, thereby paving the way for the removal of judicial mechanisms from the system for resolving conflicts of an exclusively economic and social nature. It also sets the stage for the separation of penal and guardianship-based legal processes, which the courts and administrative mechanisms have traditionally mixed together.

Thus, it is important to alter policies and amend legislation relating to infringements of penal law as a means of upholding civil rights, with such rights being understood within a social context that must also be governed by social rights. The focus on civil rights makes it necessary to set up a system of guarantees that will keep state action within certain bounds based on its purposes and on the legitimacy or illegitimacy of the mechanisms used.

In sum, specific public policies for preventing and reacting to juvenile criminality necessarily entail the restitution of the principle of legality and the construction of a complex system of safeguards in relation to the adjudication of legal consequences in the case of adolescents who are found to have violated penal law.

This system of guarantees will make it possible to guide and limit state decision making and, in so doing, will serve as a highly useful frame of reference for other public policies as well. The welfare- or assistance-based approach used in the case of juvenile criminality, on the other hand, does not permit legally rational decision making. It provides no basis for seeking to provide greater "assistance," shall we say, to a person who has committed murder than to one who has committed theft; in the welfare-based approach, the act that has been committed—the violation of a legal right vouchsafed under the penal system—is irrelevant, inasmuch as it is seen as nothing more than a symptom that the juvenile in question has "gotten off on the wrong track," and in fact, such an infringement is not even a precondition for the legitimization of state intervention. The main point in terms of welfare or care services is to determine what needs exist so that appropriate social benefits may be provided.

The Contribution Made by the Convention on the Rights of the Child: The Model of Legal Responsibility of the Adolescent

Addressing infringements of penal law with an approach based on children's rights offers a way out of the critical situation in which the guardianship-based juvenile justice system has found itself. The doctrine of the integral protection of the rights of children and adolescents is an approach that has paved the way for the proposal of a new juridical model that could be described as a "model of legal responsibility."

In Latin America, the term "doctrine of integral protection" is often used to refer to the series of principles, guidelines, and rights set forth in the international instruments formulated by the UN to protect the rights of children. Four main instruments are generally considered to have shaped this new doctrine, which has taken the place of former approaches to the rights of children:

1. The 1989 CRC, which, by virtue of its comprehensive content and normative character, is the supreme authority in this respect and serves as a framework for this series of instruments.

2. The UN Standard Minimum Rules for the Administration of Juvenile Justice (hereafter referred to as The Beijing Rules, adopted by General Assembly resolution 40/33 of November 29, 1985).

3. The UN Rules for the Protection of Juveniles Deprived of their Liberty (hereafter referred to as The Riyadh Rules, adopted by General Assembly resolution 45/113 of April 2, 1991).

4. The UN Guidelines for the Prevention of Juvenile Delinquency of 1991 (hereafter referred to as The Riyadh Guidelines, adopted by General Assembly resolution 45/112 of April 2, 1991).

Defining Subjects at Law

The starting point for the model of legal responsibility based on the CRC is the consideration of the child and adolescent as subjects at law who occupy a special position (as is recognized in a number of human rights instruments) vis-à-vis the legal system. In constructing this model, it is important to remember that it is to be applied only to adolescents, not children, since according to the CRC itself, the latter occupy a different legal position.

The model based on the CRC goes beyond the types of limited guarantees contained in traditional penal law as applied to juveniles or in minimalist penal laws for minors because it adds a legally recognized concept of the subject at law to which such guarantees are to apply: the adolescent. It is impossible to fashion a body of minimalist penal law for adolescents that observes all the necessary limitations and guarantees without a correct understanding of the legal status of the adolescent in relation to the state.

The CRC's invaluable contribution in this respect has been incorporated into a variety of comprehensive Latin American laws, codes, and statutes for children and adolescents, which thus explicitly acknowledge the legal status of children and adolescents vis-à-vis the state, their families, and society.

One essential component of the legal status of children and adolescents is their position in terms of laws that classify certain types of assaults against legal rights as punishable offenses; another crucial element is the consequences of engaging in such acts. Nonetheless, these definitions cannot be taken out of the context of the overall status of children and adolescents under the laws of a given society. The question of how the system should react to juvenile delinquency is not a matter that can be resolved exclusively on the basis of legal theory and its associated limits, but must instead be addressed from the standpoint of a broad range of judicial, social, and political considerations.

If the system for reacting to juvenile delinquency is confined to declaring the juvenile's lack of imputability under penal law and fails to address the matter from an overall legal perspective, then the justice system's response ignores the commission of an unlawful act and focuses on psychological traits of the individual, of his or her ability to love or understand, or the extent to which he or she may constitute a "threat to society."

The absence of any genuine legal and social policy to safeguard and promote the exercise of children's and adolescents' rights generates hypertrophy within the systems for controlling and reacting to juvenile delinquency, which thus expand beyond their spheres of action into social spheres of activity, where, under the guise of what is purported to be an educational function, they seek to turn themselves into complex systems for achieving the proper socialization of children and adolescents who have been labeled "deviant" or "needy."[26]

Consequently, what is being censured is not an act but rather the deviant subjectivity of the individual;[27] the reproach implicit in the imposition of any kind of measure—regardless of whether it is educational in nature or a penalty—on a person not classified as imputable is shifted from the act to the person who committed the act, from disapproval of a specific act committed by an adolescent to a condemnation of that individual's personal traits. The systems of control engendered by this kind of approach—which may or may not be humanitarian, depending on the surrounding circumstances—emphasize the separation of the individual from his or her social environment and base themselves on the idea that the individual's return to that environment may or should occur only after the system has managed to rectify or "amputate" the unsuitable or deviant traits that originally brought the individual to its attention.[28]

As discussed earlier, the guardianship-based juvenile justice system embodies many of these ideas; they are also in evidence in Germany's juvenile criminal justice system. Although Germany's system is based on the notion of juvenile responsibility and the protection of legal rights, it justifies state intervention for educational ends, thereby weakening its system of safeguards, since this means that it is not placing limits on state intervention on the basis of the rights of young individuals, but instead derives them from the educational functions of the state itself.

Such safeguards are also undermined by the existence of provisions regarding the disposition of cases involving juvenile offenders that disregard the act or event and instead focus on the person who committed the act. In Maurach's view, these types of provisions transform the penalties meted out by the juvenile justice system from a "punishment of the act" in question into a "punishment of the person" who committed the act and, paradigmatically, lead to the use of indeterminate sentencing, which is justified on the grounds that this is the form taken by the penal system's adaptation to special preventive aims within an educational framework.[29]

In contrast, if the system for dealing with infringements of penal laws is in keeping with a true theory of the "citizenship" of children/adolescents as expressed in a recognition of their rights vis-à-vis the state and their right to participate as an active subject at law in decisions affecting them, then it will be a system based on the existence of specific safeguards that guide and limit the state's control over them.

This entails an increasing differentiation of juvenile justice (appropriate to children and adolescents) and a reduction in coercive/punitive intervention by the state, which, at the most, would intervene only in relation to the same kinds of acts that legitimize its intervention when committed by adults; ideally, its intervention should be cut back even further and be limited to those acts that are not only punishable when committed by adults, but are, moreover, of an especially unlawful character for adolescents.

In addition—and this is the most difficult element to attain, as well as the most novel aspect of the model—the objective of the state's intervention will be the development of responsibility and strengthening of the individual so that the adolescent will be able to exercise his or her rights appropriately and fulfill the obligations deriving from the rights of others (art. 40, CRC) that is, the promotion of what Albrecht calls "legal behavior," rather than "socialization" or reeducation, which are not aims that can be legitimately pursued through the mechanisms provided for the administration of criminal justice.[30]

The model of legal responsibility presupposes that, within a parallel and differentiated sphere, the justice system will develop mechanisms to safeguard the integral expression of children's and adolescents' rights, that is, their integral development, through a set of mechanisms that bears no relationship whatsoever to the system for the adjudication of responsibility for infringements of the law.

Commensurate Systems of Responsibilities and Guarantees

The second pivotal element of the CRC arising out of the recognition that the subjective rights of children and adolescents constitute a limitation upon the state, is that the system for reacting to penal offenses is founded on the identification of the system of responsibility with a system of guarantees.

The notion of guarantees, or safeguards, as used here is based on Ferrajoli's analysis of "suitable normative links for ensuring the effective expression of subjective rights,"[31] and the subjective rights that need to be guaranteed or protected are the human rights that are the child's birthright as a human being, in addition to those additional rights to which he or she is entitled because of being a child.

I have proposed the name "model of legal responsibility" for two reasons: the first, and less important of the two, is to differentiate it from any positivist brand of social responsibility and to underscore the legal character of the action to be taken, in contradistinction to welfare- or assistance-based, therapeutic and educational models; the second and fundamental reason is because a legally defined concept of responsibility demands an integral consideration of the legal status of children, the full range of their rights and obligations, and their relationships with the state, the family, and society.

The Foundations of the Model of Legal Responsibility

The Principle of Progressivity and the Distinction between Children and Adolescents

Much has been said about the fact that the CRC and the associated enabling legislation have transformed the child from an object of protective measures into a subject at law who enjoys a number of rights. In applying this concept to penal offenders, it must be noted not only that the child has rights, but also that the exercise of those rights is a progressive development based on the child's evolving capacities (art. 5, CRC) and that the child's progressively greater autonomy in the exercise of those rights goes hand in hand with an increasing degree of responsibility for his or her acts.

If children are subjects at law who exercise their rights with a degree of autonomy that increases in step with their evolving capacities, then their degree of responsibility must also be progressive. This is a question of evaluating or judging children's acts on the basis of their legal status and position—not on the basis of a comparison with those of adults. It is thus no longer possible to maintain—as do laws intended for juveniles that are based on the idea of their legal incapacity—that an equivalent degree of nonimputability exists between the ages of zero and 18, or whatever other age limit may be established.

Under the provisions of penal codes intended for adults, the nonimputability of a person of 3 years of age is exactly equal in degree to that of a person at the upper age limit set for that condition; under the body of law intended for children and adolescents, the two are in strikingly different positions in terms of both their rights and their obligations.

In the interest of greater conceptual accuracy, the CRC stipulates that states should seek to promote "the establishment of a minimum age below which children shall be presumed not to have the capacity to infringe the penal law" (art. 40.3.a). This limit does not apply to the matter of responsibility, but rather to the attribution of a material act to a child, as may be deduced from article 40.1, which assumes the existence of a distinction between infringing the penal law and being responsible for its violation.[32]

An analysis of these two articles, taken together, demonstrates that the idea of an interval of gradated responsibility is contained in international instruments on children's rights, inasmuch as it is recommended that, below a certain age, states should consider children to lack the legal capacity to engage in the specified acts as described in the relevant laws (violating the law in an objective or material sense) and that, between that age and 18, a system of gradated responsibility should be established.

In order to draw that distinction, in Latin America a tendency has emerged, as noted earlier, to differentiate between children (usually up to age 12 or 14) and adolescents (over that age limit but under age 18).

The model of legal responsibility is based on this distinction and is thus applicable only to those individuals that the law defines as adolescents; it also requires that children (individuals under age 14 or 12) be declared legally incapable of infringing the penal law and that only those measures associated with a finding of responsibility for a penal offense may be applied to adolescents.

The Principle of Responsibility

The second cornerstone of the model is the legal practice of assigning or attributing specified consequences to particular acts. In other words, it refers to a formalized (justice) system for ascribing responsibility for participation in a legally described act. This responsibility leads to the application of certain legal consequences, as set forth in the law, which are usually referred to as "measures."

The new legislative trend taking hold in Latin America since the ratification of the CRC is to affirm the responsibility of the child while seeking to "reconcile" the child's right to protection with his or her position as an individual entitled to the exercise of certain rights,[33] thereby moving beyond the bounds of guardianship-based systems founded on notions of irresponsibility and education. In the sphere of penal law, this movement is expressed in the recognition of a system of juvenile responsibility for acts that, if committed by adults, would be subject to penal sanctions.

The most difficult theoretical step is to move beyond the identification of the child or minor as "nonimputable"; to this end, it has been proposed that a distinction be drawn between nonimputability and an absence of responsibility; this position has been explored by Bustos, Baratta, and García Méndez, among others.[34] From a normative standpoint, this distinction has already been made in the juvenile penal system, particularly in Germany, and in my view there is no doubt about the fact that it has been taken up in the CRC (art. 40) and the other UN rules cited earlier.

This distinction is consistent with the representation of the child as a subject at law who actively takes part in the life of society, who has rights and obligations, and who acquires a progressively greater ability to exercise those rights and fulfill those obligations. This has also made it possible to modify the terminology and make the shift—and not merely as a semantic exercise— from the idea of a nonimputable minor (from zero to 18 years of age) to that of a responsible adolescent; the child is penally nonimputable and does not bear responsibility, whereas the adolescent is not imputable in a general penal or criminal sense, but is responsible for his or her acts.[35]

To clarify the debate, I propose that this question should be approached from an overall vantage point that begins with the theory of law, rather than with one or another of the disciplines that have traditionally dealt with the matter (i.e., the penal system or the juvenile justice system).

Hans Kelsen emphasizes that the connection between offense and sanction is not a causal relationship, but rather one of imputability that consists in saying that "the penalty should follow upon the unlawful act," that is, the unlawful act calls into being—via the applicable provision—a legal consequence: a sanction.

The relationship among an unlawful act, imputability, and responsibility is explained by Kelsen in the following manner:

> We have dubbed this relationship [between an unlawful act and its sanction] with the name of Zurechnung and propose that in French the term imputation should be used, since the sanction is "imputed" to the unlawful act. We also say that a subject is zurechnungsfähig (responsible) when a sanction may be imposed upon him or her, or unzurechnungsfähig (not responsible) when a sanction may not be imposed upon him or her because the subject is a child or is mentally incapacitated. It is important, therefore, to specify that the relationship between an unlawful act and a penalty presupposes that the perpetrator of the act is responsible for his or her conduct.[36]

Thus, "the real problem which the attribution of imputability is called upon to resolve," says Kelsen, "is that of determining who is responsible for a good deed, a sin or a crime; in other words, who should be rewarded, do penitence or be penalized. . . . This attribution of imputability cannot, in actuality, be addressed without reference to the person committing the good deed, sin or crime, since that person is the one who needs to be rewarded, do penitence or be punished."

He therefore concludes that, in order to link together the act, sanction, and offender, the subject must be considered in relation to the act and must be given just as much consideration as the criminal act itself. The penalty is not a reaction to the offense per se, but is rather a consequence of the offense that is legitimately imputed to the individual responsible for its commission.

Thus, the imputability of an individual is an attribute that is legally determined by, in most cases, a legislative act, although in some cases it is a judicial decision (as in those systems in which the judiciary decides which system should be applied in each specific case, depending on the age of the person in question).[37] In this respect, imputability serves as a political-criminal barrier or dividing line between two systems: the adult criminal justice system and the system for reacting to offenses committed by adolescents. This sets aside the more traditional view of the absence of imputability on the part of a minor as signifying the young person's inability to comprehend the unlawfulness of the act in question or to act in accordance with that understanding, which entails disregarding the adolescent's identity as a person vouchsafed certain rights and obligations under the prevailing legal order.

This evolution of the concept of culpability opens the way for a body of legal theory that focuses on the criminal act, inasmuch as, since the adoption of a normative theoretical view of culpability, a consensus has been reached to the effect that a statement of culpability is not founded on a psychological link between the offense and the offender (as maintained by psychological theories of culpability) or on the deviant subjectivity of the offender (the positivistic negation of culpability), but instead on the "normative" criterion of culpability that, in the final analysis, relates to the legally recognized position of the offender vis-à-vis the normative system and the system of legal consequences.[38]

This conclusion agrees with the earlier observations concerning the need to look at the overall legal status of an adolescent when deciding whether or not to find him or her responsible for an infringement of penal law. In the same vein, Juan Bustos proposes that the idea of culpability may be defined as responsibility:

> If we assert that culpability is responsibility, then we must necessarily look at the specific individual involved, and it consequently becomes a matter of examining the person responsible for the act in question. We therefore have a theory regarding the element of injustice (the offense) and, on a different and independent basis, a theory regarding the element of responsibility (the person or offender) in which the two elements are joined by a common element, since just as the element of injustice relates to an act (not the person who committed it), so too does the element of responsibility refer to the person in relation to the act (s)he committed (not to the person in relation to his or her personality, character, or lifestyle).[39]

To conclude this analysis of imputability, we should also look at another approach derived from criminal theory and the study of Latin American writings on penal law. The concept of imputability, understood as legal capacity under penal law or as a set of biopsychological features exhibited by a minor, has no clear normative basis in the penal codes of the region, which generally go no further than making references to "those who are not punishable or are exempt from responsibility," without differentiating among categories of such elements as grounds for justification or exoneration. Thus, there are authors who say that, in the existing legal formulations, age would constitute "personal grounds for precluding responsibility."[40]

This diversity of arguments reaffirms the assertion that the "age of criminal responsibility"—based upon nonimputability, preclusion, or some policy criterion relating to criminal law—acts as a barrier or dividing line between the system of adjudication for adults and juveniles. It must not be forgotten that the aim of constructing a theory of criminal law as such is to provide elements to use in limiting the punitive power of the state and safeguarding the individual's subjective rights, rather than to create separate categories of people based on whether or not they can be penalized.

Accordingly, the concept of "age of criminal responsibility" is not intended as a means of denying an adolescent his or her identity as an autonomous person having rights and responsibilities, but rather as a means of preventing a given sanction—the punishment that would be imposed on an adult—from being levied against the adolescent.

This theoretical argument finds its clearest and most solid normative basis in the formula used by the CRC to refer to penal offenses committed by adolescents (this formula appears in the heading of article 40, which refers to "every child alleged as, accused of, or recognized as having infringed the penal law . . .") and to stipulate in article 40.3.a, as previously cited, that it is necessary to establish a minimum age below which children shall be presumed not to have the capacity to infringe the penal law.

These interpretations of the concept of responsibility contain the essential elements of the model:

1. The concept of responsibility is a mechanism for limiting the State's punitive power, that is it functions as a safeguard.

2. The notion of responsibility makes it possible to establish a legal link between the act and the person who committed that act and between that person and the legal consequence ascribed thereto.

3. The "responsible subject" should be considered within the context of that individual's legal and social status; a responsible adolescent is not a theoretical abstraction, but a subject at law who gains that identity on the basis of an effective recognition of the fact that the individual's social relationships are established on the basis of the attribution of rights and obligations.[41]

As a safeguard, the idea of responsibility calls for the full application of the requirements established under general penal law regarding the attribution of responsibility, proof of the commission of the act defined under penal law, absence of grounds for justification that would expunge the illegality of the act, absence of grounds for excluding culpability other than minority, and the possibility of having acted otherwise. The idea of responsibility also ensures that the sanction will bear relation to—and, indeed, that its maximum degree will be proportionate to—the act proven to have been committed. Finally, the consideration of the status of the specific offender ensures that the responsibility ascribed will be commensurate with the actual stage reached by the offender's evolving legal capacities and the social conditions under which the act was committed.

In sum, the primary function of the concept of responsibility is to permit the incorporation, in a particularly extensive and intensive manner, of the guarantees that the justice system has developed to curb the power of the state.

The Principle of Recognition of a Judicial-Penal Conflict: The Principle of Legality

In a guardianship-based juvenile justice system, an abandoned juvenile and a juvenile offender are functionally interchangeable, since both may be subject to the same legal consequences. The basis for equating the two is the concept of crime as a pathology and of penalties as a form of treatment. The system based on responsibility, on the other hand, is founded on a strict definition of infringement of penal law as the only admissible grounds for the imposition of the legal consequences (measures) of a declaration of responsibility.

In addition to acknowledging the child as a subject at law and recognizing the principle of responsibility, it is equally important to bear in mind that the circumstances leading to intervention by the state constitute a conflict or dispute that is regulated by penal law. It is a conflict involving legal rights that are protected by the threat of punishment, as well as specific actions that threaten or impair those rights and that are expressly defined in penal law.

Thus, to say—as advocates of the guardianship-based juvenile justice system have sought to do—that juveniles have been removed from the sphere of penal law[42] is an unjustifiable euphemism. What is actually occurring is that these conflicts are defined—or identified—in penal law, while their consequences, and the conditions under which they are to be applied, are to be found in other legal instruments, such as those of the juvenile penal justice system or laws designed for minors. Such legal conflicts are thus regulated by a series of heterogeneous provisions and standards drawn from different parts of the legal system.

An awareness that a serious conflict has arisen with regard to a person's rights calls for action on the part of the state, since "the administration of justice is justified by the formalization of the conflict, i.e., by the system's ability to examine and resolve serious inter-personal conflicts or disputes in an atmosphere of relative calm, from a removed stance, while guaranteeing the rights of the parties involved."[43]

Once it has been established that the state should intervene in order to resolve the conflict of interests, it is important for the state to consider the matter in its entirety, from the vantage point both of the adolescent and of the social and individual interests involved. The legal system's response to juvenile offenders must not be partial or unilateral, but must instead integrate, insofar as possible, the different components of the conflict. The response should therefore take the form of adjudication, since through due process a judge can afford effective protection for these opposing interests, as well as rank them and thus determine which should prevail, taking into consideration the special rights of the child and the child's degree of responsibility.

This perspective allows us to separate two areas of juvenile law that are usually confused with one another: that of the guardianship of the rights of children when those rights are threatened or have been violated, and the reaction to infringements of penal law. The spheres of law and of social welfare or assistance should be clearly separated, with attention being devoted to the nature of the circumstances that have motivated the intervention of the state in each of these areas.

Only on the basis of an exact, accurate analysis of the legal conflict to be resolved by the courts can limits be set on the possible legal consequences to be ascribed to the adolescent. In particular, the possible deprivation of liberty, as a last resort, will be effective if and only if the law authorizes its use only in the case of the most serious types of conflicts under penal law, that is, those that place persons in real danger or do them actual harm.

The link between punishable conduct and the principle of legality is analyzed by Ferrajoli:

> Punishable forms of deviant behavior . . . are not those which, because of their intrinsic or ontological nature, are recognized in each case as being immoral, as being naturally abnormal or as being socially harmful. Rather, they are those which are formally indicated by law as required grounds for the imposition of a penalty, according to the classic formulation of nullum crimen nulla poena sine lege.[44]

The application of the principle of legality to the sphere of juvenile delinquency places an absolute limit on the possibility of applying sanctions in cases that have not previously been strictly and precisely described and sanctioned by the law. The fact that this must predate the commission of the specific act to be penalized is an imperative that extends to the judiciary (the principle of legality in its restrictive sense, i.e., that there is no crime except as provided by law) and to legislators, who are therefore bound to formulate bills of law in limitative terms and with empirical precision (the principle of legality in its strict sense).[45] Viewed in this light, such legal terms as "irregularities" and "deviant conduct" contained in the laws applying to juveniles are clearly illegitimate.

The principle of legality requires that there must be a certain minimum degree of judicial certainty, thereby preventing the finding that a wrongful act has been committed—and hence that the imposition of a punishment is a possibility—from being entirely at the discretion of the magistrate.

The CRC accords express recognition of this principle in article 40.2.a:

> States Parties shall, in particular, ensure that: a) No child shall be alleged as, be accused of, or recognized as having infringed the penal law by reason of acts or omissions that were not prohibited by national or international law at the time they were committed.

In article 37.b the principle is applied to limit the use of punitive measures: "No child shall be deprived of his or her liberty unlawfully or arbitrarily. The arrest, detention or imprisonment of a child shall be in conformity with the law and shall be used only as a measure of last resort and for the shortest appropriate period of time."

The American Convention on Human Rights (art. 9) also provides that no one may be convicted of acts or omissions that were not unlawful under the applicable legal provisions at the time they were committed. This provision is also found in article 15.1 of the International Covenant on Civil and Political Rights.

The specific instruments in this area recognize and recommend a "delegated" form of legal definition or description or, in other words, the application of the definitions of penal offenses applying to adults in defining infractions under the juvenile system. A correct application of this technique prohibits the legal definition of forms of conduct that are punishable only if they are committed by minors.

On the contrary, there is an increasingly clear trend in legal doctrine toward the establishment of a shorter list of offenses for juveniles by decriminalizing acts for juveniles that would be punishable when committed by an adult. Hence, the list of punishable offenses for juveniles will never be longer than the list for adults, but it is indeed recommended that it should be shorter.

The reasons for proposing this primary form of decriminalization in the case of adolescents is based on the peculiar legal status of adolescents in relation to the state and its laws. The existence of certain human rights that are specific to children and adolescents constitutes a set of special protective standards for them. The extent of these protective standards for children, for which the CRC is the basic instrument, is designed to protect their integral development by ensuring their enjoyment of a series of wholly interdependent rights, all of which must be upheld in order to permit their genuine development. Given the interdependent nature of these rights, integral protection of the rights of the child[46] must be afforded, and any violation of, threat to, or restriction of those rights must be considered from the standpoint of its effects on those rights as an integral whole and in terms of the state's obligation to promote and safeguard children's and adolescents' development.

Thus, childhood and adolescence are stages in life during which individuals enjoy special protection under the law, and greater tolerance is called for in dealing with infringements of the law committed by adolescents, especially in view of their diminished capacity in terms of the commission of wrongful acts, the fact that the offenses they commit are often minor ones and are unpremeditated, and that, as a rule, complex forms of conduct are involved in which they are unlikely to be directing the course of events giving rise to criminal acts.[47]

Application of the Principles of Opportunity

The fourth pillar of the model is that the state's prosecution of violations of penal laws by adolescents is governed by the principle of opportunity rather than by the principle of legality. According to the principle of legality, government authorities have an absolute duty to prosecute and punish the guilty, which precludes any sort of discretion on the part of the authorities whose job it is to prosecute such cases.

Guardianship-based juvenile justice systems did not even try to apply the principle of legality to the prosecution of offenses; however, no rational screening of cases was made either. Indeed, most of the laws applying to minors included some sort of "filtering" clause about the social or material position of the child that contained references to "a healthy home environment," "material or moral danger," or similar terms.

In short, the system was encouraged to set up screening mechanisms, generating a form of selectivity that has since been well documented and whose end result was that middle- and upper-class adolescents could commit unlawful acts with impunity, whereas adolescents from underprivileged segments of society were subjected to expanded and reinforced punitive control mechanisms. Laws based on the CRC have dealt with this issue by providing for the application of the principle of opportunity either as a rule or an exception, using as a model the "diversion" provided for by rule 11 of the Rules of Beijing and article 40.3.b of the CRC, which holds out the possibility of adopting measures for dealing with child offenders "without resorting to judicial proceedings, providing that human rights and legal safeguards are fully respected."

This is more a case of diversion than of applying the principle of opportunity, because it opens the door to a system of adjudication without trial. It is important to point out, however, that the CRC itself restricts the possibility of applying certain kinds of measures without judicial review, including separation from parents (art. 9) and deprivation of liberty (art. 37). In order for this principle to be applied correctly, it is important for national laws to contain a provision that explicitly states that the legal consequences deriving from a finding of responsibility for the infringement of penal law may be established only by means of judicial adjudication under due process of law and that no form of coercion may be employed by any authority whatsoever as a consequence of the commission of an act defined as an infringement of penal law except by means of adjudication under due process of law.

It is important to note the existence of evidence to the effect that the application of the principle of opportunity does not contribute to an increase in criminal activity among juveniles; indeed, the commission of crimes by juveniles actually decreased in Germany during the 1980s, when this principle was being applied, as the federal government itself has acknowledged.[48]

Nevertheless, it is evident (and research findings show this to be true) that the application of the principle of opportunity can give rise to arbitrary practices and may heighten the selectivity of the juvenile penal justice system. The principle of opportunity must not be used as a means of sidestepping the minimum standards of equality that must be observed if a punitive system is to maintain its legitimacy.

Thus, the principle of opportunity is nothing more than a means of supplementing the decriminalization efforts of legislators who, as noted earlier, may not extend the list of punishable acts for adolescents by including acts that are not offenses if committed by an adult, but who can, on the other hand, shorten that list.

The Intensive Application of Penal and Procedural Safeguards: Due Process

Penal and procedural safeguards are closely interrelated and constitute an integrated group of techniques for defining and verifying the suppositions on which the state's reaction is based; their purpose is to keep arbitrary action to an absolute minimum by determining what assumptions underlie a judgment of responsibility and by setting up conditions that help to ensure that this judgment will not be arbitrary, but will instead be based on determinations referring to facts and standards that can be empirically corroborated.[49] The system of responsibility being proposed calls for an intensive use of mechanisms that will protect the rights of the adolescents concerned.

As regards substantive matters, the principles of legality and of humanity must be upheld, and a principle needs to be formulated that will guarantee that findings of culpability are well founded. The principle of humanity will be addressed as part of the discussion of legal measures; the basic elements of the principles of legality and responsibility have already been analyzed.

The use of procedural safeguards will ensure that due process is observed in criminal proceedings involving adolescents. The CRC sets forth, expressly and restrictively, a series of guarantees whose purpose is to ensure due process:

1. Presumption of innocence (40.2.b.i)

2. Legal proof, the right to present evidence in one's defense and to contest adverse evidence (40.2.b.i and iv)

3. Attribution and notification of charges (40.2.b.ii)

4. The right to legal and other appropriate assistance in preparing and presenting a defense (40.2.b.ii and 37.d)

5. A competent, independent and impartial authority or judicial body (40.2.b.iii)

6. Determination of the case without delay (40.2.b.iii)

7. A fair hearing according to law (40.2.b.iii)

8. The right to call witnesses on one's behalf and to examine adverse witnesses or have them examined (40.2.b.iv)

9. The right not to be compelled to give testimony or to confess guilt (40.2.b.iv)

10. The right to appeal judicial decisions and have them reviewed (40.2.b.v)

11. The right to personal integrity and privacy during the proceedings (40.2.b.vii)

12. The right to alternatives to institutionalization during the proceedings (37.b and 40.4)

13. Principle of treatment proportionate to the offense and the juvenile's circumstances (guidelines for adjudication)

14. The right to be judged according to laws, in proceedings and by authorities specifically intended for dealing with children who are alleged to, accused of, or recognized as having infringed the penal law.

The long list of such guarantees that are explicitly set forth in the CRC—together with the application, in accordance with the principle of benefit of penal law, of any other safeguard that may be asserted in any other national or international instrument containing procedural guarantees—attests to the fact that the model of legal responsibility is equipped with sufficient normative mechanisms to ensure due process.

The existence of this array of mechanisms suggests that it is indeed possible to move beyond the inquisitional, authoritarian proceedings prevailing in guardianship-based juvenile justice systems, which are based on the power vested in the magistrate to make a determination and devise judicial formulas for the disposition of cases without any participation on the part of the individual in question and in reference to vague classifications not amenable to empirical verification (e.g., dangerousness, "irregular situations," and readaptive capacity).

Just as the courts, as a repository of power and decision-making authority, have been the central component of the guardianship-based juvenile justice system, the task of building safeguards into the model of legal responsibility will surely pave the way for proceedings based on the participation of the accused, the recognition of guarantees, the search for an empirically verifiable truth, and judicial decisions that strictly adhere to the law.[30]

The Legal Consequences of Responsibility

Foundations and Guidelines

Article 40 of the CRC contains what I feel is the most comprehensive synthesis yet developed of criminal policy as it relates to the nature and purposes of the legal consequences for adolescents who are found to be responsible for a criminal offense. This article relies on three fundamental principles for directing intervention:

a. Intervention should foster the adolescent's sense of dignity and self-worth, and the measures taken must therefore not seek his or her degradation or subjugation; accordingly, this principle constitutes a supplementary guarantee for the prohibition of torture or other forms of cruel, inhumane, or degrading treatment or punishment (principle of humanity and human dignity).

b. Intervention should strengthen the young person's respect for the rules of social coexistence based on a respect for the rights of others; in other words, if the adolescent is involved in social relationships governed by rights and duties, then the consequences of an infringement of the latter should be such as to foster a sense of respect for social coexistence.

c. The specific objective of intervention is to promote young people's integration into society and to encourage them to play a constructive role in society. This is a positive principle in that it structures the content of such interventions. It is also limiting, however, because it blocks the application of desocializing or depersonalizing measures that jeopardize the integral development of the adolescent.

There is another principle to be drawn from the general tenets of the CRC that, although it is not explicitly stated in that instrument, can be deduced from a number of its provisions: the principle of the intangibility of rights, which signifies that the adolescent may not be deprived of any rights other than those expressly restricted by the sanction imposed on him or her.

This principle is of pivotal importance when the time comes for the judge to decide on some sort of measure, seeking to choose the least severe measure in terms of the adolescent's rights, to resort to the deprivation of liberty only in those cases where the use of that measure is specified, and to safeguard the rights of adolescents who are deprived of their liberty so that the deprivation of their right to liberty does not turn into the deprivation or restriction of all of their rights.

Hence, even when a juvenile offender is deprived of liberty, he or she is not deprived of the right to education, to recreation, to learn a vocation, or of any other right except those expressly restricted by the adjudication of the case in which the juvenile is found to be responsible.

The grounds for placing this series of demands on the juvenile criminal justice system are not that juvenile offenders are "less guilty" than adult offenders, that their behavior is the result of societal neglect, or that they suffer from some form of deviance or irregular condition. The responsibility borne by adolescents is different from that borne by adults not only because the adult criminal justice system could do irrevocable harm to the lives of juvenile offenders, but also, and most importantly, because adolescents have a different legal status from adults, and the maximum expression of that status is that it is the state's duty to ensure children's well-being and integral development and to see to it that they achieve an appropriate form of social integration. This aim should not be interpreted in a restrictive sense (as relating to material or physical conditions alone), but rather in the broadest possible terms, that is, as relating to human dignity in general (inter alia, art. 6.2 and art. 27 of the CRC).

Objectives and Classifications: Deprivation and Nondeprivation of Liberty

A correct application of the proposed system requires a suitable concept of the measures that may be applied to juvenile offenders. Taking into consideration the aims set forth in article 40 of the CRC as analyzed above, the chief objective of such measures is to strengthen the adolescent's sense of responsibility or, as some have termed it, the adolescent's "responsibilization."[51]

Society's response to juvenile offenders should be profoundly and intrinsically educational in nature, rather than starting from a repressive or punitive stance, which eventually leads to the adoption of an "educational" or "formative" measure. The system must cease to be a catalog of "protective measures" and become instead a comprehensive system encompassing every part of the system, from the police force to those responsible for implementing the measures adopted, from the state to the community. We must cease to view the system of "rehabilitation and protection" as the final reparative stage of a harmful process that has been exacerbated by state intervention.

Whereas, in the past, attempts were made to base the effectiveness and legitimacy of the measures to be adopted on their educational/reformatory character (in the case of the advocates of a medically oriented therapeutic system) or on their ability to deter or preclude certain types of behavior (in the case of the supporters of a punitive model), the legitimacy and value of the measures to be applied under the model based on the CRC should be afforded by their effectiveness in fostering a sense of personal dignity, responsibility, and social integration.

The personal dignity of adolescents should be understood as respect for their rights and their ability to exercise those rights independently in keeping with their evolving capacities. The important point in such cases is to limit any abusive restriction of adolescents' rights and the independent exercise thereof.

Article 37.a of the CRC, in particular, states that no child shall be subjected to torture or other cruel, inhuman, or degrading treatment or punishment and prohibits the imposition of capital punishment or imprisonment without possibility of release for any person below age 18.

The social integration of adolescents may be defined as the exercise of their rights and obligations based on an adherence to the values predominating in a democratic society: respect for human dignity and for the rights of others, and the use of legitimate means of expressing their differences and securing the benefits of being a member of society. The measures to be applied should seek not only to refrain from hindering this process of social integration but to actively promote it, in accordance with the obligation to protect the adolescent's integral development.

The concept of responsibility may be understood, according to De Leo, as a "process for governing responsive interactions leading to the development of a sense of ownership of one's own acts and of authority over oneself, [which] is an inalienable right of young persons."[52]

The process of learning how to take part in the life of a society governed by the rule of law cannot be based on the idea of irresponsibility; it is a gradual process involving the acquisition, step by step, of a feeling of ownership over one's own acts and of self-control. Depriving young people of the opportunity to learn this is to deny them the chance to develop within an atmosphere of harmonious social coexistence. The measures to be employed should instead foster this process.

If the idea of the "development of the child's personality" (one of the central guidelines of the CRC) has to do with the formation of an "identity" and if this personal identity is the result of a "social process" in which the value system (expressed in rules and norms) and the system of coexistence (expressed in rights, means of control, and social obligations) are an integral scheme with which the individual interacts, then in order to develop, young people need to acquire a sense of responsibility, and the only way for them to do so is through social experience.

The inevitable conclusion, then, is that the acquisition of a sense of personal responsibility hinges on the individual's interaction with socializing agents; the adolescent's relationship with society's normative systems and formal mechanisms of social control, in particular, will take on great importance, and these are primarily experienced in the form of the legal system's rule-making functions and role in regulating life in society.

In summary, establishing the idea of responsibility in relation to adolescents can be seen as a way of linking up society's reaction to an act that, under the laws applying to adolescents and adults, constitutes a criminal offense; the objective of this approach is to ensure that the adolescent will acquire a feeling of ownership over his or her own acts together with a sense of their social relevance, and to respect (and foster) the development of his or her personality and full integration into the life of society through the application of certain legal consequences commonly referred to as "measures."

Given this discussion, the concept of responsibility or of "responsibilization," cannot only serve as a safeguard, as already mentioned, but must also be an appropriate expression of the content of intervention, and any measures that may be applied—covering the entire range, from reprimands to deprivation of liberty—are delimited and guided by this orientation toward the promotion of a sense of responsibility. If a system for classifying the possible measures is to be devised on this basis, it will be observed that there are a number of types of measures that, aside from any other features they may have, seek to promote the acquisition of what we have called "responsibility."

Considered from this standpoint, the now classic distinction made by the German legal system between educational or formative measures, disciplinary or corrective measures, and punishments stands in contrast to the placement of all the measures to be used under the heading of "socioformative" measures, as in the model employed for Brazil's Estatuto da Criança e do Adolescente.

The advantage of this three-fold distinction is that it permits a clear differentiation between legal consequence and treatment, therapy, or cures for a sick person. This nomenclature delineates the incompatibility of the concepts of punishment and assistance by reminding us of the impossibility of resolving the paradox as to how to treat people or teach them to handle freedom while they are confined and deprived of their liberty.

The term *socioformative measures* has the virtue of expressing the fact that all measures (even those that involve deprivation of liberty), while they may not be used for educational or formative purposes, should uphold the principles of personal dignity and responsibility and should be oriented toward achieving genuine social integration. The difficulty with this option is that, since the term *socioformative* is not adequately defined, there may be a tendency to interpret measures placed under this heading as a form of psychosocial intervention undertaken for behavior modification purposes.

I suggest that the measures to be used should be classified according to the degree of restriction they entail, with the major division being between those that involve the *deprivation of liberty* and those that do not. This criterion would appear to be the most appropriate from the standpoint of rights and safeguards, since it precludes any sort of "false advertising" that would conceal the true nature of measures that restrict the individual's rights by mislabeling them as welfare-oriented or educational measures.

The CRC strictly limits the restriction of the right to personal liberty, stipulating that such restrictions must be used only as a measure of last resort and for the shortest appropriate period of time, and that they must be ordered and carried out in conformity with the law (art. 37.b). This provision of the CRC has been put into effect through the promulgation of new laws in Latin America which require that in juvenile cases a standard of proportionality must be maintained between the act and any measure involving the deprivation of liberty. Such measures may be applied only in the case of serious offenses that have caused personal harm, and even then are never mandatory; the judge always has the option of applying a measure that does not deprive the juvenile of his or her liberty.

In addition, with regard to the implementation of such measures, article 37.c provides that

> Every child deprived of liberty shall be treated with humanity and respect for the inherent dignity of the human person, and in a manner which takes into account the needs of persons of his or her age.

Specifically, the CRC provides that any child who is deprived of his or her liberty has the right to:

- be separated from adults (37.c)

- maintain contact with his or her family (37.c)

- have prompt access to legal assistance (37.d)

- challenge the legality of the deprivation of his or her liberty before a court or other competent, independent and impartial authority, and to a prompt decision on any such action (37.d).

These same rights are also contained in the Beijing Rules, which state (rule 13.3): "Juveniles under detention . . . shall be entitled to all rights and guarantees of the Standard Minimum Rules for the Treatment of Prisoners adopted by the United Nations."

The UN Rules for the Protection of Juveniles Deprived of Their Liberty constitute a complete catalog of definitions, principles, and rights of minors deprived of their liberty and should serve as guidelines for the drafting of laws and regulations on the subject.

These rules define juveniles as "any person under eighteen years of age" and do not differentiate between persons who are imputable and those who are not. For purposes of applying the rules, deprivation of liberty is defined as "any form of detention or imprisonment, or internment in a public or private institution from which the juvenile may not leave on his own free will by order of any judicial or administrative authority or other pubic authority" (rule 11, subparagraphs a and b). This definition is of great significance because most national legislation provides for measures such as internment or institutionalization that clearly do deprive the juvenile of his or her liberty. With regard to the requirements pertaining to the deprivation of liberty, the rules state that such measures should "be determined as a last resort and for the minimum amount of time necessary and shall be limited to exceptional cases. The duration of the sanction shall be determined by the judicial authority without excluding the possibility that the juvenile may be released before that time" (rule 2).

The rules contain provisions regarding the following matters:

- special rules applying to juveniles in preventive custody (rules 17–18)

- rules on administration, induction, registration, mobility, transfer, and classification (rules 19–30)

- rules regarding the physical facilities in which the juvenile is held while deprived of his or her liberty (rules 31–7)

- rules on education, vocational training, work, recreational activities, and worship (rules 31–48)

- rules on health care (rules 49–58)

- rules that guarantee contact with the family, attorneys, and community (rules 59–62)

- rules limiting the use of physical coercion and force, and rules concerning disciplinary and complaint procedures (rules 63–78).

Measures could also be classified by the length of time for which they will be applied, with different categories: for such measures as probation, which are applied over some period of time; for those that are completed at the time they are issued, such as reprimands; and for measures whose implementation takes place at a subsequent time, such as fines, the repair of damage caused, or community service. This classification would serve a fundamental purpose in structuring the justice system's mechanisms for overseeing the application of such measures with a view to ensuring their suitability and effectiveness.

Conclusions: Responsibility as a Safeguard for the Rights of Adolescents

The concept of responsibility is a more effective means of providing safeguards than the idea of education is. Responsibility for acts committed, safeguarding the right to personal development, and avoiding exclusion from society are the basic guidelines for the measures to be taken in relation to juveniles.

Ultimately, the limiting effect of the model should be gauged by its capacity to restrict the deprivation of liberty, which, as Albrecht says, "is deprivation of life within society."[53] Deprivation of liberty cannot be used as a specific method—a treatment—for achieving responsibilization; on the contrary, the concept of responsibility provides a means of limiting its use on the basis of the principle of proportionality at the same time that it endows the measure's application with substantive content while impeding excessive interference with the personality of the adolescent.

An attempt has been made to demonstrate that the idea of responsibility has a solid legal foundation and that, as such, it can be limited and regulated so that it may be increased by degrees and with the sole aim of fostering law-abiding behavior on the part of juveniles and preventing state intervention — whether punitive or formative — from adding to the damage already done and to the juvenile's marginalization from society.

Accordingly, a basic principle of the new model is a sharp reduction in the likelihood of incarceration, coupled with an explicit injunction against any attempt to legitimize it by depicting it as a formative measure. In the final analysis, the reason for resorting to incarceration, whether we like it or not, is society's refusal to deal with assaults on certain kinds of legal rights by any means less harsh than deprivation of liberty or other punitive measures.[54]

Serious consideration should be given to the evidence that segregation and differentiation are not responses that promote the social integration of juveniles who have suffered serious social and personal damage. The alternative model, however, seeks to promote a real increase in the juvenile's degree of social integration based on the exercise of his or her rights and on the formation of social relationships founded on mutual respect and acceptance — in short, on genuine personal development.

It should be stated that acknowledging juveniles as subjects at law means that we must renounce the practice of forming vertical relationships with them under the aegis of the authoritarian brand of guardianship whose most glaring example is the incarceration of juveniles in institutions, reformatories, and jails. The rights-based approach, in contrast, entails rebuilding our relationships with juveniles and supplanting authoritarian forms of intervention with a reaction that, as has been emphasized, will tend to increase their sense of responsibility by promoting their social integration and the exercise of their rights.

Finally, it may be appropriate to describe the overall context within which the justice system's dealings with children and adolescents should take place. Such a description is provided in rule 1.4 of the UN Standard Minimum Rules for the Administration of Juvenile Justice:

Juvenile justice shall be conceived as an integral part of the national development process of each country, within a comprehensive framework of social justice for all juveniles, thus, at the same time, contributing to the protection of the young and the maintenance of a peaceful order in society.

NOTES

1. See R. Cantarero, "Derecho Penal y Procesal de Menores," Ed Montecorvo, Madrid, 1985, pp. 85 y ss; M. Barbero Santos, "Delincuencia Juvenil," Universidad de Santiago de Compostella, 1973; J. R. Mendoza, *La Protección y el Tratamiento de los Menores*, Buenos Aires, 1969, pp. 1–7.

2. See A. Bunster, "Sobre el Régimen Tutelar para Menores Infractores," in *Escritos de Derecho Penal y Política Criminal*, México City, 1994, p. 237; and R. Cantarero, op. cit., n. 1, pp. 92 et seq.

3. See E. García Méndez, *Derecho de la Infancia y Adolescencia en América Latina. De la Situación Irregular a la Protección Integral*, Forum-Pacis, Bogotá, 1994 ; P. Veerman, *The Rights of the Child and the Changing Image of Childhood*, Martinus Nijhoff Publishers, Ad Dordrecht, The Netherlands, 1992, pp. 3–11; G. Therbron, "Los Derechos de los Niños desde la constitución del concepto de menor. Un estudio comparado de países occidentales," in *Intercambio Social y Desarrollo del Bienestar*, L. Moreno compi-

lator, Consejo Superior de Investigaciones Científicas. Instituto de Estudios Sociales Avanzados, Madrid, 1993, pp. 77–143; M. Cillero, "Leyes de Menores, Sistema Penal e Instrumentos de Derechos Humans," in *Sistema Jurídico y Derechos Humanos. El Derecho Nacional y las Obligaciones de Chile en materia de Derechos Humanos*, C. Medina and J. Mera (editors), Diego Portales University, Santiago, 1996, pp. 477–543.

4. The reference to naturalist positivism alludes to the school of thought that developed out of organicist sociological evolutionism and to the explanations for the phenomenon of criminality proposed by criminological anthropology. In both Europe and the United States, there is evidence of the influence exerted by the theories of such authors as Herbert Spencer, Cesare Lombroso, Enrico Ferri, Rafael Gárfalo, and others in the emergence of special legislation regarding minors in the late nineteenth and early twentieth centuries. See A. Platt, *The Child Savers: The Invention of Delinquency*, 2a., ed. 1977. A Spanish translation of this publication is available under the title *Los Salvadores de los Niños o la Invención de la Delincuencia* Ed. S.XXI, 1a. ed, Mexico, 1982, pp. 44 et seq., regarding the United States, and G. De Leo, *La Justicia de Menores*, Ed. Teide, Barcelona, 1985, regarding Italy.

5. E. García Méndez, op cit., n. 3, p. 82.

6. Examples of this legislative reform movement include the new laws passed since 1989 in Bolivia, Brazil, Costa Rica, Ecuador, El Salvador, Guatemala, and Peru, all of which have been based on the Convention on the Rights of the Child.

7. See A. Platt, op. cit., n. 4, pp. 120 et seq.; G. De Leo, op. cit., n. 4, pp. 8 et seq.; E. García Méndez, op. cit., n. 3, p. 44; E. Giménez-Salinas, "La Justicia de Menores en el S. XX, Una Gran Incógnita," in *Un Derecho Penal del Menor*, J. Bustos Ramírez, Director, Ed. Conosur, Santiago, 1992, pp. 11 et seq.

8. Juvenile Courts were created in 1905 in England, 1908 in Germany, 1911 in Portugal, 1912 in France, 1921 in Argentina, 1922 in Japan, 1923 in Brazil, 1924 in Spain, and 1928 in Chile. By 1928, only two states in the United States did not have such courts. See E. García Méndez, op. cit., n. 3, p. 44, and A. Platt, op. cit., n. 4, p. 154.

9. C. Cuello Calón, *Tribunales para Niños*, Madrid, 1917, p. 38.

10. L. Jiménez de Asúa, *Cuestiones de Derecho Penal*, Talleres Gráficos Nacionales, Quito, 1953, p. 85.

11. In this connection, see A. Platt, op. cit., n. 4, p. 153, which cites cases in the courts of Pennsylvania and Illinois that upheld the constitutionality of these laws.

12. *In re Gault*, 378, USA, 1967, cited in A. Platt, op. cit., n. 4, pp. 173 et seq.

13. This is the manner in which a solution was found for the problem posed by the question of the application of procedural guarantees to minors who, because they "could not be held accountable," could not be considered to be "persons charged with a crime." This is the Commission's interpretation of article 14.2 of the International Covenant on Civil and Political Rights, in Salgar de Montejo with Colombia (No. 64/1979), paragraph 10.4, cited in D. O'Donnel, *Protección Internacional de los Derechos Humanos*, Lima, 1989, p. 327.

14. C. González Zorrilla, "Los Menores entre Protección y Justicia. El Debate sobre la Responsabilidad," in *Un Derecho Penal del Menor*, J. Bustos Ramírez, Director, Ed. Conosur, Santiago, 1992, p. 133.

15. *Sistemas Penales y Derechos Humanos en América Latina. Informe Final*, Eugenio Zaffaroni (coord.), IIDH, Depalma, 1986, pp. 239 et seq.

16. In this connection, see E. García Méndez and E. Carranza (comps.), *Infancia, Adolescencia y Control Social en América Latina*, a study sponsored by UNICRI (United Nations Interregional Crime and Justice Research Institute) and ILANUD (Instituto Latinoamericano de las Naciones Unidas para la Prevención del Delito y el Tratamiento del Delincuente), De Palma, 1991; F. Pilotti and I. Rizzini, *A Arte de Gobernar çs*, IIN, University of Santa Ursula, Rio de Janeiro, 1995; M. Cillero (coord.), *Evolución Histórica de la Consideración Jurídica de la Infancia en Chile*, IIN (Instituto de Investigación Nutritional), Montevideo, 1994, pp. 75–138; H. D. McKay, "Report on the Criminal Careers of Male Delinquents in Chicago: Task Force Report—Juvenile Delinquency and Youth Crime," pp. 107–13, cited in A. Platt, op. cit., n. 4, p. 173; M. Cillero and P. Egenau, "Administración de Justicia Juvenil y Daño Psicosocial," in *Los Derechos del Niño en una Sociedad Democrática*, Ed. SENAME (Servicio Nacional de Menores), Santiago, pp. 272–89.

17. In this connection, see M. Cillero, "Leyes de Menores, Sistema Penal e Instrumentos de Derechos Humans," in *Sistema Jurídico y Derechos Humanos. El Derecho Nacional y las Obligaciones de Chile en Materia de Derechos Humanos*; see also R. Schurmann, "El Grado de Eficiencia en Uruguay del Sistema Penal Minoril como Límite del Control Social," and R. Maxera, "La Legislación Penal de Menores a la Luz de los Instrumentos Internacionales: El Caso de Costa Rica," both in *Del Revés al Derecho* (various authors), sponsored by UNICEF, UNICRI, and ILANUD, Ed. Galerna, Buenos Aires, 1992.

18. See E. García Méndez, op. cit., n. 3; G. De Leo, op cit., n. 4. Along the same lines, most of the existing historical studies on legal provisions applying to minors indicate that one of the main reasons why legislative reforms are undertaken is the existence of signs of an increase in juvenile crimi-

nality. See also M. Cillero op. cit., n. 3; A. Platt op. cit., n. 4; E. García Méndez and E. Carranza, op. cit., n. 16.

19. Lechner contends that fear of criminal violence may, above and beyond its objective validity, constitute a reflection of society's internal fears. N. Lechner, *Los Patios Interiores de la Democracia. Subjetividad y Política*, FCE, Mexico City, 1988. It is quite likely that no symbolization of society's collective imagery fits this interpretation so well as that of juvenile delinquency, which is emblematic—by virtue of its irrationality and unpredictability—of a society beset by the tensions associated with senseless violence whose true causes are unknown and that erupts, according to mainstream theory, out of the heart of society, the cities, and the family with an apparently irresistible force. This may account for the social impact of criminal acts committed by adolescents and the strength of public repercussions, which, in many cases, are blown out of proportion when compared with concerns about adult criminality, corruption, illegal drug traffic, and other forms of violence that affect Latin America.

20. A distinguished Brazilian educator who is an expert on policies relating to children.

21. See D. Melossi, *The State of Social Control: A Sociological Study of Concepts of State and Social Control in the Making of Democracy*, 1990. A Spanish translation of this publication is available under the title *El Estado del Control Social*, Siglo XXI Editores, Mexico City, 1992, pp. 15–20. Melossi bases his discussion of this issue on the writings of Kelsen, who asserts that the only possible definition of the "state" is one founded upon a juridical-normative conceptualization. Kelsen refutes the sociological attempt to distinguish between a "juridical State" and a "sociological State," contending that human actions are not considered to be part of the "state" except where the evaluative criterion is the juridical-normative order of the state. According to this (sociological) theory, there is indeed such a thing as a state as viewed from a "sociological" standpoint, that is, as a construct of a specifically oriented common endeavor, while some people devote their efforts toward objectifying the existence of the state as a juridical-normative order, or in other words, the existence of a system of wholly valid norms. Following this line of reasoning, rather than the usual contraposition of the law and the state, a distinction is drawn between a juridical state and a sociological state; the author concludes that nothing can justify a terminology that uses a single word to designate what are supposed to be two such entirely different concepts. H. Kelsen, Allgemeine Staatslehre, 1925 (Spanish translation: Teoría General del *Estado*, Editora Nacional, 15th edition, Mexico City, 1979, pp. 24–5).

22. On the subject of active and reactive social control, see D. Melossi, op. cit. n. 17, p. 17.

23. The main methods employed for these purposes have been techniques based on the positivist criminological concept of preventing delinquency by "amputating" those characteristics that lead delinquents to act as they do, on the one hand, and, on the other, correctional techniques directed toward achieving rehabilitation. In this regard, see N. Morris. *The Future of Imprisonment* (Studies on Crime and Justice), University of Chicago, 1974. A Spanish translation of this publication is available under the title *El Futuro de las Prisiones*, SXXI, C, de México, 1978. See also A. Platt, op. cit. and R. E. Zaffaroni, *Criminología. Aproximación desde un margen*, Ed Temis, Bogota, 1993, and the classic *Surveiller et punir*, M. Foucault, 1975.

24. The nature of the relationship between violence and the state's response has been brought to light by a number of the approaches taken to justify the punitive role of the state. Hegel asserted that violence is nullified by violence and that it was therefore not determined judicially but rather by necessity, that a second act of violence eliminated the first act of violence. G. F. Hegel, *Grundlinien der Philosophie des Rechts*, 1821 (Spanish translation: *Fundamentos de la Filosofía del Derecho*, Siglo XX, Buenos Aires, 1987, paragraph 93). Resta, for his part, highlights the ambivalent nature of violence, likening it to the Greek pharmakon, with violence serving as both poison and antidote: ". . . violence committed by the sovereign . . . as the only remedy, the only effective antidote for violence." E. Resta, *La Certezza e la Speranza. Saggio su Diritto e Violenza*, 1992 (Spanish translation: *La certeza y la esperanza. Ensayos sobre el Derecho y la Violencia*, Paidos, Buenos Aires, 1995, pp. 28–30).

25. Chile was once such an extreme case in this respect that in 1994 it was actually necessary to promulgate a law specifically designed to prohibit the "protective" incarceration of persons under 18 years of age in jails intended for adults under the provisions of a statute dating from 1967 that permitted this to be done even when the adolescent or child had not even been charged with a penal offense.

26. As early as 1892, V. Listz brought the problem to light when he noted that the kindness done to individuals by promoting their "betterment" should clearly be independent of the commission of a punishable act. He posed the question as to whether it was not a serious mistake to afford the care of the state only to those who had lapsed into criminal behavior. Cited in P. A. Albrecht, *El Derecho Penal de Menores* (first edition in German, 1987), first edition in Spanish, Promociones y Publicaciones Universitarias, Barcelona, 1990, p. 95.

27. Ferrajoli provides a broad-ranging discussion of what he calls an "inquisitional epistemology" that is generically opposed to safeguards and downplays the role of the law. This approach does not impose sanctions on

criminal behavior as such, but rather focuses on the individual or offender and classifies that person as a delinquent from an ethical, natural, or social — and in any case, ontological — perspective. L. Ferrajoli, *Diritto e Ragione. Teoría del Garantismo Penale*, 1989 (Spanish translation: *Derecho y Razón. Teoría del Garantismo Penal*, Ed. Trotta, Madrid, 1995, pp. 41 et seq.).

28. Ferrajoli describes three schools of thought that embrace or represent different facets of these ideas: pedagogical theories focusing on the alteration of behavior, therapeutic doctrines based on the idea of protecting society, and forms of teleological pragmatism that emphasize the resocialization of the individual, one of whose exponents is Von Liszt. Ferrajoli contends that the conclusions reached by these three schools of thought are remarkably consistent. They all consider criminal acts to be pathologies — and place little importance on whether these pathologies are moral, natural, or social in character — and regard penalties as a politically based form of therapy applied either by curative means or via "amputation." Ferrajoli, op. cit., n. 27, pp. 264–70.

29. R. Maurach, *Tratado de Derecho Penal*, Ed. Ariel, Barcelona, 1962, pp. 603 et seq. In a more recent criticism of German legislation in this area, Albrecht states that the legal practice of handing down more or less indeterminate sentences for juveniles (from 6 months to 4 years) is a sign of the orientation of German criminal law toward the "education" of the offender. This type of penalization, which is entirely absent from general criminal law, was introduced by National Socialist legislators and is based on the presumed existence of "harmful tendencies" on the part of the offender and the impossibility of determining how long it will take to "educate" the juvenile in question. He also argues that the indeterminate duration of the penalty is an additional penalty in and of itself and is used in cases where it seems unlikely that the juvenile will be easily influenced by the system. He ends his analysis by recommending the abolishment of indeterminate sentencing on the grounds that it is a questionable mechanism in a state operating under the rule of law. P. A. Albrecht, "El Derecho Penal de Menores," op. cit., n. 26, pp. 351 et seq.

30. P. A. Albrecht, "Respecto del Futuro del Derecho Penal de Menores — Peligros y Chances," in *Un Derecho Penal del Menor*, J. Bustos, op. cit., n. 7, p. 63: "The only constitutionally-sanctioned objective of juvenile criminal justice is the partial guidance of behavior towards legal forms of conduct. From a socio-scientific perspective, this is not "education" (socialization) but simply social control."

31. See L. Ferrajoli, op. cit, n. 27, p. 28.

32. For a history of the drafting of this part of article 40, see Sh. Deetrick, *The United Nations Convention on the Rights of the Child*, Martinus Nijhoff, The Netherlands, 1992, pp. 478–79.

33. In this connection, see the interesting essay authored by J. Eekelaar, "The Interests of the Child and the Child's Wishes: The Role of Dynamic Self-Determinism," in *The Best Interests of the Child*, Philip Alston (editor), UNICEF, Oxford University Press, 1994, pp. 42–61.

34. Regarding this difference, see J. Bustos, "Imputabilidad y Edad Penal," in *Homenaje a Antonio Beristain*, San Sebastian, 1989, pp. 449–52, in which he distinguishes between criminal and noncriminal penal responsibility; A. Baratta, "Elementos de un Nuevo Derecho para la Infancia y la Adolescencia a Propósito del Estatuto del Niño y del Adolescente de Brasil," in *Capítulo Criminológico*, vol. 23, No. 1, January–June 1995, Zulia University. Also see E. García Méndez, *Adolescentes en Conflicto con la Ley Penal: Seguridad Ciudadana y Derechos Fundamentales*, op. cit., second edition, Bogota, 1997, pp. 209–27.

35. The question of how to define the type of responsibility ascribed to young people has been, and probably will continue to be, one of the most heatedly debated aspects of the model. Be that as it may, the categorical statement made by Albrecht in the prologue to the German edition of *El Derecho Penal de Menores*, op. cit., n. 26, is of interest: "The juvenile penal system is the penal system. It is not a system of social law. It is not designed to 'help' but only to serve the purposes of 'social control.'" In our opinion the characteristics of the mechanisms at the system's disposal (particularly the deprivation of liberty) and the objective normative presuppositions underlying its operation (a lack of criminal justice) place what we have called the model of legal responsibility squarely within the sphere of the state's criminal justice system; consequently, all the guarantees that limit the state's punitive power should not only be applied but also reinforced.

36. H. Kelsen, *Reine Rechtslehre*, 1934 (Spanish translation: *Teoría Pura del Derecho*, Eudeba, Buenos Aires, tenth edition, 1971, p. 19).

37. The most typical example of these types of systems bases responsibility on the faculty of discernment, which is still in use in Chile today. Argentina's system also permits the imposition of alternative (successive) penalties or measures on persons above age 16, although it does not rely on the criterion of discernment as a justification.

38. For a brief synopsis of the debate on this issue, see E. R. Zaffaroni, *Manual de Derecho Penal*, general section, sixth edition, Ediar, Buenos Aires, 1991, pp. 511–15.

39. J. Bustos, *Manual de Derecho Penal Español. Parte General*, Ed. Ariel, Barcelona, 1984.

40. See, e.g., E. R. Zaffaroni, *Manual de Derecho Penal*, op. cit., n. 38, p. 109.

41. The constitutive nature of the notion of culpability is brought out by Hassemer, who, following a historical review of the concept's evolution,

concludes that "the object of culpability ceases to be an obvious and measurable fact and becomes instead a construct." W. Hassemer, *Fundamentos de Derecho Penal*, Bosch, 1984, p. 288.

42. This assertion was bandied about and became something of a slogan for the Spanish correctionalist, Dorado Montero: "Penal law has disappeared for child and adolescent offenders and has been turned into a charitable, humanitarian institution overtaken, if you will, by pedagogy, by psychiatry and by the art of governance." Dorado Montero, *Los Peritos Médicos y la Justicia Criminal*, Madrid, 1906, p. 211. More recently, this argument has been turned back on itself with the assertion that what actually disappeared for juveniles were only the safeguards vouchsafed under penal law, with the guardianship-based juvenile justice system taking on the identity of a reinforced penal system. P. Andrés Ibáñez, "El Sistema Tutelar de Menores como Reacción Penal Reforzada," in *Psicología Social y Sistema Penal*, F. Jiménez Burrillo and M. Clemente (compilers), Alianza Universidad, Madrid, 1986, pp. 209–28.

43. W. Hassemer, op. cit., n. 41, p. 300.

44. L. Ferrajoli, op. cit., n. 27, p. 34.

45. L. Ferrajoli, op. cit., n. 27, p. 35.

46. The statement, which is frequently heard in Latin America, that the region's legislation is based on the "doctrine of integral protection" alludes to this idea. In this regard, see E. García Méndez, op. cit., n.3 ; at the normative level, the reader may wish to review Brazil's Estatuto da Criança e do Adolescente, which was promulgated as a federal law on July 13, 1990.

47. For a similar discussion of this subject, see P. A. Albrecht, "Respecto del Futuro del Derecho Penal de Menores — Peligros y Chances," op. cit., n. 30, p. 63.

48. P. A. Albrecht, "Respecto del Futuro del Derecho Penal de Menores — Peligros y Chances," op. cit., n. 30, p. 57. See also C. Roxin et al., Buenos Aires, 1993, particularly, "Facultades discrecionales del Ministerio Público e investigación preparatoria: El principio de oportunidad," Fabricio O. Guariglia, pp. 83–95.

49. See Ferrajoli, op. cit., n. 27, pp. 36 and 40.

50. In this connection, see L. Ferrajoli, op. cit. n. 27, and A. Binder, "Menor Infractor y Proceso . . . Penal? Un Modelo para Armar," in *La Niñez y la Adolescencia en Conflicto con la Ley Penal*, San Salvador, 1995, pp. 83–98.

51. See J. Funes and C. González, "Delincuencia Juvenil e Intervención Comunitaria," in *Revista Menores*, No. 7, January–February 1988, Juvenile Legal Protection Bureau, Ministry of Justice, Spain; G. De Leo, op. cit., n. 4, and R. Cantarero, op. cit., n. 1.

52. G. De Leo, *Responsabilitá: Definizioni e Aplicacioni nel Campo della Giustizia Minorile*, Milan, 1985.

53. P. A. Albrecht, "Respecto del Futuro del Derecho Penal de Menores—Peligros y Chances," op. cit., n. 30.

54. See W. Hassemer, op. cit., n. 41, p. 300.

12 | State Response to Children and Adolescents in Trouble with the Law

EUGENIO RAÚL ZAFFARONI

Two Ideologies Guiding the Response

If we understand "ideology" to mean a system of ideas, that is, something akin to what is sometimes called a "philosophy" in English-speaking circles, and if we disregard the pejorative meaning sometimes given to the term (as concealing reality in some instances and meaning a lack of realism in others), we can say that government responses to the problem of children and adolescents in trouble with the law cover a wide range but can be categorized into two prevailing currents of thought: that of *guardianship* and that of *rights*.

a.   For the guardianship ideology, the child and the adolescent who get into trouble with the law must be placed (materially and formally) outside criminal law and receive specialized treatment from a court that largely takes on a guardianship role, replacing the family, which has failed in its socializing role.

b.   For the rights-oriented ideology, no matter what extenuating or even excusing circumstances might be introduced and adopted and whatever punishments other than imprisonment might be envisioned, or any of the departures from the criminal process that might be proposed, children and adolescents in trouble with the law may not be deprived of their individual rights and guarantees as established in international and constitutional legal agreements for any person accused or convicted of a crime.

Having formulated the problem in these terms and noting in advance that we are very firmly persuaded of the latter position, we will now set forth the reasons for that option, which is indeed that of current international law.

What Is Guardianship in Criminal Law and What Model of State Does It Fit?

Guardianship is not a waiving of criminal law; it does not depart from the framework of punishment, but rather it is one kind of discourse used to exercise the power of punishment: it is the exercise of the power of punishment, justified discursively on the grounds that something is thereby being *safeguarded*; it may be society, the state, the legal system, but also the one being punished. Almost all criminal law discourse is about guardianship at least insofar as the aim is to legitimize punishment, and certainly almost all forms of penal discourse legitimize punishment and the power to punish.

When guardianship discourse seeks to legitimize the power to punish by claiming that the latter is intended to protect the person who is the object of that power, it is implying that the power to punish is beneficial for that person, and, therefore, since it is beneficial, there is no need for controls or limits: when someone is receiving a benefit, the more there is of the benefit, the better off he or she will be.

When this is the starting point taken, it suffices that a government body be imparting the benefit; there is no need for control by any other state body or by the public, unless the benefit is insufficient. The logic of such reasoning leads inexorably to the *inquisition*: an administrative body or a judge or court operating by imparting the benefit (the punishment) and not allowing the presence of prosecutors, defense attorneys, the public, and the news media. Such a body does not even need to be independent of the executive branch, which acts without a prosecutor's office, with no defense, behind closed doors, and in secret.

Such a legal procedure was used in history whenever the people subject to the power to punish were regarded as inferior persons who had to be protected because of their inferiority. Such was the situation of Indians during colonial times, by reason of their theological inferiority (infidels), which required that they be instructed; that of women in the Middle Ages by reason of their genetic weakness, which made them easy prey of Satan, and who were guarded to prevent greater damage from being done to their own souls and those of others; that of the Indians under neocolonialism, when they were subjected to security measures by reason of their genetic or acquired biological inferiority; that of blacks who were brought in as slaves while the white slave master simply kept them in the status in which he had received them; and that of a woman whose goods until a few decades ago were handled by her husband or who could not dispose of her own goods without his consent.

More refined and indirect ways of a guardianship curtailing rights occur through the classification of actions that harm inferior persons: threats of punishment for sexual relations with psychologically incompetent persons who are regarded as being subjectively incapable of enjoying them have the effect of depriving such persons of sexual relations; the criminalization of any contract or dealing with minors and those who are incompetent, the classification of an undefined "seizure of the will," and the like have the effect that in practice such persons—particularly the aged—are deprived of their property rights and their rights to acts of marriage, donation, and last will. In both cases, the claim of guardianship translates into the deprivation of the rights of the supposed victim.

The inquisition likewise assumes that the exercise of the power of punishment need not be subjected to strict material limits: if punishment benefits its recipient, legal formalities need not be observed and general guidelines are enough. As a rule, guardianship is exercised in connection with what is lacking in the person being punished, which can be diagnosed like a disease: when on the basis of one or two symptoms the physician is certain of the disease, there is no need to verify the other symptoms in order to be sure that all are present.

By analogy, or by completely ignoring the principle of legality in the field of basic criminal law, the principle that in the criminal process charges must be presented is denied. When the charge fits a well-described defined crime, it must take the form of a charge that specifies facts of the case, to which the defense will respond, and the person on trial may be accused of nothing else. When there is no criminal classification or material legality, but instead a benefit is being imparted because of information indicating the need to do so, none of this is necessary.

Criminal legal procedure (*nullum crimen nula poena sine proevia lege penale*) and the process of bringing charges (clear separation among the functions of rendering judgment, accusing, and defending, that is, among judge, prosecutor, and defense attorney) are characteristics of the rule of law anywhere, while the assumptions of lack of need for legal process and the inquisitory approach—where judge, prosecutor, and defense lawyer are the same person—are proper to a police state or authoritarian state.

The former is a state that respects the sphere of moral autonomy of each inhabitant and strives to have all regarded as persons and treated without discrimination, and therefore recognizes that punishment is an evil for the person undergoing it; the latter is paternalistic, and thinks that it must step into the moral sphere of its inhabitants, discriminates between them, and considers punishment to be beneficial for inferiors. The former regards itself and the law that it produces as instruments at the service of human beings (nontranscendent idea of the law); the latter regards itself and therefore the law that it produces as instruments of suprahuman ends (transcendent concept of the law).

When inquisitorial procedures are claimed and, correspondingly in the penal realm, legal guarantees are suspended, instead of observing criminal procedure with formal presentation of charges, what is at stake is not simply a matter of policy for criminal procedure, but an option between types of state: either a police state or the rule of law. If the option is for the former, the decision is being made for a type of state in which all inhabitants are subjected to the will of the one who rules. If the option is for the latter, the choice is for a kind of state in which all, rulers and ruled alike, are under the law.

Why Were Children and Adolescents Removed from Criminal Law and Criminal Process?

The penal system of the past century wielded the power to punish with the structural characteristics of selectivity, violence, and corruption that it always had and still has, but which it rationalizes or hides with regard to adults. In the case of children and adolescents, the cruelty could not be disguised, and hence such power inevitably lost its legitimacy. The claim in discourse that they were exempt from criminal law, far from being a way of protecting them from the cruelty of the system, was a way of protecting the system from a crisis of legitimacy. By eliminating children and adolescents from its discourse, it was delivered from one of its features that was hardest to justify. Hence, it has by no means faced up to its guardianship discourse about them, but it has continued to claim it for over a century.

The power to punish thereby gained one of its best deals in history, riding high on naiveté and humanitarian and philanthropic intentions, while really mocking them: it continued to exercise the power of punishment over children and adolescents with no limit or control whatsoever, taking criminal law and criminal procedure with respect to them back to preindustrial or medieval times; at the same time, by removing them from its discourse it was not compromised by this use of power, which was not regarded publicly as punitive.

It is usually said that the first juvenile courts (Chicago, etc.) were created at the urging of philanthropic groups. That is only half-true; these groups fell prey to naiveté, because the penal establishment plainly took advantage of them and bureaucratically sought to dispose of children and adolescents, about whom it did not know what to do, because treating them just like adults would place the entire legitimacy and public trust of such groups in crisis.

Punitive Power Is Extended to All Children and Adolescents

Nevertheless, the benefits for the penal system entailed in the exit of children and adolescents from its discourse did not end with its increased power to punish (with neither material nor formal limits) being exercised on those who violate the law and its protection from blame (through the exclusion of certain discourse), but thereby astonishingly increased its ability to wield punishment: the way was opened for it to arbitrarily criminalize and institutionalize all children in dire need. That is not all: it became possible to enter into the private life of the entire population under the guise of protecting children from their own families. Religious behavior patterns, traditions, habits, life-style choices, and so on can be judged by the state on the grounds that they may affect children and adolescents, and therefore anyone can be threatened with the punishment of removing and institutionalizing children and adolescents, decided by a superpaternalistic state, which alone knows what is good for one's children. The parent state is expressly enshrined: the exercise of the right of trusteeship by the state as an actor.

Children who are abandoned (or designated by another more or less pejorative term), and poor children or adolescents in general, are also subject to juvenile court, while the violator of the law, under the guise of humanitarianism is subjected to the same court by reason of the claim of guardianship. As discourse, the claim is quite acceptable: the child or adolescent violator is treated as one in need. The violation is the result of a need—usually material, although it can be of another nature—and hence should not receive other institutional treatment.

However, the discourse conceals something quite different: guardianship becomes an agency of punishment without limits. The result is the exact opposite of the discourse: the child or adolescent violator is treated as a violator, but without the adult violator's guarantees and limits; the child or adolescent nonviolator, said to be "abandoned," ends up being treated in the same manner. While the discourse seeks to treat the violator humanely and therefore likens him or her to a nonviolator, in actuality the nonviolator is treated like a violator, who is treated as an adult violator, but without the guarantees and limitations that the criminal justice system affords the latter.

Anyone examining the legislation on children and adolescents in Latin America for the guardianship stage prior to the Convention on the Rights of the Child will see that the principle of legality was entirely lacking. Any child or adolescent could be institutionalized whenever the state so wished (for bad behavior or for problems of behavior, personality, abandonment, or need, i.e., for any reason). It will also be plain that such a child or adolescent had no defense or only a very limited one, and that secrecy ruled, under the guise of protecting the child. Usually there was not even a role for the office of the government attorney. The agencies responsible for making a presentation to the one making the judgment tended to be bureaucratic and to act in accordance with always predictable guidelines, to be guided by personal criteria and subjective values, to appeal to middle-class moral values for cases of children and adolescents from the humblest and most outcast groups, and so forth. In some countries the agencies making decisions were not judicial in nature and the fact that they were called "courts" tended to be formal; that is, they were sometimes simply administrative agencies: they were not only unfamiliar with legal standards and the presentation of charges, but they were sometimes even ignorant of judicial procedure. There is no criminal and procedural guarantee enshrined in the republican constitutions of Latin America and universally enshrined in the International Agreement on Civil and Political Rights (nor regionally by the American Convention on Human Rights) that is not directly violated by such bodies of law.

Institutionalizing a Child or Adolescent Is Worse Than a Prison Sentence for an Adult

The claim is that in this case punishment is beneficial and ought not to be called punishment. Many years ago Kohnrausch referred to the fraudulence entailed in labels, and Binding noted the danger entailed in giving punishment another name. Punishment is such whenever its content is burdensome, regardless of what it might be called. Institutionalizing a child or adolescent is not qualitatively different from institutionalizing an adult, except for its effects, which may do even greater damage.

For several decades, there has been talk of the effect of total institutions, a classification covering both prisons and boarding institutions. Both are known to cause a person to deteriorate; in adults they lead to symptoms of regressive situational neurosis, increase all kinds of risk of violent death and illness, and the like. In the case of putting children in boarding institutions (however they might be called), the effects are more serious, because while adults suffer situational neurosis, if their prior experience and previously attained maturity has been healthy enough and the period of institutionalization is not too long, they may be able to emerge from the situation without harmful consequences. The problem is that children and adolescents are at a stage of growth where, by definition, such healthy experience and maturity do not exist or are frail, and so the consequences of institutionalization are likely to be more serious. To hold that this is not a punishment is an unspeakable euphemism.

Can the Judge and the Institution Replace the Family?

To claim that the judge, court, or institution can replace the family is simply one more piece of discourse, an absurdity from the standpoint of the social sciences, which is used for sheer rhetorical purposes by the guardianship ideology. Neither the institution nor the judge can replace the family or the community. The family is a primary institution in society, while the state and all its agencies are secondary institutions: the primary institutions operate spontaneously, in a specific manner for each case or situation, and their actions or decisions are not regulated. Secondary institutions act according to standardized rules and must act that way.

Bureaucracy is not a term of contempt or a pejorative expression, but something absolutely necessary for the existence of the state: without bureaucracy there is no state, and the better it is, the better the state and its services operate. But as secondary institutions, bureaucracies must conform to established rules that are applicable to all cases or to objectively defined groups of cases. That is not a defect, but a need of the state and society.

The personalized decision of a primary institution cannot be transferred to a secondary institution because it undermines and destroys it: the father and mother know when the child should go to bed without desert, go to the movies, and watch television, or when to give preference to the needs of grandmother or one's brother, but a bureaucracy cannot react in this manner because it would cease to be operating under the rule of law, because the demands are massive and it cannot personalize its attention and its response to them, because it must observe certain basic formalities, and because its basis for operation must be that everyone deserves to receive equal treatment and consideration.

Neither the court nor institutions can operate otherwise: their members cannot act in accord with their feelings or by sheer intuition, but by observing generalizing laws, regulations, and guidelines. Otherwise there would be chaos, and caprice would reign supreme.

Moreover—and granting the absurdity, that is, the possibility that the state through its agencies actually could perform the family's function—it should be said that in legal discourse a power of guardianship is granted, that is, a supplementary and sometimes exclusive parental power, with the aim of replacing the family: it should be asked toward which model of person would the task of raising a child or adolescent strive, which social class or which cultural groups within the multicultural societies of our contemporary world it would imitate, and on what grounds one kind of religious upbringing would be imparted rather than another, and so forth. In short, it is not only institutionally and socially impossible to replace the family, but it is ethically impossible as well.

Possible Solutions within the Framework of the Current Convention

What is called the "issue of the minor" began with industrialism. It did not exist with the extended family in the countryside: the godparent relationship and other such institutions arose so that if children or adolescents were orphaned or left abandoned, other family members would take them into their own families, albeit temporarily. Children were protected (as were old people). Vulnerability has increased with the nuclear family in the urban setting: children come to depend solely on their parents. It reaches an extreme with the single-parent household centered on the mother, on whom everything rests.

The state, as we have seen, cannot compensate for this abandonment of the child and adolescent. The key to this issue cannot be anything but the strengthening of civil society, the community, and urban recreation, with the conditions that were lost along with the rural environment. This seemingly utopian objective is the great civilizing challenge of our time; either we overcome the fragmented and shrunken society of anonymity, where people do not know one another and live in mutual fear, or a great deal of what is said in the decadent and reactionary thinking of Spengler will turn out to be true. I wager on the former, with the reempowering of the state through its secondary and tertiary manifestations (provinces and municipalities) with the ability to promote new social relationships and encourage the growth of society.

The point is that the community must reassume its function of protecting children and adolescents, which was lost with industrialization and crowding into cities. This is not a wild idea in a world with extra time, where the old are institutionalized, where grandchildren and grandparents alike are in jeopardy. The impoverishment of the existing values will give rise to others as cultural alternatives, because information cannot be monopolized, societies are becoming increasingly multicultural, national states are weakening, local governments are becoming stronger, decisions are being placed closer to people, and control over government administration is more direct.

And child violators? At the close of a century of guardianship, it has become necessary to universally declare the principle that no child or adolescent can be deprived of the criminal, procedural, and judicial rights and guarantees that would be his or hers as an adult who had committed the same violation. That this principle has become enshrined is the clearest proof of the fallacy of guardianship: not only was it not good, but because it is a punishment, it became necessary to declare that it cannot be imposed without guarantees.

The institutionalization of children must be the last resort, when all other alternatives have failed. This is no new principle and it is not limited to children: the same principle ought to be in effect for adults as well. Its enshrinement here is simply an acknowledgment that the state has a clientele that it serves in accord with its ability to imprison, ensuring the continuation of its penal system: every state has the number of prisoners that it wants to have and the number of institutionalized children and adolescents that it wants to have. It is not very clear why, but it has them. This arbitrariness of number, which does not depend on the frequency or seriousness of conflicts but on the state's need to reproduce its penal system, becomes particularly intolerable in the case of children, and hence for them it is emphatically necessary to invoke the ultima ratio clause. That seems correct, but it is always good to recall that it is not limited to children but applies to the institutionalization of any person.

I am not going to pause here on the different legislative techniques for ameliorating the punishment of children and adolescents, to obviate it, to appeal to alternatives or punishments that do not deprive them of their freedom, to divert the penal process when there are adequate models of nonpunitive solutions for problems, and so forth. That is, all these procedural devices are sound, but the important thing is that, in any case, the law and judges fully observe the Constitution and international human rights law, keeping in mind that children and adolescents are persons and inhabitants of our nations, that they enjoy the same rights and guarantees as any other inhabitant, that institutionalizing them or removing them from their family is a punishment; that there is no punishment that can be imposed without a prior law that classifies the behavior and establishes its nature and duration, that it cannot be imposed without a legal procedure that respects the right to challenge and the general process of bringing charges, and that it must be decided by a judge who ought to do so in accord with legal arguments and not merely with subjective moral considerations wielded arbitrarily and loosely. The state of law is not the exclusive property of adults, but belongs preeminently to children and adolescents.

13 | From Minors to Citizens

Social Policies for Children within the Context of the Integral Protection Doctrine

EMILIO GARCÍA MÉNDEZ

Introduction

"From minors to children" is one of the best descriptions of the change in the legal and social conceptions of children in the wake of the UN Convention on the Rights of the Child (CRC). Recent years have witnessed this fundamental qualitative change in the perception of children implied by the Convention. In this sense, I am convinced that all descriptions are insufficient to reflect the revolutionary potential of this international human rights agreement, which has generated more political-legal and, above all, social consensus than any other agreement in the history of humanity.

If the 1959 Declaration of Children's Rights can be considered an ethical minimum with respect to the young, the CRC—adopted 30 years later—may be seen as a legal maximum. Transformed into substantive law at national and international levels, it highlights the enormous gap between the new legal status of children and the difficult material and social conditions in which they continue to live.

It is not uncommon for international awareness to anticipate and greatly exceed national recognition of problems and solutions. The CRC perception of children as subjects with rights, which has consequences as yet to be determined, is one of the best examples of this international awareness. Converting the new culture for children into specific action depends largely on two conditions: (1) the capacity to reproduce this new culture broadly and coherently, that is, the power to transform it into policies developed for and by children, and (2) the extent to which governmental and nongovernmental entities and people subject to that policy are able to overcome recurrent Manichaean thinking and the restrictive corporate nature of their immediate demands. In short, this refers to the ability to link children's problems to the fundamental problems of democracy.

From this standpoint, the CRC is both a cause and a consequence of a certain decline in the traditional idea of social policy, that is, the constant tension existing between the technocratic view, which sees policy as the exclusive domain of specialists, and the democratic view, which regards it as everyone's concern.[1] However, I will not attempt an exhaustive or general analysis of politics and policies, since I consider it more important to stimulate a wider debate on more specific perspectives. This reflects the decline of traditional ideas about participation in implementing social policy, primarily policies for children in Latin America.

My aim is therefore to contribute to the current discussion on social policy from the perspectives posed by the political and legal dimensions of social policy. Consequently, a brief summary of the evolution of social policies for children in Latin America seems appropriate at this point.

Origins of Social Policy in Latin America

In their modern version, social policies for children are relatively new in Latin America. Generally, patterns for the region indicate that until the 1920s and 1930s, the state shared responsibility, especially with the Catholic Church, for designing and carrying out activities concerning children (particularly the poorest). In fact, all programs and policies for the young originated with the question of what to do with the children of the poor? Obviously, the extent to which this question is evident depends on the type of policy being discussed. State participation is stronger and occurs earlier in the case of so-called universal policies (health and education), to the extent that measures of this type are linked to the formation of nation-states. However, in the case of public welfare or compensatory policies, the church exercised undeniable leadership until the 1950s. Although, after the crisis in the 1930s, Latin America's subordinate but privileged insertion into the world market opened the way for universal social policies, it was not until the 1950s, under the influence of distributive populism, that the states began to intervene more forcefully in the area of public welfare policies.

The Authoritarian Period

An exclusively governmental policy was implemented under the name of "public policy." Society's participation in this policy almost always developed through the charitable approach. In the area of children's affairs, nongovernmental organizations (NGOs), in the modern sense of the term, did not exist until well into the 1970s. NGOs were born during the authoritarian era of that decade, a time when most countries of the region had virtually no channels of communication between government and civil society. NGOs emerged as a form (perhaps the only one at the time) of response and viable resistance to the more or less brutal political and social conditions imposed by authoritarianism. Needless to say, nearly every NGO established in the region was associated with a nongovernmental institution in one of the world's industrialized countries. The specific consequences of this mark of origin have yet to be analyzed. However, particularly in the case of NGOs involved with children, two obvious tendencies came together. One was a vocation for service that implied direct attention to especially vulnerable children. The other was an implicit or explicit criticism of the prevailing type of social policy.

Since authoritarianism deliberately erases or eliminates the limits between government and state, NGOs seemed at the time to be the most appropriate and effective response to the conditions imposed by authoritarianism. In this context, it is easy to see why NGOs were more antigovernmental than nongovernmental. Erasing the differences between government and state also obliterates the differences between antigovernmental and antistate positions. Manichaeism was a fundamental component of the ideological cement that legitimized these practices. Reflecting on this period, it is indeed difficult to contradict the idea that society represents the good and state government the bad.

Antonio Carlos Gomes da Costa outlined a clear picture of this process in authoritarian Brazil. With some exceptions, much of his reasoning can be applied to other countries in the region. Obviously, children's policies implemented under military rule in Brazil were bound to reflect the general features of the prevailing system of government: authoritarianism, verticalism, hypercentralization, bureaucratism, and a preference for responses that might imply institutionalization (a euphemism for deprivation of liberty). These were basic features of children's policy during the authoritarian period. The alternative response encouraged by NGOs represents the other side of the coin. Democratic decentralization, use of community resources, and rejection of traditional forms of institutionalization are what best describe the alternative model. A variety of innovative work with children and adolescents was developed during the period. However, it was not long before the more progressive NGOs recognized the major drawback to this model: the difficulty—even the impossibility—of reproducing small, successful experiences on a broader scale. This posed a dilemma for those who perceived the problems of the children they worked to benefit as invariably linked to those of all children. Generally speaking, the demise of alternativism in the region coincided with the depletion of the authoritarian model. Among other effects, democracy—even its most fragile and doubtful versions—does away with many of the Manichaean "truths" of the past. What was good and what was bad settled on movable and vague frontiers. Good and bad began to be shared "democratically" between government and civil society.

With the decrease of alternativism and the return to democracy, a third element came into play that made a decisive contribution to change and helped initiate the process in which we are now immersed. I refer to the legal-social potential of the CRC, which started to operate at the end of 1989.

Democracy and the CRC

That moment saw a radically new relationship between children's legal and material conditions. Laws that applied to "minors" and that were based on the "irregular situation" doctrine had established a legal and cultural hegemony lasting more than 70 years. The CRC inspired a most important and radical break with that pattern.

Under alternativism, laws and rights were considered the exclusive patrimony of judges, lawyers, and, in a more diffused way, government authorities. For the most part, this was not without good reason during the authoritarian period. Among its many merits, the CRC is also the first specific legal instrument written in comprehensible language that involves social movements dedicated to children's problems. As an instrument of children's human rights, it transforms needs into rights. To put it in another way, the CRC allows needs to be interpreted as rights, and brings the problem of the liability for rights to the forefront, in both a legal and a political-social sense. From this standpoint, the legislative form of the CRC began to be viewed as a very appropriate and potentially suitable means of broadly reproducing the best alternative microexperiences developed in the 1970s and most of the 1980s.

Current processes for legislative reform in the region, and their immediate consequences in terms of institutional reform, do away with all myths and false dilemmas concerning the exclusive subjects for whom the production and social use of the law are intended. The unprecedented nature of grassroots involvement in the legislative reform, intended to substantially adapt national law to the spirit and text of the Convention, contains unusual lessons that go beyond the narrow field of social policy for children. If children's legislation based on the "irregular situation" doctrine (which ruled between 1919 and 1990) was the result of small and surreptitious recommendations of so-called experts, new legislative reform processes show that it is impossible to alter the content of the law without transforming the social mechanisms that create it. Paradoxically, certain theoretical problems that once caused concern for the sociology of law are, to some extent, being resolved by movements involved in the struggle for children's rights.

New Legislation for Children

Children's new legality develops automatically as a democratic one. This implies the use of democratic process in formal procedures, as well as in unprecedented forms of involvement and the creation of new legal institutions motivated by grassroots participation. As examples, I would like to mention two cases resulting from new legislation for children in Brazil,[2] which have influenced other countries of the region (e.g., Guatemala). Both examples deal with innovative legal-social institutions created under Brazilian law; namely, the Councils for Children's Rights (at federal, provincial, and municipal levels) and the Guardian Councils (municipal level). The Councils for Children's Rights are deliberative bodies whose purpose is to design and draft children's policy in the various areas of Brazil's political-administrative organization. There are now more than 3,000 councils of this type (serving the country's 5,000 municipalities), averaging 12 members each,[3] half of whom represent civil society. The overall impression is that only a small portion of the civil representatives are associated with NGOs that are organized and structured in the traditional sense of the term. In this case, the new legality has quantitatively and qualitatively broadened the concept of grassroots participation in social policy for children in an unprecedented and original way. This is a clear example of the law becoming an appropriate tool for institutionalizing the democratic basis of policy.

Acting within the field of public law, the Guardian Councils are autonomous, nonjurisdictional bodies comprised of citizens selected by the community to perform social functions that do not involve legal conflicts (but do imply a genuine and concrete process of judicial simplification). These fully-vested public bodies challenge theorists of administrative law and represent one small way in which children's new legality has substantially affected the traditional way social policy is designed and implemented. However, little or no thought has been given to the consequences of such changes.

Children's new legality faces unprecedented problems, the contradictory complexity of which must be understood fully in order to draft political strategies to overcome current impasses in the social field. One such problem is cultural resistance, which flourishes even in sectors that regard themselves as progressive. Cultural resistance makes it impossible to construct nondiscretional relations between the child and the state, or between the child and the world of adults.[4] There is also a contradiction between the legality that confirms and consolidates a new form of citizenship for children (the contents of which must be spelled out) and the uncommon economic crisis that is characterized more by social (and political) exclusion and spiraling distributive inequity than by a net decline in overall resources, particularly those earmarked for social spending.

Levels of Children's Policy

In 1993, based on statements by Antonio Carlos Gomes da Costa, I developed a dual in-depth analysis (static and dynamic) of the way social policies for children[5] are being conceived of and applied. Having the advantage of new political evidence, I wish to update the analysis, focusing on how the various levels of social policy for children operate. Four distinguishable levels can (and must) be identified.

A Static View

Basic Social Policies

Basic social policies are universal by definition; that is, they are obligations of the state corresponding to the rights of every person. To one extent or another, basic social policies have constitutional status in nearly every country of the region. They refer almost exclusively to fundamental services in health and education.

Public Welfare Policies

Though not as extensive as basic social policies, public welfare policies also constitute a state obligation and refer to rights to which only those in need are entitled. Policies of this type (e.g., emergency programs to combat poverty, special services for the physically or mentally disabled) do not always have constitutional status, except in countries with modern charters inspired by social responsibility.

Special Protection Policies

More limited than public welfare policies, special protection policies are designed to handle emergency situations involving children and adolescents who are subject to the risks of abandonment, sexual abuse, mistreatment, underage labor, exploitation, armed conflict, or other hazardous circumstances.

Policies on Civil Rights

Policies on civil rights apply particularly to children and adolescents who are in trouble with the law. Policies of this type invariably have legal constitutional backing.

A Dynamic View

Basic Social Policies

Effective universalization of these policies reached its peak in the 1950s, during the era of distributive populism. Health and education rights for all children were almost exclusively handed down "from above" as state services. Demand had little or no impact on their availability. Despite their limitations and restrictions, these policies managed to create a quasi-welfare state in some countries of the region.

Due to the mounting fiscal crisis facing the state in the late 1960s, the negative effects of such policies were evident in the decreased supply of public services. This process was also hastened by the fact that the need for services almost completely lacked any organized expression.

In the 1970s, the situation was further aggravated by authoritarianism, the result being an increase in the number of "minors" (defined as children with totally or partially unsatisfied basic needs) and a decline in the number of children and adolescents whose basic needs were satisfied. Specific resistance to the diminished coverage of basic social policies began to take shape. However, this resistance was still a by-product of the anti-authoritarian political struggle. Opposition to the government automatically became opposition to the state. The need for basic social services was then voiced by new social movements (narrowly considered NGOs). In their view, the alternative to government-provided services also became an alternative to state sponsorship as well (alternative health and education services originating with and for grassroots sectors). The provision of health services began to be privatized upward and their application downward to disappear. Education services fell victim to economic asphyxia from above and growing social distrust from below.

Public Welfare Policies

Until the 1930s, public welfare policies were designed and implemented almost exclusively by the Catholic Church. They were not undertaken by governments until the 1940s. Public welfare programs were generally fragmentary in approach and subject to political patronage. Social assistance was viewed more as a handout than as a right.

Special Protection Policies

It also proved difficult to develop special protection policies beyond pilot programs. For a long time, their very limited coverage—considering the magnitude of the problems at hand—was legitimized by their "pilot" nature. Mistrust in the government and state during the authoritarian period remained virtually intact during the difficult and complex return to democracy. The anti-statist culture even penetrated the workings of national projects and programs not directly affected by authoritarianism. This also demonstrated the cultural hegemony of alternativism, which only began to be questioned in the wake of legislative and social transformations based on the CRC.

The development of special protection programs were limited by two factors: the strong alternative-minded tendency that prevented their success, and the very way that government strategies articulating the problems were designed. From the government's perspective, its strategies seemed to be the most efficient way to resolve quantitative disparities between the demand for programs and the real potential for response to that demand under the alternative perspective.

Once the euphoria motivated by the fall of authoritarian governments subsided, many programs for children at risk faced the problem of limited coverage. Basically, this was resolved in two ways. One was to ignore the subject of coverage as a major difficulty. Consequently, these initiatives remained pilot programs indefinitely. This perspective obviously coincides with steps taken to limit the state's role in the social field, and it transformed many alternative projects into little more than cheap labor for underfunded programs to help the impoverished. Second, in being aware of the qualitative leap demanded by the quantitative dimensions of the problems at hand, some NGOs began a slow, complex, and difficult process of critical discussion with the government sector. The challenge was, and continues to be, to upscale successful programs already developed.

Policies on Civil Rights

Although policies on civil rights have constitutional status in almost every country (e.g., all have a constitutional expression stating generally that "no citizen of the country may be detained unless in flagrante delicto or by written order of a competent authority"), rights derived from the general principles of law (due process, equality in the eyes of the law, etc.) have never been applied, even nominally, to children under age 18. Legislation for "minors," based invariable on the "irregular situation" doctrine, explicitly provides for the denial of constitutional rights. As a result, law enforcement mechanisms become a means by which public welfare policies are instigated and sustained. In fact, the juvenile justice system has customarily designed (and executed to the extent possible) a policy for poor children in Latin America, who are euphemistically called "minors in irregular situation."

The usual, systematic, and legal ways by which poverty is criminalized (by institutionalization or declaration of child abandonment) are the objective outcome of laws intended to "protect minors." But these laws constitute little more than a series of insubstantial measures to control segments of the population that are considered socially dangerous.

Where Do We Stand and Where Are We Headed? A Hypothesis

There are reliable indications today that confirm these trends, particularly the qualitative and quantitative decline of basic social policies and the growing volume and influence of public welfare policies. The causes for this are, however, anything but simple and linear. That is, they do not correspond to a mere reduction in the overall volume of social spending. The reasons are far more complex and they deal more with political than economic motives.

Of course, I am fully aware of the obstacles for demonstrating this hypothesis. The first consists of the difficulty, if not the impossibility, of identifying the true quantitative dimension of social expenditure. In the political context that generates and allows this situation, the fact that a school-age child crosses a bridge is often enough reason for automatically crediting the cost of the bridge to social spending on education. These are strictly technical difficulties, but all sorts of "effective" political maneuvering is engineered around them. As so aptly noted in a recent article, electoral cycles are fundamental to understanding the meaning and development of social policy.[6]

Without ignoring this gray area in the nature of social expenditure, what we see is a major reorganization particularly with respect to type of social expenditure. From this standpoint, the current crisis in social policy amounts to a conflict between targeted assistance and the universal nature of basic social policies. It is also a conflict between bureaucratic discretion and self-determination. If discretion is essential to understanding this conflict, then the following is also true: the basic criterion for distinguishing a universal policy and a welfare policy is the degree of mediation exercised by the political apparatus of the government or the party (and not necessarily of the state) to effectively implement a particular service or benefit. Paradoxically, the growing crisis in the legitimacy of political action is supported by this "new" type of social policy, which finds an ideal breeding ground in the tradition of *caudillismo* and political patronage.

In this perspective, which oils the political machine via social policy, the dismantling of objective entitlement—coupled with almost automatic development of universal policies, the implementation of which is subject to bureaucratic discretion (another name for political patronage in a state that is unable to constitute itself as such)—is indispensable to securing and/or keeping political power. The rationale for discretion collides head-on with the rationale for the self-determination of rights. However, if the crisis is defined in terms of social exclusion, overcoming it will imply just the opposite—the right of social integration understood as the nonmediated capacity for access to services. This is convincingly outlined in a recent study based on an intelligent and in-depth analysis of the extent and caliber of relations between democracy and social policy. It maintains that "social rights can no longer be understood merely as 'rights to something,' 'entitlements' or passive rights to compensation. We must go beyond this point, or be content with a broad array of assistance rather than social participation for all. The struggle against exclusion invites us to explore a third type of rights: those of integration."[7]

In my opinion, the backdrop of this crisis is not new. Two centuries of unresolved tension—originating with the French Revolution—between the rights of man and those of citizens[8] probably contain the key to moving ahead, not toward something superior to democracy but toward a better type of democracy.

Having exhausted its revolutionary role against the old feudal order, the concept of citizenship was reshaped as a suitable political-legal means of legitimizing the exclusion of certain people (women, children, those who do not own property, foreigners, etc.). Accordingly, it is the social structure, in which all citizens are people but obviously not all people are citizens, that defines "natural" rights. Citizenship is a necessary condition for effective exercise of rights (not only political ones) to which all people are potentially entitled. This route also takes us to the conflict between bureaucratic discretion and self-determination. As a specific instrument of the human rights of individuals whose only distinction is being under age 18, the CRC might provoke a positive solution to the crisis and to the tensions just mentioned.

If we manage to transform the CRC into an instrument for closing the gap between the rights of all people and those of citizens, we will confirm our willingness to take all rights seriously, in addition to verifying the force and effectiveness of the most legally ratified, as well as socially accepted and disseminated, instrument of human rights in the history of humanity.

NOTES

1. On this point, see A. Baratta, "La Niñez Como Arqueología del Futuro," in *El Derecho y los Chicos*, María Carmen Bianchi, compiler. Editorial Espacio, Buenos Aires, 1995.

2. I refer to the Child and Adolescent Act, the first national law in Latin America to be adapted substantially to the CRC. Approved in July 1990, it took effect in October of the same year.

3. The law stipulates only that representation on these councils be equal. The number of members vary, according to the size of the municipality.

4. On the subject of the CRC as an instrument that radically redefines the type of relationship between the child and the state, and between the state, the child, and adults, see M. Cillero, "El Interés Superior del Niño en el Marco de la Convención Internacional sobre los Derechos del Niño," mimeographed. Santiago de Chile, 1997.

5. E. García Mendéz, "Informe Final Reunión de Puntos Focales, Area Derechos del Niño," Paipa, Colombia, December 6–9, 1993 (internal document of the UNICEF Regional Office for Latin America and the Caribbean).

6. E. Bustelo and A. Minujín, "La Política Social Esquiva," mimeographed. Buenos Aires, 1997.

7. J. P. Ftoussi and P. Rosanvallon, *La Nueva Era de las Desigualdades*, Editorial Manantial, Buenos Aires, 1997, p. 219.

8. I am indebted to L. Ferrajoli for this distinction and the possibility of using the concept (and instruments) of human rights to close the gap between the rights of man and those of citizens.

14 | Comments on "From Minors to Citizens"

JUAN E. MÉNDEZ

Introduction

The Convention on the Rights of the Child (CRC) is a truly remarkable achievement by the international community, especially if viewed from the perspective of those of us who are professionally interested in the promotion of new standards of behavior by states toward their own citizens. Standard setting in international law is a laborious and often unrewarding task because nation-states are the legislators and the prevailing majorities among them are resistant to adopting meaningful constraints on their discretion to act within their jurisdiction. In this, the CRC is a stunning exception. Not only was it drafted and adopted in record time, but in only a very few years it has been signed and ratified by virtually every state in the international community.[1] Given that impressive record, a casual observer could be forgiven for believing that the language of this international instrument must be necessarily bland, compromising, or otherwise not creating any real obligation on states.

In fact, the opposite is true. By its terms, the CRC is a genuine step forward in international lawmaking, since it goes further than better known instruments in formulating affirmative and negative obligations on the part of states. It goes a considerable way toward breaking the damaging dichotomy created in the 1950s of civil and political rights (drafted as negative obligations and therefore immediately enforceable) versus economic, social, and political rights (subject to "progressive realization" by states in accordance with their capabilities).[2] In the case of rights that are eminently economic, social, and cultural, like the rights to health, education, and social security, the CRC incorporates language that makes the "appropriate measures" required of states (i.e., the "progressive realization" obligation) measurable by objective standards. For example, article 24 mandates that such measures be directed to "diminish infant and child mortality," which means that a country whose rate of infant mortality grows from one year to the next is in breach of an international obligation (unless, arguably, it can show that factors beyond its control are to blame for the rise). Primary education is to be made compulsory and available free to all children (article 28) and social security benefits must be made available to all children (article 26). And the CRC also tackles controversial and pressing social issues like the right to an identity, intercountry adoption, child labor, children in warfare, and juvenile justice with prescriptions that are by no means ambiguous or inconsequential.

Ground-Breaking International Instrument

We learn from Emilio García Méndez that, when it comes to public policy toward children, the spirit and orientation of the CRC, which he calls the "comprehensive protection doctrine," is no less sweeping in its dramatic overhaul of the attitudes prevailing before the CRC was adopted, the "irregular situation doctrine." If so, it is interesting to note that this aspect also sets this international instrument apart from all other human rights treaties. For the most part, human rights treaties reflect a consensus about ideas and values that are not prevalent everywhere, but have certainly been tried and proved successful in some countries or regions. This, I think, is what is meant in the preamble to the Universal Declaration of Human Rights, when this ground-breaking instrument is called "a common standard of achievement." It is meant to be a statement of what humanity has already accomplished, without prejudice to its also being a call to states that do not live up to that common standard to endeavor to come up to speed. In contrast, the chapter I am commenting on seems to me to describe the CRC as an ideal model. I do not mean "ideal" in the sense of unrealistic or unachievable, but rather in the sense of a creation of the mind that does not point to any practical example as an existing paradigm.

If I have understood this point correctly, that fact is also significant. The CRC represents a determined effort to use international law to guide and drive the development of public policy in each country, rather than the establishment of a high-water mark that some countries may well have achieved and even passed already. The fact that an effort that reaches for so much also yields such good results in terms of acceptance should provide a useful lesson to the eternal "realists" in standard-setting exercises, who advise us to propose only what country representatives are willing to accept—which is only what they are already practicing. Even more stunning is to realize that, according to García Méndez, the strategy seems to be working: not only are countries ratifying the CRC, they are also adopting its major tenets and profoundly affecting their own internal policies toward children.

Limitations of the CRC

Where are the weak points in what sounds like such a promising picture? There may well be none or very few, but since I understand my role at least in part to be the skeptic, let me raise some issues that are, in any event, common to many other international human rights instruments and not particular to the CRC. First, I should take issue with García Méndez's characterization of the CRC as a "legal maximum," unless all he means by it is that this is a very comprehensive legal instrument (in contrast to the 1959 Declaration, which he calls an "ethical minimum"). All multilateral treaties that protect rights are meant to be minimum commitments, from which governments are free to depart as long as by doing so they provide broader and deeper protections of those rights. Repeating a formula found in all other instruments, the CRC expressly so states in article 41. After adoption of the CRC, the solemn obligations thus assumed have become each state party's minimum legal and ethical obligation.

Second, I do find fault in the CRC in the area of freedom of expression. Article 13 tracks the language in the International Covenant on Civil and Political Rights (ICCPR; art. 19), which is less progressive than the relevant protections found in the American Convention on Human Rights. In the latter, restrictions that are allowed to be imposed on the exercise of this fundamental freedom are limited to postpublication sanctions, thereby explicitly forbidding prior censorship, with the only exception being restrictions on access by underage persons to certain public spectacles on the basis of public morals. In contrast, article 13 of the CRC (and art. 19 of the ICCPR) allow for prepublication restrictions under certain circumstances if prescribed by law and necessary in a democratic society for the protection of the rights or reputations of others or to protect national security, public order, or public health or morals. Even with the qualifications inserted in the text (which have been the subject of authoritative interpretations), this clause leaves open a giant loophole that may well prevent children from exercising their free expression. This point is relatively minor, of course, since children in countries that are parties to the

American Convention will enjoy the enhanced freedom of expression this other treaty affords, and children in other countries appear to have the same freedom of expression that adults have in the same countries.

The CRC is deficient, however, in one vital aspect: its mechanisms of implementation. This being the major weakness of this expanding area of international law, it is a pity that the framers did not take advantage of the clear momentum they had and provide this instrument with a better system of international monitoring and protection. As it is, the CRC contemplates creation of a Committee on the Rights of the Child, with members elected from experts nominated by state parties. The jurisdiction of this Committee is limited to receiving country reports from state parties and—presumably, though nothing specific is stated to that effect—commenting on those periodic reports. This is the system adopted for several other conventions, a self-monitoring and self-reporting scheme with a relatively passive body at the receiving end.[3] It has proved a dismal failure.[4] In comparison, the ICCPR includes an optional protocol by which signatory countries choose to allow its organ of implementation, the Human Rights Committee, to hear individual complaints brought against such states alleging specific violations of the covenant.[5] The women's rights movement is active as we speak in promoting an optional protocol to CEDAW that would enable its Committee to hear individual complaints.[6] In fact, a better system yet would have been to create a judicial approach to case complaints brought under the treaty, as has been put in place in regional systems.[7] If the intent of the committee format is to generate pressure from the international law community on domestic jurisdictions to move policy on children in the direction of the comprehensive protection doctrine, a highly authoritative body applying that doctrine to specific cases brought on behalf of children around the world could be a formidable, persuasive force.

Implementation

A more definitive judgment on the relative success of the CRC, however, must rely less on the effectiveness of international mechanisms of protection and more on the degree to which its substantive norms are incorporated into domestic law in each country. Latin American countries automatically incorporate treaties into domestic law without the need for implementing legislation; in most of these countries, international treaties occupy a hierarchical place between the constitution and the laws, so that acts of the national congress cannot amend or abolish them; recently, many Latin American countries have elevated human rights treaties to the status of constitutional provisions. All of this means that provisions of a treaty are directly enforceable before the courts. This, however, is only true in general and as a matter of legal technicality. Most courts in the region are unaware of legal obligations arising under treaties, are not ready to learn about them, and will just as soon find jurisdictional arguments to refuse to grant relief under a treaty provision. It is fair to say that things have begun to change for the better in this respect, but we are still far from being able to rely on our courts for strong, consistent protection of treaty-based rights.

The next step in incorporation, though it should not be necessary, is implementation through national legislation. We learn from García Méndez that prospects here look better; some states have actually amended their legislation on children to adapt to the CRC standards, and others are in the process of doing so. Nevertheless, it seems to me that the legislation needed requires not only clear statements of substantive principle and administrative directives, but most importantly, appropriate jurisdictional norms to empower courts to enforce these rights. Only when these rights are shaped and interpreted by application to real-life cases can we be certain of the legal stability of the newly acquired rights. This is especially true in those areas of the CRC that relate to economic, social, and cultural rights. It is imperative that we find ways, in both domestic and international law, to overcome the limitation of the "progressive realization" dodge that governments can so easily take refuge in. For the rights to health, education, and social security to be effective rights, they have to be justiciable, either as collective or individual rights. If, in drafting legislation on children, we design jurisdictional and procedural rules to protect these rights via the courts, we will take a giant step toward deleting the dichotomy of civil and political versus economic, social, and cultural rights.

Even if we do not strongly mandate courts to deal with these rights in implementing legislation, that should not prevent us from trying to obtain landmark court opinions defining the scope of the rights contained in the CRC. Activist lawyers and nongovernment organizations dedicated to children can find ways to overcome formalistic and archaic objections to jurisdiction and force courts to act on the principle that the protection of rights (including direct application of rights found in treaties) is the ultimate raison d'être of the courts of justice of any country. There is now an unsteady but discernible trend in Latin American judiciaries to understand this role and apply it creatively, and the overwhelming popularity of children's rights should provide a good vehicle to expand and consolidate the trend. This is an area where the democratic waters of our hemisphere deserve much further testing. Our democracies will be much stronger and meaningful to all if we go beyond elections and obtain powerful, independent, and impartial judiciaries. We will know we have courts with those fundamental attributes when we see them stand up to various sources of power and defend the rights of the underprivileged with sound, lasting legal precedents. A major first step in this direction is to meet the challenges offered by the CRC.

The Comprehensive Protection Doctrine

García Méndez's thesis is that the CRC's profound philosophical innovation is to force policymakers to stop treating children as "minors" and to recognize them as "citizens." To those of us who are used to the language of human rights law, this is a rather surprising choice of words. We think of rights as fundamentally attributed to persons because of their inherent dignity as human beings and without regard to the status they may enjoy with respect to the particular political community in which they live or where they are at a given moment. In this sense, citizenship represents only some additional rights that some persons in that community acquire by virtue of a relationship to the nation-state, rights more specifically associated with voting and running for office. In García Méndez's chapter, however, citizenship is used to indicate a degree of inclusion or integration into the community, a substantive and not simply formal belonging to that community in terms of equality with other members and the absence of invidious de facto or de jure discrimination. In fact, the women's rights movement has increasingly insisted on asserting the rights of citizenship in this more fundamental sense, which obviously goes beyond the fact that women have had the vote for several decades.

This is, I think, a very useful way to describe the fundamental requirements of a true democracy and to point out the limitations of our real-life democracies. In this view, a citizen is someone who, in law and in practice, has achieved the highest degree of integration and inclusion into the community and who suffers the least degree of invidious discrimination in the exercise of his or her rights. Even at the risk of sounding like a rhetorical device, treating underage persons as citizens offers the radical advantage of forcing us to look at their interests fundamentally as rights. This means that we leave behind the tendency to guard the interests of children by means of "protective measures" inspired in the conviction that they are persons who are, by definition, incapable of forming and manifesting their will and who require special protection. In the past, this way of protecting the interests of categories of persons led to policy and law that allotted women and indigenous people a second-rate citizenship. These special categories of protected persons were to be guarded even against themselves, since the state knew better where their real interests lay; in the end, protective measures prevented people from making their own choices and discerning for themselves what their interests were and how to pursue them.

The comprehensive protection doctrine is very welcome if it overcomes this attitude. As reflected in the CRC, this doctrine certainly breaks with the paternalistic attitudes of the irregular situation doctrine. To give only a few important examples, the CRC sets forth the principle that the child must be heard in any proceeding to adjudicate or determine his or her rights and interests. It also gives the child direct access to the court in matters affecting those rights and interests. And it unmistakably states that children enjoy freedom of expression, including the right to seek and impart information, which has been described as the most fundamental right necessary to act in a community with the full attributes of citizenship.

Critical Comments

This major shift in vision, from irregular situation to comprehensive protection, leaves us, nonetheless, with questions that García Méndez and others must have already thought about. The new doctrine appears to be, among other things, an attempt to get rid of the arbitrary presumptions in the law as to when a person is mature enough to form his or her will and reach decisions consistent with his or her best interest; or at least it is an attempt to limit the legal effects of such arbitrary determinations in the law. Even so, it seems inevitable that some limits on citizenship will have to remain and that those will—also inevitably—be imposed with a high degree of arbitrariness. I refer here to citizenship in the classic sense related to voting rights. Political communities will continue to establish ages of maturity before which persons will not be allowed to vote. In this sense, the nonbinding and voluntary exercises to poll the opinions of children on a variety of matters, conducted with encouraging success by UNICEF and others in the context of recent Latin American elections, are a partial effort to break down this barrier to participation. The "vote" of a child may not be counted in tallying the results of the election, but the collective and diverse opinions of many children voicing their concerns on issues relevant to the same election undoubtedly add to the quality of the democratic exercise itself.

There will remain questions as to the proper balance of children's rights and parental authority, as well as on the degree to which a more profound view of the rights of children is consistent with a policy to strengthen the family. The CRC's provisions that relate to parental duties and rights and to the child's right to family relations, to know and to be cared for by his or her parents, and so on seem to leave no doubt that the intent of the CRC is to incorporate parents and family into the picture. Whether the proper balance has been struck, and more importantly, if it will be struck in national legislation and judicial decisions implementing this new vision, will be up to specialists in this area to decide. At this point I only wish to raise it as a concern, if for no other reason than because it seems to me that the ideological attack on the new doctrine, and the defense of the old concept of protective measures, will continue to come from those purporting to defend the absolute rights of parents and family.

Finally, I wish to state a concern about the application of this doctrine (or maybe of wayward interpretations) to juvenile justice. It is most welcome to see the child who is caught in the justice system referred to as a person who enjoys due process rights and fair trial guarantees, and not as the object of protective measures that, as García Méndez describes, have often trampled over such rights. But in developed countries, a get-tough-on-crime attitude by prosecutors is leading to the trend to try some juvenile suspects as adults. Invariably, the result is not to broaden the scope of the children's citizenship, but to restrict their rights as criminal defendants to the most favorable penal law available to them. That this trend enjoys public opinion support and is fueled by the perception that violent crime among youthful offenders is on the rise only adds to the concern that we need a better answer to this problem. A different point about juvenile justice systems that I will make has to do more with impressions: in some Latin American countries, progressive legislation along the lines of the CRC has been adopted, but without a concerted effort to explain to administrators and society the actual contours of the new rules. The result is that there is a simplistic though persistent impression, held by police and society, that the new rules mean that children cannot be arrested or will not be investigated. As a result, police refrain from acting in response to hooliganism and even minor violent acts, and the community reacts, demanding a restoration of their sense of security. Public sentiment against the more progressive aspects of laws based on the new doctrine cannot be far behind.

These critical comments are meant to raise flags and signal pitfalls to avoid, by no means to diminish the merits of the CRC and the revolutionary vision about children's rights it represents. The comprehensive protection doctrine must be defended if it is to prevail beyond its consecration in a multilateral treaty. Its best defense is its consistency with a modern idea of democracy and with the features that many recent theoreticians of democracy have insisted on: accountability, decency in the way institutions treat citizens, and an honest and sustained effort to eliminate exclusionary barriers to full participation by all.[8] All of these features are patently missing in our existing democracies in Latin America, no matter how many other important achievements we have derived from them. For this reason, such features also constitute the pressing agenda of our time to make democracy meaningful for all, and children's rights are the best place to start.

NOTES

1. One of two states that have not yet ratified is Somalia, which at present has no recognized government representing it in international fora; the other country is the United States. Ratification by more than 180 nations has taken place in the comparatively short span of years since adoption of the CRC by the UN General Assembly on November 20, 1989.

2. Cf. art. 2, International Covenant on Economic, Social and Cultural Rights (adopted in 1966, entered into force in 1976), with art. 2, International Covenant on Civil and Political Rights (adopted in 1966, entered into force in 1976).

3. Convention on the Elimination of all Forms of Racial Discrimination (CERD), art. 8; CEDAW (Convention on Elimination of Discrimination Against Women), art. 17.

4. Philip Alston, editor, *The United Nations and Human Rights: A Critical Appraisal.* Oxford: Clarendon Press, New York: Oxford University Press, 1992. See also: Anne Bayefsky, "Making the Human Rights Treaties Work," in Louis Henkin and J. Hargrove, eds., *Human Rights: An Agenda for the Next Century.* Washington: ASIL, 1994; and Henry Steiner and Philip Alston, *International Human Rights in Context.* Oxford: Clarendon Press, 1996, pp. 500–20, 556–61.

5. Optional Protocol to the ICCPR (adopted in 1966, entered into force in 1976).

6. The Optional Protocol to CEDAW was finally adopted and opened for signature in March 1999; see UN Document E/CN.6/WG/L.2. See also *IIDH, Protocolo Facultativo: Documento de Trabajo,* San José, Costa Rica: IIDH (Instituto Interamericano de Derechos Humanos), 1998.

7. American Convention, art. 33; European Convention for the Protection of Human Rights and Fundamental Freedoms (adopted in 1950, entered into force in 1953), art. 19, and nine successive optional protocols.

8. Philippe Schmitter and Terry Lynn Karl, "What Democracy Is . . . and Is Not," *Journal of Democracy,* Vol. 2, No. 3, summer 1991, pp. 75 et seq.; Avishai Margalit, *The Decent Societ.* Cambridge: Harvard University Press, 1996, cited in note 85 of Guillermo O'Donnell, "Polyarchies and the (Un)Rule of Law in Latin America," in Méndez, O'Donnell, and Paulo Sérgio Pinheiro, eds., *The (Un)Rule of Law and the Underprivileged in Latin America.* Notre Dame: Kellogg Institute Series with the University of Notre Dame Press. See also: German Bidart Campos, "Libertad y Participación Política en el Marco de los Derechos Humanos," *Revista IIDH,* No. 14,

January–June 1991; Manuel Alcántara, "Sobre el concepto de países en vía de consolidación democrática en América Latina," in *Boletín Electoral Latinoamericano* VI, IIDH-CAPEL (Instituto Interamericano de Derechos Humanos-Centro de Asesoría y Promoción Electoral), July–December 1991; and Ricardo Valverde, "El Derecho de Participación Política y la Consolidación Democrática en el Sistema Universal de Protección y Promoción de los Derechos Humanos" (mimeo). IIDH, XVII Inter-Disciplinary Course on Human Rights, San José, Costa Rica, June 1999.

D | Children, Citizenship, and Democracy

15 | The Child as Subject of Rights and as Participant in the Democratic Process

ALESSANDRO BARATTA

Democracy and Public Policies
on the Protection of Children's Rights

The "democratic context" of public policies on the protection of children's rights varies in meaning and relevance depending on whether children are considered a party to democratic relations or not, and how the relationships between children and adults are understood.

There are two possible formulations of the concept of democracy. From the point of view of the relations between subjects, a distinction can be made between social and political dimensions of democracy,[1] depending on whether we consider the institutions of civil society (families, schools, associations) or those of the state or the international legal order (state or public territorial entities, institutions of the international community). From the point of view of territorial extension, democracy has local, central (national), and global (international) dimensions.

Taking these two formulations into account, five dimensions of democracy and other aspects of functional relations between the democratic context and public policies can be distinguished. Before examining these, there are a few general remarks on public policies to protect children's right to positive action by the state worth noting.

Public Policies

A systematic interpretation of Part I, article 3, of the Convention of the Rights of the Child (CRC) of 1989 demands, as we shall see, that we cross out the restriction suggested by the text in section 1, "In all actions concerning children," on the assumption that normally all measures "undertaken by public or private social welfare institutions" have a direct or indirect bearing on children. The criterion of the "child's best interests"[2] thus becomes a principle of universal relevance to children that implies public policies and international measures aimed at the protection of children's rights. This means that the protection of these rights is not necessarily incumbent only on particular institutions with a specific competence, but also on a general strategy that potentially concerns every public and private institution, every organ of the state or its territorial entities, and the international community. It demands the coordination and synergy of every potentially competent subject.

The difference between public and private domains does not necessarily coincide with the one between public and private subjects. Private subjects can carry out or help to fulfill a public function. Civil society's participation in social policies is an essential step in the development of participative democracy and can play a major role in the policies on the protection of children's rights.

In the broadest possible sense, the public policies on the protection of the child within the CRC occur on four levels, illustrated in a diagram by Emilio García Méndez.[3] The four levels take on the shape of a pyramid, tapering upward. The largest section consists, quite rightly, of *basic social policies* (e.g., those concerning schools and health). As we move upward we find *social support policies* (protective measures in the strictest sense), then *correctional policies* (e.g., social-educational measures against juvenile delinquency), and, finally, *institutional policies* (dealing with administrative and judicial organizations and children's fundamental procedural rights).

The fundamental principle of every strategy aimed at implementing the integral protection of children's rights is to reestablish the primacy of basic social policies with respect to the proportions set out in the CRC. This means, in the first place, that basic social policies have a universal function and that all other policies should be residual and, second, that the dynamic conception of the principle of equality imposes on the state parties, respectively, a minimum of conformity to the principles of the welfare state, and imposes on the international community an adherence to a concept of economic development regulated by the criteria of human development.[4]

The norms of the CRC offer eloquent examples of a dynamic conception of equality[5] regarding the rules of the welfare state and the principle of international solidarity,[6] which points to a different kind of globalization from the one we know today.[7]

The catalog of the fundamental rights of the child, which the CRC demands that states parties protect, is perhaps the largest to have been in force to date, due to the detailed and specific manner in which it has been formulated. The reservation clause that constitutes article 41 allows this catalog to be considered as extended and rectified in conformity with the best interest of the child: it conforms with all those domestic and international norms valid in a state party (before or after the CRC) that are more favorable to children than the norms contained in the CRC.[8] This clause, which, in my opinion, was amplified and connected in favor of children's interest, also applies to every document of international or domestic law in which fundamental human rights are defined and protected, regardless of age. The convention thus makes the relevance of the whole system of children's fundamental human rights clear and, in the end, dispels any possible doubt on this crucial point.

The extent of the catalog of a state's right to positive action in the CRC is due not only to its length and specificity, but also to the fact that parts of the civil rights and rights of freedom that children enjoy in the system of the CRC are not merely negatively protected, that is, as rights to protection,[9] but are also complementary rights to positive action by the state itself.[10]

The protection of children's rights from offences by third parties is also provided with a series of specific norms that make up a particular group of the rights to receive state protection against offences by third parties.[11]

If, in addition to the rights accorded by the basic social policies considered so far, we consider the rights accorded by positive state actions as social support policies,[12] the norms that establish correctional policies,[13] and the volume of institutional policies that the state has to fulfill, then the issue of human and financial means to be allocated becomes of crucial importance.

These observations illustrate why the "democratic context" must be considered a basic framework for the development of adequate strategies to implement the CRC. In listing these reasons I shall refer to the five dimensions of the concept of democracy mentioned above.

The Dimensions of Democracy

1. *Municipalization of and participation in public policies* (which, to give an excellent example of a legislative translation of the CRC, was applied by the Brazilian Estatuto da Criança e do Adolescente)[14] can be successfully accomplished only if the network of democratic relations of power and participation are sufficiently developed within the social institutions of the local community. On the other hand, experience has shown that

children's needs and the perception of their needs as rights can turn into a constructive and evolutionary moment in the culture of democracy and in the development of democratic legality within the local community.

2. At the central, or national, level of civil society, stress should be laid on the role of political institutions, including the importance of their level of democratic organization. Also important is the role they play in developing popular participation in and control over the processes of lawmaking and law implementation in the field of children's rights. At this level, a fundamental political discussion on the themes of children's rights can become an important element in the consolidation of a society's democratic principles.

Pluralism and democratic control of the media, as well as freedom of access to them, are essential factors in the formation of a critical public opinion and the liberation of a social imagination capable of seeing below the surface. Not only the subject of children's rights, but also children themselves could turn into an extraordinary source to renew and positively transform adults' concepts of democracy, provided we listen to and learn from them.

It would be convenient to consider social democracy, at a national level, as *ethnic and cultural pluralism*, as a respect for minorities, and as a capacity to learn from them. An adequate development of this dimension of social democracy would implement children's right to a cultural and ethnic identity.[15] The respect of children's cultural and ethnic identity is, in turn, a condition for the existence and reproduction of a pluralistic dimension of social democracy.

3. Let us consider the political dimension of democracy at its *local level*. In the context of the current transformation of the state and the crisis concerning its sovereignty, conditioned by the growing and rapid globalization of the economic system and its decision-making structure, we are witnessing a localization of the political system and a reevaluation of local autonomy, which is centered above all on the city. Instead of a technocratic decentralization—a movement of power delegated from above and working downward—the phenomenon of localization, in its newest and most promising aspects, takes the form of a democratic decentralization, or reform of the foundations of power, tending to produce an upward movement of reform. This movement appears in three forms: federalism, participative local public policies, and city networks for the coordination of specific sectors of local policies.

It is extremely important to take into consideration localization—and its concomitant potential—to reform the community political network (which is much more difficult to accomplish at a central level) by considering the strategies being used to implement the CRC in the process of localization. Localization is favorable to the development of multiagency and interinstitutional relations that improve social and political democracy at the local level. So far, the potential of public policies to implement the CRC at this level is far from being exhausted, both in Latin America and in Europe.[16]

4. By no means do the importance acquired by local democracies and the crisis of sovereignty of nations mean that the role of the latter in fulfilling public policies is diminished. The possible change resulting from federalism and localization may modify the forms of intervention of central institutions, but not their importance. Local policies of empowerment and of alternative development require not a weak state, but a strong one, a state that will support local policies through legislative and financial action.

It is at a central level, rather than at a local one, that the main problem for the welfare state emerges: the financing of public policies. This problem is dramatically aggravated by the crisis of the welfare state. Constitutional law considers the fundamental rights to positive state action—economic, social, and cultural rights—to be subjected to a general reservation concerning what is economically achievable.[17] This reservation seems to limit the state's obligation to ensure that adequate policies are implemented. Even the CRC refers to this.[18]

Nevertheless, we should avoid an interpretation of the reservation that could provide an alibi for, or a legitimization of, a lack of state accomplishment. A correct interpretation of the reservation, which takes the fundamental rights of citizens seriously, supposes that it comes into force only when the state has exhausted all the possibilities of fully accomplishing its duty to provide the necessary resources by means of fiscal and financial policies. This reservation does not apply if the state does not seriously attempt to regulate the systems of the production and social distribution of wealth, as well as to technically rationalize and legally control its allocation.

On the other hand, it is not correct to place all the variables on which the problems of financing public policies depend within the radius of the state's actions. Indeed, the fundamental variables rest on the economic development of the world and its relationships of complementarity with or opposition to human development, that is, on the system of human needs and fundamental rights.[19]

Questions about social equality and justice, on the one hand, and about economic and human development, on the other, are strictly interdependent. Both are largely excluded from the state's internal decision-making system and are only very insufficiently controllable with the present forms of international organization and cooperation. The task of state democracy ends where that of international democracy begins.

5.   The most serious lack of democracy lies in its international dimension, which is where it is especially needed today. The growing interdependence of national societies and states goes hand in hand not with a decrease in the gap between rich and poor, but with an increase in that gap. The "economic" growth of the global village and the universalization of the market may not immediately seem to have any positive impact on children's global tragedy. However, children pay more than anyone else for the distortions of development—for example, due to absolute poverty (affecting 240 million children) and famine and disease (40,000 children die every day). Within economic development that is structurally separated from human needs, the production and distribution of food is conditioned by the logic of the market. Human needs do not necessarily correspond with either the demand for goods or the priorities of supply.

If we observe the international community in its social dimension, it is similar to an anarchic oligarchy in which real power is highly concentrated in a few hundred financial centers that compete against each other and whose volume of economic activities has surpassed the total sum of the budgets of half the world's nations. The need for technical and financial support from the international community for public policies on children's rights is still disproportionately larger than the present degree of satisfying that need.

The Course of Development

Considering the vastness of this discourse, I shall have to limit myself to an outline of three of its possible directions.

1.   As with the local and national levels, improving the level of democracy within the global-level power structure is a condition that cannot be neglected in the process of defining strategies for a policy to implement the CRC.

2. The control of global conditions for implementing the CRC—and not only structural or emergency actions to protect children's rights—depends on the competence and responsibility of all international institutions for policy and social solidarity. The most general and important of these conditions are peace and international economic order, which, in my opinion, the CRC contains an implicit reference to.

3. Faced with tasks such as these, it is necessary to consider amplifying the competencies, improving the structure, and strengthening the power of the above-mentioned international institutions and organizations. Though their democratization is a necessary condition, it must be followed by further qualitative change; without peace and an economic order capable of ensuring that the production and distribution of wealth is oriented toward human needs and development, the structural and financial requirements for the implementation of the CRC will not be met.

However, ensuring peace in a more fair international economic order presupposes that the legal order and the international organizations exercise a just and efficient control over the centers of power within the global civil society—centers that have largely emancipated themselves from state control and that partially control the states themselves. This makes a critical reexamination of the subordinate relations between states and the international community unavoidable.[20]

The restricted and unsatisfactory manner in which the CRC has so far called for international collaboration and for UN intervention regarding the financing[21] and control[22] of state policies is an eloquent sign of the need to carry out this reexamination.

The argumentation developed so far can be considered valid even if we conceive of the "democratic context" in a way that does not include children. Nonetheless, the argumentation shows the importance of democracy—if it is exclusively for adults—for defining and implementing the public policies demanded by the CRC. It also shows that taking children's fundamental human rights seriously can become a way of enriching adults' concepts of democracy. But what effect would the application of a democracy that includes children have on the way of understanding and practicing democracy and the democratic context of public policies?

Comparative Reflections on Children and Democracy
in Latin America and Europe

We are often forced to relativize the significance of the valuable maxims that we use to live by. This is the case of two contrasting propositions that have become classic in the discourse on children's rights.

It has been stated that "democracy is good for children."[23] Others have stated that "children are good for democracy."[24] I must confess that, having gradually encountered these efficient formulations, I realized that, in their opposition and complementarity, they bear witness both to the present importance of the child issue in the democratic system and to the historical exclusion of children and adolescents from the concept of democracy's programs of action.

Concerning this present importance, the crisis of authoritarian regimes — first in Europe, between the 1940s and the end of the 1970s, and later, toward the end of the 1980s, in Latin America — has enabled us, among other things, to measure the importance of reestablishing and developing the democratic constitutional state for the normative recognition and actual protection of children's and adolescents' rights at both international and national levels. In the past decade, the topic of children has been the object of and driving factor in a mobilization of civil society and the democratic process in various Latin American countries.

In the second half of this century, both in Europe and in Latin America, the new discourse on human rights has been extended to children's and adolescents' rights, according to an international trend expressed in the doctrine and documents of the UN. In this doctrine, as we know, children are not seen as objects of protection/repression by the state and adult society, but rather as *subjects* with original rights in regard to these institutions.

Given the historical exclusion of children, the need for their entitlement to human rights as a prerequisite is clear, but this alone does not extend the concept and regulations of democracy to children and adolescents: they would have to participate actively in what I suggest we call the "social or political relationship of autonomy, democracy, and self-rule." This relationship is *social* when it refers to the institutions of civil society — such as family, schools, factories, and associations — and it is *political* when it refers to state and other territorial political bodies — such as provinces, municipalities, or districts. It is a *relationship of autonomy* when it refers to regulations that allow decisions to be made in the name of the community, and it is one of *self-rule* when it refers to certain individuals' competence to make such decisions or to participate directly in decision making. The social or political relationship of autonomy and self-rule could be called more concisely the "social or political relationship of democracy."

A class of subjects has a political or social democratic relationship with other subjects if agreement among the members of that class plays an essential role in producing or validating the rules that regulate the decisions made on behalf of the community in a certain institution of civil society, in the state, or in any other territorial political organization, and if that class can participate in the decision making, either directly or by proxy. It is clear that this definition embraces the two poles—which only appear to be opposite—between which the present theories on democracy can be placed: the formal-procedural pole[25] and the substantial-participatory one.[26]

With the above-mentioned definition, democracy is an "ideal type," rather than a classifying concept. An ideal type does not describe reality, but stylizes it by indicating a regulatory criterion, that is, an aim that admits various phenomenological interpretations of civil society and of political territorial organizations, and their ongoing evolutionary processes, by evaluating them according to how close they get to the ideal type.

It is also obvious that the degree of similarity between Latin American and European societies varies greatly, even between particular countries, according to the various institutions and territorial bodies, the class of subjects (men and women, white and colored, rich and poor, native and foreign, adults and children), and the historical period, as well as a combination of these variables.

Let's go back to our two valuable propositions: that democracy is a favorable occasion to strengthen children's rights and that children's rights are or can be a favorable occasion to strengthen democracy. This does not necessarily mean, however, that children and adolescents are the subjects of political or social relations, of autonomy, and of self-rule.

Taken literally, our two propositions actually point above all to an external functional relationship of importance between children and democracy: they do not generally indicate that the progress of democracy can favor the participation of children and adolescents in activities of political and social democracy, or that the democratization of the relationship between children and adults in general can favor the progress of democracy. It is not a question of the functional relationship between the democratic system and one of its subsystems, but of the mutual importance between the democratic system and children that includes the superior interest of children. But this interest, as well as the concomitant rights of children, necessarily correspond to their democratic participation in the social and political spheres.

Let us now consider two familiar transitions in children's development: "from child and adolescent to minor" and "from minor to citizen."[27] With the first transition, it is as though a century of having institutionalized the exclusion of a wide minority of children and adolescents (in Europe) or even the majority of them (in some Latin American countries) from the normal school-family system were to pass before our eyes.

The second transition, in contrast, underlies the shift in the premise of policy toward children from one based on an irregular situation, as described earlier, to one based on the protection of the rights of children and adolescents as adopted by the UN in the 1989 Convention and its precursors. Thus, the global approach to protecting children's rights seeks to abolish the social classification that separates minors from children. This approach therefore refers to children and adolescents as subjects with original human rights in order to reintegrate delinquent juveniles, or "minors" who are in unfavorable situations, into the normal child and adolescent system as quickly as possible.[28]

The doctrine of the global protection of children's rights was also brought about by a wide social movement in favor of children's rights and by the reformation of children's rights that has taken place and is still under way in Latin America and in Europe. Not only have the concept and the role of central public institutions for children changed dramatically, including courts for minors, but language about children has been revolutionized: this is an important sign of transformation on the normative level. There is less and less talk of minors and more and more of children and adolescents and their rights.

The adoption of the formula "from minor to citizen" places us within an ongoing process, as yet incomplete. This open character of the process obviously does not refer solely to the actual implementation of the international and national norms and the theoretic principles that express the new doctrine, but also to the very process of normative and doctrinal definition. The saying "from minor to citizen" thus expresses what the author of the other statement appropriately called "our memory of the future."[29] Going back to being a child alone would not suffice to turn a minor into a citizen. Let us remain on the normative level: to what degree are children and adolescents citizens in the system of the Convention? The answer will enable us to establish whether there is more memory or more future in this memory of the future. It is important to do so in order to know how long the process of developing norms and doctrines will take.

Freedom, Participation, and Representation in the UN Convention on Children's Rights

Citizenship is the juridical state of full participation in the state community or in other territorial political organizations. In its integral form, it presupposes the de jure and de facto applicability of the constitutional norms and principles typical of the social and democratic constitutional state and the entitlement to all the fundamental rights that characterize this form of state, including political rights and those of political participation.[30] On the other hand, as we shall see, proper use of these rights can be made only under the condition that all other fundamental rights (civil, economic, social, and cultural) are exercised. Citizenship and democracy are not identical, but one cannot exist without the other.

Citizenship includes political relations of autonomy and self-rule, but not social relations, at least not directly. Nevertheless, in a complex and pluralist society such as ours, democratic policies cannot exist without social democracy. Citizens who enjoy democratic rights in the political sphere (who can influence the community with their opinions and decisions) but are subject to autocratic relations in the various societal institutions (family, school, factory, or civil or religious associations) would only be half-citizens. It is hard even to hypothesize a situation in which political power could exist without social power.

This was widely recognized in the political theory of empowerment developed by John Friedmann. He showed that the political exclusion of individuals of the poorest social classes was conditioned by their social exclusion. He wrote, "To be economically excluded is, for all practical purposes, to be politically excluded."[31] The strategy of alternative development that Friedmann proposes, based on his long experience with development programs in Latin America and elsewhere, is founded on the increase of social power and the transformation of the latter into political power, starting from the strengthening of the economic and communicative capacity of the poor, beginning with the family nucleus and the local community.[32] This, according to Friedmann, is the main way of realizing the model of "inclusive democracy."[33] Yet this is but an actual extension of active citizenship, that is, participation by all individuals in the decisions of the political and social spheres on which their conditions of life depend.

The history of democracy in Latin America and Europe is likely to portend the future history of democratic empowerment. With some reflection, the political theory of empowerment could be extended to all categories of subjects who are de jure or de facto excluded from fully exercising their political rights, that is, whose status as citizens is seriously limited. The story is an old one, as old as Western history, but its latest decisive phase began with the theory and practice of the social pact that characterizes modernity. In other works I have explained how this pact can be considered one of exclusion since, despite the declared universal potential of its principle, it was a pact among white, wealthy, male adults to exclude women, children, have-nots, and people of color—that is, those who possessed nothing but their labor force—from the exercise of citizenship in the new state that was being created with the pact.[34] The development of the modern social pact in the formal and material constitution of Latin American and European countries is characterized by the struggle of the excluded to attain citizenship and become integrated in democracy.

The history and future role of democracy is that of transforming social exclusion into social inclusion, that is, of extending the social basis of the exercise and legitimacy of decisions made on behalf of the community. This history, we saw, is not homogeneous because so far the democratic process has been discontinuous and fragmentary with regard to social groups and geographic areas. There are also some fundamental elements of unity that depend above all on the functional relationship between what is commonly called the "center" and the "periphery" of the capitalist social and economic formation. There are noticeable differences between the development of democracy in Latin America and in Europe, which I shall not deal with here, limiting myself to the differences between social groups. There are at least three anomalies that make the historical role of children in the development of democracy disharmonious if not incongruous with the history of all other social groups.

First, children's ongoing exclusion from the social pact appears as an explicit and planned exclusion from the social pact of modernity, not only a de facto, but also a de jure exclusion from the exercise of citizenship. Children and adolescents, like all humans, have access to civil rights and rights of freedom, as established in the declaration of human rights. Yet they are not a contracting party in the pact: they have neither the power nor the natural duty to be a party. This is obviously due to the differentiation between rational and irrational beings that is an ontological and ethical foundation of the theories of natural law and of contractualism in modern times: adults on one side and children and animals on the other. All creatures—and all organizations, inasmuch as they are centers of life and existence—are centers of value, but only adult humans are subject to the juridical and moral code.[35]

Children can find protection in the civil state, a product of the social pact, but they are not part of it. The contradiction of being excluded from the pact is the accepted norm for children, one that excludes them from fully exercising their citizenship rights. They have a much longer way to go to obtain recognition of their rights than other groups excluded from the modern social pact.

Second, children's struggle for equality of rights is not tied to their fight for the acknowledgment of their difference, whereas the recognition of difference in gender, culture, and position in the world of production is the climax in the struggle for equality of the other excluded people: women, nonwhite ethnic groups, and the labor class.

For children, the issue of their difference has produced benefits in terms of protection, at the price, however, of their equality, while the issue of equality has had negative effects inasmuch as it refers to the identity between children and adolescents—as the various exceptions and reservations made by the signatory states with regard to the CRC show, exceptions that have allowed states to equate adolescents and adults with regard to work, military recruitment, and penal age, not only de facto, as is often the case, but also from a juridical point of view.

I cannot help thinking that the distinction between children and adolescents is not a structural separation between two lines of development—equality and identity—but a delay, an ideological holdover that could even be a signal (in spite of the great progress made in the past decades) that the struggle for children's rights has not reached its climax, that (to use a metaphor of Gomez da Costa again)[36] there is still a wide gap between the future and memory. The historical delay, which refers to the relation between the movements for equality and for difference, requires children's right to a different citizenship to be placed in the forefront in the development of the democratic constitutional state.

Third, the struggle for children's and adolescents' rights, unlike those of other excluded groups, has been unfair in being dependent on adult discourse and action. This is paradoxical if we bear in mind that it is the adults who exercise power over children and yet it is adults to whom the demand for the equality, freedom, physical and moral integrity, and respect of children's rights is addressed.

Similar claims by other social groups have had a positive outcome on condition when (1) they were led by members of the group or of a significant sector of the group, (2) they were led collectively and publicly, (3) they transformed needs into rights, and, finally, (4) action was taken against the power of the antagonistic groups. Thus, women's struggle was directed against men's power, colored people's struggle against white power, and workers' struggle against the power of capitalists.

Nevertheless, we should bear in mind that the fight for emancipation and justice has lost (at least partly) the dimension of specific antagonism that has characterized the historical class struggle and has taken on the characteristic of a more general conflict for freeing individual identity and transforming the typical structure of relations based on power, as analyzed by Michel Foucault.[37]

In light of Foucault's theory on power and the struggle for power, which strives to change our world, we can perhaps understand the anomaly and paradox of the ongoing struggle for children's rights. In the struggle for children's rights witnessed in Latin America and in Europe, children are not the protagonists, but merely those to whom such rights refer. Children have not become a collective subject or the cause of a public movement, nor have children created a discourse on their needs redefined as rights, though there have been a few very valuable isolated experiences in this regard (such as the movement of the *pibes unidos* in Argentina and Uruguay, that of the *meninos da rua* in Brazil, and several school movements in Europe).[38]

These anomalies have largely conditioned the movement for children's rights and its present outcome. The adults who have taken charge of the movement have granted ample space to children's civil, social, and economic rights, but hardly any room to children's political rights and rights of political participation.

Adults have reformulated the rules of the game and the procedure with which decisions that directly or indirectly determine children's conditions can be made, but they have not agreed to share with children the power to formulate the rules of the game and the procedure, to name representatives, or to participate directly in decision making in the name of the community. They have granted children all citizens' rights but the right to participate in the rule of the "polis." Democracy has turned into a limit to children's citizenship, but as we shall now see, childhood has become democracy's frontline issue. In other words, democracy will not move out of its childhood phase until it starts dealing with the issue of children's rights as an internal question, not as a merely external problem.

First, it should be pointed out that such an inclusive conception of democracy is incompatible with historical limits, which becomes evident by examining the most renowned theories on democracy. To my knowledge, none of the great contemporary theories on democracy have ever offered children or adolescents the chance to exercise political rights. This exclusion is explicitly formulated by both Bobbio and Dahl,[39] who are at opposite poles of this wide range of theories. On the other hand, as to the external relations between democracy and children's rights, there is a lack of symmetry between the two groups of authors who deal with these subjects: those who write about children's rights also talk about democracy, whereas those who write about democracy do not mention children's rights at all. This historical limit is even present in the text of the CRC.

Nevertheless, in my opinion, both the theories of democracy and the CRC contain important elements (if they are considered in the context of a dynamic and systematic interpretation)[40] for the construction of a theoretical, normative discourse that can take us beyond this limit. If we examine the CRC in the literal sense of its articles and in a fragmentary and static manner, the traces left by this historical limit will come to light. These traces are evident, especially when they affect the meaning and scope of the fundamental innovative principle introduced by the CRC through article 12:

children capable of forming their own views have the rights to express themselves freely, to be heard, and to have due importance attached to their opinions.

Children's autonomy and subjectivity, the weight that their opinions can and must have in adults' decisions, had never been acknowledged so explicitly before the CRC. This new principle is also present in articles 9.2, 13.1, and 14.1.[41] However, two broad series of norms are provided to counterbalance this with an opposing principle.

The first of these assures adults the right to determine the best interests of the child in an objective and definitive manner[42] and to determine what promotes his or her social, spiritual, and moral well-being and physical and mental health.[43] The second series of norms conditions the child's exercise of his or her rights, not only according to the rights and freedoms of others[44] — which is just and necessary — but also depending on the interpretation given by adults of general clauses or vague concepts such as national security, public order, and public health or morals.[45]

Yet the internal limits of these rights (to express oneself freely, to be heard, and to be given due attention) are nonetheless relevant. First, the scope of the three rights decreases from the first to the second and from the second to the third. The freedom to form one's own view has no limitation of content. Indeed, it refers to children's attitude toward the world. The right to express their own views, however, does not include their entire view of the world. Its scope is limited to matters that affect them directly. In this respect, article 12.1 merely sets forth that the child's opinion shall be given due weight, but "due" according to what? The answer is "in accordance with the age and maturity of the child."[46]

The right of the child to be heard — a right set forth in article 12.1 — is much more restricted. It does not refer to children's global experience, to what they think about the decisions adults make for them; it refers merely to those decisions that adults make at an institutional level in the case of "any judicial and administrative proceedings affecting the child." Any? Yes, but only those that affect the child, of course.

Second, the strength of the rights set forth in article 12 is weak. We know from the doctrine of fundamental rights that the strength of rights can vary depending on the case, that there are strong rights and weak ones, that only some have the strength of "definitive" rights (rights that can be defended in court), according to the expression used by Robert Alexy.[47] The rights provided by article 12 of the CRC are not "definitive" but weak ones, because they are characterized by a lack of symmetry between the state's duties and the expectations of those entitled to them. This is due to the formulation of rights and the application of explicit or implicit conditions to those rights, such as the reservation concerning what is "economically possible." Finally, we know that, in general, the rights of service—those that correspond to the state's positive duty toward those entitled to them—are weaker than rights of protection, which relate instead to the state's obligation not to interfere (as, e.g., to refrain from prejudging the citizens' life and freedom).

The right to form one's own opinion is presented as a state duty of service (to guarantee a child the necessary conditions to form his or her own opinion), but it does not refer to a subjective juridical position concretely determined in the child, and furthermore, it is subject to the reservation of what is economically possible. The right to have one's opinions heard has been formulated without specifying whether those who should listen to them are the officials or the adults responsible for the child. Finally, the right to be heard, the only one presented as a child's right and not as a general duty of the state or of other subjects, is formulated by referring back to the national legislation on proceedings, without setting any limitations.[48] This is also why the CRC adopts a relatively weak formulation, employing the term "opportunity" instead of "right."[49]

The third aspect is the most important one because it regards the functional connection between the rights laid down in article 12 and the state and societal democratic structure, as well as that between these rights and the child's position within this structure. There is no explicit relationship between these rights and the functioning of the democratic system. On the contrary, as we have seen, the importance of children's opinions is strictly limited to the situations and the proceedings that affect their interests. It does not extend to general interests, and children's opinions that could relate to general concerns are not considered important. The only time the CRC explicitly draws a functional relationship between the exercise of children's rights to freedom and the principle of democracy is in article 15.2; it does not, however, do so to point out the democratic function of children's freedom—in this case, freedom of association—but to allow limits to be set to this freedom, that is, "that they are necessary in a democratic society."[50]

On considering the albeit fragmentary literary tenor of the preamble and of the specific articles, we should come to the conclusion that the CRC protects the rights of children—even the ones that could play a major role in their participation in the democratic process within society and the state (like those provided in article 12—not like the rights of citizens who participate in relations of autonomy and self-rule, but like the rights of half-citizens, or rather of potential or future citizens. In the meantime, children would be guaranteed the possibility of developing freely, of enjoying civil, economic, social, and cultural rights (with the above-mentioned restrictions and counterweights) under adults' rule and regulations, but only when they became full citizens, like adults, will they will enjoy, eventually, the rights of political participation.

Human Development and the Politics of Rights:
Children's Role in the Future of Democracy

The future of democracy, to use the title of a famous book by Norberto Bobbio, is fundamentally connected to the recognition of the child, not as a future citizen, but as a full-fledged citizen. To back this statement, I would like, first of all, to present three theses.[51]

First, by using a systematic, dynamic interpretation of the CRC—instead of a fragmentary, static one—that is, by developing its spirit with all due respect to its letter, children, in any given phase of their development, even when very young, would enjoy full citizenship. Second, this citizenship is entirely compatible with the due consideration of their difference from adults, that is, their identity as children. Finally, the differences in the way that democratic powers and functions of children and adults are exercised—as far as the positions of adults and children in the particular functioning of the system of political representation are concerned—compensate in favor of children within the system of rights implied by the CRC and in children's central position in the foundation of a new democratic welfare state. In this last sense, the principle of children's absolute priority does not concern only the aims of an alternative democratic development, but the means itself, the communicative methodology of this development, which is what is meant by "inclusive democracy."

As to the first point, we should bear in mind that the most advanced theory of fundamental rights allows us to consider democratic principles as the focal point for the classification and systematization of rights within the framework of the welfare state. Let us take the systematization proposed by Klaus Stern as an example. According to his theory, fundamental rights can be divided into four groups: (1) civil rights and the right of freedom (rights of protection against the state), (2) economic, social, and cultural rights (rights of positive action from the state), (3) political rights and rights of political participation, and (4) fundamental procedural rights.[52]

If we take such a classification as a starting point, we can establish three important premises for our discourse. First, as stated above, the first and second categories of rights are prerequisites to exercise the third group of rights: political and participation rights. The system of political democracy cannot function if life, personal freedom, and freedom of opinion and association are not truly guaranteed, if the economic, social, and cultural development of individuals and groups is not ensured. Second, it is the exercise of political and participation rights that in turn condition and guarantee all other rights. Without a voice and access to avenues of information, communication, and decision making in all the state's and civil society's spheres of life, individuals and groups could not concretely exercise the necessary influence concerning the conditions on which the exercise of their civil, economic, social, and cultural rights depends.

The democratic development of the communicative and decision-making structure of the family, school, church, and political, economic, and cultural associations, as well as the active participation in them by every citizen, are important and decisive indicators of a country's political freedom, no less so than the quality and the good implementation of the rules on elections and the appointment of civil servants. The exercise of what can be called the "public use of freedom" depends on this. This is why the rights of participation are strongly functionally interrelated with the rights of freedom and especially with the so-called communicative rights of freedom, which concern the freedom of thought, information, association and reunion, and access to the media.

Even within the public sphere of the state and its functional and territorial entities, as well as the so-called parastate, citizen participation is important for the development of participatory democracy. This regards, on the one hand, the dynamics of the formalized, semiformalized, or informal processes of interaction between the public administration and citizenship and, on the other hand, the so-called procedural fundamental rights that guarantee citizens participation and representation in all kinds of judicial proceedings—civil, administrative, and penal. In Stern's classification, procedural fundamental rights thus make up a fourth group strictly tied to the third one (political and participatory rights).

While the citizens' *status negativus* (according to Georg Jellinek's terminology) is fulfilled by the classic civil rights and rights of freedom, their *status positivus* is achieved by the rights of positive action by the state. The *status activus* is fulfilled by the last two groups of rights mentioned.[53]

Following the model of an "inclusive democracy," the *status activus* represents the culminating moment of the whole system of fundamental rights. An exhaustive and systematic analysis of the CRC enables us to establish that the child is entitled—not only in an integral way, but also in a privileged manner with respect to the adults—to all the fundamental rights that constitute his or her *status negativus* and *status positivus* and that, in what concerns the *status activus*, the child fully enjoys the fundamental procedural rights and a significant part of the rights of participation.

The CRC thus grants children all those rights the exercise of which is the prerequisite to be able to exercise any political and participatory rights, as is the case with adults. The specific manner in which children's full citizenship is built in the system of the CRC depends on the difference in identity and development between children and adults.

My second thesis is that recognition of children's different identity is expressed in the specific and privileged way in which the civil rights of freedom—the economic, social, cultural, procedural, and, in particular, the communicative rights—are afforded them. These differences, of advantage to children, are established considering the special needs of protection and care that the preamble of the CRC has derived from the Declaration of the Rights of the Child adopted by the UN General Assembly in 1959. However, they can also be interpreted in light of children's positive prerogatives, and not only of their weakness and lack of physical and mental maturity.

The third thesis is that not only the privileges enjoyed by children regarding the three groups of fundamental rights I have just pointed out, but also the prerogatives of their rights to participate in the communicative and decision-making processes provide ample compensation for the handicaps that affect children in the sector of classic political rights, due to their different identity and to their specific situation in the context of social relationships. This thesis would mean that children's citizenship—their active participation in social and political democracy—is different from, but just as important as, adults'.

Supporting these three theses implies an interpretation of the rights formulated in article 12 of the CRC, which grants children's rights to be heard the greatest possible scope and a new and fundamental meaning. To be consistent with this new construction, we must have a broader understanding of the idea of freedom, as articulated in article 12: rather than a private use of freedom, our view should be oriented toward a *public use of freedom*. This can be achieved by placing the freedom implied in article 12 in a functional relationship with the concept of freedom expressed by the CRC in the third paragraph of the preamble. The latter mentions the concept of a "larger freedom" and relates it to two basic principles: a person's dignity and human development, the latter expressed with the formula "social progress." In light of this concept, we can arrive at the following systematic interpretation of article 12 together with articles 13 and 17: children's freedom and right to form their own opinion and express it entails an obligation on behalf of the adults (all of them, not only the authorities or those who are responsible for the child) with the same extension of that freedom.

The necessary reinterpretation of the letter of the norm in order to establish this relationship and symmetry between children's rights and adults' duties is logically reached by correctly extending the meaning of the concept of "proceedings affecting the child." Every proceeding, both social and institutional, in which adults intervene with their decisions and actions affects and concerns children, whether directly or indirectly. And indeed, what would the proceedings that do not affect them be? Thus, a *principle of the universal relevance of children's interests* is established, which, in turn, implies a *principle of structural reciprocity between children's rights and adults' rights*.

One of the results is a change in perspective in the application of article 12. The criterion of the universal relevance of the childhood issue corresponds not only to the matters defined as their interests, but also to the adults' interests, that is, everybody's. By extending their duty to take children's opinions into consideration, adults thus achieve a principle of evaluation and a method of decision making that they have made very little use of so far, to the disadvantage of all.

Let us take one step further, beyond the letter of article 12, and we shall realize that children's right to be heard has the same scope as the right to express their own views. We reach this conclusion by carrying out the following two operations of systematic interpretation: first, by amplifying the content of the expression "administrative proceedings" as far as possible so as to include every formal, semiformal, and even informal interaction between any civil servant or official and the child-citizen, and second, by considering the phrase in article 12.2—"the opportunity to be heard . . . either directly, or through a representative" in the procedures—as a specification of a general principle that covers the whole of article 12 and includes all the other relationships between children and adults. This principle implies children's general and fundamental right to be heard and adults' symmetrical duty to hear them.

On the other hand, this duty cannot be simply reduced to children's freedom to communicate their experience with regard to other children and adults. If we interpret children's right to be heard as adults' duty to hear them and *learn from them*, to listen to their voices and to consider them to be decision makers,[54] so that they can define their interests autonomously (i.e., their concrete needs as subjects entitled to autonomous rights and juridical personality of their own),[55] the principle contained in article 12 becomes the nucleus of the CRC, directing the way for future relations between children and adults. This is also the way to the future of democracy.

To realize this, we must reflect on how the child's rights to be heard or the adult's duty to learn from the child are related to the concepts of participation and representation. Citizenship as a means of expressing political freedom takes the form of both direct and indirect participation in public decisions. Indirect participation can be carried out by representative mandate. However, the concept of representation is more general than that of mandate.

Adults and authorities that make decisions based on fulfilling their duty to learn from children carry out a form of representation without mandate, but do so with a communicative duty that is not isolated from other means of representation by which modern democracy works. Scientific research and institutional knowledge as the research activities of universities and other institutions of society, the state, and the international community also represent the needs, opinions, and interests of citizens. Exercising children's right to be heard in the form of adults' doing their duty of learning from children can also be understood as a form of participation by the child in political or social democracy by means of representation. The quality and legitimacy of the forms of representation without mandate depend mainly on accomplishing the duties of communication and interaction, which I see as a constitutional principle that regulates the action of the representative societal institutions.

The communication and reciprocity between adults and children determine the quality and legitimacy of the decisions that adults make on behalf of the community. Considering the diversity of situations present in the relation between children and adults with regard to various informal and institutional contexts and children's various stages of development, we should go a step further by taking into account the varied consequences of children's right to be heard, beyond its possible representational meaning. In dealing with this aspect of the issue, I suggest that we begin by acknowledging that the general validity of children's right to be heard can be made compatible with all the possible ways of achieving this. There is no age and no institutional or informal sphere of the child-adult relationship in which the applicability of the normative principle is less intense. Nevertheless, such an assertion requires the principle to be extended beyond the intellectual and verbal sphere of the opinions and actual judgment that children are capable of formulating and expressing.

The principle incorporated into article 12 is valid as the general principle of the CRC. It refers not only to verbal expression and views, but to any sign of children's intellectual and emotional experiences, as well as their need to be heard in any situation, at all ages, and in every micro and macro social context.

It is adults' duty to learn from children in order to orient or modify attitudes or actions with regard to both the public and the private exercise of their freedom; by freedom we mean children's very development, which at the same time presupposes a lack of hindrance and all kinds of positive conditions—material, emotional, social, and cultural. Even premature babies who have to be checked by a doctor with a stethoscope have the right to be heard, as do adolescents who want to make their presence known in class. Finally, the child's right to be heard also means the right to be respected in one's capacity of autonomous orientation, a capacity that starts at a vegetative level and continues into the intellectual and moral sphere.

The idea is not to deny parents and educators the right to encourage and follow the physiological, affective, intellectual, and moral development of the child, but rather to recognize restrictions on care and education in order to prevent such restrictions from turning into the manipulation and repression of children's (especially of very young children's) capabilities.

For years, Alice Miller has been pointing out the drawbacks suffered by children owing to diverse forms of manipulation and repression that seriously hinder them from taking the greatest possible advantage of their natural ability to learn by experience, solve conflicts, and work on their anguish. These are not trivial inconveniences that trouble children. Alice Miller and other authors have pointed out that the taboo imposed by adult society on children who elaborate and express the violence suffered in their closest environment (especially within the family) is fundamentally responsible for reproducing those who support violence in our society.[56]

Peace is a prerequisite for democracy. According to a valuable definition by Johan Galtung,[57] peace is the absence of violence in any form, be it individual or structural, physical or psychological. Grown-ups, the family, the school, and the church offer children opportunities to free themselves of the burden of the taboo and thus the inheritance of violence inflicted on them. Taking seriously children's right to elaborate and express their experiences as victims of violence is a central aspect of adults' collective self-analysis needed, among other things, to interrupt the cycle of violence — its reproduction throughout the generations.

In a book on the limits of democracy, Etienne Balibar shows how difficult it is to introduce the principle of politics as a politics of rights into the discourse and the practice of the social constitutional state. The fact is, writes Balibar, that the politics of rights is what makes democracy face up to its limits, that is, the line that divides the present from the future.[58] A dynamic vision of democracy — one that includes children at the core of an alternative form of development that is compatible with human development — implies a transformation of the very concept of politics: from politics as an administration of society's status quo to politics as a project of society. In politics as a project, the subject is society itself seen as a constituent part, rather than a constituted form of the state; the state and the social alliance are always being founded anew. The politics of rights — the dynamic realization of the constitution of the social state and the international conventions that integrate it — is what permits new rights to be defined, allowing the state–society alliance to renew itself continuously. The policy of implementing children's rights and the realization of the innovating principle contained in article 12 of the CRC thus indicate that a change in paradigm is taking place that could lead democracy away from its childhood stage and toward a mature and human society.

The Reflective Dimension of Development: Scientific Knowledge and the Representation of Needs in the Democratic System

In a democratic conception of the functional relationship between knowledge and society, scientific research and institutional knowledge are forms of representation of citizens without mandate, that is, forms that articulate their needs and rights.[59] This is also true of scientific research and institutional knowledge that deal with children's situation and rights and help the public and private institutions that aim to protect them.

Scientific and institutional knowledge are also forms in which children's right to be heard and adults' duty to hear them and learn from them are accomplished. Institutional knowledge occurs on three levels: local, national, and global. Each level produces knowledge that is directed toward the construction of action programs and their evaluation.

At a local level, a participative methodology following the principles of action research has proved to be very efficient. At the central and global levels, institutional knowledge can be used to diagnose situations in the national and international spheres and to create programs or strategies of technical support and evaluation of local and national policies. At every level higher than the local one, we will find a twofold goal of institutional knowledge: one, the monitoring and support of action carried out at lower levels, and the other, self-monitoring.

It is of great importance that institutional knowledge be accompanied by free scientific research and that the national and international institutions that produce institutional knowledge collaborate with centers of free investigation or even have their own. Scientific knowledge can indeed integrate and orient the production of institutional knowledge. But unlike institutional knowledge, it is free of the tasks of monitoring and self-monitoring, characteristic of action programs, and must have the freedom to choose autonomously its own targets and methodologies, even if its objects are action programs and the social needs they address.

Scientific knowledge, as institutional knowledge, but in a different manner, listens to children and represents their needs. Its relation to programs and administrators at each level can be described as a lung that breaths in freely the experiences of the programs and their social context and can transmit knowledge to every cell of the planetary organism formed by these programs. The promotion and even the organization of free scientific research is one of the tasks of the institutions dedicated to implementating the CRC, particularly those belonging to the international community. Scientific research is an important and indispensable means through which the voice of children can be heard in public policies designed to protect their rights.

NOTES

1. Bobbio (1991: 50).
2. Alston (1994: 13–23), An-na'im (1994: 76–80), Dorsch (1994: 103–8), Eekelaar (1994), Ronfani (1997).
3. García Méndez (1997: 241 ss).
4. This concept is used by the UN. The three most important dimensions of human development are "to lead a long and healthy life, to acquire knowledge and to have access to resources needed for a decent standard of living." With their annual report, the researchers of the UN Development Programme describe the development of some indicators to quantify the degree of human development worldwide. For the definition of "human development," see UNDP, "Human Development Report, 1990," New York (1991: 9–16), esp. 10; on the "right for development," see Denninger (1990: 221).
5. CRC, article 2.
6. CRC, articles 4, 18 (par. 2 and 3), 20, 22–8, 31, 32, 38 (par. 4), and 39. For particular reference to the principle of equality, see CRC, articles 23 (par. 3), 28, and 31 (par. 2).
7. This perspective of a global interaction "from above" through initiatives of the subordinate states, regions, and social classes and groups has been newly described as "cosmopolitanism" in an impressive text by De Sousa Santos. He understands this cosmopolitanism as the biggest promise for a democratic development on the international level through a cosmopolitan policy on human rights, in which human rights must be redefined in a "*mestiza* conception (mixed conception)" in opposition to the false Western concept of universalism (Santos, 1997: 32–43); see the discussion on international solidarity and political alliance in a cosmopolitical perspective concerning the foundation of a "halfbreed state" (Baratta, 1996; Baratta and Giannoulis, 1996: 237–40, 253–66).
8. See, e.g., Dorsch (1994: 123–6).
9. CRC, articles 13, 14, 15, 16 (par. 1), 30, 38 (par. 2 and 3), and 40.
10. CRC, articles 10, 37 (sec. c), and 39.
11. CRC, articles 11, 16 (par. 2), 19, 21, 32–6, and 38 (par. 2).
12. CRC, articles 17 (par. 2 and 3), 20, 22–6, 28, and 38 (par. 4).
13. CRC, articles 37 (secs. c and d), and 40.
14. Baratta (1995a: 49–50), Cury et al. (1992: 405–27), García Méndez (1994: 103–12).
15. CRC, articles 29 (par. 1, sec. c) and 30.
16. Szanton Blanc (1995), Cornia and Sipos (1991).

17. For an example of this in a decision of the German Federal Constitutional Court, see Alexy (1986: 457) and Murswiek (1992: 267–8).

18. CRC, articles 4 and 27 (par. 3).

19. Baratta (1993, 1997) and Heller (1976).

20. See, e.g., Pieper (1994: 170–1).

21. CRC, articles 4, 24 (par. 4), and 28 (par. 3).

22. CRC, articles 43, 44, and 45.

23. Declaration of James P. Grant, executive director of UNICEF (see García Méndez, 1994: 178).

24. Emilio García Méndez quoted in Gomez da Costa (1995: 110); see the discussion on these statements in Baratta (1995a: 19–22).

25. Bobbio (1991: 4–7, 63–84).

26. Dahl (1990) and Friedmann (1992).

27. Gomez da Costa (1992).

28. See, e.g., Viccica (1989).

29. Baratta (1995b: 20–1) and Gomez da Costa (1992).

30. This is a strict concept of citizenship that refers above all to the exercise of potential rights in a state. Apart from this legal or political definition, there is also a sociological concept, often used when referring to children's rights, in which citizenship is defined as "access to full economic, social and cultural rights" (Rizzini et al., 1995: 96); in this case, citizenship is synonymous with the concept of participatory democracy. On this interpretation, see, e.g., Leca (1994), Marshall (1950), and Turner (1994).

31. Friedmann (1992: 20).

32. Ibid., 136–66.

33. Ibid., 74–84.

34. Baratta (1995b: 15–20; 1996).

35. Baratta (1996: 406–8).

36. Gomez da Costa (1992).

37. Foucault (1987); cf. Deleuze (1986: 77–88), Baratta (1994).

38. On the various projects involving "street children," see the reports in Szanton Blanc (1995). Also see the outcome of projects to protect children in the completely different conditions of Norway regarding the institution of the "Ombudsman for Children" (Flekkoy, 1991)—also mentioning the situation in other developed countries (pp. 199–209; cf. Wolff, 1992).

39. Bobbio (1991: 5–6, 52), Dahl (1990: 129). In practice, children's rights are restricted in three ways, (1) *indirectly* (in family law, children's rights are largely placed under their parents' care), (2) *conditionally* (the nonavailability of funds is more often alleged than when implementing adults' rights), and (3) *completely* (certain rights are only granted to adults; Flekkoy, 1991: 178–9).

40. See Strempel (1996: 82): "The core of the convention is the 'triangle of rights': wealth of children, non-discrimination, and participation."

41. If the interpretation of the first of these articles is correct, children form one of the parties to be taken into account in the proceedings that will decide a possible separation from the parents against children's will.

42. Articles 9.1, 18.1, 21, and 40.2.b.iii.

43. Articles 17.1.e and 40.4.

44. Articles 10.2, 13.2.a, and 14.3.

45. Articles 10.2, 13.2.b, 14.3, and 15.2.

46. Without a comprehensive interpretation of the CRC, we would make the same mistake as paternalism, which holds the wrong assumption that, though children have their own view of the world, adults have nothing to learn from it. This occurs when decisions are made as to what is best for children without consulting them, under the pretext that they are too young or immature.

47. Alexy (1986: 91–2, 456).

48. See Dorsch (1994: 259–60).

49. Article 12.2.

50. It is not unusual in international declarations to apply the worrisome strategy of mentioning democracy as a barrier to the exercise of human rights (be it, as is here the case, as a barrier-barrier), which cannot however conceal the character of a liberal, representative democracy as a means of limiting human rights in favor of the ruling order. Several articles of the European Commission on Human Rights thus refer to the clause "necessary in a democratic order" to regulate the restriction of human rights (see e.g., Cohen-Jonathan, 1989: 549–50); furthermore, the law also directly advances the argument of the "democratic order" as a barrier to human rights (see the decision by the European Court of Human Rights in the Klass case, 1978, § 42).

51. Bobbio (1991).

52. Stern (1992: 70–4).

53. Jellinek (1979: 87, 94–105).

54. Flekkoy (1991: 224–8).

55. The most advanced doctrine, which rejects state and parental paternalism in defining children's interests as an ideological concept, is of the same opinion (Eekelaar, 1994; Ronfani, 1997: 91–3).

56. Miller (1983, 1991a, 1991b).

57. Galtung (1975: 32–6).

58. Balibar (1993: 201–6, 219–20).

59. These forms can be classified under a comprehensive "human right to (global) knowledge" (Sandkühler, 1991: 370–91, according to whom a

democratic form of society is an essential prerequisite of the scientific quest for truth).

BIBLIOGRAPHY

Alexy, Robert. 1986. *Theorie der Grundrechte*. Frankfurt: Suhrkamp.

Alston, Philip. 1994. "The Best Interests Principle: Towards a Reconciliation of Culture and Human Rights," in Philip Alston (ed.), *The Best Interests of the Child: Reconciling Culture and Human Right*. Oxford: Clarendon Press, 1–25.

An-na'im, Abdullahi. 1994. "Cultural Transformation and Normative Consensus on the Best Interests of the Child," in Philip Alston (ed.), *The Best Interests of the Child: Reconciling Culture and Human Rights*. Oxford: Clarendon Press, 62–81.

Balibar, Etienne. 1993. *Die Grenzen der Demokratie*. Hamburg: Argument.

Baratta, Alessandro. 1993. "Die Menschenrechte zwischen struktureller Gewalt und strafrechtlicher Strafe," in *Festschrift für Günther Jahr*. Tübingen: Mohr, 9–24.

_____. 1994. "Panoptische Subjektiverung. Zur Ideologie aktueller Drogenpolitik," in: *Tüte. Zur Aktualität von Michel Foucault*. Tübingen: *Wissen und Macht*, 60–5.

_____. 1995a. "Elementos de un nuevo derecho para la infancia y la adolescencia," in Alessandro Baratta and Sneider Rivera (eds.), *La ninez y la adolescencia en conflicto con la ley penal*. San Salvador: Editorial Hombres de Maìz, 47–62.

_____. 1995b. "La niñez como arqueología del futuro," in María del Carmen Bianchi (ed.), *El derecho y los chicos*. Buenos Aires: Espacio editorial, 13–22.

_____. 1996. "Der Mischlings-Staat und die plurale Bürgerschaft. Überlegungen zu einer weltlichen Theorie der Allianz," in John Milios (ed.), *Social Policy and Social Dialogue in the Perspective of the Economic and Monetary Union and of the "Europe of Citizens*," Athens: European Cultural Centre of Delphi/Kritiki, 403–24.

_____. 1997. "Bedürfnisse als Grundlage von Menschenrechten," in *Festschrift G. Ellscheid* (forthcoming).

Baratta, Alessandro, and Christina Giannoulis. 1996. "Vom Europarecht zum Europa der Rechte," *Kritische Vierteljahresschrift für Gesetzgebung und Rechtswissenschaft*, 3: 237–66.

Bobbio, Norberto. 1991. *Il futuro della democrazia.* Torino: Einaudi.

Cohen-Jonathan, Gérard. 1989. *La Convention Européenne des Droits de l'Homme.* Paris: Economica.

Cornia, Giovanni Andrea, and Sándor Sipos (eds.). 1991. *Children and the Transition to the Market Economy: Safety Nets and Social Policies in Central and Eastern Europe.* Avebury: Aldershot.

Cury, Munìr, et al. (eds.). 1992. *Estatuto da Criança e do Adolescente comentado.* Sao Paulo: Malheiros editores.

Dahl, Robert. 1990. *Democracy and Its Critics.* New Haven: Yale University Press.

Deleuze, Gilles. 1986. *Foucault.* Paris: Minuit.

Denninger, Erhard. 1990. *Der gebändigte Leviathan.* Baden-Baden: Nomos.

Dorsch, Gabriele. 1994. *Die Konvention der Vereinten Nationen über die Rechte des Kindes.* Berlin: Duncker und Humblot.

Eekelaar, John. 1994. "The Interests of the Child and the Child's Wishes: The Role of Dynamic Self-Determinism," in Philip Alston (ed.), *The Best Interests of the Child: Reconciling Culture and Human Rights.* UNICEF/Oxford: Clarendon Press, 42–61.

Flekkoy, Malfrid Grude. 1991. *A Voice for Children: Speaking Out as Their Ombudsman.* London: Jessica Kingsley.

Foucault, Michel. 1987. "Das Subjekt und die Macht," in Hubert Dreyfus and Paul Rabinow (eds.), *Michel Foucault: Jenseits von Strukturalismus und Hermeneutik.* Frankfurt/M.: Athenäum, 243–61.

Friedmann, John. 1992. *Empowerment: The Politics of Alternative Development.* Cambridge: Blackwell.

Galtung, Johan. 1975. *Strukturelle Gewalt, Beiträge zur Friedens- und Konfliktforschung.* Reinbek b. Hamburg: Rowohlt.

García Méndez, Emilio. 1994. *Derecho de la infancia-adolescencia en America Latina.* Santa Fé de Bogotá: Forum Pacis.

———. 1997. *Derecho de la infancia-adolescencia en América Latina: De la situación irregular a la protección integral,* 2ª ed. Santa Fé de Bogotá, Forum Pacis.

Gomez da Costa, Antonio Carlos. 1992. "Del Menor al Ciudadano Niño y Ciudadano Adolescente," in: Emilio García Méndez and Elias Carranza (eds.), *Del Revés al Derecho.* Buenos Aires: Galerna, 131–53.

———. 1995. "La infancia como base del consenso y la democracia," in Alessandro Baratta and Sneider Rivera (eds.), *La ninez y la adolescencia en conflicto con la ley penal.* San Salvador: Editorial Hombres de Maìz, 99–110.

Heller, Agnes. 1976. *Theorie der Bedürfnisse bei Marx*. Westberlin: VSA.

Jellinek, Georg. 1979. *System der subjektiven öffentlichen Rechte*, 2nd ed. 1919, reprint. Aalen: Scientia Verlag.

Leca, Jean. 1994. "Individualism and Citizenship," in Bryan Turner and Peter Hamilton. *Citizenship. Critical Concepts*, London: Routledge, 148–87.

Marshall, Thomas H. 1950. *Citizenship and Social Class and Other Essays*. Cambridge: Cambridge University Press.

Messner, Claudius. 1995. *Soziale Lage und kultureller Kontext italienischer Jugendlicher im Saarland. Eine Pilotstudie*. Saarbrücken: Arbeiten aus dem Institut für Rechts- und Sozialphilosophie.

Miller, Alice. 1983. *For Your Own Good: Hidden Cruelty in Child-Rearing and the Roots of Violence*. New York: Farrar.

_____. 1991a. *Banished Knowledge: Facing Childhood Injuries*. London: Virago.

_____. 1991b. *Breaking Down the Wall of Silence: To Join the Waiting Child*. London: Virago.

Murswiek, Dietrich. 1992. "Grundrechte als Teilhaberechte, soziale Grundrechte," in Josef Isensee and Paul Kirchhof, (eds.), *Handbuch des Staatsrechts*, vol. 5. Heidelberg: C.F. Müller, 243–88.

Pieper, Stefan Ulrich. 1994. *Subsidiarität*. Köln: Heymanns.

Rizzini, I., et al. 1995. "Brazil: A New Concept of Childhood," in Cristina Szanton Blanc (with contibutors), *Urban Children in Distress: Global Predicaments and Innovative Strategies*. Luxembourg: UNICEF/Gordon and Breach, 55–99.

Ronfani, Paola. 1997. "L'interesse del minore: Dato assiomatico o nozione magica?" *Sociologia del diritto*, 1: 47–93.

Sandkühler, Hans Jörg. 1991. *Die Wirklichkeit des Wissens*. Frankfurt/M.: Suhrkamp.

Santos, Boaventura de Sousa. 1997. "Toward a Multicultural Conception of Human Rights" *Sociologia del diritto*, 1: 27–45.

Stern, Klaus. 1992. "Idee und Elemente eines Systems der Grundrechte," in Josef Isensee Paul Kirchhof (eds.), *Handbuch des Staatsrechts*, vol. 5. Heidelberg: C.F. Müller, 45–100.

Strempel, Rüdiger. 1996. "Fünf Jahre Geltung der Konvention über die Rechte des Kindes," *Zeitschrift für Rechtspolitik*, 3: 81–4.

Szanton Blanc, Cristina (with contibutors). 1995. *Urban Children in Distress: Global Predicaments and Innovative Strategies*. Luxembourg: UNICEF/Gordon and Breach.

Turner, Bryan. 1994. "Outline of a Theory of Citizenship," in Bryan Turner and Peter Hamilton *Citizenship: Critical Concepts*. London: Routledge, 199–237.

Viccica, A. D. 1989. "The Promotion and Protection of Children's Rights through Development and Recognition of an International Notion of Juvenile Justice and Its Child-Centered Perspective in the United Nations," *Nordic Journal of International Law*, 58, 68–93.

Wolff, Reinhart. 1992. "Hilfe ohne Kontrolle. Der 'neue Kinderschutz' als Pionier für zeitgemäßere Konzepte sozialer Arbeit," *Deutsche Zeitschrift für Sozialarbeit*, 6: 165–8.

16 | Children, Rights, and Democracy

A Commentary
on Alessandro Baratta

GUILLERMO O'DONNELL

Introduction

It is quite a challenge to comment on the complex and interesting paper written by an eminent authority on the rights of children such as Professor Alessandro Baratta. Being myself a political scientist who has done some work on issues of democracy and citizenship, I will limit my comments to this perspective, thus overlooking other aspects of his chapter.

In the paper he presented at the seminar from which this volume originates, Baratta made an important point that I miss from the version I am presently discussing (Chapter 15). He noted that "those who write about children's rights also talk about democracy, whereas those who write about democracy do not mention children's rights." This is the kind of statement that once it is made sounds obvious, even though it was not obvious at all before it was said, and, furthermore, it soon becomes apparent that it is loaded with important implications. Simply put, democratic theory has been neglectful of children and their rights, as if they did not pertain to the purview of this theory. Baratta argues forcefully that, instead, children and their rights should be recognized as central elements of both the theory and the practice of democracy. I find this view entirely persuasive although, as will be seen below, I have some doubts and disagreements concerning the way Baratta substantiates and develops his arguments.

Overview

In summarizing Baratta's arguments, I believe they have a four-pronged structure: (1) children should be recognized as having important rights deriving from their human condition, including their condition as full members of society; (2) any political arrangement that calls itself democratic has the obligation of recognizing and protecting these rights; (3) such recognition and protection is due not only children; it is also for the benefit of democracy itself, insofar as it improves its scope and quality; and (4) in order for this to happen, the preexistence of a democratic context, even if it is an imperfect one, is a necessary condition. This reasoning, with which I agree, may sound tautological, but it is not. Rather, it has a dynamic character: the effective incorporation of rights is made possible by some existing—partial but not irrelevant—degree of democratization, and in turn, such incorporation improves that same democracy, opening the way to the further broadening and specification of rights.

This, as Baratta notes, is homologous to the arguments made in the past for recognizing the rights of rural and urban workers, ethnic minorities, and women. In these cases it was argued not only that those agents had a clear right to full citizenship; it was also claimed that endorsing these demands meant improving democracy and that, consequently, such acceptance was in the interest of all those who claimed allegiance to democracy. Today most political scientists, myself included, agree that political democracy exists when full political rights (not necessarily socioeconomic ones) are enjoyed by (at least) all the native-born or naturalized adults under the jurisdiction of a given state.

The resulting political regimes are representative: citizens do not govern directly. Rather, through fair and competitive elections citizens decide who will "represent" them in various governmental roles. I use "represent" in quotation marks because what is represented and how, even if there is any representation at all, is one of the most muddled and disputed issues in contemporary democratic theory.[1] But one aspect is clear. Citizenship does not entail only the right of choosing representatives, but also that of being chosen. The right of being elected is no less constitutive of citizenship than the right of electing.

Baratta sidesteps the complications that spring from what I have just noted. Whatever the rights of children, including political ones, we could hardly imagine a society—even if fully democratic—that did not establish a minimum age threshold for running for governmental office, as well as for occupying other social roles that carry important collective responsibilities. In this context, the "paradoxes," "insufficiencies," and "anomalies" that Baratta states concerning the recognition of children's rights in relation to other previously excluded (adult) groups are not as they seem, but a recognition of this crucial difference.

Justly praising the Convention on the Rights of the Child (CRC) but at the same time criticizing it for what he sees as its restricted scope in this matter, Baratta proposes that children should be considered "full-fledged citizens" (p. 291). That this statement cannot be taken à la lettre is shown when, further on, Baratta asserts that children participate socially and politically under "forms of representation without mandate" (p. 294), and when he comments (p. 292) that "in what concerns the status activus, the child *fully* enjoys the fundamental procedural rights and a *significant part* of the rights of participation" (emphasis added), without spelling out what that significant part is, or how it could be determined, though obviously it is something less than the "full citizenship" of children that he already mentioned. This kind of indeterminacy of the caveats introduced for qualifying sweeping assertions also hinders the broad array of "necessary conditions" and "requisites" (which span from ideal conditions in the family to full democratization at the international level) that Baratta identifies for the full effectiveness of the rights of children.

Partial versus Full Citizenship

In terms of citizenship, I believe that this chapter would gain in clarity, and eventual persuasiveness, by distinguishing this theme from two other ones. One is Baratta's argument that children's rights should be given priority, not only when those rights seem to be directly concerned, but also in all spheres of social and state activities. But this injunction, with which I basically agree, derives its force not from the fact that children are full citizens, but precisely because they lack such condition—including, as noted, that they cannot run for election as adults claiming to represent class, ethnic, and gender identities. It does not necessarily follow from the fact that the rights of A should be given precedence over the rights of B, or that B has special obligations of care and protection toward A, that A is as full a citizen as B is—usually the opposite is true.

The second argument, with which I also agree, is about the obligation of listening to children. As Baratta eloquently argues, there is much that we adults have to learn from this. All social forms, from families to national societies, are enriched when adults listen carefully and lovingly to what children say—not just because it is useful but because it is an act of respect due every human being, adult or child. In this sense, Baratta is on the mark when he criticizes article 12, paragraph 2, of the CRC for restricting this right to be heard to "judicial and administrative proceedings affecting the child," instead of making of this an overall legal and moral obligation. But I cannot agree when Baratta uses this argument to support his argument for the full citizenship of children. Again, I do not think that it necessarily follows that B's obligation to carefully and respectfully listen to A means that A and B are equal qua citizens.

Paternalism

Underlying the reservations I have presented is my impression that, in order to make a more fully rounded argument, Baratta would have to tackle with an issue missing from his paper: paternalism. This is an extremely complicated topic, which has recently raised a lot of attention in moral and political theory. In regards to adults, most liberal and democratic theorists are reluctant to validate paternalism, except in very well specified and justified situations. Democracy is premised on nonpaternalistic assumptions about the autonomy and responsibility of every adult, and strives to create such conditions for those who for some temporary (i.e., children) or socially determined reason (say, destitution or severe mental illness) lack these conditions. Paternalism, in this view, is justifiable only for preventing serious harm and when it is practiced with the intention of becoming unnecessary, because those who are temporarily subject to paternalism gain sufficient autonomy and responsibility.

This, it seems to me, is particularly applicable to children. The priority given to their rights and the obligation to listen to them are *in nuce* what the core meaning of democracy is about: an effective concern for the rights of others, particularly of those who are in a weak or otherwise disadvantaged situation, on the one hand, and the respectful exchange of reasoned arguments, on the other. But in relation to children, this is not because they are, or should be considered, full citizens. It is because it is the duty of a democratic society to prepare all children to be future full citizens. This criterion meets the requirement for acceptable paternalism I stated above.

Trusteeship

The preceding reflections put in a somewhat different context Baratta's analysis about the representation of children. Having accepted the author's argument about children's right to be heard well beyond judicial and administrative proceedings, I depart from Baratta by believing that, instead of the idea of "representation without mandate" that he proposes, a better concept is the traditional one of trusteeship. The trustee, in the guise of parents or tutors, represents (makes actual to other relevant agents) what in her informed and disinterested opinion are the best interests of the represented (for which she is obliged to take into serious consideration whatever opinions the latter is able to express), and must hold those interests as paramount in the decisions she makes as such trustee. This is a kind of representation, but one that is premised (as against the representation of adult citizens in the political sphere) in the lack of full autonomy and responsibility of the represented. Again, precisely because it is thus based, another fundamental responsibility of the trustee is to act with the aim of helping the represented develop the conditions that in the future will make effective the assumption of autonomy and responsibility of the human being the trustee is, in this specific sense, representing.

This more restricted view of the kind of representation entailed in the case of children leads me to a skeptical note on Baratta's concluding remarks in the sense that "scientific research and institutional knowledge are forms of representation of the citizens without mandate [prominently including children, O'D]" (p. 294). This may or may not be the case. The very temptations to ignore or distort the views and interests of children (sometimes cloaked as authentic concern for them) that Baratta denounces, may also appear under the guise of scientific research or institutional concern. Nothing guarantees better against this danger than applying to our own work and institutions the same critical view we cast outside of them.

NOTE

1. For cogent recent discussions see Adam Przeworski, Susan Stokes, and Bernard Manin, eds., *Democracy, Accountability, and Representation* (New York: Cambridge University Press, 1999).

E | Children and
Social Policy
in Latin America

*Successes, Failures,
and Challenges*

17 | Child Survival and Development

Challenge for the New Millennium

MICHAEL B. HEISLER and COREY ANDERSON

The twentieth century will be remembered chiefly, not as an age of
political conflict and technical inventions, but as an age in which
human society dared to think of the health of the whole human race
as a practical objective. Our age is the first since the dawn of history
that has dared dream it practical to make the benefits of civilization
available to all.

—Arnold Toynbee

Introduction

The quality of life for children and families around the world has improved
more significantly in the past 50 years than in all previous recorded history.
At times it seems reasonable to dare to think not only of the health but of
the education, safety, and economic security of every child as a practical objective. James Grant, the former executive director of UNICEF, often quoted
Thoreau, who said, "If you have built a castle in the air, you need not be lost.
That is where they should be. Now put the foundations under them." The
achievements of the past 50 years have come about because so many dared to
dream that every child could be healthy, safe, educated, and loved and then

built the foundation necessary to transform vision into reality. Our task is to stand with those realists and ask: What has actually been achieved? What challenges remain? How should the new science about early child development affect policy? Is there any guide, based on the past 50 years of efforts, that can help policy makers, nongovernmental organizations (NGOs), and communities in Latin America and around the world who remain committed to effective, sustained improvement in the lives of children, especially in the face of diminishing resources?

Fifty Years of Progress

The improvement in the lives of children over the past five decades is remarkable. Child mortality rates have decreased by two-thirds, from around 300 to 100 per 1,000 live births. Average life expectancy has increased from approximately 40 years in 1950 to 62 years in 1990. Adult literacy rates have doubled to almost 70%. Over the past 20 years, the number of children, especially girls, completing primary school has increased from 38 to 68%. The number of children living in poverty has diminished dramatically around the world, especially in Southeast Asia and the Americas, as economies have expanded and GDPs have increased. From 1980 to 1990, immunization rates around the world against childhood diseases increased from a low of 10% in some regions to over 80%. An estimated 2.5 million fewer children are expected to die in 1997 than in 1990 from these preventable afflictions. Children also have greater protection from developmental delay, physical disabilities, blindness, and mental retardation. The World Summit for Children in October 1990, the 1989 Convention on the Rights of the Child, and the series of UN Global Summits on the environment, population and reproductive health, the status of women, and social justice set specific targets for improving the quality of life of children, women, and families. Many nations, including those in the Americas, adopted recommendations from the summits and incorporated them into national policy. This gives us reason to celebrate what can be done when there is global commitment and political will.

The Challenges that Remain

Global statistics do not, unfortunately, reveal the lives of suffering and hopelessness of many children from that segment of society that has not benefitted from the improvements of the past decades. These are the victims of the growing disparity between the haves and have-nots in every region of the world. Immunization rates have improved, but 1 million children still die each year from measles. Infant mortality rates have decreased dramatically but are still nearly seven times higher in developing countries than in the industrialized nations of the world. Neonatal tetanus causes 700,000 infant deaths a year, most of them newborns who had never seen a physician. The AIDS virus is threatening to undo the gains made in child survival over the past decade, especially in Africa and Asia. Babies born to HIV-positive mothers have a 20 to 40% chance of contracting the virus through breast milk, and almost all who do will die before the age of 5. In the past decade, 2 million children have been killed in wars, more than combatants themselves. More than 4 million have lost limbs, suffered brain damage, or had sight or hearing loss. An estimated 110 million land mines remain buried around the world, and children, playing innocently, are often the victims. Despite the improvement in education rates, 110 million 6- to 11-year-olds do not attend school.

The Situation in Latin America

There has been significant progress for children in the Americas during the past 30 years as well, but again there are disparities. Some 87% of the world's children currently live in developing countries, including about 10% in Latin America. Policy making in Latin America is difficult because of the unique circumstances of poverty in the region. In contrast to the rest of the developing world, the poor in Latin America are more likely to reside in urban rather than rural areas, creating problems different from the challenges facing the rural poor. The challenges will only increase as the urban population of Latin America rises from 66% of the region's total population in 1985 to a projected 78.3% in 2010.

When compared with other regions of the developing world, Latin America and the Caribbean rank consistently near the top for most of the basic indicators of nutrition, health, education, economics, and the status of women. At the same time, great disparities between and within individual Latin American and Caribbean countries remain.

Health

The Latin America and the Caribbean region has been a model for the rest of the world in the effort to immunize children. The Americas were first in the world to eradicate polio (there have been no cases of wild polio virus in the region since October 1991), and it is well on its way to achieving the same success against measles. The region has an under age 5 mortality rate of 47%, the lowest in the developing world. However, this rate is almost six times that of industrialized nations. There is great disparity in the under age 5 mortality rates in individual Latin American countries, as seen in Table 1. Between 1960 and 1993, the infant mortality rate in the region fell by more than half, from 107 per 1,000 live births to 45. At 10%, the proportion of underweight children is the lowest in the developing world, but there are still 6 million malnourished children in the region. There is 1 doctor per 1,000 people compared with 1 per 6,000 in the developing world as a whole. In urban areas, 90% of the people have access to safe water; in rural areas only 56% do. Two million people in Latin America are infected with HIV.

Table 1.   Under Age 5 Mortality Rates

Country	Percent
Cuba	10
Jamaica	13
Chile	15
Guatemala	15
Bolivia	105
Haiti	124

Economic Disparity

Latin America's per capita GNP is US$3,139, highest by far of any region of the developing world (Table 2). However, that figure is one-eighth the GNP of industrialized countries, and 110 million people in the region continue to live in poverty. Again, there is great variation between countries. Table 3 reveals a wide range of per capita GNP, with Haiti lowest at $230 and Argentina highest at $8,110. The gulf between rich and poor within countries has also increased. In Canada, the wealthiest 20% of the population has an income that is seven times greater than that of the poorest 20%. The ratio is 9:1 in the United States, 32:1 in Brazil, 31:1 in Guatemala, 30:1 in Panama, 24:1 in Honduras, and 20:1 in Ecuador. These data have importance beyond pure economics: poverty levels are directly linked to health and social status indicators. Low birth weight, infant mortality, and deaths from acute diarrheal disease in children under age 5, for example, all increase with the decrease of per capita GNP. As income levels vary within a country, human development indicators vary as well. In Mexico City, infant mortality rates range from 13.4 to 109.8 per 1,000 live births. In Lima, Peru, the rate is 50 per 1,000, but some of the country's rural areas have rates as high as 140 per 1,000.

Table 2. World Comparison of Per Capita GNPs

Region	1994 US$
Latin America and the Caribbean	3,139
CEE/CIS and Baltic states	2,121
Middle East and North Africa	1,662
East Asia and Pacific	962
Sub-Saharan Africa	503
South Asia	325
Industrialized countries	24,300
Developing countries	1,023
Least-developed countries	233
World average	4,498

Table 3. Regional Comparison of Per Capita GNPs

Country	1994 US$	Country	1994 US$
Argentina	8,110	Paraguay	1,580
Uruguay	4,660	Jamaica	1,540
Mexico	4,180	El Salvador	1,360
Trinidad and Tobago	3,740	Dominican Republic	1,330
Chile	3,520	Ecuador	1,280
Brazil	2,970	Guatemala	1,200
Venezuela	2,760	Cuba	1,170
Panama	2,580	Bolivia	770
Costa Rica	2,400	Honduras	600
Peru	2,110	Nicaragua	340
Colombia	1,670	Haiti	230

Education

Latin America's primary school enrollment rate of 86% is relatively high, but secondary school enrollment drops off to 45% for males and 49% for females, lower than any other region of the developing world except sub-Saharan Africa. Between 1960 and 1990, secondary school and higher education enrollment increased nearly eightfold, but nearly 20 million boys and girls at the secondary level are still out of school. Less than half the entrants to grade one reach grade five. Primary and secondary school enrollment again shows the disparity within and between countries, as seen in Table 4.

Table 4.   Regional Percentage of School Enrollment

Country	Primary school		Secondary school		Country	Primary school		Secondary school	
	Male	Fem	Male	Fem		Male	Fem	Male	Fem
Argentina	108	107	70	75	Paraguay	114	110	36	38
Uruguay	109	108	61	62	Jamaica	109	108	62	70
Mexico	114	110	57	58	El Salvador	79	80	27	30
Trin. & Tob.	94	94	74	78	Dom. Rep.	95	99	30	43
Chile	99	98	65	70	Ecuador	124	122	54	56
Brazil	101	97	31	36	Guatemala	89	78	25	23
Venezuela	95	97	29	41	Cuba	104	104	73	81
Panama	108	104	60	65	Bolivia	99	90	40	34
Costa Rica	106	105	45	49	Honduras	111	112	29	37
Peru	123	118	66	60	Nicaragua	101	105	39	44
Colombia	118	120	57	68	Haiti	58	54	22	21

What Have We Learned?

What do these statistics really mean for policy makers in the Americas? Have we learned anything over the past 20 years about child survival and development that can guide our actions into the next millennium? The answer is yes with a word of caution: any list of "lessons learned" is only as useful as the commitment, ability, and tenacity of the individuals and organizations who use them as a guide. Many involved in improving children's lives have made the false assumption that the political and financial resources to give every child the opportunity for a "healthy start" would materialize simply based on altruism. As Martin Luther King said, however, "Human progress is neither automatic nor inevitable. Even a superficial look at history reveals that no social advance rolls in on the wheels of inevitability. Every step towards the goals of justice requires sacrifice, suffering, and the tireless exertions and passionate concern of individuals."

Those who are serious about sustained improvement for children must be passionate and tireless in their effort to shift their and others' thinking and focus on three points.

1. Investment in the health, education, safety, and welfare of children results in a significant and measurable return on investment. It should be among the highest priorities of responsible policy makers to make decisions based on economic and social indicators, not altruism. There is clear evidence that investment in people, in "social capital," has been an integral component of every successful economic development story in the past 30 years.

2. Child advocates, whether they are from Boston or Buenos Aires, must be as adept as every other interest group when competing for limited resources. They must develop and use the skills of generating public opinion, working legislatively, stimulating political action, and incorporating positive change into budgets and law.

3. Good policy is more often than not based on good science. The science that has become available in the past 10 years about early childhood development, for example, is nothing less than dramatic. Neurobiological research has made it clear that children's ability to learn, function within society, and reach their maximum potential, and therefore their ability to contribute to society, is based on stimuli and inputs in the first 5 years of life. This information crosses social, economic, and racial barriers. Policy makers who are aware of these data and attempt to make decisions based on good science are often able to make choices that effect real change.

Knowledge to Action:
Using Neurobiology as the Basis for Policy Decisions Affecting Children

Regarding the third point, let us explore how the science of child development can and should have a major impact on policy decisions affecting children and families in the Americas and the rest of the world. There is no better example of how good science can help policy makers make sound choices affecting their constituency and the short- and long-term interests of their nation. "Of all of the discoveries that have poured out of neuroscience laboratories in recent years, the finding that the electrical activity of brain cells changes the physical structure of the brain is perhaps most breathtaking."[1] This finding may also be very important for families, communities, and policy makers.

How the brain develops and the role of genetics versus environment have long been the subject of philosophical debate. That debate is of less and less interest to most developmental neurobiologists. They are much more interested in how genes and the environment interact. That interaction, that "dance" as Dr. Stanley Greenspan from George Washington University calls it, begins around the third week of gestation when a thin layer of cells fold in on themselves forming the neural tube. Cells in the neural tube then proliferate at the amazing rate of 250,000 per minute giving rise to the brain and spinal cord. At birth a baby's brain contains approximately 100 billion neurons, about as many stars as there are in the Milky Way. Basic connections between these neurons or brain cells are already in place, allowing functions necessary for life, like breathing, heartbeat, and primitive reflexes. Most of those connections seem to be laid down genetically. Then an amazing process begins. External stimuli that result in electrical impulses at the cellular level play a larger and larger role in establishing the connections between brain cells.

Shortly after birth, a baby's brain produces trillions more connections between neurons than it will ever use. Then, depending on the frequency and nature of stimuli, connections are eliminated, leaving in place a brain that is unique in thought pattern and emotion. Without a stimulating environment, a baby's brain suffers. As noted in *Time* magazine, researchers have found that children who do not play much or are rarely touched develop brains 20 to 30% smaller than normal for their age. Rats raised in toy-strewn cages exhibit more complex behavior than rats confined to sterile uninteresting boxes. They also develop brains that contain as many as 25% more synapses per neuron. "Rich experiences, in other words, really do produce rich brains."[2] Additionally, there is a growing body of information about "windows of opportunity," periods in a child's brain development when stimuli are critical if the child is to develop his or her full capacity—for language, emotion, cognitive ability, music. "It is the experience of childhood, determining which neurons are used that wire the circuits of the brain as surely as a programmer at a keyboard reconfigures the circuits of a computer. Early experiences are so important that they can completely change the way a person turns out."[3] Since most of these windows close before the end of elementary school, is there any hope for children who did not receive appropriate stimulation and nurturing? As Joseph Sparling has said, "You never want to say that it is too late, but there does seem to be something special about those early years."[4]

This is not simply interesting science. It has a profound impact on policy makers faced with allocating diminishing resources. Investment in early childhood—nutrition, preschools, health, and education—have a direct, measurable impact on the productivity of the workforce, on public and private social sector costs, and on the perception of equity, social justice, and, therefore, stability within a country. The final paragraph from the *Time* article is worth repeating:

Just last week, in the US alone, some 77,000 newborns began the miraculous process of wiring their brains for a lifetime of learning. If parents and policy makers don't pay attention to the conditions under which this delicate process takes place, we will all suffer the consequences—starting around the year 2010.[5]

A Growing Consensus

Returning to the question What have we learned? there is a growing consensus based on neurobiology and experience in child development over the past 20 years concerning the interventions for children and families that work and lead to the highest "return on investment" in an environment of diminishing economic resources. If the conclusions and recommendations from the series of UN World Summits held since 1990 are compared with the annual reports of the World Bank, UNICEF, WHO, the UN Development Program, and the UN Population Fund, as well as reports from other development organizations over the same period, there is remarkable convergence. The following nine conclusions appear again and again:

1. Human development is directly linked to economic development; one cannot progress without simultaneous advancement in the other. Economic and social sector policy are directly linked and must be considered simultaneously rather than separately. Human development efforts must directly encourage policies that strengthen economic growth, open markets, and increased employment, thereby creating a stable economic base on which children and families can build a more promising future.

2. The economic development and health of a population are directly linked. Health policy must guarantee the provision of cost-effective, essential health services and basic public health packages, rather than continue to invest in expensive, hospital-based curative services. As summarized in its Table 1, the *World Development Report*, 1993 made specific recommendations about both essential services and basic public health. They should be used as guidelines for health sector reform throughout the developing world, including in the Americas. The World Summit for Children outlined a list of "goals for the year 2000" (see Appendix 1). These are achievable, cost-effective, and measurable outcomes. *The Progress of Nations*, 1997 provides a summary of what has been accomplished in the Americas compared with other regions of the world. The Americas have accomplished a great deal, but much work remains.

3. Education is a major determinant of successful development and is yet another example of the benefit of investing in people. According to the *Economist* magazine, "Education is the key to getting rich—for countries as well as individuals. It is widely believed that one of the main reasons why 'tiger' economies like Singapore and South Korea have grown so quickly is that their governments have made determined and successful efforts to raise educational standards."[6] Investment in education for children, adolescents, and young people is shown to be so profitable for themselves, their families, society, and the economy that it offers a compelling reason for allowing them to devote full time to their studies for at least 10 years of schooling and preferably until they complete their full secondary education (12 years). At current pay levels, putting children through 3 additional years of primary or secondary school will enable them to earn over six times the cost of the additional education. Education is more profitable the earlier it is offered. Giving adolescents 4 years of secondary education is a much better investment than attempting to provide the equivalent through compensatory programs for adults at 1.5 to 5 times the cost. Girls must be assured equal access to both primary and secondary education not only because it is just, but because there is no better determinant of a child's survival than the education level of its mother.

4. Protecting the environment is not a luxury. For example, access to safe water is a major priority and an essential service that affects children's health and economic development. An example of the importance of safe water to communities is included in the *1997 UNICEF Annual Report*. Ten years ago, members of the marginalized communities living on the hilly fringes of Tegucigalpa, Honduras's capital city, heard that municipal authorities had left them out of a plan to upgrade and expand the city's water supply. Leaders of a small group demanding change, most of them women, refused to give in. They were tired of seeing their children suffer from diarrhea and other waterborne diseases, illnesses responsible for one-fourth of all child death in Honduras. They were also tired of spending as much as 30% of their income to buy water from private vendors. In collaboration with UNICEF, the National Water and Sanitation Agency developed a compromise plan that is still in place. The agency supplies water to marginalized communities and the communities provide free labor and some construction materials, eventually repaying all construction costs. In 1996, communities helped construct 21 new water systems serving over 32,000 people, bringing to 125,000 the total number of people obtaining safe water at half the former price.

5. Children must be secure, not the victims of community and family violence and war. The banning of personnel land mines is an example of a specific objective that has received much attention and would have a direct impact on children. A landmark document, the *Convention on the Rights of the Child* was presented for the first time at the World Summit for Children in 1990. Besides addressing the right of every child to be secure and free from violence, it reaffirms the fact that children, because of their vulnerability, need special care and protection, and it places special emphasis on the primary caring and protective responsibility of the family. Every country in the world should not only ratify the Convention, but incorporate it into national plans of action. As of September 1997, only two countries in the world had not ratified the Convention, the United States and Somalia. Every country in Latin America has ratified the Convention. As noted in the *1997 UNICEF Annual Report*, at the Caribbean Conference on the Rights of the Child (Belize, October 1996) 16 heads of state or government agreed to harmonize national laws with the principles of the Convention and 9 countries (Bolivia, Brazil, Costa Rica, Dominican Republic, Ecuador, El Salvador, Guatemala, Honduras, Peru) reformed legislation in 1996 to incorporate the rights set forth in the Convention. All countries in the region should do so.

6. Equality for women must be ensured—economically, educationally, and legally. Every woman should have the right to choose if and when she will bear children. The major recommendations from the 1995 Beijing Women's Summit should be incorporated into national policy.

7. Children, families, and communities must be actively involved in designing and implementing development strategies that have an immediate impact on their lives. Lao Tsu said it well in 700 B.C.:

    Go to the people. Live with them, learn from them, love them. Start with what they know, build with what they have. But with the best leaders, when the work is done, the task accomplished, the people will say, "We have done this ourselves."

Virginia Abernathy has been a bit more direct:

Let the globalists step aside. One world solutions do not work. Everywhere people act in accord with their own interests. People are adept at interpreting local signs to find the next move needed.

The international community should support policies that empower local communities and strengthen participatory government. Again this is not based on altruism, but on sound politics with the greatest potential for sustainability. Two examples:

- For the past 25 years, primary health care services have been provided to the Esmeraldas area in northwest Ecuador through a series of community-based health posts situated within the Rio Santiago basin, a part of the Amazonian river system that drains out of Ecuador to the Pacific Ocean. Communities select their own health worker, provide the funds necessary to maintain their community clinic, and serve on the governing board of the regional health system. Most of the health workers are women. Integrated primary health care is the strategy employed throughout the region. The system is self-sustaining and is a source of genuine pride to the multiple communities that can be seen along the riverbank as you glide by in dugout canoes. The system works because the people own it, philosophically and practically.

- The Grameen Bank in Bangladesh, which provides microcredit to women, is an example of effective community participation in development. Since its formation in 1983, the bank has given out nearly 16 million loans of an average $100. The bank lends only to the poorest of the rural landless poor, remains women-focused (94% of its customers are women), provides loans without collateral or security, and helps and supports the borrower in succeeding. The borrower, not the bank, decides the business activity the loan will be utilized for and the interest rate required to keep the bank self-reliant (i.e., not dependent on grants or donations). The Grameen Bank enjoys an unparalleled customer loyalty. The on-time loan repayment rate exceeds 98% and defaults (bad debts) are less than 0.5% of loans. This bank of the poor thus outperforms all other banks in Bangladesh and most banks around the world.

Both of these examples of community participation should be examined for their applicability in other areas of the Americas.

8. Successful, sustainable development is increasingly the result of effective public–private partnerships that include the government, the communities, corporations, NGOs, donors, and international, regional, and local lending agencies. "Partnership" implies a common objective and the willingness to negotiate a common strategy. "Sustainability" depends on each partner's ability to meet clearly stated vested interests. Two examples of partnerships with direct impact in Latin America:

- River blindness affects the poorest of the poor in communities in six Latin American countries: Brazil, Columbia, Ecuador, Guatemala, Mexico, and Venezuela. The parasite *Onchocerca volvulus* enters the blood of a person via the bite of a black fly and over time produces an inflammatory reaction with severe itching and, eventually, scarring of the anterior and posterior chamber of the eye, causing blindness. In 1987, Merck & Co., Inc., decided to donate the drug Mectizan® for the treatment of river blindness "for as long as needed to as many as necessary." Merck asked the Task Force for Child Survival and Development to implement a distribution program on its behalf. PAHO (Pan American Health Organization), all six national governments, the InterAmerican Development Bank, the River Blindness Foundation, multiple NGOs, local businesses, the Carter Center, and others formed a coalition that has now significantly decreased the incidence of river blindness in the region and is well on its way to meeting the year 2007 target of eliminating the disease as a public health problem in the Americas.

- Malaria is a leading cause of morbidity and mortality around the world, including in the Americas. It kills over 1 million children under age 5 every year—a child every 30 seconds. Prevention is difficult and throughout malaria-endemic regions there is a resurgence of the disease as *Plasmodium falciparum*, the parasite that causes most of the problem, develops resistance to current therapy. In the Americas, Bolivia, Brazil, Columbia, Ecuador, Panama, Paraguay, Peru, and Venezuela now have malaria that is resistant to the standard treatment of chloroquine. In 1997, Glaxo Wellcome established a program to donate its new drug, Malarone®, free of charge, to target populations who could benefit from the medication but who could not afford it. As with Mectizan®, this private sector initiative has led to partnerships with host governments, donors, NGOs, and others. It is too soon to assess the impact of the program, but the importance of the public-private model is clear.

The Americas, perhaps more than any other region in the world, has a huge, untapped potential for public–private partnerships. These partnerships should be pursued. The World Bank publication *Business as Partners in Development* is an excellent resource document.

9. UN agencies and funds devoted to children and families have an important role to play in child survival and development. They provide technical expertise, funding, the ability to generate political will, skill in program implementation, and expertise in advocacy. At the country and regional level, however, they have not always coordinated their efforts

efficiently. Where they do not yet exist, effective, functional strategic planning committees at the national level should be formed with responsibility for coordinating cross-sectional, integrated developmental assistance in partnership with national governments.

The conclusions and recommendations can be summarized as follows:

- Establish economic and social sector policy with the constant appreciation that they are interdependent. Encourage policy that strengthens economies, opens markets, and increases employment.

- Implement the Essential Health Services and Public Health Package from the *World Development Report, 1993* as a basis for health sector reform.

- Provide the resources and political will necessary to achieve the Year 2000 Goals outlined at the 1990 World Summit for Children.

- Establish national policy to ensure that all children, especially girls, have access to full primary and secondary education.

- Implement the Convention on the Rights of the Child as national policy.

- Implement the recommendations from the 1995 Beijing Women's Summit.

- Include families and communities as full participants in planning and implementing development strategies.

- Actively seek expanded public–private partnerships for sustainable development throughout the region and in every sector.

- Establish effective mechanisms to coordinate the activities of all UN agencies at the country level to increase impact, diminish duplication and unnecessary competition, and maximize benefit for children and families.

There is much around the world and in the Americas to be hopeful about. The understanding of the relationship between knowledge, policy, and action, the appreciation of the "interdependence" of all areas of development, the new tools available to improve the health and quality of life of children around the world—all are encouraging. The Americas are as poised as any region of the world to achieve real improvement in the lives of children. The challenge is to develop and sustain true political commitment and to remember, as Margaret Mead has said so well, that "the solution of adult problems tomorrow depends in large measure upon the way our children grow up today. There is no greater insight into the future than recognizing when we save our children, we save ourselves."

Appendix 1: Goals for the Year 2000

1. A one-third reduction in 1990 death rates for children under age 5 (or to 70 per 1,000 live births, whichever is less).
2. A halving of 1990 maternal mortality rates.
3. A halving of 1990 rates of malnutrition among the world's children under age 5 (to include the elimination of micronutrient deficiencies, support for breast-feeding by all maternity units, and a reduction in the incidence of low birth weight to less than 10% of all births).
4. The achievement of a 90% immunization rate among children under age 1, the eradication of polio, the elimination of neonatal tetanus, and a 90% reduction in measles cases and a 95% reduction in measles deaths (compared with pre-immunization levels).
5. A halving of child deaths caused by diarrheal disease.
6. A one-third reduction in child deaths from acute respiratory infections.
7. Basic education for all children and completion of primary education by at least 80% of them—girls as well as boys.
8. Clean water and safe sanitation for all communities.
9. Acceptance of the Convention on the Rights of the Child in all countries, including improved protection for children in especially difficult circumstances.
10. Universal access to high-quality family planning information and services in order to prevent pregnancies that are too early, too closely spaced, too late, or too numerous.

NOTES

1. Nash, J. Madeleine, "Fertile Minds," *Time*, February 3, 1997.
2. Ibid. p. 51.

3. Begley, Sharon, "Your Child's Brain," *Newsweek*, February 19, 1996.
4. Ibid. p. 62.
5. Nash, op. cit, n. 1, p. 56.
6. "Education and the Wealth of Nations," *Economist*, March 29, 1997.

18 | Facing the New Millennium

Children and Rights in Latin America and the Caribbean

ALBERTO MINUJIN and RAQUEL PERCZEK

As witnesses of the turn of the millennium, we have the opportunity to reflect on the political, social, cultural, economic, and technological developments that have transformed our world and that make our lives radically different from those of our ancestors. Observing the transition to the new millennium likewise gives us a chance to question ourselves about our yearnings for the future and what we aspire for ourselves, our children, and the generations to come.

This millennium, and this century in particular, has witnessed great advances by humankind, as well as the persistence of unacceptable situations of suffering and backwardness. Global trends today indicate more rapid technological progress, expanded communications, more dynamic trade, further privatization, and the gradual recognition of human rights. Yet they also indicate the formation of segmented societies in which major portions of the population are surviving in conditions of poverty and vulnerability and are affected by institutional corruption, environmental decline, imbalances in the labor market, and acts of violence that disregard their human rights. It is also clear that during this final period of the century, contrary to what was hoped for, inequalities between and within countries have been increasing, and situations of vulnerability and social exclusion are on the rise.

As the century ends, we see that some of its paradigms have been overturned, giving rise to uncertainty in the face of new possibilities. Focusing on the social realm, we could mention the end of wage labor as a mechanism of social inclusion, and the simultaneous crisis of the welfare state and the failure of "socialist" experiments. At the same time, there have emerged political, economic, and social processes that will largely determine the global trends of the next century. We could point out—even while emphasizing that this claim forms part of an ongoing discussion—that perhaps one of the significant legacies for the twenty-first century has been the expansion of human rights with the incorporation of social rights during this century. The Convention on the Rights of the Child (CRC), passed by the UN General Assembly on November 20, 1989, is one of the clearest and most effective examples of the advances by humankind: clearest inasmuch as it makes children and adolescents, who make up 37% of the world population and around 40% of the population in developing countries, full subjects with rights;[1] and most effective, because it provides specific guidelines for acting in the legal, institutional, and social realms.

One of the greatest challenges of the twenty-first century may be that of shaping an international "emancipated citizenship" in the context of globalization. What this chapter proposes is that society's main challenges may be expressed in terms of building a global ethic of respect for human dignity and democracy, establishing sustainable equitable development, and shaping cohesive, inclusive democratic societies in which the full exercise of rights, particularly social rights, is the expression of such inclusion and of democracy at work. Such a democracy must be conceived of as embodying "first-generation" (i.e., civil and political) rights, "second-generation" (i.e., social and economic) rights, and "third-" and "fourth-generation" rights, namely those having to do with safeguarding the environment, peace, and development.

A fundamental tenet of this process is that boys, girls, adolescents, and women are essential for social change. This is not an empty formula, a contemporary version of some cliche; childhood and adolescence are essential because they represent the primary periods for shaping values, human capital, social and cultural capital, and citizenship.

Women and families are also fundamental elements of this transition process. Full participation by women in the economic, social, political, and cultural spheres and their access without discrimination to the fruits of development are not simply a result of, but a necessary condition for, building this new type of society. The family is the basic unit of social cohesion; it is here that the primary socialization of children and adolescents takes place. We need effective policies to strengthen the family if we are to reach the "social horizon" that we seek. The problem here is not simply of an instrumental nature, but has to do with the basic paradigms that guide social policy. A radically different model of social policy must be set in motion, one that builds on what has been achieved, corrects mistakes that have been made, and leads toward more equitable societies centered on the accumulation of social capital as the basis of development. A new economic and social policy based on the recognition of rights as empowering persons, whether they are women or men, adults or children, must be generated through a consensus between the state and civil society, based on an analysis of the situation and a set of priorities that have been set collectively.

This chapter begins with an overview of the recent evolution of economic and social conditions in Latin America, stressing the issues of poverty, the labor market, income distribution, and social spending. The second section briefly examines the status of children's survival, development, and protection. The third section discusses children's rights and introduces the concepts of "paternalistic citizenship" and "autonomous or emancipated citizenship," the latter making it possible to move toward new kinds of public policies that comply with human rights. Finally we identify some of the remaining challenges that must be dealt with in moving toward a social citizenship in the twenty-first century.

Latin America from the "Lost Decade" to the Present

Crisis, Adjustment, and Stabilization

At the dawn of the 1990s, one found a climate of marked optimism in Latin American countries. It reflected initial economic advances signalling an end to the crisis that lasted through the 1980s and extended to all countries in the region. This crisis was primarily due to the inability of countries to service their swollen foreign debt, which in combination with multiple crises in both production and fiscal matters caused instability and stagnation.

In terms of growth, the effects were dramatic: between 1981 and 1990, per capita GDP in the region fell by 9.6%, leading to lower employment, evident in the rate of urban unemployment, which rose significantly in most of the countries on which information is available. After waves of recession, the major efforts by countries of the region to stimulate the economy caused inflation to get out of hand to the point where, in 1985, it reached an average of 275% a year.

Prompted by the issue of foreign debt, on top of external restrictions and internal imbalances, Latin American countries implemented a number of adjustment packages to reestablish macroeconomic equilibrium. They did this by stabilizing the interest rate and the exchange rate and reducing fiscal deficits. It was hoped that this adjustment, although harsh and demanding, would not last long. However, the measures proved ineffective and were replaced by new approaches designed to make a medium- or long-range adjustment that would produce substantial changes in the economy and in the development model. This led to a package of measures, commonly known as the "Washington Consensus," set forth by the World Bank and the International Monetary Fund.

Actually, this Consensus was not explicitly created, but combines a series of interrelated and interdependent measures of political economy. By way of summary, such measures include: (a) liberalization of foreign trade, (b) fiscal discipline, which has a noteworthy influence on inflation levels and, hence, on relative prices, (c) focusing of public spending on areas with high rates of social return, (d) fiscal reform, (e) liberalization of the financial market, (f) competitive exchange rates, (g) free entry of foreign investment, and (h) privatization of government-owned companies and deregulation of the market. According to their proponents, these measures would ensure sustainable high growth rates in the long run, which would lead to improved living conditions for the people and diminished poverty.

Application of the Consensus in Latin America initially prompted renewed economic growth and improvement of the supply of social services in many countries during the first half of the 1990s. Indeed, despite financial market instability, in 1997 the region displayed the greatest economic growth in the past 25 years and the lowest inflation rate in the past 50 years, thanks to a coherent and solid economic policy. These gains in the macroeconomic realm occurred as trade, financial, tax, and labor reforms were taking place and privatization processes were firmly advancing. Today, restrictions on imports have been practically eliminated and tariffs have declined significantly; in the finance area, interest rate controls have been gradually eliminated, and in the area of taxes, reforms to modernize the sector have been introduced. Among other things, this encouraged new technologies and major innovation in the area of communications.

Despite these advances in the macroeconomic area and in the implementation of reforms, gains in the social realm have been minimal and insufficient to counteract many years of deteriorating social conditions. While it is true that, prior to the 1980s, major sectors in Latin America were excluded from the fruits of development, with income and wealth distributed unequally, the crisis and subsequent adjustment processes helped worsen the situation for a vast proportion of the population, aggravating poverty and social exclusion and widening the already existing social and economic gaps. Unemployment, declining real wages, high inflation rates, and the exclusion of broad groups from the benefits of social spending are some of the reasons that poverty rose significantly and a new, unequal, and excluding social structure took shape.

X-Ray of the Social Situation in Latin America

The "lost decade," as the 1980s are commonly called in Latin America, witnessed a dramatic reversal of the economic and social gains achieved in the 1970s. According to the Economic Commission for Latin America and the Caribbean, between 1980 and 1990, those subject to poverty rose from 35 to 41% of the population, which means that over a 10-year period, more than 61 million people joined the ranks of the poor (CEPAL 1997a). In Latin America today, there are around 209 million people whose incomes are insufficient to meet their basic needs and almost 100 million of them—one out of every six households—lack the means to cover even their food needs (see Figure 1).

Figure 1. Trends in Poverty and Extreme Poverty in Latin America (millions of people)

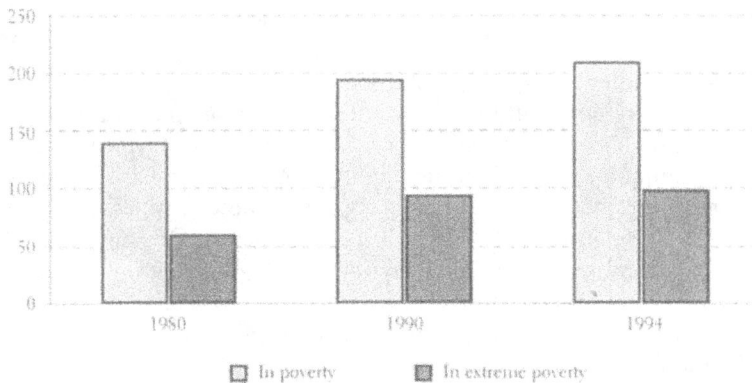

Source: CEPAL (1997a).

Major differences with regard to poverty can be seen from country to country within Latin America. Poverty levels today are the result of uneven development across the region and of improvements and setbacks within each country. According to the Economic Commission for Latin America and the Caribbean (ECLAC) estimates for 12 countries in the region in the decade thus far, the poverty rate rose in 3 countries, held steady in 1, and fell in the others. In only half of the latter was the decline sufficient to bring rates below what they were prior to the crisis of the 1980s. Currently, the poverty rate varies from less than 10% of households (Uruguay) to 73% (Honduras). In general terms, the poverty rate can be placed at between 30 and 50% for a major group of countries, which is significantly higher than the international rate (CEPAL 1997a). The disparities observed between the countries of the region are also mirrored within them: once a rural phenomenon, poverty is now a predominantly urban problem, with almost two-thirds of the poor concentrated in cities.

Youth under age 15 are among those most affected by poverty. Almost 60% of all young people are poor, and they constitute 35% of those suffering from poverty in the region (Van Der Gaag & Winkler 1996). Inasmuch as childhood and adolescence are stages when the capabilities essential for participating in the productive economy and in society are acquired, it is obvious that eradicating poverty for children and young people must be a priority for governments and civil society so that the cycle of poverty may be halted.

An important aspect of the new social framework in Latin America over the past decade is the transformation suffered by middle-income groups as a result of the application of stabilization and adjustment policies. Besides suffering from the general decline in income, these groups are particularly affected by the rise in taxes, changes in the labor market, and the decline of social services. There is no question that the poorest, those who have historically been poor, are worse off than before. However, a significant number of families, while perhaps not exhibiting some of the deficits and typical features of the poor, do not have sufficient income to cover the basic basket of goods and have growing needs that are not being met. These families, known as the "new poor," manifest new needs and social demands. Obviously, society is being affected by new forms of marginalization and social disaffiliation connected with the prevailing model of growth. Moreover, conflicts resulting from land tenure, violence, drug trafficking, corruption, unequal access to education and health care, and vast inequalities have added to the issues producing poverty and now threaten stability and hinder economic growth in the region (Wolfensohn 1997).

Income Inequality

One of the central problems of the region, very much correlated with poverty, is the substantial and growing inequality in the distribution of income and wealth. It is worth asking whether this trend toward inequality is observable only in Latin American economies. In theoretical terms, the best kind of development is that which increases incomes across the population while simultaneously causing inequality to decline. That should translate into an increase of per capita GDP along with a decline in the Gini index.[2] However,

Figure 2. Trends in Income Level and Distribution in Selected Countries

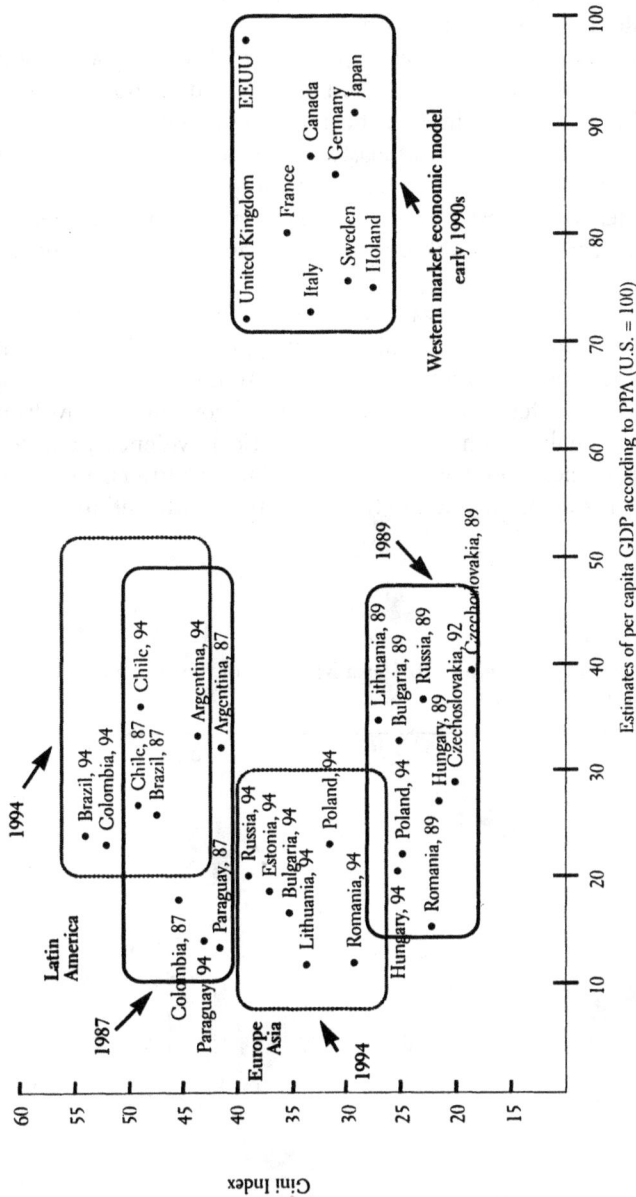

Note: Data for the Gini index of the initial year for Argentina, Colombia, and Paraguay are for 1986; for Mexico 1984; and for Brazil 1979. *Source:* MONEE Database; UNICEF (1994, 19). Data for Latin America were taken from CEPAL (1996) for the Gini index, and from the World Bank (1996) for per capita GDP.

that has not happened in Latin America and in some countries in Eastern Europe. Figure 2 indicates that these countries have advanced toward higher rates of inequality in a move that some authors (e.g., Thurow 1996) regard as an overall "natural" effect of capitalism.

Historically, Latin America has displayed a highly unequal income distribution. In the late 1960s, after a period of sustained economic growth, income inequality in the countries of the region was higher than that of developing countries in East and Southeast Asia.[3] According to some, this is one of the reasons why Latin American countries despite their growth and good productivity rates in the past, could not overcome the worst features of poverty, which now seems to be stubbornly persisting and even deepening in most countries.

The crisis of the 1980s negatively affected income distribution in the countries of the region, while the subsequent application of the Washington Consensus, which involves the transition from an import substitution model toward an export-oriented one with lower levels of government involvement, helped make inequality even worse. The empirical evidence indicates that many of those policies—such as the lowering of trade barriers, and labor and financial reforms—are connected to the widening of distribution gaps.

Figure 3.   Income of the Richest 20% as a Multiple of the Income of the Poorest 40%, 1990–96

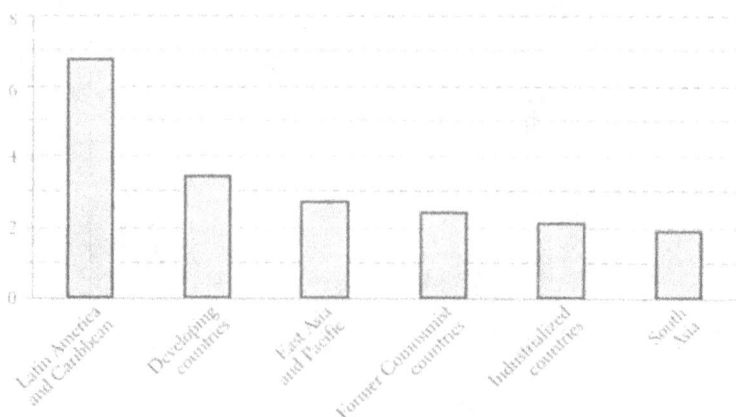

Source: UNICEF (1998c).

Currently, estimates of the Kuznets curve—which predicts levels of inequality vis-à-vis level of development—calculated for a sample of 102 countries, shows that on average Latin American countries display Gini indices that are 4.1 points higher than those of other countries with a similar per capita income. Recent data from some countries apparently show a simultaneous and contradictory increase in average per capita income and the Gini index—that is, despite higher income the already grave differences in income have become worse. Londoño and Székely (1997) estimate that the arithmetic average of the Gini indices of the countries in the region is 0.49, which is 15 points higher than that of developed countries and Southeast Asian countries, and is comparable only to the average of African countries; the region thus has "extra" inequality. An analysis of the ratio between the income of the richest 20% and the poorest 40% of the population reinforces the fact that Latin America and the Caribbean have the largest income inequality of any region in the world (see Figure 3).

Employment Inequality

Generating quality employment is another crucial problem.[4] Persistent high rates of poverty in the region also reflect recent developments in employment largely due to economic expansion, privatization and deregulation, labor flexibility, and the overhaul of the state. There has emerged a highly productive sector with highly qualified professional or technical salaried and non-salaried workers, but the number of jobs is very small. At the same time, low productivity and informal employment has expanded most rapidly, is estimated to account for 8 of every 10 new jobs created in the first half of this decade (Tokman 1996). Likewise, the salary gap between export-oriented and "niche" economic sectors and other sectors of the economy has recently grown wider. It is estimated that the income gap between professionals and technicians and people employed in low-productivity sectors rose 40 to 60% in the first four years of this decade, as can be seen in Figure 4. Research being done in Central America seems to indicate that even in modern sectors of the economy, the new features of employment (short-term jobs, piecework, and so forth), also help deepen the inequalities between wage-earning men and women, to the disadvantage of the latter. As well, unemployment, particularly among youth and heads of households, has tended to rise in several countries in the region.

A more positive side to recent development in Latin America and the Caribbean is that in 11 of the 15 countries for which comparative data exist, funds allocated for social spending increased during the early 1990s, even rising above the levels of the early 1980s. Hence, government social spending as a percentage of GDP rose 1.8% on average, and the increases took place primarily in the areas of education and social security (CEPAL 1996). However, the level of public spending varies widely across the region. Social spending in a significant number of countries is less than US$54 per capita, which is quite low compared with the average in Latin America, which is US$242 or with the average of industrialized countries, US$3,600 (Zevallos 1997). Those countries with the highest per capita social spending regionally dedicate proportions of GDP that are similar to those in a number of industrialized countries. In absolute terms, however, those per capita figures are much lower than those in more developed countries, due to the great differences in GDP. Thus, it is not surprising that even in the better-off countries in the region, social spending is by no means adequate to achieve the increases of coverage and quality of social services needed for equitable development. The countries with the lowest social spending are far from the internationally recognized recommendation by the World Summit on Social Development that governments allot 20% of their budgets to basic social services.[5] Besides inadequate levels of spending, Latin America must also deal with problems of efficiency and fairness.

In short, the extreme inequality that characterized the region in the 1970s has increased, rather than decreased, not only during the crisis of the 1980s, but even while economic development in the 1990s was being implemented. Today the high poverty rate, unequal distribution of income and

Figure 4.   Disparity of Labor Incomes, 1990–94

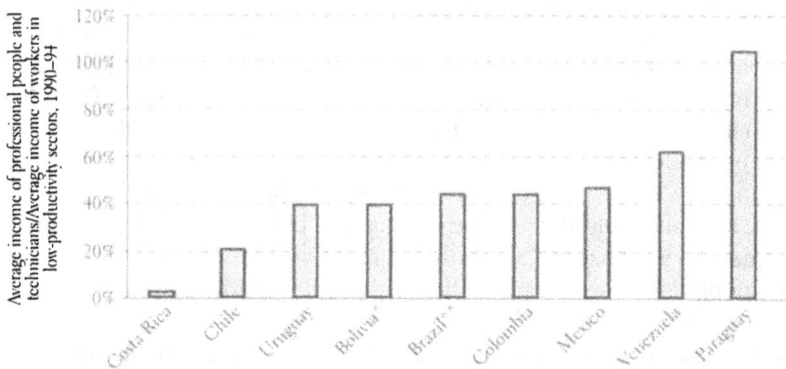

* 1989–94
** 1987–93
Source: CEPAL (1997b).

wealth, unemployment, lack of access to basic services, and persistent in-equalities of gender, race, ethnic group, and geographic region make it clear that the main challenge faced by the countries of the region is to combat the exclusion of a large proportion of the population from economic develop-ment. This exclusion is a manifestation of what is called poverty of citizen-ship—the absence of basic material conditions, codes for emancipation, and notions of cooperation and reciprocity as elemental dimensions of a shared social arrangement (UNICEF 1998).

Moving toward more inclusive societies requires bolstering the process of acquiring rights and exercising them. Within the area of social policy and programs, those that are most effective for achieving that objective, those that really deal with the challenges facing Latin America in the social realm, must be identified. Such a social policy must (1) be an integral part of economic policy, not an afterthought, (2) must ensure some level of living standards for the population and not be restricted to cushioning the harmful effects that development may have on those who are poorest and most vulnerable, and (3) must actually play a decisive role in growth and contribute to building citizenship and developing democracy. The latter point is crucial for most countries in Latin America, where the transition to democracy is underway or where democracy itself is being shaped. A social policy that is guided by human rights is one of the essential elements for building inclusive societies where individuals can exercise full citizenship.

Childhood and Adolescence in Latin America

The adverse economic and social climate in Latin America in the 1980s, and the recent processes tending to aggravate socioeconomic inequality and exclu-sion of broad elements of the population have affected children and adoles-cents in the region.[6] Concerning the welfare and development of boys and girls in Latin America, one can scarcely ignore the vast discrepancies between and within countries that make the region quite heterogeneous. Indeed, the social advances that have made the region relatively better off than some other regions in the world have not been felt equally across its countries and populations.

With regard to children under age 5,[7] the picture is both encouraging and discouraging. It is encouraging because in the past 40 years major ad-vances have been made: 3 out of every 20 children in the region used to die before reaching the age of 5 in 1960, while today this ratio is down to 1 in 20. Although this means that there were 484,000 deaths of children under 5 in 1996—most of them easily preventable with low-cost technology—the mortality rate of children under 5 in Latin America and the Caribbean is the lowest in the developing world (see Figure 5). The situation is discouraging because this decline in mortality has not been uniform—the disparities across countries in the region are becoming ever sharper. In 1960, the ratio of highest to lowest mortality rates in the region was 6:1. Today this ratio is 78:1, a thirteenfold increase. Moreover the ratio between the death rate in Latin America/Caribbean and in the industrialized world has also increased from 3:1 in 1950 to 6:1 in 1996. Similar disparities are also noteworthy within countries. In Brazil, for example, infant mortality varied between 25 per thousand in the south to 74 per thousand in the northeast (IGBE 1992). Similar inequalities can be seen in several other countries in the region, where the decline in infant mortality has been concentrated in particular locales or economic strata.

Figure 5.   Mortality Rate of Children under Age 5, 1960 and 1996

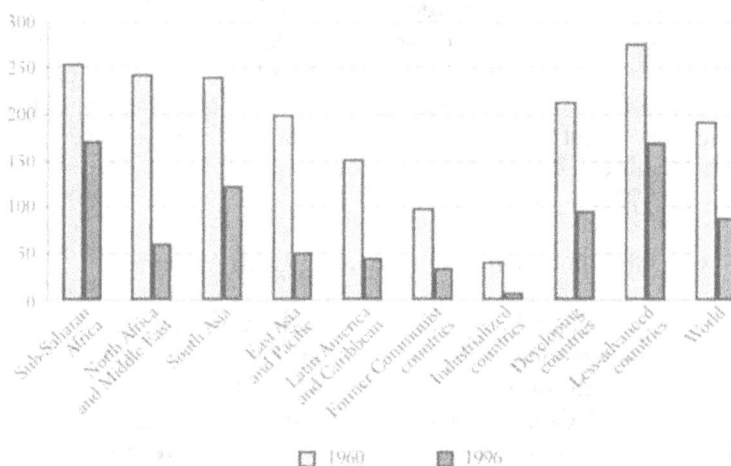

Source: UNICEF (1998c).

Mortality rates in childbirth display similar trends. Available information shows that in Latin America and the Caribbean, around 22,000 women a year die because of complications related to pregnancy and childbirth. This means that a woman dies every 25 minutes—for reasons that are regarded as preventable over 90% of the time—with devastating effects on the survival of the child. Disparities between countries are significant. The ratio of maternal death rates of some Latin American countries (such as Costa Rica, Cuba, and Uruguay) and that of developed countries is 4:1, whereas in countries like Haiti and Bolivia, this ratio is around 75:1.

Regarding education, Latin America and the Caribbean have a net elementary school attendance rate of 91.9% for boys and 85.7% for girls, which is relatively high compared with the rate in other developing regions. However, the disparities between countries are huge. The rate is below 90% in the Dominican Republic, El Salvador, Guatemala, Haiti, Honduras, Nicaragua, and Trinidad and Tobago. The gaps become wider in secondary education, with rates varying from over 60% to under 30% across the region.

Inequalities in access to quality education are obvious. The poor sectors of the population — indigenous people and other minorities — are often excluded from the education system, and when they do manage to go to school, the education they receive is of poor quality. This is reflected in performance tests, which show that most children attending public schools do not learn even the basic minimum requirements.

Another problem associated with education is the high dropout rate. Eighty percent of the students in the region who enter the first grade reach the fourth grade, and 73% the fifth grade. Having to repeat a grade is also common. Of the approximately 9 million children who enter primary school each year, 44% fail the first grade, and 29% repeat the year. The poor school performance and high dropout rates prevailing in Latin America are also associated with scant availability of preschool education and a general low investment in child development. Only 17% of children between 4 and 5 years of age have access to preschool education and most of them are found in upper-income families. Access to preschool education varies significantly between countries and subregions: approximately 31% of children in the Caribbean and 37% in Central America.

With regard to protecting children, while it is true that all countries in the region have ratified the Convention on the Rights of the Child and several of them have finished the process of adapting their legislation to Convention standards,[8] children and adolescents continue to be victims of acts that violate their human rights. Child labor constitutes a clear example of such violations. Children have been found doing high-risk work in 15 countries in the region, with serious repercussions for their health, education, development, and overall welfare (see Figure 6). Only a fourth of all adolescent workers in Latin America urban areas are attending school. On average, children and adolescents who are working achieve a lower education level and hence earn lower incomes throughout their adult life than those who do not work.

Forms of violence often affect vulnerable segments of the population severely, including children and adolescents/young adults. In over half the countries of the region, homicide is the second cause of death in 12- to 24-year-olds. Sexual exploitation, mistreatment, abuse, and abandonment are flagrant violations of the rights of children. Although these violations are common and affect a high percentage of children in the region, they have received little attention in the form of government policies for monitoring

Figure 6.   Children Aged 13 to 17 Who Work, 1995

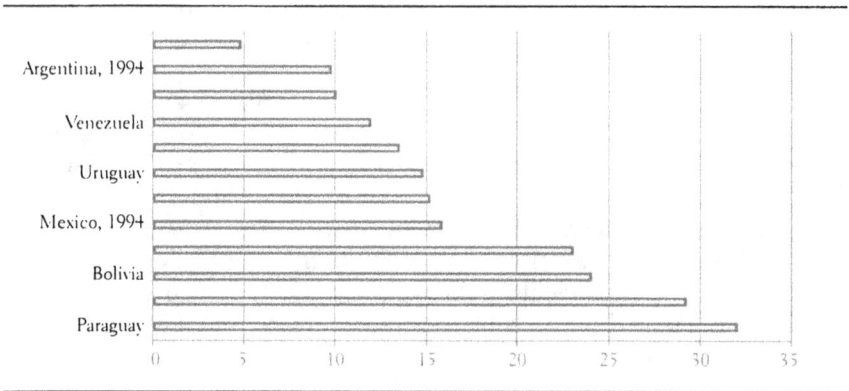

Source: CEPAL (1997a).

their occurrence and protecting children. Instead, children and adolescents are often blamed for the high incidence of violence, criminality, and insecurity in society, and government efforts to resolve such problems tend to be limited to the use of force and punishment through the court system.

Children's Rights:
The Path to a Social Inclusion Model

As can be concluded from the preceding section, the challenge for Latin America and the Caribbean is to address the substantial patterns of inequality, marginalization, and exclusion that prevent the population as a whole from participating in social development efforts and their fruits. Building inclusive societies is not an alternative that can be easily implemented, especially in what are called "developing" regions or countries. Many segments of society must agree to implement a variety of factors, including the establishment of a new conception of social policy and the acceptance of the basic elements of what can be called "autonomous or emancipated citizenship."

Models of Citizenship[9]

Projecting this focus toward the future and taking into account the macroeconomic framework and current trends in social policy, it can be stated that two models of citizenship are currently in competition. One of the models could be called "paternalistic citizenship" and it is typical of the prevailing trends in social policy in the region. The other is "autonomous or emancipated citizenship," which is now emerging from the social policy of some countries in the region (Draibe 1995; Guimaraes de Castro & Azerado, Minujin 1997; Raczynski 1994).

The paternalistic citizenship (PC) model is set within the more conservative tradition of economic and social policy and can be recognized in the theoretical formulations of Friedrich von Hayek (1944) and Milton Friedman (1962). This is the prevailing notion associated with the economic adjustment and economic liberalization models now in ascendancy in Latin America, particularly in connection with the so-called Washington Consensus (Williamson 1996).[10] The starting point for this model is an atomized notion of society in which individuals with interests are recognized as the basic organizing principle of any human association. The model archetype is the Homo economicus, who by maximizing his or her personal benefit automatically benefits the whole of society. The negative freedoms magisterially explained by Sir Isaiah Berlin in his *Four Essays on Liberty* (1969) constitute the most profound theoretical articulation of the PC model. It is the negative freedoms that serve to ensure the full exercise of individual freedoms without interference from the state, other persons, or, in general, from claims based on public reason. Thus, what is called for is a minimum state bureaucracy that must not alter or interfere with the basic self-regulating mechanism in which the interests of millions of sellers and consumers are found and socially optimized — namely, the market. The market is conceived as a self-regulating mechanism, apart from politics and social policy; its logic is paramount and must always be "heeded." This model does not allow the possibility of situations in which cooperation is advantageous, in the sense that the advantage always goes to the "free riders"[11] as described well by Mancur Olson (1965) in *The Logic of Collective Action*. Since there is no such thing as the public good (other than the market) in the sense of something higher than the interest of individuals, there is no possibility for public policies either.

In the PC model, citizenship is conceived of as essentially civic in nature. Political citizenship refers only to formal rights, primarily the right to elect and be elected. Social rights may not be demanded in a positive sense unless they are based on contributions, for example, as a kind of social security that establishes in an individual account the contributions of each person together with benefits calculated on an actuarial basis. Social rights, if they can be fulfilled by social services, are subject to the availability of resources: that is why they are actually only "conditional opportunities" (Barbalet 1988).

There is no concern for distributing income and wealth because inequalities are natural and the result of the triumph of the fittest. Therefore, state policies must be marginal and neutral with regard to redistribution. So-called social policies must not seek income distribution but rather target poverty and form "safety nets" for the most vulnerable social groups. On this point, PC social policy links up with the old ideas of electoral clientelism and social paternalism (of citizenship "guided" by a "leader") that have traditionally operated in Latin America. With the current economic adjustments based on the open economy model, social policy is necessary to lay the foundations for governability so as to ensure the legitimation of reforms required by the market. The various types of revenue transfers to the poor involving social policy are based on an ethic of compassion: assisted citizenship is essentially a subsidized citizenship. In terms of economic calculation, subsidies are a disincentive, and therefore must be used only as exceptions and only temporarily.

Minimum state health and education policies based on human capital can be implemented. Their structure should not go beyond the logic of individuals investing in themselves by calculating the future return on such investments. Likewise, in order to deal with the unexpected and with risks to their lives, individuals ought to capitalize a portion of their incomes in private funds or forms of insurance that observe an individual actuarial logic. Here, social policy meshes with economic policy, inasmuch as it provides the funds needed to increase savings that are channeled to investment through the capital market.

The emancipated citizenship (EC) model recognizes another conceptual tradition extending from the early utopian thinkers, including socialists, and culminating in the so-called welfare state with the social reforms pressed by the Fabians and Beveridge in England, by G. Moller in Sweden (Olsson and Sven 1993), and in the academic realm by the contributions of Thomas Marshall and Richard Titmuss. Social equality, understood primarily as the right of persons—envisioned as members and partners in a framework of social cooperation—to have equal opportunities of access to socially and economically important goods, is of central importance to this tradition. Equality means equity—proportionality in access to the benefits and costs of development—and also redistributive justice based on collective solidarity.[12]

Social cooperation implies the existence of a collective "we" for making a particular human society viable. The existence of individuals is not denied, but society is acknowledged and hence there is a public sphere in the sense of a concern for what individuals have in common, for what is shared, for the interest of all. The first-person *plural* is commensurate with what is "social"; "we" are "associates," the set of "partners" who are mutually involved in an effort at cooperation. Making "us" a concrete proposal means simply sharing a community of discourse, a shared set of arguments that essentially consists of defining the direction that is to be taken and how to proceed. The plural subject is thus constituted in the founding dimension of a society; it becomes more relevant in a globalized world where there is competition with other proposals for production and society. Individual freedoms in the form of negative freedoms are important, but equally relevant are positive freedoms: persons' improved access to the opportunities that will allow more people to make progress and develop. Equality is therefore about enabling rather than leveling.

Thus presented, the EC model is by definition socially inclusive. Everyone is part of the conversation through which a community of arguments is developed. And in the community of arguments, some people are crucial for reducing the multiple ways in which exclusion is reproduced—for example, by improving access to productive employment, a quality education, and the socially relevant codes that enable women and men to participate and widen the field of their rights and responsibilities. In the EC model, persons are not "patients"—objects to be treated or acted on by governments—but actors in their twin roles of individuals and members of society: emancipation is individual because individuals are autonomous. But emancipation is not counted one by one; it is not singular. It entails, as was stated, a community of arguments and a responsibility for the whole: that is why emancipation is democratic.

The market and the logic of profit are not inherently blameworthy, but they are clearly instrumental. Here all political, economic, and social institutions are analyzed in terms of their effects on persons, on women, men, and new generations, all of whom have a right to equal opportunity. Institutions are judged according to whether they help emancipate or create dependency; whether they degrade, humiliate, and exploit; whether they concentrate or distribute power and wealth.

Investigating models of citizenship makes it possible to visualize new kinds of public policies linking government and civil society, establishing an unbreakable tie between economic policy and social policy, and moving from handout-type aid to fulfilling the rights of all, men and women, boys and girls.

Transformations and Challenges for Building an Emancipated Citizenship

It is interesting to examine, from the standpoint of childhood, what steps must be taken to establish in society the key elements that would in combination shape an emancipated citizenship and what challenges face Latin America and the Caribbean in setting such changes in motion.

Childhood represents a privileged opportunity for implementing the transformations that might lead to the preeminence of inclusive societies for three main reasons. First, inasmuch as exclusion is the result of a process of cumulative disadvantages that begin at the outset of life itself, childhood represents a very favorable time for acquiring knowledge and developing creativity, as well as for gaining the tools necessary for guaranteeing that this population group be properly included in the economy and society. Second, childhood emerges as an ideal time for implementing the changes that, in terms of the Convention on the Rights of the Child, can strengthen the values of equity, solidarity, and tolerance, which are key factors for building up social capital and are necessary for advancing toward a society of rights. Finally, from an economic standpoint, various studies have shown a high rate of return on early investment in childhood, as well as the importance of investment in human capital for economic development.

It is worthwhile examining what these transformations are, particularly those that have a greater capacity for synergistically stimulating progress toward the type of society desired. They may be grouped into three dimensions, which are not exhaustive or exclusive: (1) survival, which includes the transformations and challenges connected to the basic material conditions that ensure a dignified standard of living for the population; (2) development of capabilities, that is, what still remains to be done so that all children may have access to a quality education and develop the creativity and abilities that will enable them to enjoy a full life, within the family, the community, and society's institutions; and (3) citizenship, which encompasses the necessary changes and the difficulties that have to be overcome in order to promote development and the strengthening of full participation and empowerment.

It must be emphasized that while numerous changes are needed so that the state can fulfill its fundamental role of ensuring that the human rights of all are respected, this section does not explicitly and comprehensively take up the changes that must be brought about within the state and that affect the institutions and the way they relate to civil society, because such issues are complex and to analyze them would go beyond the purposes of this chapter.

Basic Material Conditions of Life

Since 1990 when the World Summit for Children[13] was held and goals were set for the year 2000 in the areas of health care, nutrition, education, and the condition of women and children in especially difficult circumstances, a firm social awareness about childhood has been established. There is an increasing acknowledgment that achieving basic material conditions and eliminating the worst manifestations of poverty are essential for human dignity. All families should be able to (1) exercise their right to food, health care, water, and shelter and (2) work and receive income in a society in which the fruits of economic growth are broadly distributed. These goals can only be attained insofar as children, adolescents, and women have access to basic services to ensure survival, as well as to health care, adequate nutrition, and a quality education (UNICEF 1998).

Major advances have unquestionably been achieved in meeting such necessities: child survival and expanded coverage of basic services have increased significantly in almost all countries in the region; infant mortality and malnutrition are at historically low levels, school enrollment in Latin America is almost universal, and during the past 10 years, millions of people have acquired potable water in their homes. Even so, at present there remain critical situations that threaten the survival of a significant percentage of children in the region; a half million boys and girls die before their fifth birthday, many of them from diseases for which inexpensive preventive measures and treatments, such as immunization and antibiotics, are available.

Education and Learning

Education and learning must create not only "human capital" for the sake of economic development, but also social capital, democracy, tolerance, and equity.

The discussion of human rights has had a considerable impact on the very idea of social policy, to the point that in addition to providing quality services, it is expected to build inclusive and democratic societies. In this context, policies in the field of education must address citizenship values, equal access to knowledge, social integration, respect for diversity, and tolerance.

While Latin America has been able to increase significantly its net rate of primary school enrollment, which is now relatively high in comparison with other developing regions, significant problems still threaten the sustainability of those achievements and the possibility of attaining a kind of education oriented toward rights and citizenship. As noted earlier, child and youth labor is one of the main obstacles to the education of children and adolescents in the region. In this regard, it has been shown that work hinders academic performance and leads to students repeating grades and dropping out of school.

The main challenges for education in Latin America concern equity in education, access to preschool education and early childhood development, and primary education and its content.

The Family as Nucleus

The family is the fundamental nucleus of society and the context in which children and adolescents are primarily socialized. In the early years of life and through everyday practices, it is where one learns and internalizes such values as solidarity, tolerance, equity, and respect, which can help sustain peaceful societies that respect diversity. It is also where one first acquires knowledge, and where, as has been amply demonstrated, adequate early stimulation spurs the learning process and awakens creativity. Therefore, the family in all its forms[14] must be strengthened and made an opportunity for building inclusive societies.

The dramatic changes taking place in Latin America and the Caribbean over the past several decades have had a significant impact on family structures, relationships between family members, and the role played by parents. Likewise, changes in the role of the state have transferred to the family a series of responsibilities proper to it, resulting in additional burdens that are difficult for poor families to bear. Policies and programs aimed at the family usually do not look on it as part of a larger context, but in a fragmented and incomplete way. In UNICEF's view, government policies must have an integrating approach whose starting point is an overall vision of the family and its relationship to society, where the family does not lose its institutional character and where it fulfills a set of wider tasks, both emotional and material, vis-à-vis the broader social system. A task for the future therefore becomes the reconsideration of the role of the state and the development of public policies to safeguard and strengthen the family.

Empowerment of Women and Girls

The observance of, and compliance with, the rights of girls and women, besides being a matter of justice, is also a prerequisite for bringing about a substantial improvement in the living conditions of the almost 500 million inhabitants of Latin America and the Caribbean. Only when children develop in an equitable society and are properly cared for, when women have a right to the full development of their capabilities, and when women work for wages on a par with those of men will we begin to be able to leave behind the age of poverty, disease, and war (UNICEF 1993).

This century has seen the flourishing of movements to value and respect women's rights. As a result of these struggles and multiple political, social, and economic changes, the participation of women in the public and private spheres has expanded, clearly demonstrating the transforming power they embody in society, the economy, and the culture. Today it is acknowledged that a growing respect for the rights of women and their increasingly active role in many spheres will be some of the main ingredients—or the main ingredients—of change in the next century.

Nevertheless, it is obvious that despite progress in gender equality, discrimination still affects girls, adolescents, and women. The future of childhood in the region is closely connected to the living conditions of women, which in turn are a reflection of how much progress has been made toward gender equity. The future of childhood also depends on the priority given to social welfare in government policies, and therefore such policies must take into account the gender perspective—recognizing that men and women play different roles in society, have different degrees of control over resources, and, accordingly, often have different needs.

Accepting Existing Legislation to the Convention on the Rights of the Child

The CRC is the most widely accepted human rights legal document in the world and has been ratified by all countries in the world except the United States and Somalia. Ratification of the CRC will soon be universal and hence it will become the first world law approved for all humankind. Nevertheless, ratification constitutes simply the first step toward full implementation of the rights of children. Both legislative and institutional reforms are needed, as well as deep social and cultural changes in our attitude toward children. Today the challenge lies in how to bring the Convention beyond initial universal ratification into the area of specific actions on behalf of children (UNICEF 1996a). Many Latin American and Caribbean countries are now involved in a legislative reform to adopt existing laws to the terms of the Convention. This has brought about a fundamental legislative shift to provide children with full rather than partial protection: laws dealing with the emergency situations of children and adolescents at risk of abandonment, sexual abuse, mistreatment, exploitative labor, armed conflicts, and so forth are being supplanted with laws safeguarding all children and adolescents in all situations.

Reform of Protective Institutions, the State, and Social Welfare Agencies

The CRC has addressed the relationship between children and the law in a new way. The Convention states that protective institutions must act in accordance with the "higher interest of the boy and girl." That means that before any measure affecting children is taken, it must be ensured that such measures will promote and protect their rights rather than violate them (Cillero Bruñol, 1997). However, for these changes to laws and institutions to be really effective, a social reform must be carried out to (1) modernize the management of social welfare agencies so that communities participate more in solving and handling their problems, (2) correct income and wealth inequalities, and (3) address the social and economic exclusion of significant groups of the population.

Building Participation and Free Expression

In recent decades, Latin American and Caribbean countries have been waging a battle against the factors that threaten the survival, development, and welfare of their children and adolescents. Although accomplishments vary from country to country, some indicators (infant mortality rate and primary education coverage, among others) show that the region has experienced a significant improvement in the quality of life of the child and youth population.

As gains are gradually made in basic rights to health care, nutrition, and education in a number of Latin American countries, there is growing support for the idea that, even though much remains to be done about children's survival and development, there are other rights enshrined in the CRC that ought to be observed and promoted, such as the right of children and adolescents under age 18 to participate in all matters affecting themselves and the right to information and free expression (arts. 12 and 13 of the CRC).

Such rights enhance human potential and enable people to have greater control over their lives: it also promotes productivity, creativity, and efficiency.[15] Many mechanisms could be useful for motivating and promoting the participation and free expression of children and adolescents, ranging from activities at the family or community level to large-scale programs.

The true challenge for the new millennium is that of opening up everyday opportunities within school and family for girls and boys to participate, so that they may transmit their perceptions, thoughts, and feelings on matters of concern to them, as well as influence decision making.

NOTES

Some portions of this chapter are found in Maurás and Minujin (1998). This chapter has been substantially enriched by the contributions and studies done by Eduardo Bustelo and Maria Maurás Pérez, to whom we are extremely grateful. The authors are solely responsible for the opinions contained here, which do not necessarily represent the viewpoint of the agency for which they work.

1. UNICEF (1998c). Those who are under 18 years of age.

2. In analyzing changes in income distribution, three complementary measurements are used: two of position, the average and the mean, and one of inequality. The Gini index is derived from the Lorenz curve and measures the distance between a completely equal income distribution and the real distribution of a country or a population. The Gini index extends from zero to one; a zero value means that the distribution is completely equal, and as it rises and approaches one, it indicates a situation of increasing inequality. The median corresponds to the value of the income that divides the population into two equal parts, and the mean indicates the average income of the population. How income distribution has changed can be analyzed on the basis of the movement of these three indicators.

3. In 1960 the ratio between the incomes of the richest 10% and poorest 10% of the population was 33.6, 21.2, 18.0, and 11.4:1 in Brazil, Colombia, Venezuela, and Argentina, respectively, while in the Philippines, Thailand, and South Korea it was 13.6, 8.9, and 7.5:1 (Andrea 1994).

4. *Productive or quality employment* is understood to be whatever provides the employee and his or her family the basic levels of security and coverage, because it no longer refers to the old paradigm of full-time salaried employee, but rather to novel arrangements that make possible both the degree of flexibility imposed by global patterns of labor demand and a basic coverage of needs in accordance with social citizenship.

5. The World Summit on Social Development, held in Copenhagen in March 1995, adopted the 20/20 Initiative, which proposes that 20% of budget expenditures and 20% of aid flows ought to be allocated to basic social services. It is based on the conviction that the delivery of basic social services is one of the most efficient and cost-efficient ways of combating the worst manifestations of poverty.

6. The data in this section are taken from UNICEF (1998c).

7. The mortality rate of children under 5 and infant mortality indicate the number of boys and girls who die before the age of 5 and before their first birthday, respectively, for every 1,000 live births. These two indicators are commonly used because they offer a general reflection of the conditions of well-being and the development of the society.

8. These countries are Brazil, Bolivia, Costa Rica, Ecuador, El Salvador, Guatemala, Honduras, Nicaragua, Paraguay, Peru, and the Dominican Republic.

9. This section draws on Bustelo (1998). For further information, see Bustelo and Minujin (1996). Here the word "model" is being used in the

sense of *paradigm*, that is, as a simple representation of a set of values and concepts structured with some degree of consistency. A model allows for recognizing and defining with relative precision the set of relevant dimensions that structure the paradigm in question. Through the various dimensions that make up a model, it is possible to understand and differentiate two paradigms of citizenship that have taken shape in the history of social policy. In actuality, models do not occur in the pure state because by definition reality is much more complex. Even so, models make it possible to differentiate the forms and/or different styles of social policy in the real world and to refer to and classify them in terms of two basic types of citizenship (Varsafsky, 1971).

10. An intelligent overview of social policy from a standpoint of economic orthodoxy can be found in Esping-Andersen (1990).

11. "Free rider" or what Hirschman (1996) calls the "parasitism of the freeloader," refers to those who make use of a particular public good or service without paying the corresponding fee or tax.

12. A similarly concise and clear discussion of equality in economic and social policy can be found in Esping-Anderson (1994).

13. The World Summit for Children was held in New York in September 1990. At that time, leaders of over 150 countries, including 71 presidents and heads of state, came together to lay the groundwork and define the goals that ought to be reached by the year 2000 to achieve a better future for the children of the world.

14. The family is here being referred to as the basic nucleus for the shared life of children not to any particular shape it may take.

15. Griffin and McKinley (1994).

BIBLIOGRAPHY

Atkinson, A. B. 1988. "Social Exclusion, Poverty and Unemployment," in Atkinson and John Hills (eds.), *Exclusion, Employment and Opportunity*. CASE paper no. 4, London.

Aylwin, Nidia. 1991. *El Análisis de las politicas sociales desde una perspectiva familiar*. Simposio Políticas de Familia. Universidad Pontificia Comillas, España. Octubre.

Barbalet, J. M. 1988. *Citizenship*. Open University Press, Milton Keynes.

Beccaria, L. 1997. "Poverty Measurement, Present Status of Concepts and Methods." Document prepared in the Division of Statistics and Economic Projections of ECLAC for the seminar Poverty Statistics, Santiago, Chile.

Beccaria, L., and Minujín, A. 1991. "Sobre la medición de la pobreza." Mimeo. UNICEF, Argentina.

Berlin, Isaiah. 1969. *Four Essays on Liberty*. Oxford University Press, Oxford.

Bobbio, N. *La era de los derechos*. Tauras.

Boltvinik, Julio. 1991. "Conceptos y mediciones de la pobreza predominantes en América Latina, evaluación critica," in *Pobreza violencia y desigualdad: Retos para la nueva. Colombia*, PNUD.

Bustelo, Eduardo. 1998. "Expansión de la ciudadanía y construcción democrática," in Bustelo and Minujín, *Todos entran: Propuesta papa sociedades incluyentes*. Editorial Santillana/UNICEF, Santafé de Bogotá.

Bustelo, Eduardo, and Minujín, Alberto. 1996. "La política social esquiva," *Espacios, Revista Centroamericana de Cultura Política*, July–December, no. 8.

Castel, Robert. 1995. *Les métamorphoses de la question sociale: Une chronique du salariat*. Fayard, Paris.

CEPAL (Comisión Económica para América Latina y el Caribe). 1996 and 1997a. *Panorama social de América Latina*. LC/G 1768, September 1993:1844, November 1994:1886, December 1995. Santiago, Chile.

_____. 1997b. *La brecha de la equidad*. Santiago, Chile.

Cillero Bruñol, Miguel. 1997. "El interés superior del niño en el marco de la Convención Internacional sobre los Derechos del niño." Presentado en el Seminario sobre Justica Penal Juvenil Adolescentes privados de libertad: Información e indicadores. Costa Rica.

Commission of the European Communities (CEC). 1993. *Towards a Europe of Solidarity: Intensifying the Fight against Social Exclusion, Fostering Integration*. Brussels.

Deacon, Bob, Michelle Hulse, and Paul Stubbs. 1997. *Global Social Policy: International Organizations and the Future of Welfare*. Sage, London.

Draibe, Sonia, Guimarães de Castro, Maria Helena, and Azeredo, Beatriz. 1995. "The System of Social Protection in Brazil," in Kellogg Institute Democracy and Social Policy Series, working paper no. 3, Spring.

Esping-Anderson. G. 1990. *The Three Worlds of Welfare Capitalism*. Polity, Cambridge, and Princeton University Press, Princeton.

_____. 1994. "Welfare States and the Economy," in J. N. Smelser and R. Swedberg (eds.), *The Handbook of Economic Sociology*. Princeton University Press, Princeton.

Fitoussi, Jean Paul, and Rosanvallon, Pierre. 1996. *Le nouvel âge des inégalités*. Éditions du Seuil, Paris.

Franco, Rolando. 1996. "Los paradigmas de la política social," *Revista de la CEPAL*, no. 58. April, Santiago de Chile.

Friedman, Milton. 1962. *Capitalism and Freedom*. University of Chicago Press, Chicago.

Gordon, Linda. 1994. *Welfare Reform: A History Lesson*. Dissent, New York.

Griffin, Keith, and McKinley, Terry. 1994. *Implementing a Human Development Strategy*. Macmillan, New York.

Hayek, Friedrich von. 1944. *The Road to Serfdom*. University of Chicago Press, Chicago.

Heller, A., and Fehér, F. 1992. *El péndulo de la modernidad*. Ediciones Península, Barcelona.

Hirschman, Albert O. 1996. *Tendencias autosubversivas, ensayos*. Fondo de Cultura Económica/Economía Contemporánea, Mexico.

IBGE (Instituto Brasileiro de Geografia e Estatistica). 1992. *Social Indicators*, vol. 4.

Iglesias, Enrique. 1998. *Exposición en la sesión inaugural de la reunión annual de las Asambleas de Gobernadores del Banco Interamericano de Desarrollo y de la Corporación Interamericana de Inversores*. Cartagena de Indias, Colombia.

Londoño, Juan Luis. 1995. "Pobreza, desigualdad y desarrollo humano en América Latina," *Coyuntura Social*, no. 13, November.

Londoño, Juan Luis, and Székely, Miguel. 1997. "Sorpresas distributiyas después de una década de reformas: América Latina en los noventa." Documento preparado para el seminario Latin America after a Decade of Reform: What Are the Next Steps? BID.

Maturana, Humberto. 1992. *El sentido de lo humano*. Ediciones Pedagógicas Chilenas. S. A. Hachette, Santiago, Chile.

Maurás, Marta, and Minujin, Alberto. 1998. "Derechos e inclusión social: Desafíos para el siglo XXI." Documento presentado en El Foro América Latina–Europa para un Desarrollo Social Sostenible en el Siglo XXI.

Minujin, Alberto. 1997. "The Formation, Growth and Downfall of the Welfare State in Southern Cone Countries and Its Difficult Rebirth in a Democratic Context." Presented at the conference "Social Policies for the Urban Poor in Latin America: Welfare Reform in a Democratic Context." University of Notre Dame, Helen Kellogg Institute for International Studies, Notre Dame, Indiana.

_____. 1998. "Vulnerabilidad y exclusión en América Latina," in *Todos entran*. Editorial Santillana/UNICEF.

Minujin, Alberto, and Kessler, G. 1995. *La nueva pobreza en la Argentina*. Temas de Hoy, Editorial Planeta, Argentina.

Olson, Mancur, Jr. 1965. *The Logic of Collective Action: Public Goods and the Theory of Groups*. Harvard University Press, Cambridge, Mass.

Olsson, Hort, and Sven, E. 1993. "Models and Countries: The Swedish Social Policy Model in Perspective," in *Social Security in Sweden and Other European Countries*. Papport till ESO. Expertgruppen för Studier I offentlig ekonomi, Stockholm.

Organización Internacional del Trabajo y Programa de las Naciones Unidas para el Desarrollo. 1996. *Social Exclusion and Anti-Poverty Strategies.* ILO.

Programa de las Naciones Unidas para el Desarrollo (PNUD). 1997. *Informe sobre el desarollo humano.*

Putnam, Robert. 1993. *Making Democracy Work.* Princeton University Press, Princeton.

Raczynski, Dagmar. 1994. "Social Policies in Chile: Origin, Transformations and Perspectives." Kellogg Institute Democracy and Social Policy Series, working paper no. 4, Fall.

Reyes, Carmen. 1989. "Programa de desarrollo familia y prevención de problemas familiares." Presented at the seminar Mujer y Familia en la Nueva Democracia. Instituto Chileno de Estudios Humanísticos.

_____. 1992. "La Familia chilena hoy: Fundamentos para políticas públicas orientada al grupo familiar." Presented at the seminar La Familia en Chile: Aspiraciones, Realidades y Desafios.

Rowntree, B. S. 1941. "Poverty: A Study of Town Life," in *Poverty and Progress.* London.

Sen, Amartya. 1992. "Sobre conceptos y medidas de pobreza," *Comercio Exterior,* vol. 42, April 4.

Thurow, Lester C. 1996. *The Future of Capitalism.* Morrow, New York.

Tokman, Victor E. 1996. "Jobs and Solidarity: Main Challenges for the Post-Adjustment in Latin America." Presented at the conference Development, Thinking and Practice. Washington, D.C.

UNICEF. 1993. *A Time for Action: Girls and Human Rights—Development Programmes for Women Unit.*

_____. 1994. "Crisis in Mortality, Health and Nutrition: Central and Eastern Europe in Transition—Public Policy and Social Conditions." Economics in Transition Studies, Regional Monitoring report no. 2, August.

_____. 1996a. *De menor a ciudadno.* UNICEF, Oficina Regional para América Latina y Caribe, Fotoletras Ltda.

_____. 1996b. *La Convención Internacional de los Derechos del Niño: Derecho democracia y realidad.* Discurso de la Directora de UNICEF para América Latina y Caribe en la IV Reunión de la Comisión Interparlamentaria Latinoamericana de Derechos Humanos, Chile, May.

_____. 1997a. *Guidelines for the Formulation of the UN Development Assistance Framework (UNDAF): Which Role for the CRC?* Working paper by Mara Santos Pais.

_____. 1997b. *Estado mundial de la infancia*. Oxford University Press, Oxford.

_____. 1998a. *Towards an Agenda for Children beyond the Year 2000: A Vision, Key Transformations, and the Strategic Role of UNICEF*. Working paper.

_____. 1998b. *Una estrategia de desarrollo centrada en los niños: UNICEF en América Latina y Caribe en los años 90*. Informa de Fin Misión de la Directora Regional de UNICEF para América Latina y Caribe. Documento aún sin publicar.

_____. 1998c. *Estado mundial de la infancia*. Oxford University Press, Oxford.

UNICEF/TACRO (United Nations Children's Fund/The Americas and Caribbean Regional Office). 1997. *Enfoque de derechos, formulación de políticas y programación*. Documento de trabajo interno escrito por Ana Mercedes Brealey.

Van Der Gaag, Jacques, and Winkler, Donald. 1996. "Children of the Poor in Latin America and the Caribbean." Presented at the World Bank annual conference on Development in Latin America, July.

Varsavsky, Oscar. 1971. *Proyectos nacionales*. Ediciones Periferia, Buenos Aires.

Williamson, J. 1996. "The Washington Consensus Revisited." Presented at the conference Development, Thinking and Practice. IDB. Washington, D.C.

Wolfensohn, James D. 1997. *The Challenge of Inclusion*. Annual meeting address, Hong Kong SAR, China.

World Bank. 1996. *World Development Report*.

Zevallos, José Vincente (ed.) 1997. *Estrategias para reducir la pobreza en América Latina y el Caribe*. Un estudio de Proyecto "Mitigación de la Pobreza y desarrollo social." Programa de las Naciones Unidas para el Desarrollo (PNUD), Ecuador.

Zolo, Danilo. 1994. "La strategia della cittadinanza," in Danilo Zolo (comp.), La cittadinanza: Appartenenza, identitià diritti. Laterza, Roma.

19 | The Rights of the Child

The Path toward a Model of Social Inclusion

MARTA MAURÁS PÉREZ

The "Washington Consensus" and Its Results

Since the debt crisis at the beginning of the decade of the eighties, the majority of the countries of Latin America and the Caribbean have applied, at varying paces and intensities, economic reforms based on policies that constitute what has been called the "Washington Consensus." In reality, this "consensus" has not been explicitly agreed upon, but rather brings together a set of policies promoted from Washington by the International Monetary Fund and the World Bank, among others, with the objective of moving from previous protectionist philosophies toward noninterventionist open market models. In the region, high external debt and the need for foreign financing were decisive factors leading to widespread acceptance of the Consensus by local governments.

The Washington Consensus is composed of a set of economic policy measures that are interrelated and interdependent.[1] These measures, according to their promoters, would ensure high rates of sustainable growth in the long term. This would result in improvement of the living conditions of the population and reduction of poverty. Perhaps this is the appropriate point to recall Keynes's famous statement "In the long term we will all be dead."

However, the adoption of the Consensus in the region has not rendered the expected results, especially in the social sphere. Even though economic growth has been restored in many of the region's countries, it has been weak and dangerously dependent on foreign capital inflows, as was evidenced by the recent Mexican crisis. In economic terms, this model has its limitations, and in social terms it has frankly failed.

The Paradox of Modernization and Exclusion

The "lost decade," as the 1980s are commonly called in Latin America, signified for the countries of the region a dramatic regression of the economic and social progress achieved in the seventies. From 1980 to 1990, according to the Economic Commission for Latin America and the Caribbean (ECLAC), the rate of those living in poverty rose from 35 to 41% of the population, which means that in those 10 years, more than 61 million people entered the ranks of the poor. In spite of the reactivation of economic growth and improvement in the provision of social services that took place from 1990 to 1994, the progress with regard to poverty reduction was minimal and insufficient to counteract the many years of deteriorating of social conditions, a partial manifestation of the long and costly processes of adjustment and economic restructuring.

At present, in Latin America there are approximately 209 million people whose income is not sufficient to satisfy their minimum needs, and almost 100 million of them—one out of six households—do not possess the resources needed merely to satisfy their nutritional needs. In our region, the equivalent of the joint populations of the United Kingdom, Canada, and Sweden lack the means to nourish themselves adequately.

Looking more closely at the region, important differences can be seen among the countries with regard to poverty. The levels seen today are the result of very unequal evolution—of improvements and setbacks—across countries. The incidence of poverty varies from less than 10% of households in the case of Uruguay, to as much as 73% in Honduras. In general terms, however, an important group of the region's countries can be classified as poor—with an average incidence of poverty of between 30 and 50% of households—which is significantly greater than the international pattern. Poverty in the region has gone from being a rural phenomenon to a predominantly urban one, with almost two-thirds of the poor gathered in the cities.

And, of course, children and adolescents—84 million of them, or around 40% of the region's poor—are among those most seriously affected by this situation. Considering that childhood and adolescence are periods in which the opportunities to obtain skills essential for productive participation in society are determined, it is evident that the eradication of poverty among children and adolescents should be a priority of governments and civil society, so as to stop the poverty cycle.

However, it must be acknowledged that even during periods of relative economic growth, there has been limited progress in reducing poverty in the region. Historically, Latin America has had a highly inequitable income distribution. At the end of the 1960s, after a period of sustained economic growth, income inequality in the countries of the region was greater than that in other developing countries of East and Southeast Asia.[2] According to some, this is one of the reasons why Latin American countries, in spite of having achieved economic growth and good levels of productivity in the past, were not able to eradicate the most severe manifestations of poverty, which seem to drag on, and at present even increase, in the majority of countries. Empirical estimates of the Kuznets Curve using a sample of 102 countries indicate that, on average, Latin America countries have a Gini coefficient 4.1 times higher than other countries with similar per capita incomes.[3] Recent data for some countries show the apparent contradiction of a simultaneous increase of both the average per capita income and the Gini coefficient; that is, in spite of increases in income, the already serious differences across the income spectrum have increased. Londoño and Székely (1979)[4] estimate that the region has an "excess of inequality" of approximately 15 Gini coefficient points with respect to the average of the rest of the world.

The persistence of high levels of poverty in the region is also due to recent trends in employment, which are, to a great extent, the result of economic liberalization, privatization and deregulation, labor flexibility, and reform of the state. On the one hand, a highly productive employment sector of professionally or technically trained salaried or nonsalaried workers has emerged, even though it has produced a limited number of new jobs. On the other hand, informal and low-productivity employment has shown the greatest growth, with 8 out of 10 new jobs estimated to be of this kind. The salary gap between the economic sectors linked to foreign markets (and certain niche economies) and other sectors of the economy has widened. Current research in Central America seems to indicate that, even in modern sectors of the economy, the new characteristics of employment (short duration, payment by the "piece" or product, etc.) also contribute to the inequalities between male and female salaried workers, to the detriment of the latter. Unemployment, especially of young people and heads of household, has tended to increase in various countries of the region.

A more positive aspect of recent development in Latin America and the Caribbean is that in 12 of the 15 countries for which there are comparative data, the resources allocated to the social sector increased during the early years of the 1990s, reaching higher levels than those registered at the beginning of the 1980s. As a result, public social expenditure as a percentage of GDP increased an average of 1.8 points.[5]

However, there are great variations in levels of public expenditure in Latin American countries. The highest rates of per capita social expenditure seen in some countries within the region are similar to those in several industrialized countries. However, in absolute terms, the total expenditure is much lower than that of the most developed countries, since regional GDPs are substantially smaller than those of developed countries. For this reason, it is not surprising that even in the best of situations regionally, social expenditure cannot achieve the increase in coverage and quality of social services that is required to bring about equitable development. The countries with the lowest social expenditure are far from the recommendation, accepted at the World Summit on Social Development, of using 20% of the federal budget for basic social services.

There can be no doubt that the recent effort of Latin America and the Caribbean to fulfill the commitments made at the World Summit for Children in 1990 (adapted and complemented by the Nariño Accord of 1994, the Santiago Accord, and the Belice Accord of 1996) has borne important results. The goals defined for the year 2000 with regard to child survival and increased coverage of services are clearly closer to being achieved. Infant mortality and malnutrition have reached historically low levels, school enrollment is virtually universal for both boys and girls (with discrimination between boys and girls on the decline), and safe water reaches the homes of several million more people than a decade ago.

But the gaps are still enormous. Poverty, inequity, and the poor quality of services forestall progress in such crucial areas as maternal mortality, sanitation, and grade repetition and dropping out of school. Other serious problems, such as child labor, the deprivation of liberty of children and adolescents, population displacement due to armed conflict, and early pregnancy, appear in the regional panorama.

Achieving the minimum goals associated with child welfare is the basis for human development. But even with the important progress toward the goals of the World Summit for Children achieved to date in the region, there remain other just as "hard" or even "harder" goals, related to reducing poverty and social inequalities. To advance this agenda requires a new kind of public policy that links the government and civil society, unites economic policy with social policy, and shifts from paternalism to fulfillment of the rights of all—men and women, boys and girls.

In summary, the extreme inequality that characterized the region in the 1970s has increased rather than diminished, not only during the crisis of the 1980s, but also during the 1990s, when economic liberalization was being implemented. Recent trends include a decreasing rate of growth, the intensification of stabilization and adjustment programs, a slow increase in social expenditure (which is as yet neither efficient, of high quality, nor universally available), an unstable employment situation, and the almost total absence of redistributive policies. These trends allow us to predict that the problem of social exclusion will tend to become more serious in the years ahead. Only with significant political-economic countertrends will we be able to transform the opportunity of modernization into a reality for all.

The Rights of the Child: The Path toward a Model of Social Inclusion

The Convention on the Rights of the Child (CRC) has been ratified by 191 countries, making it the most internationally accepted instrument of human rights.

Historically, human rights, and among them the rights of children, adolescents, and women, have been conceived of as an important element of the legal framework, one that bespeaks a fundamental ethical character more than anything else, but in practice such rights have not translated into policies for exercising those rights. In the identification and formulation of national policy, explicit mention is rarely made of the rights that will be exercised through such policy. With the CRC and the Convention on the Elimination of All Forms of Discrimination Against Women (CEDAW) it is now possible to develop public policy language that refers to the rights of children and women. These two conventions have established an important foundation for change in the culture of public policy decisions. That change, little by little, will make it normal to refer to rights when the state and the private sector and civil society formulate policies and define strategies for public action. There are several ways to reflect on these issues to help interpret a new socioeconomic policy based on the recognition of rights as the entitlement of the individual, whether woman or man, adult or child. First, the supreme interest of the child—the basic principle of the CRC—needs to become one of the guiding principles of socioeconomic policy. That interest is not a blank check to be filled out by each person according to his or her subjective interpretation. The supreme interest of the child should be translated into nondiscretional rules and policies, consistent with the guarantor spirit of the CRC. That is, the social rights of children are sustainable only in the context of an economic policy that guarantees the allocation of the resources needed for fully exercising those rights.

Second, the achievement of enduring progress in the application of human rights depends upon effective public policy—both national and international—that contributes to economic, political, environmental, and social improvement based on respect for the cultural values and traditions of each nation. The state is, and should continue to be, the principal guarantor of the rights of all, but it should act in accord and cooperation with civil society, through public policies that include, in addition to the adequate provision of basic services, more efficient and effective fiscal and tax measures that contribute to reducing inequities in the distribution of income and wealth. That is, it is recognized that action by the state through its various agencies is necessary and irreplaceable, but it must also be pointed out that society should become increasingly capable of participating in and controlling such action and demanding an accounting from the government, as well as assuming its inherent responsibility for the fulfillment of rights.

Third, making civil and political rights real and guaranteeing economic, social, cultural, and environmental rights are both part of a whole. It is not possible to speak of a relative hierarchies of rights, since there exists not only an interdependence of, but also a synergistic relationship among, rights. Economic, social, and cultural rights create the conditions necessary for full exercise of civil and political rights, and vice versa. Although the full exercise of rights may appear impossible to reach, such a synergistic relationship establishes the foundations for policies of universal coverage while paying due attention to those people who are most vulnerable, without becoming "poor policies for the poor," that is, policies that propose to satisfy the basic needs of all, without discrimination, but that give priority to the most disadvantaged.

In this regard, both the CRC and the International Covenant on Economic, Social, and Cultural Rights[6] define a level of social protection and welfare whose achievement should be sought by all states, regardless of their systems and circumstances. That endeavor should visualize the full exercise of rights as the result of the progressive development of public policy, legislation, and practical action. For this to occur, it is necessary to define a minimum basic content for each right, which can contribute to the formulation of appropriate policies for advancing toward such fulfillment.

Human rights require from the state actions that ensure respect for them (abstaining from acting against them), protect them (through measures that prevent and punish their violation), and make them real (through measures that ensure they are exercised in reality). The complement of state action, in the area of the rights of children and women, is the existence of a culture and will of the people with regard to rights and their fulfillment. In the construction of a day-to-day culture and a basic set of positive reactions regarding the rights of children and women, there is a great deal of work to be done by governments and society.

Here a fourth idea emerges: a modern social policy is, therefore, a policy of building citizenship, acknowledging rights and responsibilities, respecting people as social subjects as opposed to "objects of treatment," and establishing transparent and equitable participation in the production and distribution of goods and services. From the perspective of children, an effective social policy is that which guarantees the rights of children, adolescents, and young people not as a matter of charity or compassion, but rather as an ethical, legal, and economic obligation of adult generations. Consider, for example, the obligation of adults to listen to children, an obligation that is symmetrical to the right of children to decide and freely express their opinions.

Finally, the strength of the system of social relations of a particular country and the measure in which relations of cooperation and solidarity take priority over extreme individualism and the promotion of competition among individuals constitute that country's social capital. In an open economy that must face increasing levels of international competition, social capital becomes the main trigger of development. Thus, between two economies with equivalent stocks of capabilities and similar levels of technological and productive development, the one that will triumph in international competition is the one that has a greater accumulation of social capital, that is, the one that educates its people the most in the knowledge of their public rights and responsibilities, the one that promotes the advantages of cooperation and equity among its people, the one that optimizes the processes of social inclusion, the one that builds citizenship not just for children, but from childhood on.

For everyone, this is the great challenge: children as the foundation of more inclusive societies in which all people live together with more solidarity and democracy—in sum, the construction of modern citizenship.

NOTES

1. In brief, these policies are based on the following basic elements: (a) liberation of foreign trade, (b) fiscal discipline, which significantly affects the level of inflation and, therefore, relative prices, (c) focussing of public expenditure on sectors having a high social rate of return, (d) fiscal reform, (e) liberation of the financial market, (f) competitive exchange rates, (g) free entry of foreign investment, and (h) privatization of state-owned companies and deregulation of the market.

2. In 1960 the ratio of the incomes of the richest 10% of the population to those of the poorest 10% had values of 33.6, 21.2, 18.0 and 11.4 in Brazil, Colombia, Venezuela, and Argentina, respectively, while in the Philippines, Thailand, and South Korea it was 13.6, 8.9, and 7.5. Cornia G. Andrea

(1994), "Macroeconomic Policy, Poverty Alleviation and Long-Term Development: Latin America in the 1990s," Innocenti Occasional Papers, Economic Policy Series, no. 40, ICDC-UNICEF, Florence.

3. Pan Yotopoulos, "The World Distribution of Income: Some Estimates," *Pakistan Journal of Economics*, 1976; Berry, Albert, Francois Bourguignon, and Christian Morrison, "The Level of World Inequality: How Much Can One Say?" in *Review of Income and Wealth*, 1983, and Margaret Grosh and Waine Nafziger (1986), "The Computation of World Income Distribution," in *Economic Development and Cultural Change*, 1986.

4. Juan Luis Londoño and Miguel Székely, "Sorpresas distributivas después de una década de reformas: América Latina en los Noventa." Prepared for the seminar Latin America after a Decade of Reform: What Are the Next Steps? March 1997.

5. CEPAL (Comisión Económica para América Latina y el Caribe), *Panorama social de América Latina, 1996* (Santiago de Chile).

6. Adopted by the UN General Assembly in 1966 and entered into force in 1976, it reaffirms the principles of the Universal Declaration of Human Rights with regard to economic, social, and cultural rights.

Appendix

The Changing Status of Children in Latin America: Issues in Health and Children's Rights

CONFERENCE

I. The Changing Face of Malnutrition in Latin America

Chair: Alex Malaspina, International Life Sciences Institute (ILSI), USA

1. Overview of Malnutrition in Latin America
   Author: Guillermo O'Donnell, CESNI, Argentina
   Discussant: Aaron Lechtig, Regional Advisor on Health and Nutrition, UNICEF, Colombia

2. Residual Undernutrition Issues: Micronutrient Malnutrition
   Panel: Wilma Freire, Pan American Health Organization (PAHO)
   Tomás Walter, INTA, University of Chile
   Nelly Zavaleta, Instituto de Investigación Nutricional, Peru

II. Feeding Practices and Environmental Sanitation

Chair: Frederick L. Trowbridge, Nutrition and Health Promotion Program, ILSI, USA

1. Breastfeeding and Appropriate Complementary Feeding Practices
   Author: Ana María Aguilar, BASICS, Bolivia
   Discussant: Helen Armstrong, Baby Friendly Hospital Initiative, UNICEF

2. Environmental Sanitation and Its Relation to Child Health
Author: Dennis B. Warner, Rural Environmental Health, World Health Organization (WHO)
Discussant: Steven Esrey, Project Information Management Unit, UNICEF

III. Bridging Issues of Child Health and Juvenile Rights

Chair: Dinah Shelton, University of Notre Dame Law School

1. The Agendas and Priorities of International Agencies Working with Children and Children's Issues
Author: Michael Heisler, Task Force for Child Survival and Development, The Carter Center, USA
Discussant: Bruce Corrie, Concordia University, St. Paul, USA

2. The Epidemic of Violence
Author: Rodrigo Guerrero, PAHO, former mayor of Cali, Colombia
Discussant: Mary Ann Beloff, Faculty of Penal Law, University of Buenos Aires, Argentina

IV. Childhood, Citizenship, and Democracy

Chair: Scott Mainwaring, University of Notre Dame

1. The Child as Citizen and the Concept of Democracy
Author: Alessandro Baratta, University of Saarland, Germany
Discussant: Guillermo O'Donnell, University of Notre Dame

2. Integral Protection of Minors as Citizens
Author: Emilio García Méndez, UNICEF, Colombia
Discussant: Juan Méndez, Inter-American Institute of Human Rights, Costa Rica

V. Violence, Delinquency, and Penal Law
Chair: Emilio García Méndez, Faculty of Penal Law, University of Buenos Aires, Argentina

1. Children and Adolescents in Conflict with Penal Law
Author: Miguel Cillero, UNICEF, Chile
Discussant: Alessandro Baratta, University of Saarland, Germany

2. Mortality Due to Violent Crimes: External Causes of Juvenile Death
Author: João Yunes, Bireme-PAHO; School of Public Health, University of São Paulo, Brazil
Discussant: Nancy Cardia, Center for the Study of Violence, University of São Paulo, Brazil

VI. Child Labor and Education

Chair: Errol Mendes, Human Rights Research and Education Centre, University of Ottawa, Canada

1. Child Labor and Education in Latin America
Author: María Cristina Salazar, Defence for Children International, Colombia
Discussant: Walter Alarcón, International Consultant on Child Labor Issues, Peru

Contributors

COREY ANDERSON
  Task Force for Child Survival and Development at the Carter Presidential Center, Atlanta, Georgia

ALESSANDRO BARATTA
  Chair in Sociology of Law at the University of Saarland, Saarbrücken, Germany

ERNEST BARTELL, C.S.C.
  Professor of Economics and former Executive Director of the Kellogg Institute for International Studies at the University of Notre Dame, Notre Dame, Indiana, USA

MIGUEL CILLERO BRUÑOL
  Professor of the Diego Portales University Law School and advisor to the National Directorship of the National Service for Children, Chile

STEVEN A. ESREY
  Senior Project Officer of the Programme Information Management Unit (PIMU) of UNICEF and member of the Standing Scientific Advisory Committee of the Thrasher Research Fund

WILMA B. FREIRE
Food and Nutrition Coordinator of the Pan American Health Organization (PAHO)

EMILIO GARCÍA MÉNDEZ
Professor of Criminology at the University of Buenos Aires, Argentina, independent consultant, and former Chief Counselor for children's rights at the regional office of UNICEF in Colombia

RODRIGO GUERRERO
Regional Advisor for Health and Violence to the Pan American Health Organization (PAHO) and former mayor of Cali, Colombia

MICHAEL B. HEISLER
Director of the Task Force for Child Survival and Development at the Carter Presidential Center, Atlanta, Georgia, USA, and Professor at the Center for International Health at Emory University's School of Public Health and School of Medicine

AARON LECHTIG
Senior Regional Advisor, Health and Nutrition, UNICEF TACRO for Latin America and the Caribbean

MARTA MAURÁS PÉREZ
Regional Director of UNICEF for Latin America and the Caribbean

JUAN E. MÉNDEZ
Director of the Center for Civil and Human Rights at the University of Notre Dame, Notre Dame, Indiana, USA, and former General Counsel for Human Rights Watch

ALBERTO MINUJIN
Regional Consultant on Social Policy, Evaluation, and Supervision, Regional UNICEF Office for Latin America and the Caribbean

ALEJANDRO M. O'DONNELL
Director of the Center for Studies on Infant Nutrition (CESNI), head of the Nutrition Unit of the National Pediatric Hospital in Buenos Aires, Argentina, Professor of Nutrition at the School of Medicine of the University of Salvador in Buenos Aires, and Associate Professor of Pediatrics of the School of Medicine at the University of Iowa, USA

GUILLERMO O'DONNELL
Helen Kellogg Professor of Government and International Studies and former Academic Director of the Kellogg Institute for International Studies at the University of Notre Dame, Notre Dame, Indiana, USA

RAQUEL PERCZEK
Senior Statistics Assistant, Regional UNICEF Office for Latin America and the Caribbean

MARÍA CRISTINA SALAZAR
President of Defence for Children International, Colombia section, Vice-chair of the International Working Group on Child Labour, and research consultant for UNICEF

TOMÁS K. WALTER
Head of the Hematology Unit at the Institute of Nutrition and Food Technology (INTA), University of Chile, and member of the American Academy of Pediatrics

DENNIS B. WARNER
Chief of Rural Environmental Health at the World Health Organization (WHO)

JOÃO YUNES
Professor of the Department of Maternal and Child Health at the School of Public Health of the University of São Paulo (USP), Brazil, and Acting Director of the Latin American and Caribbean Center of Health Sciences Information, BIREME-PAHO

EUGENIO RAÚL ZAFFARONI
Congressman for ALIAN, Buenos Aires, Argentina, and former Director of the Program of Penal Systems and Human Rights of the Inter-American Institute for Human Rights and General Director of the UN Latin American Institute for Crime Prevention and Treatment of Delinquents (ILANUD)

NELLY ZAVALETA
Principal Investigator of the Institute for Nutritional Research in Peru

TAMARA ZUBAREW
Professor of the Department of Pediatric School of Medicine, Catholic University of Chile

Index

www.ingramcontent.com/pod-product-compliance
Lightning Source LLC
Chambersburg PA
CBHW050624280326
41932CB00015B/2510